A Longman Cultural Edition

Rudyard Kipling's
KIM

Edited by

Paula M. Krebs
Wheaton College

Tricia Lootens
University of Georgia

Longman

Boston   Columbus   Indianapolis   New York   San Francisco   Upper Saddle River

Amsterdam   Cape Town   Dubai   London   Madrid   Milan   Munich   Paris   Montreal   Toronto

Delhi   Mexico City   Sao Paulo   Sydney   Hong Kong   Seoul   Singapore   Taipei   Tokyo

Senior Sponsoring Editor: Virginia L. Blanford
Editorial Assistant: Rosie Ellis
Executive Marketing Manager: Joyce Nilsen
Production Coordinator: Scarlett Lindsay
Project Coordination, Text Design, and Electronic Page Makeup: Grapevine
    Publishing Services, Inc.
Cover Design Manager: Wendy Ann Fredericks
Cover Art: Smithsonian American Art Museum, Bequest of Emily Tuckerman
Senior Manufacturing Buyer: Roy L. Pickering, Jr.
Printer and Binder: Courier Corporation / Westford
Cover Printer: Demand Production Center
Library of Congress Cataloging-in-Publication Data

Kipling, Rudyard, 1865–1936.
    [Kim]
    Rudyard Kipling's Kim / edited by Paula M. Krebs, Tricia Lootens.
        p. cm. — (A Longman cultural edition)
    Includes bibliographical references and index.
    ISBN-13: 978-0-321-43583-5 (alk. paper)
    ISBN-10: 0-321-43583-4 (alk. paper)
    1. Irish—India—Fiction. 2. Boys—Fiction. 3. Orphans—Fiction. 4. India—Fiction.
5. Lamas—Fiction. 6. Kipling, Rudyard, 1865–1936. Kim. I. Krebs, Paula M. II. Lootens,
Tricia A. III. Title.

PR4854.K4 2010
823'.8—dc22
                                                                    2009044861

2 3 4 5 6 7 8 9 10—CRW—13 12 11 10

Longman
is an imprint of

ISBN 13: 978-0-321-43583-5
ISBN 10:   0-321-43583-4

www.pearsonhighered.com

Contents

List of Illustrations

Cover: Edwin Lord Weeks (1849–1903), *Hindu Merchants*, n.d.

p. xxi. Edwin Lord Weeks, from *McClure's Magazine* serialization of *Kim*. Permission of University of Georgia Libraries.

p. xxii. Map of the geography of *Kim*.

p. 157. L. A. Waddell, *The Wheel of Life: Picturing the Buddhist Theory of the Universe*. From *The Buddhism of Tibet*. W. H. Allen, 1895.

p. 235. John Lockwood Kipling, *The End of the Search*. From *Kim*. Permission of Princeton University Library.

p. 253. Edwin Lord Weeks, page from *Harper's Magazine*.

p. 254. Advertisement for the 1971 reissue of the 1950 film as a Children's Matinee. *Kim* © Turner Entertainment Co. A Warner Bros. Entertainment Company. All rights reserved.

About Longman Cultural Editions

Inspired by the innovative *Longman Anthology of British Literature*, the Longman Cultural Editions are designed to illuminate the lively, ever variable intersections of literature, tradition, and culture. In each volume, a work or works of literary imagination gather new dimensions from materials that relate to informing traditions and debates, to contemporary conversations and controversies, and to later eras of reading and reaction. While the nature of the contexts varies from volume to volume, the reliable constants (in addition to handsome production and affordable pricing) are expert editing and helpful annotation throughout; a stimulating introduction; a table of dates to track composition, publication, and reception in relation to biographical, cultural, and historical events; illustrations guaranteed to spark conversation; and a guide for further browsing and study. Whether you are reading this volume along with the *Anthology*, or in a different or more specialized kind of course, or reading independently of any coursework, we hope you'll encounter much to stimulate your attention, curiosity, and pleasure.

SUSAN J. WOLFSON
General Editor, Longman Cultural Editions
Professor of English, Princeton University

About This Edition

"He sat, in defiance of municipal orders, astride the gun Zam-Zammah on her brick platform opposite the old Ajaib-Gher—the Wonder House, as the Natives call the Lahore Museum": Thus the story of *Kim* begins. Grounded in Rudyard Kipling's childhood in India, *Kim* draws together strands from a rich, controversial career. Our selections from Kipling's autobiography, poetry, travel writing—and crucially, his journalism—offer new ways of exploring Kipling's most successful novel, both in the context of its author's varied writing career, and in relation to larger literary, cultural, and political concerns.

Set in the vivid, imaginary realm known as "Kipling's India," *Kim* focuses fantasies and debates over colonialism and imperialism toward the end of the century and beyond. Our notes offer new ways to connect the novel to global as well as British imperial politics; our contextual selections include British Indian Survey documents; journalism on border tensions by Indian civil servant Muhammad Mafiz Ali and by Kipling himself; and an intimate, radically ambivalent account from 1897, in which Sir Hugh Clifford, a British imperial administrator, reflects on his career in Malaya in terms partly set by Kipling's writing.

When the narrator of *Kim* addresses readers as "we," who are "we" supposed to be? This is a question that plays out on many levels: cultural, political, epistemological, spiritual, and—of course—linguistic. Indeed, even the narrator's opening sentence seems calculated to remind readers of their own widely differing cultural locations and literacies. Readers new to Kipling's literary world may be startled by a narrator who apparently hasn't quite finished translating "Ajaib-Gher," to "Wonder House," much less to "Lahore Museum"; bilingual readers might feel equally struck by the narrator's casual assumption of imperial linguistic authority. In either case, the speaking of English becomes—and remains—an issue.

As generations of readers have found, allowing oneself to be confused, tantalized, rewarded—and perhaps even taunted—by Kipling's vocabulary can be one of the great pleasures of reading *Kim*. Here, we have tried to protect such pleasure. Readers who prefer to immerse themselves in Kipling's language may do so, uninterrupted by the usual round of explanatory glosses. Those who seek clarification or reminders may use the glossary, in which definitions of complex, shifting terms have been streamlined with an eye to the specifics both of the novel itself and of late nineteenth-century Anglo-Indian culture.

First serialized in New York's *McClure's Magazine* between December 1900 and October 1901, and in London's *Cassell's Magazine* from January through November 1901, *Kim* began by straddling two centuries and two continents. Our edition, whose text comes from the book's first British publication in volume form, by Macmillan, in 1901, with obvious errors corrected, emphasizes how dramatically Kipling's novel is poised at other boundaries as well, be they cultural, political, historical, linguistic, or generic.

The story of Kim begins with a boy astride a gun. *Kim* the novel, however, opens differently: that is, with a poetic epigraph. Here, we offer an excerpt from the source of that quoted stanza—Kipling's newspaper reportage of a trip to Japan. Such reprinting is another unusual aspect of this edition. By presenting possible sources, including earlier poems and stories in which figures from *Kim* appear, we cast new light both on what the world of *Kim* encompasses and what it may reframe, elide, or omit. A short-story Lispeth comes of age (p. 281); a fully comic Hurree Chunder Mookerjee dies, in a poem of hostility towards the Indian National Congress (p. 269); a crueler, simpler Mahbub Ali appears as a mere exotic storyteller (p. 274); and Strickland, the wryly humorous, surprisingly gentle model imperialist of *Kim*, turns to torture (p. 286). Temporal boundaries, too, become more flexible and suggestive, as histories of composition and serialization come to the fore. In our annotations, we emphasize the origins and afterlives of poetic chapter headings, providing pointers for further textual study. Our contextual selections supplement Kipling's account of composing *Kim* with a never-before-printed excerpt from the British Museum draft "Kim o' the Rishti," a scene whose brutal language, like its violent subject matter, should help inspire new discussions of Kipling's revision processes, as well as his representations of racial and religious violence.

In *McClure's*, *Kim* appeared with two sets of illustrations: one by Kipling's father and one by distinguished American Orientalist painter Edwin Lord Weeks, whose work appears on our cover. Here, for the first time, we reprint one of Weeks's contributions, along with a brief extract from his travel writing for *Harper's Magazine*. Weeks's images of India suggest new ways of connecting *Kim* to popular American culture, from Mark Twain to Cold War filmmaking. Set alongside the iconography addressed in our discussion of J. L. Kipling's closing bas-relief, Weeks's work also helps illuminate the functions of illustration within the shifting cultural life of *Kim*.

This speaks to a final, unusual focus of our text: that is, on Kipling's intense, controversial engagements with visual beauty. Writing for the *Pall Mall Gazette* in 1904, for example, George Moore suggested that the narrator's gaze in *Kim* betrayed a shameless avidity more befitting a divorce-case detective or a spy than a great writer. Yet in 1907, the Nobel Prize Committee wrote that Kipling's "landscapes appear to the inner vision as sudden apparitions do to the eye."[1] As the son of an artist, designer, art teacher, and museum curator and the nephew of both renowned Pre-Raphaelite painter Edward Burne-Jones and Sir Edward John Poynter, President of the Royal Academy, Kipling might have been expected to take his own passionate pleasure in the visual for granted. Still, as our excerpts from "Edge of the East" and "Home" suggest, his writing is steeped in anxieties over "the lust of the eye."

All our contextual resources invite you to appreciate the extent to which Kipling's imperial concerns intensify, rather than limit, his complex engagement with other issues of his day. Directly, though uneasily, connected to India's emergence as a center of global, English-speaking literary culture, *Kim* continues to focus our attention on the vibrancy of Kipling's insistently, yet not exclusively, imperial imagination.

We would like to thank our students at the University of Georgia and Wheaton College: Their strong, articulate opinions helped shape this volume. A Wheaton-Mellon fellowship and Wheaton College research awards funded Paula Krebs's research in London and Bloomington, Indiana; a University of Georgia Franklin College Faculty Development Assignment enabled Tricia Lootens to travel to Providence, Rhode Island for weeks of hard, satisfying collaborative work.

UGA research assistants Melanie King, Lisa Ulevich, Annalee Edmondson, and Doreen Thierauf hauled books, kept lists, and made photocopies; Doreen Thierauf painstakingly reviewed *Kim* for material to be glossed. At Wheaton, Kati Mather served as an able researcher and bibliographic assistant; Robin Doss valiantly worked through the *McClure's* edition. Paula Smith-MacDonald cheerfully photocopied and shipped on a moment's notice. Tricia's and Paula's shared readings were made immeasurably more pleasurable by Sam Dastor's splendid Audible.com audio recording. Thank you to proofreaders Joy Bracewell, JoEllen Childers, Julia Rende, and, especially, Kevin Durr.

[1]<http://nobelprize.org/nobel_prizes/literature/laureates/1907/press.html>.

This edition owes much to colleagues, at our universities and beyond. We are especially grateful for the support and hospitality of Lisa Lewis, as well as for her excellent work on the manuscript of *Kim*; for the generous conversation of Parama Roy; and for Susan Dearing's expertise on Buddhism. Thanks, too, to Jan Montefiore and Kaori Nagai of the University of Kent for organizing the valuable Kipling Conference 2007, where key aspects of our approach first came together. We also thank the dedicated members of the Kipling Society, as well as the staffs at the British Library Manuscripts Reading Room, the Madeline Clark Wallace Library at Wheaton College and the University of Georgia Libraries.

Thanks to those who photographed and digitized our illustrations (Alexander Bandazian for the MGM film advertisement; Andrew Howard, for the Wheel of Life; and Mark Dodson, for work from *McClure's* and *Harper's Magazine*). Thanks, too, to Cambridge University Press for permission to reprint an excerpt of Kipling's "Home" essay, from Rudyard Kipling, *Writings on Writing*, ed. Sandra Kemp and Lisa Lewis (1996), and to Palgrave, for allowing us to quote from Thomas Pinney's edited *Letters of Rudyard Kipling* (2004). And thanks, especially, to A. P. Watt, on behalf of the National Trust, for generously granting us permission to reproduce a portion of the draft of "Kim o' the Rishti," from a manuscript preserved in the British Library [© The British Library Board]. This volume would not have been possible without the sharp-eyed, frank, and efficient editing of Susan Wolfson; the technical support and permissions-digging of Rosie Ellis, and the creativity of Dianne Hall, who not only designed our pages but also drew our map of Kim's travels. Thanks, too, for Ginny Blanford's shepherding and Leslie Ballard's diligent editing.

And finally, thanks to Claire Buck, who has lived with this project for as long as we have, and has provided incredible support as well as proper perspective when it was most helpful (and a Google Docs tutorial); to Ruth Krebs Buck, who has been endlessly willing to watch and critique the 1950 film of *Kim* and has been extremely patient with us; and to JoEllen Childers, who has cheerfully walked (and washed) dogs, consulted long-distance, and run many kinds of interference back in Georgia so that we could work together elsewhere. We have been sustained by the memory of Barbara Lootens and George Krebs and the support of Bernard Lootens and Dorothy Krebs.

TRICIA LOOTENS
University of Georgia

PAULA M. KREBS
Wheaton College

Introduction

Rudyard Kipling's Kim, "the Little Friend of All the World," is comfortable in the company of just about anybody, from an old woman from the hills of Kulu in Tibet to an English colonel to a Bengali babu. *Kim*, the novel, too, shifts according to its companions. As children's literature, it joins Kipling's *Jungle Books*, *Just So Stories*, and *Stalky and Co.*; as a "tale of India," it joins his *Plain Tales from the Hills* or *Mine Own People*. In history, religion, and postcolonial studies courses, *Kim* illustrates aspects of British imperialism. In literature courses, it stands alongside Joseph Conrad's *Heart of Darkness*, George Eliot's *Daniel Deronda*, Salman Rushdie's *Midnight's Children*, Rabindranath Tagore's *Gora*, or the poetry of Swinburne, Tennyson, and Elizabeth Barrett Browning. In cinema studies, *Kim* can be linked to such 1950s adventure films as *The Crimson Pirate* or *King Solomon's Mines*, to children's films such as *Treasure Island*, and Cold War films from *The Day the Earth Stood Still* to the James Bond franchise.

Kim is a British novel, yet it is a novel of India; a Victorian novel, yet a twentieth-century novel. It is colonial; it's postcolonial. It is a novel; it's a loose series of adventures. It is a film. Its readers include children, adults, English, Indians, Americans, Irish, magazine readers, novel lovers, and fans of Nobel Prize-winning authors. The central question asked by our boy hero, "Who is Kim?" could just as well read "What is *Kim*?" *Kim* can be read in so many different ways, in part, because Kim himself can be read in many different ways. The child of long-dead Irish parents, fending for himself on the streets of Lahore, Kim learns to be whoever his companions need him to be: traveling doctor or skilled, subtle spy, or acolyte to a Tibetan lama. The world of *Kim* is one in which Jat, Bengali, Pathan, and Kamboh have distinct ethnic and regional characteristics—yet all are equally intelligible to Kim, who moves amongst all peoples with comfort.

Only Teshoo Lama, whom Kim comes to love more than anyone else, is not immediately transparent. Kim, who can predict everyone else's behavior, is astonished by the lama's gentle ways: "I have never seen anyone like to thee in all this my life," he tells him.

Part of the lama's unfamiliarity springs from his Buddhism. The religion had originated in India in the sixth century BCE, then spread to Tibet and China and beyond, while dying away in its birthplace. Tibet was gaining new importance for Victorians curious about comparative religions, while British colonial authorities focused on the region's strategic importance in relation to Russia. Three years after *Kim* was published, British troops, aided by L. A. Waddell, the primary British scholar of Tibetan Buddhism, invaded Tibet, inflicting heavy casualties on woefully underprepared Tibetan troops, including monks.

Whoever and whatever Kim may be, he belongs to "Kipling's India"—the "India" which late-Victorian England came to know through the sharp, vivid, nostalgic—and imperial—gaze of an Indian-born author who had not lived there in decades by the time he wrote his greatest novel. It had been a real India that first sparked Kipling's imagination and memory; negotiating in the 1920s with American actress Maude Adams about a film adaptation (not made in his lifetime), Kipling insisted—unusually, for the time—that the filming be done in India. What is more, many characters in *Kim* apparently do correspond to Kipling's contemporaries—the museum director is modeled on Kipling's father; Lurgan Sahib, on Alexander M. Jacob; Hurree Chunder Mookerjee, on Sarat Chandra Das, an Indian surveyor/spy for the British and writer about Tibet. Yet as Kipling's tour of Lahore, in his essay "Home" (p. 255) suggests, even at its most tangible, Kipling's "India" was always fictional. India as an emerging and contested political formation eluded Kipling.

Unlike the heroes of the Victorian Bildungsroman, Kim never achieves a strong adult sense of self. "Who is Kim? What is Kim?" he asks, but he never does answer. The afterlife of *Kim*, in its many editions, the film versions of 1950 and 1984 (the latter featuring Ravi Sheth as Kim), and fictional and critical reconceptions by Indian writers, reconfirms its cultural and literary significance. A novel that's not exactly a novel; a book about a child, which is really for adults; a Bildungsroman that doesn't allow its hero to grow up: *Kim* is a nineteenth-century work that continues to speak to the concerns of the twenty-first, especially imperialism.

India and Empire

Kim is an imperial novel, written at the height of Britain's empire, and set in Victorian India, the "jewel in the crown" of that empire. The British presence in India had begun during Elizabeth I's reign with the establishment of the spice trading firm that would become the British East India Company. The company effectively ruled India for Britain until the sepoys, the British Army's Indian troops, staged a massive revolt in 1857, prompted by Hindu and Muslim soldiers' suspicion that they were being required to violate religious strictures in handling rifle cartridges greased with animal fat. Known variously as the Sepoy Rebellion, the Indian Mutiny, or the First Indian War of Independence (depending on one's political perspective), the events that followed shocked Britain's sense of its relations with its most important colony. Combat deaths and murder on both sides, most infamously the murder of more than 100 British women and children in the "Bibighar Massacre" at Kanpur (Cawnpore), met brutal reprisals by the British, who executed captives by blowing them from the mouths of cannons.

In 1858 the British government took over the East India Company's functions, inheriting a fully developed military and administrative system, which came to be known as the Raj. By the time Kipling was born in 1865, significant shifts in attitude had also taken hold. Many colonial authorities were questioning the view promulgated by Parliamentarian and literary figure Thomas Babington Macaulay, in his 1835 "Minute on Indian Education," that Indians should be taught English language and culture: "We must at present do our best to form a class who may be interpreters between us and the millions whom we govern," Macaulay had written: "a class of persons Indian in blood and colour, but English in tastes, in opinions, in morals, and in intellect."

Inspired, in part, by the emerging force of "scientific" racism, which posited essential, unchangeable differences among races, colonial authorities came to see "blood and colour" as insurmountable barriers to becoming truly "English": that is, capable of independent, civilized existence. English-educated Indians now posed a particular challenge for the British. Once an honorific title, "Babu" had become an insult. As Hurree Chunder Mookerjee suggests, even to speak as a "babu" or "baboo," was to risk aggressive ridicule (see p. 149). Although by 1885, the Indian National Congress was fostering a movement for independence, the world of *Kim* is resolutely, benignly colonial.

Hurree Chunder Mookerjee both reinforces and challenges the babu stereotype, and he does so on the field of the "Great Game." That Hurree and Kim should join forces in the Great Game—the cat-and-mouse game of espionage, here especially with Russia beyond India's borders, makes sense.[1] Because Kim's own family came from Ireland, he, too, is linked to a history of ethnic stereotyping. Kim's collaboration with Hurree reflects the makeup of British Indian regiments, where sepoys fought alongside British troops and officers, many of whom were Scots or Irish, as was Kim's father's regiment, the Mavericks.

Critics have sometimes forgotten, in their desire to read *Kim* as a novel of the British Empire, that Kim is not just a child of the empire—he is the Little Friend of *All* the World. The novel constantly points out beyond empire, invoking Afghanistan, Tibet, and China. Its key characters, after all, include an Irish boy, an Afghani horse trader, and a Tibetan lama, and some of the most important events happen outside India. The Great Game of *Kim* plays out in a global context, within which Britain contends with such other powers as Russia and China.

Military operations in Central and South Asia—especially the first and second Sikh Wars (1845–46; 1848–49) for control of the Punjab, and the first and second Afghan Wars (1839–42; 1878–80)—strengthened Britain's position. In the Second Afghan War, Britain invaded Afghanistan to establish a buffer zone against Russian expansion. The operations of the Great Game, including surveying and mapping, and the expansion of the railway, all helped cement British sovereignty in the region.

The administration of the British Empire had been shaken by the 1857 Rebellion, but the empire faced challenges elsewhere as well. British governor Edward John Eyre's violent, controversial reprisals in Jamaica after the 1865 Morant Bay Rebellion and the Boer Wars (1880–81; 1899–1902), waged for political control over gold- and diamond-producing regions of South Africa, helped undermine the vision of Britain as the benevolent ruler of contented imperial subjects. The consequences of British imperial conflicts were far-reaching, as *Kim* shows: The Mavericks have looted their regimental mascot, the bull, from the Chinese emperor's summer palace. The impact of China's humiliation in the mid-century Opium Wars, which the British waged to force China to allow the opium trade, was long-lasting. The burning of the emperor's Summer Palaces in Beijing in October 1860 lived long in national memory; the defeat of General Charles George Gordon (who had been present at the destruction of the Summer Palaces) at Khartoum in 1885 cemented a Chinese friendship with the Sudan that has consequences even in twenty-first century Darfur.

Although *Kim* contains much historical and cultural specificity, Kipling's references are quite selective. Kipling himself, for example, had strong ties to the British presence in South Africa. In 1898, the Kipling

---

[1]For such imperial maneuvering see also David Damrosch's Longman Cultural Edition of Conrad's *Heart of Darkness* and Kipling's *The Man Who Would Be King* (2007).

family began to spend winters at the Cape Colony, where Kipling met the mining magnate, former Cape Colony prime minister and imperialist extraordinaire Cecil Rhodes, who advocated British control of Africa from "Cape to Cairo." The two hit it off immediately, and Rhodes built the Kiplings a house, "The Woolsack," on his estate. When, just before *Kim* was published, the British began a war against the white settler population in South Africa, Kipling, by then a world-famous author and the "Unofficial Poet Laureate of Empire," worked to combat the strong antiwar movement that had sprung up in England. Publishing anti-Boer propaganda in the *Times* of London and elsewhere, he even edited a British troop newspaper in Bloemfontein, South Africa, for a short time.

Kipling's own experience gave him an understanding of and an ability to write about empire that was unmatched in his day, and the richness of the story of Kim, as well as its limitations, may be in part attributed to the richness—and limitations—of the story of Kipling.

Kipling's Life

Joseph Rudyard Kipling was born in Bombay on December 30, 1865, to John Lockwood Kipling—artist, craftsman, and instructor at the Jeejeebhoy School of Art in Bombay, and Alice Macdonald Kipling, whose sister, Georgiana, was married to the painter Edward Burne-Jones. In *Something of Myself*, he reports that, in an idyllic first five years, his nurse had to remind him to "'Speak English now to Papa and Mamma.' So one spoke 'English,' haltingly translated out of the vernacular idiom that one thought and dreamed in." In 1871, he and his sister Alice ("Trix," born in 1868) were sent to England for school (this was customary with the British in India). The years at Lome Lodge, Southsea (he later called it "The House of Desolation") were miserable, and his eyesight and morale grew worse and worse. In 1878, he entered the United Services College at Westward Ho! in Devon (the setting for his 1899 novel *Stalky and Co.*), where he was editor of the school magazine. In 1882, at age seventeen, he returned to India to work as a journalist.

While reporting for the Lahore *Civil and Military Gazette*, he began publishing poems and short stories. These proved extremely popular: *Departmental Ditties* (1886) went into a second edition immediately; *Plain Tales from the Hills* came out in 1888, along with the series of Railway Library editions of his Indian short stories. The next year he became a roving correspondent for another newspaper, the *Pioneer*, traveling to Burma, Singapore, Hong Kong and Canton, Japan, and San Francisco. Poetry and journalism remained intertwined throughout his life, and both are strong influences on *Kim*, his most important novel.

In 1892, he married the sister of his good friend Wolcott Balestier, with whom he had written the novel *The Naulahka*, and settled in Brattleboro, Vermont. Throughout the 1890s, Kipling wrote, published, and struggled to maintain control of his work against U.S. pirate publishers who took advantage of lax international copyright. As his fame grew, he moved back to England in 1896. *Kim* was already in the works. In 1892 Kipling had proposed a short story, "Kim o' the Rishti" in a letter to Mary Mapes Dodge, the editor of the American children's magazine *St. Nicholas*. The story never materialized, but Kipling's memoir, *Something of Myself* (see p. 262) recounts the shaping of *Kim* in conversations with his father. In May 1899 the Kiplings took a trip to Vermont, and Kipling and their eldest child, Josephine, developed pneumonia. Josephine, the "Best Beloved" of the *Just So Stories*, died, leaving a very ill and bereft father, who managed to complete *Kim* in late summer. First serialized from December 1900 into 1901, *Kim* was published in volume form in 1901.

In 1907, Kipling became the first Englishman (and first English-language writer) to win the Nobel Prize for Literature (in 1913, Rabindranath Tagore, whose novel *Gora*, in part, rewrites and refutes the premises of Kipling's, would become the first Indian writer to achieve that honor). The Great War of 1914–18 marked Kipling profoundly. His only son, John, was killed just after his eighteenth birthday, in his first battle. Kipling subsequently wrote the history of John's regiment, the Irish Guards, and worked for the Imperial War Graves Commission. He wrote much about the war, including *The War in the Mountains* and *Sea Warfare*. His last collection of short stories, *Limits and Renewals*, was published in 1932, and Kipling died, following a hemorrhage from a duodenal ulcer, on January 18, 1936. His memoir, *Something of Myself, for my Friends Known and Unknown*, was published the following year.

In many ways, Kipling's critical reputation peaked in the years shortly after the publication of *Kim*, with his Nobel Prize. Kipling's blunt, aggressive imperialism, especially after the Great War, won him few new fans. By the 1940s, only a few years after Kipling's death, George Orwell could declare: "Kipling *is* a jingo imperialist, he *is* morally insensitive and aesthetically disgusting. It is better to start by admitting that, and then to try to find out why it is that he survives while the refined people who have sniggered at him seem to wear so badly" (*Critical Essays*, 1946). Kipling's writing has provoked fierce divisions: Derided by many for its crudeness and jingoism, it has also won praise (sometimes from the same readers), for its passion and artistry. In recent years, Kipling and his works, especially *Kim*, have come to inspire increasing critical debate about their aesthetics, their politics, and their power.

Table of Dates

1876	Queen Victoria named Empress of India. Famine in India.
1878	RK enters the United Services College at Westward Ho! in Devon. Summer in Paris, where his father has organized the Indian section of the arts display at the International Exposition. Second Afghan War.
1879	Zulu War in Africa, in which the British defeat the proud and militaristic Zulu nation.
1880–81	First Anglo-Boer War: British fight Dutch-descended Afrikaners (Boers), who had emigrated to southern Africa generations before and had in December 1880 declared independence from the United Kingdom, which controlled southern Africa. This results in partial independence for the Boers.
1881	RK edits the *United Services College Chronicle*. His parents publish his poems, *Schoolboy Lyrics*, for private circulation.
1882	RK sails for India in the autumn, to work as assistant editor of the *Civil and Military Gazette*, a newspaper in Lahore, where his father is principal of the Mayo School of Art and the curator of the Lahore Museum. His summer holidays are spent in Simla, the primary British retreat in the hills. British Occupation of Egypt.
1882–99	Mahdi Uprising in Sudan: British eventually retake the Sudan, at the Battle of Omdurman, where better-equipped British forces crush rebel Egyptians.
1885	Indian National Congress formed. An earthquake centered about 12 miles west of Srinigar claims some 3,000 lives.
1886	RK publishes *Departmental Ditties and Other Verses*, which immediately sells out; enters Lahore Masonic Lodge Hope and Perseverance, no. 782, EC.
1887	November: RK moves to Allahabad where he works at the newspaper, *The Pioneer*, and writes a series of articles about trips to Rajputana (Rajastan), later collected in *Letters of Marque*.

1887	British East Africa Co. charter awarded by British government, for trade and control of the region. Victoria's Golden Jubilee, celebrating 50 years on the throne.
1888	*Plain Tales from the Hills*, RK's first collection of short stories, published in January in Calcutta.
1888–89	Further collections of tales: *Soldiers Three*; *The Story of the Gadsbys*; *In Black and White*; *Under the Deodars*; *The Phantom Rickshaw*; *Wee Willie Winkie* published in Indian Railway Library Series.
1889	RK leaves India in March; visits Rangoon, Singapore, Hong Kong, and Japan en route to San Francisco. His articles about his travels across the U.S. are later collected in *From Sea to Sea*. In New York he meets his hero Mark Twain. Leaves for London in the fall and enters its literary scene.
	British South Africa Co. charter awarded, modeled on the British East India Company's, allowing diamond-mining magnate Cecil Rhodes to use militias to take control of land in southern Africa, and leading to his establishment of the colony of Rhodesia for Britain.
1890	RK publishes his first novel, *The Light That Failed*, which is not a success. RK begins close friendship with American literary agent Wolcott Balestier; suffers depression and a nervous breakdown from overwork. Remains close to Balestier until the latter's sudden death from typhoid in 1891.
1891	*Life's Handicap,* collection of stories including "Jews in Shushan," "The Mutiny of the Mavericks," "The Mark of the Beast," "Namgay Doolah," and "Without Benefit of Clergy," published in London. For the sake of his mental and physical health, RK leaves England for South Africa, New Zealand, Australia, India, and Ceylon.
1892	Marries Wolcott Balestier's sister Caroline (Carrie). They move to Vermont after they lose most of their money in a bank failure. Daughter Josephine born in December.
	Barrack Room Ballads and Other Verses (first series) collected and published. Poems include "The Ballad of

East and West," "The Ballad of the King's Jest," "Danny Deever," "Gentleman Rankers," "Gunga Din," "Ford o' Kabul River," "Tommy," and "The Widow at Windsor."

1894   RK publishes *The Jungle Book.*

1895   *The Second Jungle Book.*

1896   February: Daughter Elsie born. RK returns to England.

The Seven Seas and Further Barrack Room Ballads. Poems include "The Ladies," "The Mother-Lodge," "The 'Eathen," "McAndrew's Hymn," and "The Native Born."

1897   Son John born. Queen Victoria's Diamond Jubilee.

1898–1908   Kiplings spend their winter holidays in South Africa.

1899   RK publishes *Stalky and Co.,* collection of stories about boys at school. Last visit to the United States. Death of daughter Josephine.

1899–1902   Second Anglo-Boer War, in which British fight Dutch-descended Boers for control over territories containing gold and diamond mines.

1900   In South Africa RK writes for the troop newspaper *The Friend.* Befriends Cecil Rhodes, Leander Starr Jameson (whose rash raid on the Transvaal in 1896 had been intended to foment revolt against the Boer government), and Robert Baden-Powell (founder of the Boy Scouts).

1900–01   *Kim* published serially, in *McClure's Magazine* and *Cassell's Magazine.*

1902   RK publishes the children's classic *Just So Stories* and buys his last residence, "Bateman's," in Burwash, Sussex.

1903   *The Five Nations.* Poems include "The Buddha at Kamakura," "Chant Pagan," "The Islanders," "Recessional," "The Sea and the Hills," "The Song of Diego Valdez," "Stellenbosh," and "The White Man's Burden."

1904   *Traffics and Discoveries,* collection of short stories that includes Boer War stories as well as the early Modernist story "Mrs. Bathurst."

1907	RK is the first English-language writer, and first Briton, to receive Nobel Prize for Literature. *Collected Verse* published.
1912	*Songs from Books* appears, including chapter epigraphs and versions of the following poems from *Kim*: "Gow's Watch," "The Fairies' Siege," "A Song of Kabir," "The Prodigal Son," "The Two-Sided Man," and "The Wishing Caps."
1913	Visits Egypt. Rabindranath Tagore, whose novel *Gora* has been linked to *Kim*, is first Indian to win Nobel Prize for Literature.
1914–18	World War I. Son John enlists just before his 17th birthday. *The War in the Mountains*; *France at War*; and other war writings.
1915	John reported missing, believed killed, in France.
1919	*Rudyard Kipling's Verse: Inclusive Edition.*
1923	*The Irish Guards in the Great War*, a history of his son's regiment.
1932	*Limits and Renewals*, last collection of stories, including "Dayspring Mishandled."
1936	RK dies, January 18.
1937	Memoir, *Something of Myself for my Friends Known and Unknown*, is published.
1937–39	*The Complete Works of Rudyard Kipling, Sussex Edition*: the definitive edition prepared by RK during his last years.
1950	MGM motion picture *Kim*.
1971	Reissue of *Kim* as MGM Children's Matinee.

"'A TICKET—A LITTLE *TIKKUT* TO UMBALLA—O BREAKER OF HEARTS! . . .
HAST THOU NO CHARITY?'"

Edwin Lord Weeks, from *McClure's Magazine* serialization of *Kim*.

The Places of *Kim*

Kim

CHAPTER I

Oh ye who tread the Narrow Way
By Tophet-flare to Judgment Day,
Be gentle when the heathen pray
To Buddha at Kamakura![1]

He sat, in defiance of municipal orders, astride the gun Zam-Zammah on her brick platform opposite the old Ajaib-Gher—the Wonder House, as the natives call the Lahore Museum. Who hold Zam-Zammah, that 'fire-breathing dragon,' hold the Punjab; for the great green-bronze piece is always first of the conqueror's loot.

There was some justification for Kim,—he had kicked Lala Dinanath's boy off the trunnions,—since the English held the Punjab and Kim was English. Though he was burned black as any native; though he spoke the vernacular by preference, and his mother-tongue in a clipped uncertain sing-song; though he consorted on terms of perfect equality with the small boys of the bazar; Kim was white—a poor white of the very poorest. The half-caste woman who looked after him (she smoked opium, and pretended to keep a second-hand furniture shop by the square where the cheap cabs wait) told the missionaries that she was Kim's mother's sister; but his mother had been nursemaid in a colonel's family and had married Kimball O'Hara, a young colour-sergeant of the Mavericks, an Irish regiment. He afterwards took a post on the Sind, Punjab, and Delhi railway, and his regiment went home without him. The wife died of cholera in Ferozepore, and O'Hara fell to drink and loafing up and down the line with the keen-eyed three-year-old baby. Societies and chaplains anxious for the child, tried to catch him, but O'Hara drifted away, till he came across the woman who took opium and learned the taste from her, and died as poor whites die in India. His estate at death consisted of three papers—one he called his '*ne varietur*' because those words were written below his signature thereon, and another his 'clearance-certificate.'[2] The third was Kim's birth-certificate. Those things, he was used to say, in his glorious

---

[1] First stanza of Kipling's "Buddha at Kamakura" (see p. 260). Later versions place "the heathen" in quotation marks. The biblical Tophet is associated with sacrificial immolation of children (Jeremiah 7.31).

[2] Documents related to Kim's father's enrollment and status as a Freemason. See "The Mother-Lodge" (p. 278).

opium hours, would yet make little Kimball a man. On no account was Kim to part with them, for they belonged to a great piece of magic—such magic as men practised over yonder behind the Museum, in the big blue and white Jadoo-Gher—the Magic House, as we name the Masonic Lodge. It would, he said, all come right some day, and Kim's horn would be exalted between pillars—monstrous pillars—of beauty and strength. The Colonel himself, riding on a horse, at the head of the finest regiment in the world, would attend to Kim,—little Kim that should have been better off than his father. Nine hundred first-class devils, whose god was a Red Bull on a green field, would attend to Kim, if they had not forgotten O'Hara—poor O'Hara that was gang-foreman on the Ferozepore line. Then he would weep bitterly in the broken rush chair on the verandah. So it came about after his death that the woman sewed parchment, paper, and birth-certificate into a leather amulet-case which she strung round Kim's neck.

'And some day,' she said, confusedly remembering O'Hara's prophecies, 'there will come for you a great Red Bull on a green field, and the Colonel riding on his tall horse, yes, and'—dropping into English—'nine hundred devils.'

'Ah,' said Kim, 'I shall remember. A Red Bull and a Colonel on a horse will come, but first, my father said, come the two men making ready the ground for these matters. That is how, my father said, they always did; and it is always so when men work magic.'

If the woman had sent Kim up to the local Jadoo-Gher with those papers, he would, of course, have been taken over by the Provincial Lodge and sent to the Masonic Orphanage in the Hills; but what she had heard of magic she distrusted. Kim, too, held views of his own. As he reached the years of indiscretion, he learned to avoid missionaries and white men of serious aspect who asked who he was, and what he did. For Kim did nothing with an immense success. True, he knew the wonderful walled city of Lahore from the Delhi Gate to the outer Fort Ditch; was hand in glove with men who led lives stranger than anything Haroun al Raschid dreamed of; and he lived in a life wild as that of the Arabian Nights, but missionaries and secretaries of charitable societies could not see the beauty of it. His nickname through the wards was 'Little Friend of all the World'; and very often, being lithe and inconspicuous, he executed commissions by night on the crowded housetops for sleek and shiny young men of fashion. It was intrigue, of course,—he knew that much, as he had known all evil since he could speak,—but what he loved was the game for its own sake—the stealthy prowl through the dark gullies and lanes, the crawl up a water-pipe, the sights and sounds of the women's world on the flat roofs, and the headlong flight from housetop to housetop under cover of the hot dark. Then there were holy men, ash-smeared *faquirs* by their brick shrines under the trees at the riverside, with whom he was quite familiar—greeting them as they returned from begging-tours, and, when no one was by, eating from the same dish. The woman who looked after him insisted with tears that he should wear European clothes—trousers, a shirt, and a battered hat. Kim found it easier to slip into Hindu or Mohammedan garb when engaged on certain businesses. One of the young men of fashion—he who was found dead at the bottom of a well on the night of the earthquake—had once given him a complete suit of Hindu kit, the costume of a low-caste street boy, and Kim stored it in a secret place under some baulks in Nila Ram's timber-yard, beyond the Punjab High Court, where the fragrant deodar logs lie seasoning after they have driven down the Ravee. When there was business or frolic afoot, Kim would use his properties, returning at dawn to the verandah, all tired out from shouting at the heels of a marriage procession, or yelling at a Hindu festival. Sometimes there was food in the house, more often there was not, and Kim went out again to eat with his native friends.

As he drummed his heels against Zam-Zammah he turned now and again from his king-of-the-castle game with little Chota Lal and Abdullah the sweetmeat-seller's son, to make a rude remark to the native policeman on guard over rows of shoes at the Museum door. The big Punjabi grinned tolerantly: he knew Kim of old. So did the water-carrier, sluicing water on the dry road from his goat-skin bag. So did Jawahir Singh, the Museum carpenter, bent over new packing-cases. So did everybody in sight except the peasants from the country, hurrying up to the Wonder House to view the things that men made in their own province and elsewhere. The Museum was given up to Indian arts and manufactures, and anybody who sought wisdom could ask the curator to explain.

'Off! Off! Let me up!' cried Abdullah, climbing up Zam-Zammah's wheel.

'Thy father was a pastry-cook, Thy mother stole the *ghi*,' sang Kim. 'All Mussalmans fell off Zam-Zammah long ago!'

'Let *me* up!' shrilled little Chota Lal in his gilt-embroidered cap. His father was worth perhaps half a million sterling, but India is the only democratic land in the world.

'The Hindus fell off Zam-Zammah too. The Mussalmans pushed them off. Thy father was a pastry-cook——'

He stopped; for there shuffled round the corner, from the roaring Motee Bazar, such a man as Kim, who thought he knew all castes,[3] had never seen. He was nearly six feet high, dressed in fold upon fold of dingy stuff like horse-blanketing, and not one fold of it could Kim refer to any known trade or profession. At his belt hung a long open-work iron pencase and a wooden rosary such as holy men war. On his head was a gigantic sort of tam-o'-shanter. His face was yellow and wrinkled, like that of Fook Shing, the Chinese bootmaker in the bazar. His eyes turned up at the corners and looked like little slits of onyx.

'Who is that?' said Kim to his companions.

'Perhaps it is a man,' said Abdullah, finger in mouth, staring.

'Without doubt,' returned Kim; 'but he is no man of India that *I* have ever seen.'

'A priest, perhaps,' said Chota Lal, spying the rosary. 'See! He goes into the Wonder House!'

'Nay, nay,' said the policeman, shaking his head. 'I do not understand your talk.' The constable spoke Punjabi. 'Oh, The Friend of all the World, what does he say?'

'Send him hither,' said Kim, dropping from Zam-Zammah, flourishing his bare heels. 'He is a foreigner, and thou art a buffalo.'

The man turned helplessly and drifted towards the boys. He was old, and his woollen gaberdine still reeked of the stinking artemisia of the mountain passes.

'O Children, what is that big house?' he said in very fair Urdu.

'The Ajaib-Gher, the Wonder House!'[4] Kim gave him no title—such as Lala or Mian. He could not divine the man's creed.

'Ah! The Wonder House! Can any enter?'

'It is written above the door—all can enter.'

'Without payment?'

'I go in and out. *I* am no banker,' laughed Kim.

'Alas! I am an old man. I did not know.' Then, fingering his rosary, he half turned to the Museum.

'What is your caste? Where is your house? Have you come far?' Kim asked.

'I came by Kulu—from beyond the Kailas—but what know you? From the hills where'—he sighed—'the air and water are fresh and cool.'

[3]Complicated system of divisions within Indian society, traditionally, though far from exclusively, associated with Hinduism. During the 19th c., highly complex and conflicted definitions of caste, which seem already to have been bound up in conceptions of "race," tradition, class, location, and occupation, came to be affected by colonial rule. Although colonial policy insisted on equality before the law, official attempts to codify caste categories, including the British imperial census beginning in 1871, may have hardened and exacerbated caste divisions.

[4]Kim now clearly speaks at least "the vernacular" (Hindustani), Punjabi, Urdu, and English.

'Aha! Khitai (a Chinaman),' said Abdullah proudly. Fook Shing had once chased him out of his shop for spitting at the joss above the boots.

'Pahari (a hillman),' said little Chota Lal.

'Aye, child—a hillman from hills thou'lt never see. Didst hear of Bhotiyal (Tibet)? I am no Khitai, but a Bhotiya (Tibetan), since you must know—a lama—or, say a *guru* in your tongue.'

'A *guru* from Tibet,' said Kim. 'I have not seen such a man. They be Hindus in Tibet, then?'

'We be followers of the Middle Way, living in peace in our lamasseries, and I go to see the Four Holy Places before I die.[5] Now do you, who are children, know as much as I do who am old.' He smiled benignantly on the boys.

'Hast thou eaten?'

He fumbled in his bosom and drew forth a worn wooden begging-bowl. The boys nodded. All priests of their acquaintance begged.

'I do not wish to eat yet.' He turned his head like an old tortoise in the sunlight. 'Is it true that there are many images in the Wonder House of Lahore?' He repeated the last words as one making sure of an address.

'That is true,' said Abdullah. 'It is full of heathen *būts*. Thou also art an idolator.'

'Never mind *him*,' said Kim. 'That is the Government's house and there is no idolatry in it, but only a Sahib with a white beard. Come with me and I will show.'

'Strange priests eat boys,' whispered Chota Lal.

'And he is a stranger and a *būt-parast* (idolator)' said Abdullah, the Mohammedan.

Kim laughed. 'He is new. Run to your mothers' laps, and be safe. Come!'

Kim clicked round the self-registering turnstile; the old man followed and halted amazed. In the entrance-hall stood the larger figures of the Greco-Buddhist sculptures done, savants know how long since, by forgotten workmen whose hands were feeling, and not unskilfully, for the mysteriously transmitted Grecian touch.[6] There were hundreds of pieces, friezes of figures in relief, fragments of statues and slabs crowded with figures that had encrusted the brick walls of the Buddhist *stupas* and *viharas* of the North Country and now, dug up and labelled, made the pride of the Museum. In open-mouthed

---

[5]Buddhism emphasizes the "Middle Way" to nirvana, or enlightenment, between sensualism and asceticism. For the holy places, see p. 8, n. 13.

[6]Once assumed by many in the West to be a crucial source of Indian artistic greatness, the influence of Greco-Buddhist art has since become a matter of intense debate.

wonder the lama turned to this and that, and finally checked in rapt attention before a large alto-relief representing a coronation or apotheosis of the Lord Buddha. The Master was represented seated on a lotus the petals of which were so deeply undercut as to show almost detached. Round Him was an adoring hierarchy of kings, elders, and old-time Buddhas. Below were lotus-covered waters with fishes and water-birds. Two butterfly-winged dewas held a wreath over His head; above them another pair supported an umbrella surmounted by the jewelled headdress of the Bodhisat.[7]

'The Lord! The Lord! It is Sakya Muni himself,' the lama half sobbed; and under his breath began the wonderful Buddhist invocation:—

> *'To Him the Way—the Law—Apart—*
> *Whom Maya held beneath her heart*
> *Ananda's Lord—the Bodhisat.'*[8]

'And He is here! The Most Excellent Law[9] is here also. My pilgrimage is well begun. And what work! What work!'

'Yonder is the Sahib,'[10] said Kim, and dodged sideways among the cases of the arts and manufacture wing. A white-bearded Englishman was looking at the lama, who gravely turned and saluted him and after some fumbling drew forth a note-book and a scrap of paper.

'Yes, that is my name,' smiling at the clumsy, childish print.

'One of us who had made pilgrimage to the Holy Places—he is now Abbot of the Lung-Cho Monastery—gave it me,' stammered the lama. 'He spoke of these.' His lean hand moved tremulously round.

'Welcome, then, O lama from Tibet. Here be the images, and I am here'—he glanced at the lama's face—'to gather knowledge. Come to my office awhile.' The old man was trembling with excitement.

The office was but a little wooden cubicle partitioned off from the sculpture-lined gallery. Kim laid himself down, his ear against a

---

[7]Buddha Shakyamuni, who, as Prince Siddhartha Gautama, abandoned his life of luxury to pursue enlightenment and to teach. He is known as the Lord Buddha or the Gautama Buddha, although he noted that there were buddhas before him ("old-time Buddhas") and buddhas who would succeed him. "Bodhisat" refers to his corporeal existence.

[8]Kipling's own words: see "The Buddha at Kamakura" (p. 260).

[9]The teachings of the Buddha, who set in motion the Wheel of the Law (doctrine), which ignores Hindu caste distinctions, asserting that life is suffering (because suffering is desire); that the cause of suffering (desire) can be known; and that it is possible to attain cessation from suffering through adherence to principles of right understanding, purpose, speech, conduct, livelihood, endeavor, awareness, and meditation.

[10]What follows here is an idealized portrait of Kipling's father John Lockwood Kipling (see p. 262).

crack in the heat-split cedar door, and, following his instinct, stretched out to listen and watch.

Most of the talk was altogether above his head. The lama, haltingly at first, spoke to the curator of his own lamassery, the Such-zen, opposite the Painted Rocks, four months' march away. The curator brought out a huge book of photos and showed him that very place, perched on its crag, overlooking the gigantic valley of many-hued strata.

'Ay, ay!' The lama mounted a pair of horn-rimmed spectacles of Chinese work. 'Here is the little door through which we bring wood before winter. And thou—the English know of these things? He who is now Abbot of Lung-Cho told me, but I did not believe. The Lord—the Excellent One—He has honour here too? And His life is known?'

'It is all carven upon the stones. Come and see, if thou art rested.'

Out shuffled the lama to the main hall, and, the curator beside him, went through the collection with the reverence of a devotee and the appreciative instinct of a craftsman.

Incident by incident in the beautiful story he identified on the blurred stone, puzzled here and there by the unfamiliar Greek convention, but delighted as a child at each new trove. Where the sequence failed, as in the Annunciation,[11] the curator supplied it from his mound of books—French and German, with photographs and reproductions.

Here was the devout Asita, the pendant of Simeon in the Christian story, holding the Holy Child on his knee while mother and father listened; and here were incidents in the legend of the cousin Devadatta. Here was the wicked woman who accused the Master of impurity, all confounded; here was the teaching in the Deer-park; the miracle that stunned the fire-worshippers; here was the Bodhisat in royal state as a prince; the miraculous birth; the death at Kusinagara, where the weak disciple fainted; while there were almost countless repetitions of the meditation under the Bodhi tree; and the adoration of the alms-bowl was everywhere. In a few minutes the curator saw that his guest was no mere bead-telling mendicant, but a scholar of parts. And they went at it all over again, the lama taking snuff, wiping his spectacles, and talking at railway speed in a bewildering mixture of Urdu and Tibetan. He had heard of the travels of the Chinese pilgrims, Fo-Hian and Hwen-Thiang, and was anxious to know if there was any translation of their record. He drew in his breath as he

---

[11]The chronologically mixed moments from the life of Siddhartha Gautama that follow serve, in part, to stress parallels to the life of Christ. Maya's "Annunciation" was the prophetic vision of her holy son's birth; the ascetic Asita, like the biblical Simeon, prophesied the child's coming greatness. Parallels to Islam also emerge through the Bodhi tree's characterization as "the Mecca of Buddhism."

turned helplessly over the pages of Beal and Stanislas Julien.[12] ''Tis all here. A treasure locked.' Then he composed himself reverently to listen to fragments, hastily rendered into Urdu. For the first time he heard of the labours of European scholars, who by the help of these and a hundred other documents have identified the Holy Places of Buddhism.[13] Then he was shown a mighty map, spotted and traced with yellow. The brown finger followed the curator's pencil from point to point. Here was Kapilavastu, here the Middle Kingdom, and here Mahabodi, the Mecca of Buddhism; and here was Kusinagara, sad place of the Holy One's death. The old man bowed his head over the sheets in silence for a while, and the curator lit another pipe. Kim had fallen asleep. When he waked, the talk, still in spate, was more within his comprehension.

'And thus it was, O Fountain of Wisdom, that I decided to go to the Holy Places which His foot had trod—to the Birthplace, even to Kapila; then to Maha Bodhi, which is Buddh Gaya—to the Monastery—to the Deer-park—to the place of His death.'

The lama lowered his voice. 'And I come here alone. For five—seven—eighteen—forty years it was in my mind that the Old Law was not well followed; being overlaid, as thou knowest, with devildom, charms, and idolatry. Even as the child outside said but now. Ay, even as the child said, with *būt-parasti*.'

'So it comes with all faiths.'

'Thinkest thou? The books of my lamassery I read, and they were dried pith; and the later ritual with which we of the Reformed Law have cumbered ourselves—that, too, had no worth to these old eyes. Even the followers of the Excellent One are at feud on feud with one another. It is all illusion. Ay, *maya*, illusion. But I have another desire'—the seamed yellow face drew within three inches of the curator, and the long forefinger nail tapped on the table. 'Your scholars, by these books, have followed the Blessed Feet in all their wanderings; but there are things which they have not sought out. I know nothing,—nothing do I know,—but I go to free myself from the Wheel of Things by a broad and open road.' He smiled with most simple triumph. 'As a pilgrim to the Holy Places I acquire merit. But there is more. Listen to a true thing. When

[12]Fu-Hiouen (Fa Hsien) and Hwen-Tsiang (Hiuen Tsiang) were 5th- and 7th-c. scholars and travelers to Northern India. British scholar Samuel Beal published a translation of Hiuen Tsiang's work in 1884; Stanislaus Julien's *Voyages du pèlerin Hiouen-tsang* appeared in 1853. Highly educated though he is, the lama can read neither Beal nor Julien; without European languages, he is barred from full knowledge of his own tradition.

[13]Kapilavastu (Kapila), near Lumbini, where Siddhartha Gautama was born; Buddh Gaya (Bodh Gaya), or Mahabodhi, where he attained enlightenment; Deer Park, where the Buddha delivered his first sermon; and Kusinara (Kusinagara), where he died.

our gracious Lord, being as yet a youth, sought a mate, men said, in His father's court, that He was too tender for marriage. Thou knowest?'

The curator nodded; wondering what would come next.

'So they made the triple trial of strength against all comers. And at the test of the Bow, our Lord first breaking that which they gave Him, called for such a bow as none might bend. Thou knowest?'

'It is written. I have read.'

'And, overshooting all other marks, the arrow passed far and far beyond sight. At the last it fell; and, where it touched earth, there broke out a stream which presently became a River, whose nature, by our Lord's beneficence, and that merit He acquired ere He freed himself, is that whoso bathes in it washes away all taint and speckle of sin.'

'So it is written,' said the curator sadly.

The lama drew a long breath. 'Where is that River? Fountain of Wisdom, where fell the arrow?'

'Alas, my brother, I do not know,' said the curator.

'Nay, if it please thee to forget—the one thing only that thou hast not told me. Surely thou must know? See, I am an old man! I ask with my head between thy feet, O Fountain of Wisdom. We *know* He drew the bow! We *know* the arrow fell! We *know* the stream gushed! Where, then, is the River? My dream told me to find it. So I came. I am here. But where is the River?'

'If I knew, think you I would not cry it aloud?'

'By it one attains freedom from the Wheel of Things,'[14] the lama went on, unheeding. 'The River of the Arrow! Think again! Some little stream, may be—dried in the heats? But the Holy One would never so cheat an old man.'

'I do not know. I do not know.'

The lama brought his thousand-wrinkled face once more a handsbreadth from the Englishman's. 'I see thou dost not know. Not being of the Law, the matter is hid from thee.'

'Ay—hidden—hidden.'

'We are both bound, thou and I, my brother. But I'—he rose with a sweep of the soft thick drapery—'I go to cut myself free. Come also!'

'I am bound,' said the curator. 'But whither goest thou?'

'First to Kashi (Benares): where else? There I shall meet one of the pure faith in a Jain temple of that city. He also is a Seeker in secret, and from him haply I may learn. May be he will go with me to Buddh Gaya. Thence north and west to Kapilavastu, and there will I seek for the River. Nay, I will seek everywhere as I go—for the place is not known where the arrow fell.'

[14]Kipling's invented phrase encapsulates Buddhist attitudes toward material life; the cycle of rebirth may be escaped through spiritual enlightenment.

'And how wilt thou go? It is a far cry to Delhi, and farther to Benares.'

'By road and the trains. From Pathânkot, having left the Hills, I came hither in a *te-rain*. It goes swiftly. At first I was amazed to see those tall poles by the side of the road snatching up and snatching up their threads,'—he illustrated the stoop and whirl of a telegraph-pole flashing past the train. 'But later, I was cramped and desired to walk, as I am used.'

'And thou art sure of thy road?' said the curator.

'Oh, for that one but asks a question and pays money, and the appointed persons despatch all to the appointed place. That much I knew in my lamassery from sure report,' said the lama proudly.

'And when dost thou go?' The curator smiled at the mixture of old-world piety and modern progress that is the note of India to-day.

'As soon as may be. I follow the places of His life till I come to the River of the Arrow. There is, moreover, a written paper of the hours of the trains that go south.'

'And for food?' Lamas, as a rule, have good store of money somewhere about them, but the curator wished to make sure.

'For the journey, I take up the Master's begging-bowl. Yes. Even as He went so go I, forsaking the ease of my monastery. There was with me when I left the hills a *chela* (disciple) who begged for me as the Rule demands, but halting in Kulu awhile a fever took him and he died. I have now no *chela*, but I will take the alms-bowl and thus enable the charitable to acquire merit.' He nodded his head valiantly. Learned doctors of a lamassery do not beg, but the lama was an enthusiast in this quest.

'Be it so,' said the curator, smiling. 'Suffer me now to acquire merit. We be craftsmen together, thou and I. Here is a new book of white English paper: here be sharpened pencils two and three—thick and thin, all good for a scribe. Now lend me thy spectacles.'

The curator looked through them. They were heavily scratched, but the power was almost exactly that of his own pair, which he slid into the lama's hand, saying: 'Try these.'

'A feather! A very feather upon the face!' The old man turned his head delightedly and wrinkled up his nose. 'How scarcely do I feel them! How clearly do I see!'

'They be *bilaur*—crystal and will never scratch. May they help thee to thy River, for they are thine.'

'I will take them and the pencils and the white note-book,' said the lama, 'as a sign of friendship between priest and priest—and now——' he fumbled at his belt, detached the open iron-work pencase, and laid it on the curator's table. 'That is for a memory between thee and me—my pencase. It is something old—even as I am.'

It was a piece of ancient design, Chinese, of an iron that is not smelted these days; and the collector's heart in the curator's bosom had gone out to it from the first. For no persuasion would the lama resume his gift.

'When I return, having found the River, I will bring thee a written picture of the Padma Samthora—such as I used to make on silk at the lamassery. Yes—and of the Wheel of Life,'[15] he chuckled, 'for we be craftsmen together, thou and I.'

The curator would have detained him: they are few in the world who still have the secret of the conventional brush-pen Buddhist pictures which are, as it were, half written and half drawn. But the lama strode out, head high in air, and pausing an instant before the great statue of a Bodhisat in meditation, brushed through the turnstiles.

Kim followed like a shadow. What he had overheard excited him wildly. This man was entirely new to all his experience, and he meant to investigate further: precisely as he would have investigated a new building or a strange festival in Lahore city. The lama was his trove, and he purposed to take possession. Kim's mother had been Irish too.

The old man halted by Zam-Zammah and looked round till his eye fell on Kim. The inspiration of his pilgrimage had left him for awhile, and he felt old, forlorn, and very empty.

'Do not sit under that gun,' said the policeman loftily.

'Huh! Owl!' was Kim's retort on the lama's behalf. 'Sit under that gun if it please thee. When didst thou steal the milk-woman's slippers, Dunnoo?'

That was an utterly unfounded charge sprung on the spur of the moment, but it silenced Dunnoo, who knew that Kim's clear yell could call up legions of bad bazar boys if need arose.

'And whom didst thou worship within?' said Kim affably, squatting in the shade beside the lama.

'I worshipped none, child. I bowed before the Excellent Law.'

Kim accepted this new god without emotion. He knew already a few score.

'And what dost thou do?'

'I beg. I remember now it is long since I have eaten or drunk. What is the custom of charity in this town? In silence, as we do of Tibet, or speaking aloud?'

'Those who beg in silence starve in silence,' said Kim, quoting a native proverb. The lama tried to rise, but sank back again, sighing

---

[15]Tibetan lamas were known for their intricate drawings of the Wheel of Life (see p. 157). Padma Samthora (Padmasambhava), the "Lotus-Born," brought Buddhism to Tibet in the 8th c.

for his disciple, dead in far away Kulu. Kim watched—head to one side, considering and interested.

'Give me the bowl. I know the people of this city—all who are charitable. Give, and I will bring it back filled.' Simply as a child the holy man handed him the bowl.

'Rest thou. *I* know the people.'

He trotted off to the open shop of a *kunjri*, a low-caste vegetable-seller, which lay opposite the belt-tramway line down the Motee Bazar. She knew Kim of old.

'Oho, hast thou turned *yogi* with thy begging-bowl?' she cried.

'Nay,' said Kim proudly. 'There is a new priest in the city—a man such as I have never seen.'

'Old priest—young tiger,' said the woman angrily. 'I am tired of new priests! They settle on our wares like flies. Is the father of my son a well of charity to give to all who ask?'

'No,' said Kim. 'Thy man is rather *yagi* (bad tempered) than *yogi* (a holy man). But this priest is new. The Sahib in the Wonder House has talked to him like a brother. O my mother, fill me this bowl. He waits.'

'That bowl indeed! That cow-bellied basket! Thou hast as much grace as the holy bull of Shiv.[16] He has taken the best of a basket of onions already, this morn; and forsooth, I must fill thy bowl. He comes here again.'

The huge, mouse-coloured Brahminee bull of the ward was shouldering his way through the many-coloured crowd, a stolen plantain hanging out of his mouth. He headed straight for the shop, well knowing his privileges as a sacred beast, lowered his head, and puffed heavily along the line of baskets ere making his choice. Up flew Kim's hard little heel and caught him on his moist blue nose. He snorted indignantly, and walked away across the tram rails, his hump quivering with rage.

'See! I have saved more than the bowl will cost thrice over. Now, mother, a little rice and some dried fish atop—yes, and some vegetable curry.'

A growl came out of the back of the shop, where a man lay.

'He drove away the bull,' said the woman in an undertone. 'It is good to give to the poor.' She took the bowl and returned it full of hot rice.

'But my *yogi* is not a cow,' said Kim gravely, making a hole with his fingers in the top of the mound. 'A little curry is good, and a fried cake, and a morsel of conserve would please him, I think.'

---

[16]Both destroyer and benefactor, and one of the greatest gods of Hinduism, Shiv (or Shiva) is represented by a bull. Cows and bulls are sacred to Hindus.

'It is a hole as big as thy head,' said the woman fretfully. But she filled it, none the less, with good, steaming vegetable curry, clapped a dried cake atop, and a morsel of clarified butter on the cake, dabbed a lump of sour tamarind conserve at the side; and Kim looked at the load lovingly.

'That is good. When I am in the bazar the bull shall not come to this house. He is a bold beggarman.'

'And thou?' laughed the woman. 'But speak well of bulls. Hast thou not told me that some day a Red Bull will come out of a field to help thee? Now hold all straight and ask for the holy man's blessing upon me. Perhaps, too, he knows a cure for my daughter's sore eyes. Ask him that also, O thou Little Friend of all the World.'

But Kim had danced off ere the end of the sentence, dodging pariah dogs and hungry acquaintances.

'Thus do we beg who know the way of it,' said he proudly to the lama, who opened his eyes at the contents of the bowl. 'Eat now and— I will eat with thee. Ohé *bhistie!*' he called to the water-carrier, sluicing the crotons by the Museum. 'Give water here. We men are thirsty.'

'We men!' said the *bhistie*, laughing. 'Is one skinful enough for such a pair? Drink then, in the name of the Compassionate.'[17]

He loosed a thin stream into Kim's hands, who drank native fashion; but the lama must needs pull out a cup from his inexhaustible upper draperies and drink ceremonially.

'*Pardesi* (a foreigner),' Kim explained, as the old man delivered in an unknown tongue what was evidently a blessing.

They ate together in great content, clearing the beggar's bowl. Then the lama took snuff from a portentous wooden snuff-gourd, fingered his rosary awhile, and so dropped into the easy sleep of age, as the shadow of Zam-Zammah grew long.

Kim loafed over to the nearest tobacco-seller, a rather lively young Mohammedan woman, and begged a rank cigar of the brand that they sell to students of the Punjab University who copy English customs. Then he smoked and thought, knees to chin, under the belly of the gun, and the outcome of his thoughts was a sudden and stealthy departure in the direction of Nila Ram's timber-yard.

The lama did not wake till the evening life of the city had begun with lamp-lighting and the return of white robed clerks and subordinates from the Government offices. He stared dizzily in all directions, but none looked at him save a Hindu urchin in a dirty turban and Isabella-coloured clothes. Suddenly he bowed his head on his knees and wailed.

'What is this?' said the boy, standing before him. 'Hast thou been robbed?'

[17]One of the attributes of Allah.

'It is my new *chela* (my disciple) that is gone away from me, and I know not where he is.'

'And what like of man was thy disciple?'

'It was a boy who came to me in place of him who died, on account of the merit which I had gained when I bowed before the Law within there.' He pointed towards the Museum. 'He came upon me to show me a road which I had lost. He led me into the Wonder House, and by his talk emboldened to speak to the Keeper of the Images, so that I was cheered and made strong. And when I was faint with hunger he begged for me, as would a *chela* for his teacher. Suddenly was he sent. Suddenly has he gone away. It was in my mind to have taught him the Law upon the road to Benares.'

Kim stood amazed at this, because he had overheard the talk in the Museum, and knew that the old man was speaking the truth, which is a thing a native seldom presents to a stranger.

'But I see now that he was but sent upon a purpose. By this I know that I shall find a certain River for which I seek.'

'The River of the Arrow?' said Kim, with a superior smile.

'Is this yet another Sending?' cried the lama. 'To none have I spoken of my search, save to the Priest of the Images. Who art thou?'

Thy *chela*,' said Kim simply, sitting on his heels. 'I have never seen any one like to thee in all this my life. I go with thee to Benares. And, too, I think that so old a man as thou, speaking truth to chance-met people at dusk, is in great need of a disciple.'

'But the River—the River of the Arrow?'

'Oh, that I heard when thou wast speaking to the Englishman. I lay against the door.'

The lama sighed. 'I thought thou hadst been a guide permitted. Such things fall sometimes—but I am not worthy. Thou dost not, then, know the River?'

'Not I.' Kim laughed uneasily. 'I go to look for—for a bull—a Red Bull on a green field who shall help me.' Boylike, if an acquaintance had a scheme, Kim was quite ready with one of his own; and, boylike, he had really thought for as much as twenty minutes at a time of his father's prophecy.

'To what, child?' said the lama.

'God knows, but so my father told me. I heard thy talk in the Wonder House of all those new strange places in the Hills, and if one so old and so little—so used to truth-telling—may go out for the small matter of a river, it seemed to me that I too must go a-travelling. If it is our fate to find those things we shall find them—thou, thy river; and I, my bull, and the strong Pillars and some other matters that I forget.'

'It is not pillars but a Wheel from which I would be free,' said the lama.

'That is all one. Perhaps they will make me a king,' said Kim, serenely prepared for anything.

'I will teach thee other and better desires upon the road,' the lama replied in the voice of authority. 'Let us go to Benares.'

'Not by night. Thieves are abroad. Wait till the day.'

'But there is no place to sleep.' The old man was used to the order of his monastery, and though he slept on the ground, as the Rule decrees, preferred a decency in these things.

'We shall get good lodging at the Kashmir Serai,' said Kim, laughing at his perplexity. 'I have a friend there. Come!'

The hot and crowded bazars blazed with light as they made their way through the press of all the races in Upper India, and the lama mooned through it like a man in a dream. It was his first experience of a large manufacturing city, and the crowded tram-car with its continually squealing brakes frightened him. Half pushed, half towed, he arrived at the high gate of the Kashmir Serai: that huge open square over against the railway station, surrounded with arched cloisters where the camel and horse-caravans put up on their return from Central Asia. Here were all manner of Northern folk, tending tethered ponies and kneeling camels; loading and unloading bales and bundles; drawing water for the evening meal at the creaking well-windlasses; piling grass before the shrieking, wild-eyed stallions; cuffing the surly caravan dogs; paying off camel-drivers; taking on new grooms; swearing, shouting, arguing, and chaffering in the packed square. The cloisters, reached by three or four masonry steps, made a haven of refuge around this turbulent sea. Most of them were rented to traders, as we rent the arches of a viaduct; the space between pillar and pillar being bricked or boarded off into rooms, which were guarded by heavy wooden doors and cumbrous native padlocks. Locked doors showed that the owner was away, and a few rude—sometimes very rude—chalk or paint scratches told where he had gone. Thus: 'Lutuf Ullah is gone to Kurdistan.' Below, in coarse verse: 'O Allah, who sufferest lice to live on the coat of a Kabuli, why hast thou allowed this louse Lutuf to live so long?'

Kim, fending the lama between excited men and excited beasts, sidled along the cloisters to the far end, nearest the railway station, where Mahbub Ali, the horse-trader, lived when he came in from that mysterious land beyond the Passes of the North.

Kim had had many dealings with Mahbub in his little life,—especially between his tenth and his thirteenth year,—and the big burly Afghan, his beard dyed scarlet with lime (for he was elderly and did not wish his gray hairs to show) knew the boy's value as a gossip.

Sometimes he would tell Kim to watch a man who had nothing whatever to do with horses: to follow him for one whole day and report
every soul with whom he talked. Kim would deliver himself of his tale
at evening, and Mahbub would listen without a word or gesture. It
was intrigue of some kind, Kim knew; but its worth lay in saying
nothing whatever to any one except Mahbub, who gave him beautiful
meals all hot from the cookshop at the head of the serai, and once as
much as eight annas in money.

'He is here,' said Kim, hitting a bad-tempered camel on the nose.
'Ohé, Mahbub Ali!' He halted at a dark arch and slipped behind the
bewildered lama.

The horse-trader, his deep, embroidered Bokhariot belt unloosed,
was lying on a pair of silk carpet saddle-bags, pulling lazily at an immense silver hookah. He turned his head very slightly at the cry; and
seeing only the tall silent figure, chuckled in his deep chest.

'Allah! A lama! A Red Lama! It is far from Lahore to the Passes.
What dost thou do here?'

The lama held out the begging-bowl mechanically.

'God's curse on all unbelievers!' said Mahbub. 'I do not give to a
lousy Tibetan; but ask my Baltis over yonder behind the camels. They
may value your blessings. Oh, horseboys, here is a countryman of
yours. See if he be hungry.'

A shaven, crouching Balti, who had come down with the horses,
and who was nominally some sort of degraded Buddhist, fawned
upon the priest, and in thick gutturals besought the Holy One to sit at
the horse-boys' fire.

'Go!' said Kim, pushing him lightly, and the lama strode away,
leaving Kim at the edge of the cloister.

'Go!' said Mahbub Ali, returning to his hookah. 'Little Hindu,
run away. God's curse on all unbelievers! Beg from those of my tail
who are of thy faith.'

'Maharaj,' whined Kim, using the Hindu form of address, and
thoroughly enjoying the situation; 'my father is dead—my mother is
dead—my stomach is empty.'

'Beg from my men among the horses, I say. There must be some
Hindus in my tail.'

'Oh, Mahbub Ali, but am *I* a Hindu?' said Kim in English.

The trader gave no sign of astonishment, but looked under
shaggy eyebrows.

'Little Friend of all the World,' said he, 'what is this?'

'Nothing. I am now that holy man's disciple; and we go a pilgrimage together—to Benares, he says. He is quite mad, and I am
tired of Lahore city. I wish new air and water.'

'But for whom dost thou work? Why come to me?' The voice was harsh with suspicion.

'To whom else should I come? I have no money. It is not good to go about without money. Thou wilt sell many horses to the officers. They are very fine horses, these new ones: I have seen them. Give me a rupee, Mahbub Ali, and when I come to my wealth I will give thee a bond and pay.'

'Um,' said Mahbub Ali, thinking swiftly. 'Thou hast never before lied to me. Call that lama—stand back in the dark.'

'Oh, our tales will agree,' said Kim laughing.

'We go to Benares,' said the lama, as soon as he understood the drift of Mahbub Ali's questions. 'The boy and I. I go to seek for a certain River.'

'Maybe—but the boy?'

'He is my disciple. He was sent, I think, to guide me to that River. Sitting under a gun was I when he came suddenly. Such things have befallen the fortunate to whom guidance was allowed. But I remember now, he said he was of this world—a Hindu.'

'And his name?'

'That I did not ask. Is he not my disciple?'

'His country—his race—his village? Mussalman—Sikh—Hindu—Jain—low caste or high?'

'Why should I ask? There is neither high nor low in the Middle Way. If he is my *chela*—does—will—can any one take him from me? for, look you, without him I shall not find my river.' He wagged his head solemnly.

'None shall take him from thee. Go, sit among my Baltis,' said Mahbub Ali, and the lama drifted off, soothed by the promise.

'Is he not quite mad?' said Kim, coming forward to the light again. 'Why should I lie to thee, Hajji?'

Mahbub puffed his hookah in silence. Then he began, almost whispering: 'Umballa is on the road to Benares—if indeed ye two go there.'

'Tck! Tck! I tell thee he does not know how to lie—as we two know.'

'And if thou wilt carry a message for me as far as Umballa, I will give thee money. It concerns a horse—a white stallion which I have sold to an officer upon the last time I returned from the Passes. But then—stand nearer and hold up hands as begging—the pedigree of the white stallion was not fully established, and that officer, who is now at Umballa, bade me make it clear.' (Mahbub here described the horse and the appearance of the officer.) 'So the message to that officer will be: "The pedigree of the white stallion is fully established." By this will he know that thou comest from me. He will then say

"What proof hast thou?" and thou wilt answer: "Mahbub Ali has given me the proof."'

'And all for the sake of a white stallion,' said Kim, with a giggle, his eyes aflame.

'That pedigree I will give thee now—in my own fashion—and some hard words as well.' A shadow passed behind Kim, and a feeding camel. Mahbub Ali raised his voice.

'Allah! Art thou the only beggar in the city? Thy mother is dead. Thy father is dead. So is it with all of them. Well, well——' he turned as feeling on the floor beside him and tossed a flap of soft, greasy Mussalman bread to the boy. 'Go and lie down among my horse-boys for to-night—thou and the lama. To-morrow I may give thee service.'

Kim slunk away, his teeth in the bread, and, as he expected, he found a small wad of folded tissue-paper wrapped in oil-skin, with three silver rupees—enormous largesse. He smiled and thrust money and paper into his leather amulet-case. The lama, sumptuously fed by Mahbub's Baltis, was already asleep in a corner of one of the stalls. Kim lay down beside him and laughed. He knew he had rendered a service to Mahbub Ali, and not for one little minute did he believe the tale of the stallion's pedigree.

But Kim did not suspect that Mahbub Ali, known as one of the best horse-dealers in the Punjab, a wealthy and enterprising trader, whose caravans penetrated far and far into the Back of Beyond, was registered in one of the locked books of the Indian Survey Department as C.25.1B. Twice or thrice yearly C.25 would send in a little story, baldly told but most interesting, and generally—it was checked by the statements of R.17 and M.4—quite true. It concerned all manner of out-of-the-way mountain principalities, explorers of nationalities other than English, and the gun-trade—was, in brief, a small portion of that vast mass of 'information received' on which the Indian Government acts. But, recently, five confederated Kings, who had no business to confederate, had been informed by a kindly Northern Power that there was a leakage of news from their territories into British India.[18] So those Kings' prime ministers were seriously annoyed and took steps, after the Oriental fashion. They suspected, among many others, the bullying, red-bearded horse-dealer whose caravans ploughed through their fastnesses belly deep in snow. At least, his caravan that season had been ambushed and shot at twice on the way down, when Mahbub's men accounted for three strange ruffians who might, or might not, have been hired for the

---

[18]Though the Survey was officially the British office for mapping out India, its work also extended beyond colonial boundaries. The Survey used Indians to map the areas outside British control, as they would be less noticeable than Europeans. The "kindly Northern Power" was Russia, Britain's rival for strategic control over the region (see p. 242).

job. Therefore Mahbub had avoided halting at the insalubrious city of Peshawur, and had come through without stop to Lahore, where, knowing his country-people, he anticipated curious developments.

And there was that on Mahbub Ali which he did not wish to keep an hour longer than was necessary—a wad of closely folded tissue-paper, wrapped in oil-skin—an impersonal, unaddressed statement, with five microscopic pin-holes in one corner, that most scandalously betrayed the five confederated Kings, the sympathetic Northern Power, a Hindu banker in Peshawur, a firm of gun-makers in Belgium, and an important, semi-independent Mohammedan ruler to the south. This last was R.17's work, which Mahbub had picked up beyond the Dora Pass and was carrying in for R.17, who, owing to circumstances over which he had no control, could not leave his post of observation. Dynamite was milky and innocuous beside that report of C.25; and even an Oriental, with an Oriental's views of the value of time, could see that the sooner it was in the proper hands the better. Mahbub had no particular desire to die by violence, because two or three family blood-feuds across the border hung unfinished on his hands, and when these scores were cleared he intended to settle down as a more or less virtuous citizen. He had never passed the serai gate since his arrival two days ago, but had been ostentatious in sending telegrams to Bombay, where he banked some of his money; to Delhi, where a sub-partner of his own clan was selling horses to the agent of a Rajputana state; and to Umballa, where an Englishman was excitedly demanding the pedigree of a white stallion. The public letter-writer, who knew English, composed excellent telegrams, such as:— '*Creighton, Laurel Bank, Umballa.—Horse is Arabian as already advised. Sorrowful delayed-pedigree which am translating.*' And later to the same address: '*Much sorrowful delay. Will forward pedigree.*' To his sub-partner at Delhi he wired: '*Lutuf Ullah.—Have wired two thousand rupees your credit Luchman Narain's bank.*' This was entirely in the way of trade, but every one of those telegrams was discussed and re-discussed, by parties who conceived themselves to be interested, before they went over to the railway station in charge of a foolish Balti, who allowed all sorts of people to read them on the road.

When, in Mahbub's own picturesque language, he had muddied the wells of inquiry with the stick of precaution, Kim had dropped on him, sent from heaven; and, being as prompt as he was unscrupulous, Mahbub Ali, used to taking all sorts of gusty chances, pressed him into service on the spot.

A wandering lama with a low-caste boy-servant might attract a moment's interest as they wandered about India, the land of pilgrims; but no one would suspect them or, what was more to the point, rob.

He called for a new light-ball to his hookah, and considered the case. If the worst came to the worst, and the boy came to harm, the paper would incriminate nobody. And he would go up to Umballa leisurely and—at a certain risk of exciting fresh suspicion—repeat his tale by word of mouth to the people concerned.

But R.17's report was the kernel of the whole affair, and it would be distinctly inconvenient if that failed to come to hand. However, God was great, and Mahbub Ali felt he had done all he could for the time being. Kim was the one soul in the world who had never told him a lie. That would have been a fatal blot on Kim's character if Mahbub had not known that to others, for his own ends or Mahbub's business, Kim could lie like an Oriental.

Then Mahbub Ali rolled across the serai to the Gate of the Harpies who paint their eyes and trap the stranger, and was at some pains to call on the one girl who, he had reason to believe, was a particular friend of a smooth-faced Kashmiri pundit who had waylaid his simple Balti in the matter of the telegrams. It was an utterly foolish thing to do; because they fell to drinking perfumed brandy against the Law of the Prophet, and Mahbub grew wonderfully drunk, and the gates of his mouth were loosened, and he pursued the Flower of Delight with the feet of intoxication till he fell flat among the cushions, where the Flower of Delight, aided by a smooth-faced Kashmiri pundit, searched him from head to foot most thoroughly.

About the same hour Kim heard soft feet in Mahbub's deserted stall. The horse-trader, curiously enough, had left his door unlocked, and his men were busy celebrating their return to India with a whole sheep of Mahbub's bounty. A sleek young gentleman from Delhi, armed with a bunch of keys which the Flower had unshackled from the senseless one's belt, went through every single box, bundle, mat, and saddle-bag in Mahbub's possession even more systematically than the Flower and the pundit were searching the owner.

'And I think,' said the Flower scornfully an hour later, one rounded elbow on the snoring carcase, 'that he is no more than a pig of an Afghan horse-dealer, with no thought except women and horses. Moreover, he may have sent it away by now—if ever there were such a thing.'

'Nay—in a matter touching Five Kings it would be next his black heart,' said the pundit. 'Was there nothing?'

The Delhi man laughed and resettled his turban as he entered. 'I searched between the soles of his slippers as the Flower searched his clothes. This is not the man but another. I leave little unseen.'

'They did not say he was the very man,' said the pundit thoughtfully. 'They said, "Look if he be the man, since our councils are troubled."'

'That North country is full of horse-dealers as an old coat of lice. There is Sikandar Khan, Nur Ali Beg, and Farrukh Shah—all heads of Kafilas—who deal there,' said the Flower.

'They have not yet come in,' said the pundit. 'Thou must ensnare them later.'

'Phew!' said the Flower with deep disgust, rolling Mahbub's head from her lap. 'I earn my money. Farrukh Shah is a bear, Ali Beg a swashbuckler, and old Sikandar Khan—yaie! Go! I sleep now. This swine will not stir till dawn.'

When Mahbub woke, the Flower talked to him severely on the sin of drunkenness. Asiatics do not wink when they have out-manœuvred an enemy, but as Mahbub Ali cleared his throat, tightened his belt, and staggered forth under the early morning stars, he came very near to it.

'What a colt's trick,' said he to himself. 'As if every girl in Peshawur did not use it! But 'twas prettily done. Now God He knows how many more there be upon the road who have orders to test me—perhaps with the knife. So it stands that the boy must go to Umballa—and by rail—for the writing is something urgent. I abide here, following the Flower and drinking wine as an Afghan coper should.'

He halted at the stall next but one to his own. His men lay there heavy with sleep. There was no sign of Kim or the lama.

'Up!' He stirred a sleeper. 'Whither went those who lay here last even—the lama and the boy? Is aught missing?'

'Nay,' grunted the man, 'the old madman rose at second cockcrow saying he would go to Benares, and the young one led him away.'

'The curse of Allah on all unbelievers,' said Mahbub heartily, and climbed into his own stall, growling in his beard.

But it was Kim who had wakened the lama—Kim with one eye laid against a knot-hole in the planking, who had seen the Delhi man's search through the boxes. This was no common thief that turned over letters, bills, and saddles—no mere burglar who ran a little knife sideways into the soles of Mahbub's slippers, or picked the seams of the saddle-bags so deftly. At first Kim had been minded to give the alarm—the long-drawn *cho-or—choor!* (thief! thief!) that sets the serai ablaze of nights; but he looked more carefully, and, hand on amulet, drew his own conclusions.

'It must be the pedigree of that made-up horse-lie,' said he, 'the thing that I carry to Umballa. Better that we go now. Those who search bags with knives may presently search bellies with knives. Surely there is a woman behind this. Hai! Hai!' in a whisper to the light-sleeping old man. 'Come. It is time—time to go to Benares.'

The lama rose obediently, and they passed out of the serai like shadows.

CHAPTER II

For whoso will, from Pride released,
Contemning neither man nor beast,
May hear the Soul of all the East
About him at Kamakura.[1]

THEY entered the fort-like railway station, black in the end of night; the electrics sizzling over the goods-yard where they handle the heavy Northern grain-traffic.

'This is the work of devils!' said the lama, recoiling from the hollow echoing darkness, the glimmer of rails between the masonry platforms, and the maze of girders above. He stood in a gigantic stone hall paved, it seemed, with the sheeted dead—third-class passengers who had taken their tickets overnight and were sleeping in the waiting-rooms. All hours of the twenty-four are alike to Orientals, and their passenger traffic is regulated accordingly.

'This is where the fire-carriages come. One stands behind that hole'—Kim pointed to the ticket-office—'who will give thee a paper to take thee to Umballa.'

'But we go to Benares,' he replied petulantly.

'All one. Benares then. Quick: she comes!'

'Take thou the purse.'

The lama, not so well used to trains as he had pretended, started as the 3.25 A.M. south bound roared in. The sleepers sprung to life, and the station filled with clamour and shoutings, cries of water and sweetmeat vendors, shouts of native policemen, and shrill yells of women gathering up their baskets, their families, and their husbands.

'It is the train—only the *te-rain*. It will not come here. Wait!' Amazed at the lama's immense simplicity (he had handed him a small bag full of rupees), Kim asked and paid for a ticket to Umballa. A sleepy clerk grunted and flung out a ticket to the next station, just six miles distant.

'Nay,' said Kim, scanning it with a grin. 'This may serve for farmers, but I live in the city of Lahore. It was cleverly done, babu. Now give the ticket to Umballa.'

The babu scowled and dealt the proper ticket.

'Now another to Amritzar,' said Kim, who had no notion of spending Mahbub Ali's money on anything so crude as a paid ride to Umballa. 'The price is so much. The small money in return is just so much. I know the ways of the *te-rain*. . . . Never did *yogi* need *chela* as thou dost,' he went on merrily to the bewildered lama. 'They would have

---

[1]These lines appear, slightly altered, in "The Buddha at Kamakura" (see p. 260).

flung thee out at Mian Mir but for me. This way! Come.' He returned the money, keeping only one anna in each rupee of the price of the Umballa ticket as his commission—the immemorial commission of Asia.

The lama jibbed at the open door of a crowded third-class carriage. 'Were it not better to walk?' said he weakly.

A burly Sikh artisan thrust forth his bearded head. 'Is he afraid? Do not be afraid. I remember the time when I was afraid of the train. Enter! This thing is the work of the Government.'

'I do not fear,' said the lama. 'Have ye room within for two?'

'There is no room even for a mouse,' shrilled the wife of a well-to-do cultivator—a Hindu Jat from the rich Jullundur district. Our night trains are not as well looked after as the day ones, where the sexes are very strictly kept to separate carriages.

'Oh, mother of my son, we can make space,' said the blue-turbaned husband. 'Pick up the child. It is a holy man, see'st thou?'

'And my lap full of seventy times seven bundles! Why not bid him sit on my knee, Shameless? But men are ever thus!' She looked round for approval. An Amritzar courtesan near the window sniffed behind her head drapery.

'Enter! Enter!' cried a fat Hindu money-lender, his folded account-book in a cloth under his arm. With an oily smirk: 'It is well to be kind to the poor.'

'Aye, at seven per cent a month with a mortgage on the unborn calf,' said a young Dogra soldier going south on leave; and they all laughed.

'Will it travel to Benares?' said the lama.

'Assuredly. Else why should we come? Enter, or we are left,' cried Kim.

'See!' shrilled the Amritzar girl. 'He has never entered a train. Oh see!'

'Nay, help,' said the cultivator, putting out a large brown hand and hauling him in. 'Thus is it done, father.'

'But—but—I sit on the floor. It is against the Rule to sit on a bench,' said the lama. 'Moreover, it cramps me.'

'I say,' began the money-lender, pursing his lips, 'that there is not one rule of right living which these *te-rains* do not cause us to break. We sit, for example, side by side with all castes and peoples.'

'Yea, and with most outrageously shameless ones,' said the wife, scowling at the Amritzar girl making eyes at the young sepoy.

'I said we might have gone by cart along the road,' said the husband, 'and thus have saved some money.'

'Yes—and spent twice over what we saved on food by the way. That was talked out ten thousand times.'

'Ay, by ten thousand tongues,' grunted he.

'The Gods help us poor women if we may not speak. Oho! He is of that sort which may not look at or reply to a woman.' For the lama, constrained by his Rule, took not the faintest notice of her. 'And his disciple is like him?'

'Nay, mother,' said Kim most promptly. 'Not when the woman is well-looking and above all charitable to the hungry.'

'A beggar's answer,' said the Sikh, laughing. 'Thou hast brought it on thyself, sister!' Kim's hands were crooked in supplication.

'And whither goest thou?' said the woman, handing him the half of a cake from a greasy package.

'Even to Benares.'

'Jugglers belike?' the young soldier suggested. 'Have ye any tricks to pass the time? Why does not that yellow man answer?'

'Because,' said Kim stoutly, 'he is holy, and thinks upon matters hidden from thee.'

'That may be well. We of the Loodhiana Sikhs,' he rolled it out sonorously, 'do not trouble our heads with doctrine. We fight.'[2]

'My sister's brother's son is *naik* (corporal) in that regiment,' said the Sikh craftsman quietly. 'There are also some Dogra companies there.' The soldier glared, for a Dogra is of other caste than a Sikh, and the banker tittered.

'They are all one to me,' said the Amritzar girl.

'That we believe,' snorted the cultivator's wife malignantly.

'Nay, but all who serve the Sirkar with weapons in their hands are, as it were, one brotherhood. There is one brotherhood of the caste, but beyond that again'—she looked round timidly—'the bond of the *Pulton*—the Regiment—eh?'

'My brother is in a Jat regiment,' said the cultivator. 'Dogras be good men.'

'Thy Sikhs at least were of that opinion,' said the soldier, with a scowl at the placid old man in the corner. '*Thy* Sikhs thought so when our two companies came to help them at the Pirzai Kotal in the face of eight Afreedee standards on the ridge not three months gone.'[3]

He told the story of a Border action in which the Dogra companies of the Loodhiana Sikhs had acquitted themselves well. The Amritzar girl smiled; for she knew the tale was to win her approval.

[2]After the hard-fought Sikh Wars of the 1840s, Sikhs sided with the British during the 1857 Rebellion. Sikh regiments from Ludhiana became famous defenders of the Northwest Frontier.

[3]Fierce, well-armed, strategically effective fighters, the Pathan Afridi tribe sought control of crucial Northwest territories including the Khyber Pass. Conflicts with British colonial troops, including Sikhs, subsided somewhat after the Second Anglo-Afghan War, exploding again in 1897.

'Alas!' said the cultivator's wife at the end. 'So their villages were burnt and their little children made homeless?'

'They had marked our dead.[4] They paid a great payment after we of the Sikhs had schooled them. So it was. Is this Amritzar?'

'Ay, and here they cut our tickets,' said the banker, fumbling at his belt.

The lamps were paling in the dawn when the half-caste guard came round. Ticket-collecting is a slow business in the East, where people secrete their tickets in all sorts of curious places. Kim produced his and was told to get out.

'But I go to Umballa,' he protested. 'I go with this holy man.'

'Thou canst go to Jehannum for aught I care. This ticket is only to Amritzar. Out!'

Kim burst into a flood of tears, protesting that the lama was his father and his mother, that he was the prop of the lama's declining years, and that the lama would die without his care. All the carriage bade the guard be merciful,—the banker was specially eloquent here,—but the guard hauled Kim on to the platform. The lama blinked, he could not overtake the situation, and Kim lifted up his voice and wept outside the carriage window.

'I am very poor. My father is dead—my mother is dead. Oh, charitable ones, if I am left here, who shall tend that old man?'

'What—what is this?' the lama repeated. 'He must go to Benares. He must come with me. He is my *chela*. If there is money to be paid——'

'Oh, be silent,' whispered Kim; 'are we Rajahs to throw away good silver when the world is so charitable?'

The Amritzar girl stepped out with her bundles, and it was on her that Kim kept his watchful eye. Ladies of that persuasion, he knew, were generous.

'A ticket—a little *tikkut* to Umballa—O Breaker of Hearts!' She laughed. 'Hast thou no charity?'

'Does the holy man come from the North?'

'From far and far in the North he comes,' cried Kim. 'From among the hills.'

'There is snow among the pine trees in the North—in the hills there is snow. My mother was from Kulu. Get thee a ticket. Ask him for a blessing.'

'Ten thousand blessings,' shrilled Kim. 'O Holy One, a woman has given us in charity so that I can come with thee—a woman with a golden heart. I run for the *tikkut*.'

[4]Mutilated.

The girl looked up at the lama, who had mechanically followed Kim to the platform. He bowed his head that he might not see her, and muttered in Tibetan as she passed on with the crowd.

'Light come—light go,' said the cultivator's wife viciously.

'She has acquired merit,' returned the lama. 'Beyond doubt it was a nun.'

'There be ten thousand such nuns in Amritzar alone. Return, old man, or the train may depart without thee,' cried the banker.

'Not only was it sufficient for the ticket, but for a little food also,' said Kim, leaping to his place. 'Now eat, Holy One. Look. Day comes!'

Golden, rose, saffron, and pink, the morning mists smoked away across the flat green levels. All the rich Punjab lay out in the splendour of the keen sun. The lama flinched a little as the telegraph-posts swung by.

'Great is the speed of the train,' said the banker, with a patronising grin. 'We have gone farther since Lahore than thou couldst walk in two days: at even, we shall enter Umballa.'

'And that is still far from Benares,' said the lama wearily, mumbling over the cakes that Kim offered. They all unloosed their bundles and made their morning meal. Then the banker, the cultivator, and the soldier prepared their pipes and wrapped the compartment in choking, acrid smoke, spitting and coughing and enjoying themselves. The Sikh and the cultivator's wife chewed *pan*; the lama took snuff and told his beads, while Kim, cross-legged, smiled over the comfort of a full stomach.

'What rivers have ye by Benares?' said the lama of a sudden to the carriage at large.

'We have Gunga,'[5] returned the banker, when the little titter had subsided.

'What others?'

'What other than Gunga?'

'Nay, but in my mind was the thought of a certain River of healing.'

'That is Gunga. Who bathes in her is made clean and goes to the gods. Thrice have I made pilgrimage to Gunga.' He looked round proudly.

'There was need,' said the young sepoy drily, and the travellers' laugh turned against the banker.

'Clean—to return again to the Gods,' the lama muttered. 'And to go forth on the round of lives anew—still tied to the Wheel.' He shook his head testily. 'But maybe there is a mistake. Who, then, made Gunga in the beginning?'

'The Gods. Of what known faith art thou?' the banker said, appalled.

---

[5]The Ganges, Hindu holy river.

'I follow the Law—the Most Excellent Law. So it was the Gods that made Gunga. What like of Gods were they?'

The carriage looked at him in amazement. It was inconceivable that any one should be ignorant of Gunga.

'What—what is thy God?' said the money-lender at last.

'Hear!' said the lama, shifting the rosary to his hand. 'Hear: for I speak of Him now! O people of Hind, listen!'

He began in Urdu the tale of the Lord Buddha, but, borne by his own thoughts, slid into Tibetan and long-droned texts from a Chinese book of the Buddha's life. The gentle, tolerant folk looked on reverently. All India is full of holy men stammering gospels in strange tongues; shaken and consumed in the fires of their own zeal; dreamers, babblers, and visionaries: as it has been from the beginning and will continue to the end.

'Um!' said the soldier of the Loodhiana Sikhs. 'There was a Mohammedan regiment lay next to us at the Pirzai Kotal, and a priest of theirs,—he was, as I remember, a *naik*,—when the fit was on him, spake prophecies. But the mad all are in God's keeping. His officers overlooked much in that man.'

The lama fell back on Urdu, remembering that he was in a strange land. 'Hear the tale of the Arrow which our Lord loosed from the bow,' he said.

This was much more to their taste, and they listened curiously while he told it. 'Now, O people of Hind, I go to seek that River. Know ye aught that may guide me, for we be all men and women in evil case.'

'There is Gunga—and Gunga alone—who washes away sin,' ran the murmur round the carriage.

'Though past question we have good Gods Jullundur-way,' said the cultivator's wife, looking out of window. 'See how they have blessed the crops.'

'To search every river in the Punjab is no small matter,' said her husband. 'For me, a stream that leaves good silt on my land suffices, and I thank Bhumia, the God of the Homestead.' He shrugged one knotted, bronzed shoulder.

'Think you our Lord came so far north?' said the lama, turning to Kim.

'It may be,' Kim replied soothingly, as he spat red *pan*-juice on the floor.

'The last of the Great Ones,' said the Sikh with authority, 'was Sikander Julkarn (Alexander the Great). He paved the streets of Jullunder and built a great tank near Umballa. That pavement holds to this day; and the tank is there also. I never heard of thy God.'

'Let thy hair grow long and talk Punjabi,' said the young soldier jestingly to Kim, quoting a Northern proverb. 'That is all that makes a Sikh.' But he did not say this very loud.

The lama sighed and shrunk into himself, a dingy, shapeless mass. In the pauses of their talk they could hear the low droning—'*Om mane pudme hum! Om mane pudme hum!*'—and the thick click of the wooden rosary beads.[6]

'It irks me,' he said at last. 'The speed and the clatter irk me. Moreover, my *chela*, I think that may be we have overpassed that River.'

'Peace, peace,' said Kim. 'Was not the River near Benares? We are yet far from the place.'

'But—if our Lord came north, it may be any one of these little ones that we have run across.'

'I do not know.'

'But thou wast sent to me—wast thou sent to me?—for the merit I had acquired over yonder at Such-zen. From beside the cannon didst thou come—bearing two faces—and two garbs.'

'Peace. One must not speak of these things here,' whispered Kim. 'There was but one of me. Think again and thou wilt remember. A boy—a Hindu boy—by the great green cannon.'

'But was there not also an Englishman with a white beard—holy among images—who himself made more sure my assurance of the River of the Arrow?'

'He—we—went to the Ajaib-Gher in Lahore to pray before the gods there,' Kim explained to the openly listening company. 'And the Sahib of the Wonder House talked to him—yes, this is truth—as a brother. He is a very holy man, from far beyond the hills. Rest thou. In time we come to Umballa.'

'But my River—the River of my healing?'

'And then, if it please thee, we will go hunting for that River on foot. So that we miss nothing—not even a little rivulet in a field-side.'

'But thou hast a Search of thine own?' The lama—very pleased that he remembered so well—sat bolt upright.

'Ay,' said Kim, humouring him. The boy was entirely happy to be out chewing *pan* and seeing new people in the great good-tempered world.

'It was a bull—a Red Bull that shall come and help thee—and carry thee—whither? I have forgotten. A Red Bull on a green field, was it not?'

---

[6]Carved and painted on rocks, walls, and monuments and enshrined in prayer wheels, this most famous of Buddhist mantras is chanted both publicly and privately throughout Tibet, by children and lamas alike.

'Nay, it will carry me nowhere,' said Kim. 'It is but a tale I told thee.'

'What is this?' the cultivator's wife leaned forward, her bracelets clinking on her arm. 'Do ye both dream dreams? A Red Bull on a green field, that shall carry thee to the Heavens—or what? Was it a vision? Did one make a prophecy? *We* have a Red Bull in our village behind Jullundur city, and he grazes by choice in the very greenest of our fields!'

'Give a woman an old wife's tale and a weaverbird a leaf and a thread, they will weave wonderful things,' said the Sikh. 'All holy men dream dreams, and by following holy men their disciples attain that power.'

'A Red Bull on a green field, was it?' the lama repeated. 'In a former life it may be thou hast acquired merit, and the Bull will come to reward thee.'

'Nay—nay—it was but a tale one told to me—for a jest belike. But I will seek the Bull about Umballa, and thou canst look for thy River and rest from the clatter of the train.'

'It may be that the Bull knows—that he is sent to guide us both,' said the lama, hopefully as a child. Then to the company, indicating Kim: 'This one was sent to me but yesterday. He is not, I think, of this world.'

'Beggars a plenty have I met, and holy men to boot, but never such a *yogi* nor such a disciple,' said the woman.

Her husband touched his forehead lightly with one finger and smiled. But the next time the lama would eat they took care to give him their best.

And at last—tired, sleepy, and dusty—they reached Umballa City Station.

'We abide here upon a law-suit,' said the cultivator's wife to Kim. 'We lodge with my man's cousin's younger brother. There is room also in the courtyard for thy *yogi* and for thee. Will—will he give me a blessing?'

'O holy man! A woman with a heart of gold gives us lodging for the night. It is a kindly land, this land of the South. See how we have been helped since the dawn!'

The lama bowed his head in benediction.

'To fill my cousin's younger brother's house with wastrels——' the husband began, as he shouldered his heavy bamboo staff.

'Thy cousin's younger brother owes my father's cousin something yet on his daughter's marriage-feast,' said the woman crisply. 'Let him put their food to that account. The *yogi* will beg, I doubt not.'

'Ay, I beg for him,' said Kim, anxious only to get the lama under shelter for the night, that he might seek Mahbub Ali's Englishman and deliver himself of the white stallion's pedigree.

'Now,' said he, when the lama had come to an anchor in the inner courtyard of a decent Hindu house behind the cantonments, 'I go away for awhile—to—to buy us victual in the bazar. Do not stray abroad till I return.'

'Thou wilt return? Thou will surely return?' The old man caught at his wrist. 'And thou wilt return in this very same shape? Is it too late to look to-night for the River?'

'Too late and too dark. Be comforted. Think how far thou art on the road—an hundred *kos* from Lahore already.'

'Yea—and farther from my monastery. Alas! It is a great and terrible world.'

Kim stole out and away, as unremarkable a figure as ever carried his own and a few score thousand other folk's fate slung round his neck. Mahbub Ali's directions left him little doubt of the house in which his Englishman lived; and a groom, bringing a dog-cart home from the Club, made him quite sure. It remained only to identify his man, and Kim slipped through the garden hedge and hid in a clump of plumed grass close to the verandah. The house blazed with lights, and servants moved about tables dressed with flowers, glass, and silver. Presently forth came an Englishman, dressed in black and white, humming a tune. It was too dark to see his face, so Kim, beggar-wise, tried an old experiment.

'Protector of the Poor!'

The man backed towards the voice.

'Mahbub Ali says——'

'Hah! What says Mahbub Ali?' He made no attempt to look for the speaker, and that showed Kim that he knew.

'The pedigree of the white stallion is fully established.'

'What proof is there?' The Englishman switched at the rose-hedge in the side of the drive.

'Mahbub Ali has given me this proof.' Kim flipped the wad of folded paper into the air, and it fell on the path beside the man, who put his foot on it as a gardener came round the corner. When the servant passed he picked it up, dropped a rupee,—Kim could hear the clink,—and strode into the house, never turning round. Swiftly Kim took up the money; but, for all his training, he was Irish enough by birth to reckon silver the least part of any game. What he desired was the visible effect of action; so, instead of slinking away, he lay close in the grass and wormed nearer to the house.

He saw—Indian bungalows are open through and through—the Englishman return to a small dressing-room, in a corner of the verandah, that was half-office, littered with papers and despatch-boxes, and sit down to study Mahbub Ali's message. His face, by the full ray of the kerosene lamp, changed and darkened, and Kim, used as every beggar must be to watching countenances, took good note.

'Will! Will, dear!' called a woman's voice. 'You ought to be in the drawing-room. They'll be here in a minute.'

The man still read intently.

'Will!' said the voice, five minutes later. '*He's* come. I can hear the troopers in the drive.'

The man dashed out bareheaded as a big landau with four native troopers behind it halted at the verandah, and a tall, black-haired man, erect as an arrow, swung out, preceded by a young officer who laughed pleasantly.

Flat on his belly lay Kim, almost touching the high wheels. His man and the black stranger exchanged two sentences.

'Certainly sir,' said the young officer promptly. 'Everything waits while a horse is concerned.'

'We shan't be more than twenty minutes,' said Kim's man. 'You can do the honours—keep 'em amused, and all that.'

'Tell one of the troopers to wait,' said the tall man, and they both passed into the dressing-room together as the landau rolled away. Kim saw their heads bent over Mahbub Ali's message, and heard the voices—one low and deferential, the other sharp and decisive.

'It isn't a question of weeks. It is a question of days—hours almost,' said the elder. 'I'd been expecting it for some time, but this'— he tapped Mahbub Ali's paper—'clenches it. Grogan's dining here to-night, isn't he?'

'Yes sir, and Macklin too.'

'Very good. I'll speak to them myself. The matter will be referred to the Council, of course, but this is a case where one is justified in assuming that we take action at once. Warn the Pindi and Peshawur brigades. It will disorganise all the summer reliefs, but we can't help that. This comes of not smashing them thoroughly the first time. Eight thousand should be enough.'[7]

'What about artillery, sir?'

'I must consult Macklin.'

'Then it means war?'

'No. Punishment. When a man is bound by the action of his predecessor——'

'But C.25 may have lied.'

'He bears out the other's information. Practically, they showed their hand six months back. But Devenish would have it there was a chance of peace. Of course they used it to make themselves stronger. Send off those telegrams at once,—the new code, not the old,—mine and Wharton's. I

[7]The Viceroy and his Council (the colonial government) will be officially consulted; but mobilizing the 8,000 brigade members stationed at Peshawar and Rawalpindi comes first.

don't think we need keep the ladies waiting any longer. We can settle the rest over the cigars. I thought it was coming. It's punishment—not war.'

As the trooper cantered off Kim crawled round to the back of the house, where, going on his Lahore experiences, he judged there would be food—and information. The kitchen was crowded with excited scullions, one of whom kicked him.

'Aie,' said Kim, feigning tears. 'I came only to wash dishes in return for a bellyful.'

'All Umballa is on the same errand. Get hence. They go in now with the soup. Think you that we who serve Creighton Sahib need strange scullions to help us through a big dinner?'

'It is a very big dinner,' said Kim, looking at the plates.

'Small wonder. The guest of honour is none other than the Jang-i-Lat Sahib (the Commander-in-Chief).'

'Ho!' said Kim, with the correct guttural note of wonder. He had learned what he wanted, and when the scullion turned he was gone.

'And all that trouble,' said he to himself, thinking as usual in Hindustanee, 'for a horse's pedigree! Mahbub Ali should have come to me to learn a little lying. Every time before that I have borne a message it concerned a woman. Now it is men. Better. The tall man said that they will loose a great army to punish some one—somewhere—the news goes to Pindi and Peshawur. There are also guns. Would I had crept nearer. It is big news!'

He returned to find the cultivator's cousin's younger brother discussing the family law-suit in all its bearings with the cultivator and his wife and a few friends, while the lama dozed. After the evening meal some one passed him a water-pipe; and Kim felt very much of a man as he pulled at the smooth cocoanut-shell, his legs spread abroad in the moonlight, his tongue clicking in remarks from time to time. His hosts were most polite; for the cultivator's wife had told them of his vision of the Red Bull, and of his probable descent from another world. Moreover, the lama was a great and venerable curiosity. The family priest, an old, tolerant Sarsut Brahmin,[8] dropped in later, and naturally started a theological argument to impress the family. By creed, of course, they were all on their priest's side, but the lama was the guest and the novelty. His gentle kindliness, and his impressive Chinese quotations, that sounded like spells, delighted them hugely; and in this sympathetic, simple air, he expanded like the Bodhisat's own lotus, speaking of his life in the great hills of Such-zen, before, as he said, 'I rose up to seek enlightenment.'

Then it came out that in those worldly days he had been a master-hand at casting horoscopes and nativities; and the family priest led

---

[8]Associated with learning and the priesthood, Brahmins form the highest of the four main Hindu castes. Sarsut Brahmins were known for ministering to all Hindus, regardless of caste.

him on to describe his methods; each giving the planets names that the other could not understand, and pointing upwards as the big stars sailed across the dark. The children of the house tugged unrebuked at his rosary; and he clean forgot the Rule which forbids looking at women as he talked of enduring snows, landslips, blocked passes, the remote cliffs where men find sapphires and turquoise, and that wonderful upland road that leads at last into Great China itself.

'How thinkest thou of this one?' said the cultivator aside to the priest.

'A holy man—a holy man indeed. His Gods are not the Gods, but his feet are upon the Way,' was the answer. 'And his methods of nativities, though that is beyond thee, are wise and sure.'

'Tell me,' said Kim lazily, 'whether I find my Red Bull on a green field, as was promised me.'

'What knowledge hast thou of thy birth-hour?' the priest asked, swelling with importance.

'Between first and second cockcrow of the first night in May.'

'Of what year?'

'I do not know; but upon the hour that I cried first fell the great earthquake in Srinagur which is in Kashmir.' This Kim had from the woman who took care of him, and she again from Kimball O'Hara. The earthquake had been felt in India, and for long stood a leading date in the Punjab.

'Ai!' said the woman excitedly. This seemed to make Kim's supernatural origin more certain. 'Was not such an one's daughter born then——'

'And her mother bore her husband four sons in four years—all likely boys,' cried the cultivator's wife, sitting outside the circle in the shadow.

'None reared in the knowledge,' said the family priest, 'forget how the planets stood in their Houses upon that night.' He began to draw in the dust of the courtyard. 'At least thou hast good claim to a half of the House of the Bull. How runs thy prophecy?'

'Upon a day,' said Kim, delighted at the sensation he was creating, 'I shall be made great by means of a Red Bull on a green field, but first there will enter two men making all things ready.'

'Yes: thus ever at the opening of a vision. A thick darkness that clears slowly; anon one enters with a broom making ready the place. Then begins the Sight. Two men—thou sayest? Ay, ay. The Sun, leaving the House of the Bull, enters that of the Twins. Hence the two men of the prophecy. Let us now consider. Fetch me a twig, little one.'

He knitted his brows, scratched, smoothed out, and scratched again in the dust mysterious signs—to the wonder of all save the lama, who, with fine instinct, forbore to interfere.

At the end of half an hour, he tossed the twig from him with a grunt.

'Hm. Thus say the stars. Within three days come the two men to make all things ready. After them follows the Bull; but the sign over against him is the sign of War and armed men.'

'There was indeed a man of the Ludhiana Sikhs in the carriage from Lahore,' said the cultivator's wife hopefully.

'Tck! Armed men—many hundreds. What concern hast thou with war?' said the priest to Kim. 'Thine is a red and an angry sign of War to be loosed very soon.'

'None—none,' said the lama earnestly. 'We seek only peace and our River.'

Kim smiled, remembering what he had overheard in the dressing-room. Decidedly he was a favourite of the stars.

The priest brushed his foot over the rude horoscope. 'More than this I cannot see. In three days comes the Bull to thee, boy.'

'And my River, my River,' pleaded the lama. 'I had hoped his Bull would lead us both to the River.'

'Alas, for that wondrous River, my brother,' the priest replied. 'Such things are not common.'

Next morning, though they were pressed to stay, the lama insisted on departure. They gave Kim a large bundle of good food and nearly three annas in copper money for the needs of the road, and with many blessings watched the two go southward in the dawn.

'Pity it is that these and such as these could not be freed from the Wheel of Things,' said the lama.

'Nay, then would only evil people be left on the earth, and who would give us meat and shelter?' quoth Kim, stepping merrily under his burden.

'Yonder is a small stream. Let us look,' said the lama, and he led from the white road across the fields; walking into a very hornets'-nest of pariah dogs.

CHAPTER III

Yea, voice of every Soul that clung
To Life that strove from rung to rung
When Devadatta's rule was young,
The warm wind brings Kamakura.[1]

BEHIND them an angry farmer brandished a bamboo pole. He was a market-gardener, Arain by caste, growing vegetables and flowers for Umballa city, and well Kim knew the breed.

[1]This stanza does not appear in complete, published versions of "The Buddha at Kamakura." The Buddha's cousin Devadatta, who began as one of his disciples, later became his mortal enemy.

'Such an one,' said the lama, disregarding the dogs, 'is impolite to strangers, intemperate of speech and uncharitable. Be warned by his demeanour, my disciple.'

'Ho, shameless beggars!' shouted the farmer 'Begone! Get hence!'

'We go,' the lama returned, with quiet dignity. 'We go from these unblessed fields.'

'Ah,' said Kim, sucking in his breath. 'If the next crops fail, thou canst only blame thy own tongue.'

The man shuffled uneasily in his slippers. 'The land is full of beggars,' he began, half apologetically.

'And by what sign didst thou know that we would beg from thee, O Mali?' said Kim tartly, using the name that a market-gardener least likes. 'All we sought was to look at that river beyond the field there.'

'River, forsooth!' the man snorted. 'What city do ye hail from not to know a canal-cut? It runs as straight as an arrow, and I pay for the water as though it were molten silver. There is a branch of a river beyond. But if ye need water I can give that—and milk.'

'Nay, we will go to the river,' said the lama, striding out.

'Milk and a meal,' the man stammered, as he looked at the strange tall figure. 'I—I would not draw evil upon myself—or my crops; but beggars are so many in these hard days.'

'Take notice,' the lama turned to Kim. 'He was led to speak harshly by the Red Mist of anger. That clearing from his eyes, he becomes courteous and of an affable heart. May his fields be blessed. Beware not to judge men too hastily, O farmer.'

'I have met holy ones who would have cursed thee from hearthstone to byre,' said Kim to the abashed man. 'Is he not wise and holy? I am his disciple.'

He cocked his nose in the air loftily and stepped across the narrow field-borders with great dignity.

'There is no pride,' said the lama, after a pause, 'there is no pride among such as follow the Middle Way.'

'But thou hast said he was low caste and discourteous.'

'Low caste I did not say, for how can that be which is not? Afterwards he amended his discourtesy, and I forgot the offence. Moreover, he is as we are, bound upon the Wheel of Things; but he does not tread the way of deliverance.' He halted at a little runlet among the fields, and considered the hoof-pitted bank.

'Now, how wilt thou know thy River?' said Kim, squatting in the shade of some tall sugar-cane.

'When I find it, an enlightenment will surely be given. This, I feel, is not the place. O littlest among the waters, if only thou couldst tell me where runs my River! But be thou blessed to make the fields bear!'

'Look! Look!' Kim sprang to his side and dragged him back. A yellow and brown streak glided from the purple rustling stems to the bank, stretched its neck to the water, drank, and lay still—a big cobra with fixed, lidless eyes.

'I have no stick—I have no stick,' said Kim. 'I will get me one and break his back.'

'Why? He is upon the Wheel as we are—a life ascending or descending—very far from deliverance. Great evil must the soul have done that is cast into this shape.'

'I hate all snakes,' said Kim. No native training can quench the white man's horror of the Serpent.

'Let him live out his life.' The coiled thing hissed and half opened its hood. 'May thy release come soon, brother,' the lama continued placidly. 'Hast *thou* knowledge, by chance, of my River?'

'Never have I seen such a man as thou art,' Kim whispered, overwhelmed. 'Do the very snakes understand thy talk?'

'Who knows?' He passed within a foot of the cobra's poised head. It flattened itself among the dusty coils.

'Come thou!' he called over his shoulder.

'Not I,' said Kim. 'I go round.'

'Come. He does no hurt.'

Kim hesitated for a moment. The lama backed his order by some droned Chinese quotation which Kim took for a charm. He obeyed and bounded across the rivulet, and the snake, indeed, made no sign.

'Never have I seen such a man.' Kim wiped the sweat from his forehead. 'And now, whither go we?'

'That is for thee to say. I am old, and a stranger—far from my own place. But that the *rêl*-carriage fills my head with noises of devil-drums I would go in it to Benares now . . . yet by so going we may miss the River. Let us find another river.'

Where the hard-worked soil gives three and even four crops a year—through patches of sugar-cane, tobacco, long white radishes, and nol-kol, all that day they strolled on, turning aside to every glimpse of water; rousing village dogs and sleeping villages at noonday; the lama replying to the vollied questions with an unswerving simplicity. They sought a River—a River of miraculous healing. Had any one knowledge of such a stream? Sometimes men laughed, but more often heard the story out to the end and offered them a place in the shade, a drink of milk, and a meal. The women were always kind, and the little children as children are the world over, alternately shy and venturesome. Evening found them at rest under the village tree of a mud-walled, mud-roofed hamlet, talking to the headman as the cattle came in from the grazing-grounds and the women prepared the day's last meal. They had passed beyond the belt of market-gardens round hungry Umballa, and were among the mile-wide green of the staple crops.

He was a white-bearded and affable elder, used to entertaining strangers. He dragged out a string bedstead for the lama, set warm cooked food before him, prepared him a pipe, and, the evening ceremonies being finished in the village temple, sent for the village priest.

Kim told the older children tales of the size and beauty of Lahore, of railway travel, and such like city things, while the men talked, slowly as their cattle chew the cud.

'I cannot fathom it,' said the headman at last to the priest. 'How readest thou this talk?' The lama, his tale told, was silently telling his beads.

'He is a Seeker,' the priest answered. 'The land is full of such. Remember him who came only last month—the *faquir* with the tortoise?'

'Ay, but that man had right and reason, for Krishna Himself[2] appeared in a vision promising him Paradise without the burning-pyre if he journeyed to Prayag. This man seeks no god who is within my knowledge.'

'Peace, he is old: he comes from far off, and he is mad,' the smooth-shaven priest replied. 'Hear me.' He turned to the lama. 'Three *kos* (six miles) to the westward runs the great road to Calcutta.'

'But I would go to Benares—to Benares.'

'And to Benares also. It crosses all streams on this side of Hind. Now my word to thee, Holy One, is rest here till to-morrow. Then take the road' (it was the Grand Trunk Road he meant)[3] 'and test each stream that it overpasses; for, as I understand, the virtue of thy River lies neither in one pool nor place, but throughout its length. Then, if thy gods will, be assured that thou wilt come upon thy freedom.'

'That is well said.' The lama was much impressed by the plan. 'We will begin to-morrow, and a blessing on thee for showing old feet such a near road.' A deep, sing-song Chinese half-chant closed the sentence. Even the priest was impressed, and the headman feared an evil spell: but none could look at the lama's simple, eager face and doubt him long.

'Seest thou my *chela*?' he said, diving into his snuff-gourd with an important sniff. It was his duty to repay courtesy with courtesy.

'I see—and hear.' The headman rolled his eye where Kim was chatting to a girl in blue as she laid crackling thorns on a fire.

[2]Complex and powerful god worshiped in many different Hindu traditions.

[3]Built and named by the British East India Company on foundations laid in the 16th c. by the Muslim invader Sher Shah Suri, who took the title Sher Khan, the Grand Trunk Road ran 1,500 miles northwest from Calcutta toward modern Pakistan and to the south through Agra to Bombay.

'He also has a Search of his own. No river, but a Bull. Yea, a Red Bull on a green field will some day raise him to honour. He is, I think, not altogether of this world. He was sent of a sudden to aid me in this search, and his name is Friend of all the World.'

The priest smiled. 'Ho there, Friend of all the World,' he cried across the sharp-smelling smoke, 'what art thou?'

'This Holy One's disciple,' said Kim.

'He says thou art a *būt* (a spirit).'

'Can *būts* eat?' said Kim, with a twinkle. 'For I am hungry.'

'It is no jest,' cried the lama. 'A certain astrologer of that city whose name I have forgotten——'

'That is no more than the city of Umballa where we slept last night,' Kim whispered to the priest.

'Ay, Umballa was it? He cast a horoscope and declared that my *chela* should find his desire within two days. But what said he of the meaning of the stars, Friend of all the World?'

Kim cleared his throat and looked around at the village graybeards.

'The meaning of my Star is War,' he replied pompously.

Somebody laughed at the little tattered figure strutting on the brickwork plinth under the great tree. Where a native would have lain down, Kim's white blood set him upon his feet.

'Ay, War,' he answered.

'That is a sure prophecy,' rumbled a deep voice. 'For there is always war along the Border—as I know.'

It was an old, withered man, who had served the Government in the days of the Mutiny as a native officer in a newly raised cavalry regiment. The Government had given him a good holding in the village, and though the demands of his sons, now gray-bearded officers on their own account, had impoverished him, he was still a person of consequence. English officials—Deputy Commissioners even—turned aside from the main road to visit him, and on those occasions he dressed himself in the uniform of ancient days, and stood up like a ramrod.

'But this shall be a great war—a war of eight thousand,' Kim's voice shrilled across the quick-gathering crowd, astonishing himself.

'Redcoats or our own regiments?' the old man snapped, as though he were asking an equal. His tone made men respect Kim.

'Redcoats,' said Kim at a venture. 'Redcoats and guns.'

'But—but the astrologer said no word of this,' cried the lama, snuffing prodigiously in his excitement.

'But *I* know. The word has come to me, who am this Holy One's disciple. There will rise a war—a war of eight thousand redcoats. From Pindi and Peshawur they will be drawn. This is sure.'

'The boy has heard bazar-talk,' said the priest.

'But he was always by my side,' said the lama. 'How should he know? I did not know.'

'He will make a clever juggler when the old man is dead,' muttered the priest to the headman. 'What new trick is this?'

'A sign. Give me a sign,' thundered the old soldier suddenly. 'If there were war my sons would have told me.'

'When all is ready, thy sons, doubt not, will be told. But it is a long road from thy sons to the man in whose hands these things lie.' Kim warmed to the game, for it reminded him of experiences in the letter-carrying line, when, for the sake of a few pice, he pretended to know more than he knew. But now he was playing for larger things—the sheer excitement and the sense of power. He drew a new breath and went on.

'Old man, give *me* a sign. Do underlings order the goings of eight thousand redcoats—with guns?'

'No.' Still the old man answered as though Kim were an equal.

'Dost thou know who He is then that gives the order?'

'I have seen Him.'

'To know again?'

'I have known Him since he was a lieutenant in the *top-khana* (the Artillery).'

'A tall man. A tall man with black hair, walking thus?' Kim took a few paces in a stiff, wooden style.

'Ay. But that any one may have seen.' The crowd were breathless-still through all this talk.

'That is true,' said Kim. 'But I will say more. Look now. First the great man walks thus. Then He thinks thus. (Kim drew a forefinger over his forehead and downwards till it came to rest by the angle of the jaw.) Anon He twitches his fingers thus. Anon He thrusts his hat under his left armpit.' Kim illustrated the motion and stood like a stork.

The old man groaned, inarticulate with amazement; and the crowd shivered.

'So—so—so. But what does He when He is about to give an order?'

'He rubs the skin at the back of his neck—thus. Then falls one finger on the table and he makes a small sniffing noise through his nose. Then He speaks, saying: "Loose such and such a regiment. Call out such guns."'

The old man rose stiffly and saluted.

'"For"'—Kim translated into the vernacular the clinching sentences he had heard in the dressing-room at Umballa—'"For," says He, "we should have done this long ago. It is not war—it is a chastisement. Snff!"'

'Enough. I believe. I have seen Him thus in the smoke of battles. Seen and heard. It is He!'

'I saw no smoke'—Kim's voice shifted to the rapt sing-song of the wayside fortune-teller. 'I saw this in darkness. First came a man to make things clear. Then came horsemen. Then came He, standing in a ring of light. The rest followed as I have said. Old man, have I spoken truth?'

'It is He. Past all doubt it is He.'

The crowd drew a long, quavering breath, staring alternately at the old man, still at attention, and ragged Kim against the purple twilight.

'Said I not—said I not he was from the other world?' cried the lama proudly. 'He is the Friend of all the World. He is the Friend of the Stars!'

'At least it does not concern us,' a man cried. 'O thou young soothsayer, if the gift abides with thee at all seasons, I have a red-spotted cow. She may be sister to thy Bull for aught I know——'

'Or I care,' said Kim. 'My Stars do not concern themselves with thy cattle.'

'Nay, but she is very sick,' a woman struck in. 'My man is a buffalo, or he would have chosen his words better. Tell me if she recover?'

Had Kim been at all an ordinary boy, he would have carried on the play; but one does not know Lahore city, and least of all the *faquirs* by the Taksali Gate, for thirteen years without also knowing human nature.

The priest looked at him sideways, something bitterly—a dry and blighting smile.

'Is there no priest then in the village? I thought I had seen a great one even now,' cried Kim.

'Ay—but——' the woman began.

'But thou and thy husband hoped to get the cow cured for a handful of thanks.' The shot told: they were notoriously the closest-fisted couple in the village. 'It is not well to cheat the temples. Give a young calf to thy own priest, and, unless thy gods are angry past recall, she will give milk within a month.'

'A master-beggar art thou,' purred the priest approvingly. 'Not the cunning of forty years could have done better. Surely thou hast made the old man rich?'

'A little flour, a little butter and a mouthful of cardamoms,' Kim retorted, flushed with the praise, but still cautious—'does one grow rich on that? And, as thou canst see, he is mad. But it serves me while I learn the road at least.'

He knew what the *faquirs* of the Taksali Gate were like when they talked among themselves, and copied the very inflection of their lewd disciples.

'Is his Search, then, truth or a cloak to other ends? It may be treasure.'

'He is mad—many times mad. There is nothing else.'

Here the old soldier hobbled up and asked if Kim would accept his hospitality for the night. The priest recommended him to do so, but insisted that the honour of entertaining the lama belonged to the temple—at which the lama smiled guilelessly. Kim glanced from one face to the other, and drew his own conclusions.

'Where is the money?' he whispered, beckoning the old man off into the darkness.

'In my bosom. Where else?'

'Give it me. Quietly and swiftly give it me.'

'But why? Here is no ticket to buy.'

'Am I thy *chela*, or am I not? Do I not safeguard thy old feet about the ways? Give me the money and at dawn I will return it.' He slipped his hand above the lama's girdle and brought away the purse.

'Be it so—be it so.' The old man nodded his head. 'This is a great and terrible world. I never knew there were so many men alive in it.'

Next morning the priest was in a very bad temper, but the lama was quite happy; and Kim had enjoyed a most interesting evening with the old man, who brought out his cavalry sabre and, balancing it on his dry knees, told tales of the Mutiny and young captains thirty years in their graves, till Kim dropped off to sleep.

'Certainly the air of this country is good,' said the lama. 'I sleep lightly, as do all old men; but last night I slept unwaking till broad day. Even now I am heavy.'

'Drink a draught of hot milk,' said Kim, who had carried not a few such remedies to opium-smokers of his acquaintance. 'It is time to take the road again.'

'The long road that overpasses all the rivers of Hind,' said the lama gaily. 'Let us go. But how thinkest thou, *chela*, to recompense these people, and especially the priest, for their great kindness? Truly they are *būt-parast*, but in other lives, may be, they will receive enlightenment. A rupee to the temple? The thing within is no more than stone and red paint, but the heart of man we must acknowledge when and where it is good.'

'Holy One, has thou ever taken the road alone?' Kim looked up sharply, like the Indian crows so busy about the fields.

'Surely, child: from Kulu to Pathânkot—from Kulu, where my first *chela* died. When men were kind to us we made offerings, and all men were well-disposed throughout all the Hills.'

'It is otherwise in Hind,' said Kim drily. 'Their gods are many-armed and malignant. Let them alone.'

'I would set thee on thy road for a little, Friend of all the World— thou and thy yellow man.' The old soldier ambled up the village street, all shadowy in the dawn, on a gaunt, scissor-hocked pony. 'Last night broke up the fountains of remembrance in my so-dried heart, and it was as a blessing to me. Truly there is war abroad in the air. I smell it. See! I have brought my sword.'

He sat long-legged on the little beast, with the big sword at his side,—hand dropped on the pommel,—staring fiercely over the flat lands towards the north. 'Tell me again how He showed in thy vision. Come up and sit behind me. The beast will carry two.'

'I am this Holy One's disciple,' said Kim, as they cleared the village-gate. The villagers seemed almost sorry to be rid of them, but the priest's farewell was cold and distant. He had wasted some opium on a man who carried no money.

'That is well spoken. I am not much used to holy men, but respect is always good. There is no respect in these days—not even when a Commissioner Sahib comes to see me. But why should one whose Star leads him to war follow a holy man?'

'But he *is* a holy man,' said Kim earnestly. 'In truth, and in talk and in act, holy. He is not like the others. I have never seen such an one. We be not fortune-tellers, or jugglers, or beggars.'

'Thou art not, that I can see; but I do not know that other. He marches well, though.'

The first freshness of the day carried the lama forward with long, easy, camel-like strides. He was deep in meditation, mechanically clicking his rosary.

They followed the rutted and worn country road that wound across the flat between the great dark-green mango-groves, the line of the snow-capped Himalayas faint to the eastward. All India was at work in the fields, to the creaking of well-wheels, the shouting of ploughmen behind their cattle, and the clamour of the crows. Even the pony felt the good influence and almost broke into a trot as Kim laid a hand on the stirrup-leather.

'It repents me that I did not give a rupee to the shrine,' said the lama on the last bead of his eighty-one.

The old soldier growled in his beard, so that the lama for the first time was aware of him.

'Seekest thou the River also?' said he, turning.

'The day is new,' was the reply. 'What need of a river save to water at before sundown? I come to show thee a short lane to the Big Road.'

'That is a courtesy to be remembered, O man of good will; but why the sword?'

The old soldier looked as abashed as a child interrupted in his game of make-believe.

'The sword,' he said, fumbling it. 'Oh, that was a fancy of mine—an old man's fancy. Truly the police orders are that no man must bear weapons throughout Hind, but'—he cheered up and slapped the hilt—'all the constabeels hereabout know me.'

'It is not a good fancy,' said the lama. 'What profit to kill men?'

'Very little—as I know; but if evil men were not now and then slain it would not be a good world for weaponless dreamers. I do not speak without knowledge who have seen the land from Delhi south awash with blood.'[4]

'What madness was that, then?'

'The Gods, who sent it for a plague, alone know. A madness ate into all the Army, and they turned against their officers. That was the first evil, but not past remedy if they had then held their hands. But they chose to kill the Sahibs' wives and children. Then came the Sahibs from over the sea and called them to most strict account.'

'Some such rumour, I believe, reached me once long ago. They called it the Black Year, as I remember.'

'What manner of life hast thou led, not to know The Year? A rumour indeed! All earth knew, and trembled.'

'Our earth never shook but once—upon the day that the Excellent One received Enlightenment.'

'Umph! I saw Delhi shake at least; and Delhi is the navel of the world.'

'So they turned against women and children? That was a bad deed, for which the punishment cannot be avoided.'

'Many strove to do so, but with very small profit. I was then in a regiment of cavalry. It broke. Of six hundred and eighty sabres stood fast to their salt—how many think you? Three. Of whom I was one.'

'The greater merit.'

'Merit! We did not consider it merit in those days. My people, my friends, my brothers fell from me. They said: "The time of the English is accomplished. Let each strike out a little holding for himself." But I had talked with the men of Sobraon, of Chillianwallah, of Moodkee and Ferozeshah.[5] I said: "Abide a little and the wind turns. There is no blessing in this work." In those days I rode seventy miles with an English mem-sahib and her babe on my saddle-bow. (Wow! That was a horse fit for a man!) I placed them in safety, and back came I to my officer—the one that was not killed of our five. "Give me work," said I, "for I am an outcast among my own kin, and my cousin's blood is wet on my sabre." "Be content," said he. "There is great work forward. When this madness is over there is a recompense."'

---

[4]See Introduction for a discussion of the 1857 Rebellion (p. xii).
[5]British victories in the Anglo-Sikh Wars (1845–46, 1848–49).

'Ay, there is a recompense when the madness is over, surely?' the lama muttered half to himself.

'They did not hang medals in those days on all who by accident had heard a gun fired. No! In nineteen pitched battles was I; in six-and-forty skirmishes of horse; and in small affairs without number. Nine wounds I bear; a medal and four clasps and the medal of an Order, for my captains, who are now generals, remembered me when the Kaiser-i-Hind had accomplished fifty years of her reign, and all the land rejoiced.[6] They said: "Give him the order of Berittish India." I carry it upon my neck now. I have also my *jaghir* (holding) from the hands of the State—a free gift to me and mine. The men of the old days—they are now Commissioners—come riding to me through the crops,—high upon horses so that all the village sees,—and we talk out the old skirmishes, one dead man's name leading to another.'

'And after?' said the lama.

'Oh, afterwards they go away, but not before my village has seen.'

'And at the last what wilt thou do?'

'At the last I shall die.'

'And after?'

'Let the Gods order it. I have never pestered Them with prayers: I do not think they will pester me. Look you, I have noticed in my long life that those who eternally break in upon Those Above with complaints and reports and bellowings and weepings are presently sent for in haste, as our colonel used to send for slack-jawed down-country men who talked too much. No, I have never wearied the Gods. They will remember this, and give me a quiet place where I can drive my lance in the shade, and wait to welcome my sons: I have no less than three—ressaldar-majors all—in the regiments.'

'And they likewise, bound upon the Wheel, go forth from life to life—from despair to despair,' said the lama below his breath, 'hot, uneasy, snatching.'

'Ay,' the old soldier chuckled. 'Three ressaldar-majors in three regiments. Gamblers a little, but so am I. They must be well-mounted; and one cannot take the horses as in the old days one took women. Well, well, my holding can pay for all. How thinkest thou? It is a well-watered strip, but my men cheat me. I do not know how to ask save at the lance's point. Ugh! I grow angry and I curse them, and they feign penitence, but behind my back I know they call me a toothless old ape.'

'Hast thou never desired any other thing?'

---

[6]The 1887 Golden Jubilee celebrated the 50th year of the reign of Victoria, who had been named Empress of India (*Kaisar-i-Hind*) in 1877. On Victoria's Diamond Jubilee, see "Recessional," p. 280.

'Yes—yes—a thousand times! A straight back and a close-clinging knee once more; a quick wrist and a keen eye; and the marrow that makes a man. Oh, the old days—the good days of my strength!'

'That strength is weakness.'

'It has turned so; but fifty years since I could have proved it otherwise,' the old soldier retorted, driving his stirrup-edge into the pony's lean flank.

'But I know a River of great healing.'

'I have drank Gunga-water to the edge of dropsy. All she gave me was a flux, and no sort of strength.'

'It is not Gunga. The River that I know washes from all taint of sin. Ascending the far bank one is assured of Freedom. I do not know thy life, but thy face is the face of the honourable and courteous. Thou hast clung to thy Way, rendering fidelity when it was hard to give, in that Black Year of which I now remember other tales. Enter now upon the Middle Way, which is the path to Freedom. Hear the Most Excellent Law, and do not follow dreams.'

'Speak then, old man,' the soldier smiled, half saluting. 'We be all babblers at our age.'

The lama squatted under the shade of a mango, whose shadow played checkerwise over his face; the soldier sat stiffly on the pony; and Kim, making sure that there were no snakes, lay down in the crotch of the twisted roots.

There was a drowsy buzz of small life in hot sunshine, a cooing of doves, and a sleepy drone of well-wheels across the fields. Slowly and impressively the lama began. At the end of ten minutes the old soldier slid from his pony, to hear better as he said, and sat with the reins round his wrist. The lama's voice faltered—the periods lengthened. Kim was busy watching a gray squirrel. When the little scolding bunch of fur, close pressed to the branch, disappeared, preacher and audience were fast asleep, the old officer's strong-cut head pillowed on his arm, the lama's thrown back against the tree bole, where it showed like yellow ivory. A naked child toddled up, stared, and, moved by some quick impulse of reverence, made a solemn little obeisance before the lama—only the child was so short and fat that it toppled over sideways, and Kim laughed at the sprawling, chubby legs. The child, scared and indignant, yelled aloud.

'Hai! Hai!' said the soldier, leaping to his feet. 'What is it? What orders? . . . It is . . . a child! I dreamed it was an alarm. Little one—little one—do not cry. Have I slept? That was discourteous indeed!'

'I fear! I am afraid!' roared the child.

'What is it to fear? Two old men and a boy? How wilt thou ever make a soldier, Princeling?'

The lama had waked too, but, taking no direct notice of the child, clicked his rosary.

'What is that?' said the child, stopping a yell midway. 'I have never seen such things. Give them me.'

'Aha,' said the lama, smiling, and trailing a loop of it on the grass:

> 'This is a handful of cardamoms,
>   This is a lump of *ghi*:
> This is millet and chillies and rice,
>   A supper for thee and me!'

The child shrieked with joy, and snatched at the dark, glancing beads.

'Oho!' said the old soldier. 'Whence had thou that song, despiser of this world?'

'I learned it in Pathânkot—sitting on a doorstep,' said the lama shyly. 'It is good to be kind to babes.'

'As I remember, before the sleep came on us, thou hadst told me that marriage and bearing were darkeners of the true light, stumbling-blocks upon the way. Do children drop from heaven in thy country? Is it the Way to sing them songs?'

'No man is all perfect,' said the lama gravely, re-coiling the rosary. 'Run now to thy mother, little one.'

'Hear him!' said the soldier to Kim. 'He is ashamed for that he has made a child happy. There was a very good householder lost in thee, my brother. Hai, child!' He threw it a pice. 'Sweetmeats are always sweet.' And as the little figure capered away into the sunshine: 'They grow up and become men. Holy One, I grieve that I slept in the midst of thy preaching. Forgive me.'

'We be two old men,' said the lama. 'The fault is mine. I listened to thy talk of the world and its madness, and one fault led to the next.'

'Hear him! What harm do thy Gods suffer from play with a babe? And that song was very well sung. Let us go on and I will sing thee the song of Nikal Seyn before Delhi—the old song.'

And they fared out from the gloom of the mango tope, the old man's high, shrill voice ringing across the field, as wail by long-drawn wail he unfolded the story of Nikal Seyn (Nicholson)[7]—the song that men sing in the Punjab to this day. Kim was delighted, and the lama listened with deep interest.

---

[7]Dublin-born John Nicholson became Deputy Commissioner of Punjab in 1851 and died while commanding the British forces in the assault on Delhi during the 1857 Rebellion. Emphasizing his larger-than-life personality, contemporary Anglo-Indian sources reported that Nicholson was even worshiped as a god by a small Punjab sect. Nicholson, who publicly supported the use of torture to punish rebels, is credited with having initiated the harshest methods of reprisal against those who mutinied in 1857, including strapping rebels to the mouths of cannons.

'*Ahi! Nikal Seyn is dead—he died before Delhi! Lances of North take vengeance for Nikal Seyn.*' He quavered it out to the end, marking the trills with the flat of his sword on the pony's rump.

'And now we come to the Big Road,' said he, after receiving the compliments of Kim; for the lama was markedly silent. 'It is long since I have ridden this way, but thy boy's talk stirred me. See, Holy One—the Great Road which is the backbone of all Hind. For the most part it is shaded, as here, with four lines of trees; the middle road—all hard—takes the quick traffic. In the days before rail-carriages the Sahibs travelled up and down here in hundreds. Now there are only country-carts and such like. Left and right is the rougher road for the heavy carts—grain and cotton and timber, bhoosa, lime and hides. A man goes in safety here—for at every few *kos* is a police-station. The police are thieves and extortioners (I myself would patrol it with cavalry—young recruits under a strong captain), but at least they do not suffer any rivals. All castes and kinds of men move here. Look! Brahmins and chumars, bankers and tinkers, barbers and bunnias, pilgrims and potters—all the world going and coming. It is to me as a river from which I am withdrawn like a log after a flood.'

And truly the Grand Trunk Road is a wonderful spectacle. It runs straight, bearing without crowding India's traffic for fifteen hundred miles—such a river of life as nowhere else exists in the world. They looked at the green-arched, shade-flecked length of it, the white breadth speckled with slow-pacing folk; and the two-roomed police-station opposite.

'Who bears arms against the law?' a constable called out laughingly, as he caught sight of the soldier's sword. 'Are not the police enough to destroy evil-doers?'

'It was because of the police I bought it,' was the answer. 'Does all go well in Hind?'

'Ressaldar Sahib, all goes well.'

'I am like an old tortoise, look you, who puts his head out from the bank and draws it in again. Ay, this is the road of Hindustan. All men come by this way. . . .'

'Son of a swine, is the soft part of the road meant for thee to scratch thy back upon? Father of all the daughters of shame and husband of ten thousand virtueless ones, thy mother was devoted to a devil, being led thereto by her mother; thy aunts have never had a nose for seven generations! Thy sister!—What owl's folly told thee to draw thy carts across the road?[8] A broken wheel? Then take a broken head and put the two together at leisure!'

---

[8]All the women of the carter's family reap abuse here, down to his aunts, who are all accused of having had their noses cut off for sexual unfaithfulness. An Indian owl is a dolt or fool.

The voice and a venomous whip-cracking came out of a pillar of dust fifty yards away, where a cart had broken down. A thin, high Kattiwar mare, with eyes and nostrils aflame, rocketted out of the jam, snorting and wincing as her rider bent her across the road in chase of a shouting man. He was tall and gray-bearded, sitting the almost mad beast as a piece of her, and scientifically lashing his victim between plunges.

The old man's face lit with pride. 'My child!' said he briefly, and strove to rein the pony's neck to a fitting arch.

'Am I to be beaten before the police?' cried the carter. 'Justice! I will have Justice——'

'Am I to be blocked by a shouting ape who upsets ten thousand sacks under a young horse's nose? That is the way to ruin a mare.'

'He speaks truth. He speaks truth. But she follows her man close,' said the old man. The carter ran under the wheels of his cart and thence threatened all sorts of vengeance.

'They are strong men, thy sons,' said the policeman serenely, picking his teeth.

The horseman delivered one last vicious cut with his whip and came on at a canter.

'My father!' He reined back ten yards and dismounted.

The old man was off his pony in an instant, and they embraced as do father and son in the East.

CHAPTER IV

Good Luck, she is never a lady,
But the cursedest quean alive.
Tricksy, wincing, and jady—
Kittle to lead or drive.
Greet her—she's hailing a stranger!
Meet her—she's busking to leave!
Let her alone for a shrew to the bone
And the hussy comes plucking your sleeve!
    Largesse! Largesse, O Fortune!
    Give or hold at your will.
    If I've no care for Fortune,
    Fortune must follow me still!
           The Wishing Caps.[1]

---

[1]In the full poem, in Kipling's *Songs from Books* (1912), these final lines appear as follows: "I'll neither follow nor flee. / If I don't run after Fortune / Fortune must run after me!" A *quean* is an impudent woman, a hussy; a *jade* flaunts transgressive sexual knowledge. *Kittle* means difficult; *busking* is cruising or performing for tips.

THEN, lowering their voices, they spoke together. Kim came to rest under a tree, but the lama tugged impatiently at his elbow.

'Let us go on. The River is not here.'

'Hai mai! Have we not walked enough for a little? Our River will not run away. Patience, and he will give us a dole.'

'That,' said the old soldier suddenly, 'is the Friend of the Stars. He brought me the news yesterday. Having seen the very man Himself, in a vision, giving orders for the war.'

'Hm!' said his son, all deep in his broad chest. 'He came by a bazar-rumour and made profit of it.'

His father laughed. 'At least he did not ride to me begging for a new charger and the gods know how many rupees. Are thy brothers' regiments also under orders?'

'I do not know. I took leave and came swiftly to thee in case——'

'In case they ran before thee to beg. O gamblers and spendthrifts all! But thou hast never yet ridden in a charge. A good horse is needed there, truly. A good follower and a good pony also for the marching. Let us see—let us see.' He thrummed on the pommel.

'This is no place to cast accounts in, my father. Let us go to thy house.'

'At least pay the boy then: I have no pice with me, and he brought auspicious news. Ho! Friend of all the World, a war is toward as thou hast said.'

'Nay, as I know, *the* war,' returned Kim composedly.

'Eh?' said the lama, fingering his beads, all eager for the road.

'My master does not trouble the Stars for hire. We brought the news—bear witness, we brought the news, and now we go.' Kim half-crooked his hand at his side.

The son tossed a silver coin through the sunlight, grumbling something about beggars and jugglers. It was a four-anna piece, and would feed them well for some days. The lama, seeing the flash of the metal, droned a blessing.

'Go thy way, Friend of all the World,' piped the old soldier, wheeling his scrawny mount. 'For once in all my days I have met a true prophet—who was not in the Army.'

Father and son swung round together: the old man sitting as erect as the younger.

A Punjabi constable in yellow linen trousers slouched across the road. He had seen the money pass.

'Halt!' he cried in impressive English. 'Know ye not that there is a *takkus* of two annas a head, which is four annas, on those who enter the road from this side-road. It is the order of the Sirkar, and the money is spent for the planting of trees and the beautification of the ways.'

'And the bellies of the police,' said Kim, skipping out of arm's reach. 'Consider for a while, man with a mud head. Think you we came from the nearest pond like the frog, thy father-in-law. Hast thou ever heard the name of thy brother?'

'And who was he? Leave the boy alone,' cried a senior constable, immensely delighted, as he squatted down to smoke his pipe in the verandah.

'He took a label from a bottle of *belaitee-pani* (soda-water), and, affixing it to a bridge, collected taxes for a month from those who passed, saying that it was the Sirkar's order. Then came an Englishman and broke his head. Ah, brother, I am a town-crow, not a village-crow!'

The policeman drew back abashed, and Kim hooted at him all down the road.

'Was there ever such a disciple as I?' he cried merrily to the lama. 'All earth would have picked thy bones within ten mile of Lahore city if I had not guarded thee.'

'I consider in my own mind whether thou art a spirit, sometimes, or sometimes an evil imp,' said the lama, smiling slowly.

'I am thy *chela*.' Kim dropped into step at his side—that indescribable gait of the long-distance tramp all the world over.

'Now let us walk,' muttered the lama, and to the click of his rosary they walked in silence mile upon mile. The lama, as usual, was deep in meditation, but Kim's bright eyes were open wide. This broad, smiling river of life, he considered, was a vast improvement on the cramped and crowded Lahore streets. There were new people and new sights at every stride—castes he knew and castes that were altogether out of his experience.

They met a troop of long-haired, strong-scented Sansis with baskets of lizards and other unclean food on their backs, the lean dogs sniffing at their heels. These people kept their own side of the road, moving at a quick, furtive jog-trot, and all other castes gave them ample room; for the Sansi is deep pollution. Behind them, walking wide and stiffly across the strong shadows, the memory of his leg-irons still on him, strode one newly released from the jail; his full stomach and shiny skin to prove that the Government fed its prisoners better than most honest men could feed themselves. Kim knew that walk well, and made broad jest of it as they passed. Then an Akali, a wild-eyed, wild-haired Sikh devotee in the blue-checked clothes of his faith, with polished-steel quoits glistening on the cone of his tall blue turban, stalked past, returning from a visit to one of the independent Sikh States, where he had been singing the ancient glories of the Khalsa to College-trained princelings in top-boots and white-cord breeches.

Kim was careful not to irritate that man; for the Akali's temper is short and his arm quick. Here and there they met or were overtaken by the gaily dressed crowds of whole villages turning out to some local fair; the women, with their babes on their hips, walking behind the men, the older boys prancing on sticks of sugar-cane, dragging rude brass models of locomotives such as they sell for a halfpenny, or flashing the sun into the eyes of their betters from cheap toy mirrors. One could see at a glance what each had bought; and if there were any doubt it needed only to watch the wives comparing, brown arm against brown arm, the newly purchased dull glass bracelets that come from the North-West. These merry-makers stepped slowly, calling one to the other and stopping to haggle with sweetmeat-sellers, or to make a prayer before one of the wayside shrines—sometimes Hindu, sometimes Mussalman—which the low caste of both creeds share with beautiful impartiality. A solid line of blue, rising and falling like the back of a caterpillar in haste, would swing up through the quivering dust and trot past to a chorus of quick cackling. That was a gang of *changars*—the women who have taken all the embankments of all the Northern railways under their charge—a flat-footed, big-bosomed, strong-limbed, blue-petticoated clan of earth-carriers, hurrying north on news of a job, and wasting no time by the road. They belong to the caste whose men do not count, and they walked with squared elbows, swinging hips, and heads on high, as suits women who carry heavy weights. A little later a marriage procession would strike into the Grand Trunk with music and shoutings, and a smell of marigold and jasmine stronger even than the reek of the dust. One could see the bride's litter, a blur of red and tinsel, staggering through the haze, while the bridegroom's bewreathed pony turned aside to snatch a mouthful from a passing fodder-cart. Then Kim would join the Kentish-fire of good wishes and bad jokes, wishing the couple a hundred sons and no daughters, as the saying is. Still more interesting and more to be shouted over it was when a strolling juggler with some half-trained monkeys, or a panting, feeble bear, or a woman who tied goats' horns to her feet, and with these danced on a slack-rope, set the horses to shying and the women to shrill, long-drawn quavers of amazement.

The lama never raised his eyes. He did not note the money-lender on his goose-rumped pony, hastening along to collect the cruel interest; or the long-shouting, deep-voiced little mob—still in military formation—of native soldiers on leave, rejoicing to be rid of their breeches and puttees, and saying the most outrageous things to the most respectable women in sight. Even the seller of Ganges-water he did not see, and Kim expected that he would at least buy a bottle of that precious stuff. He looked steadily at the ground, and strode as steadily hour after hour, his soul busied elsewhere. But Kim was in the seventh heaven of joy. The Grand Trunk at this point was built on an embankment to guard against winter floods from the foothills, so that one walked, as it were, a little above the country, along a stately corridor, seeing all India spread out to left and right. It was beautiful to behold the many-yoked grain and cotton waggons crawling over the country roads: one could hear their axles, complaining a mile away, coming nearer, till with shouts and yells and bad words they climbed up the steep incline and plunged on to the hard main road, carter reviling carter. It was equally beautiful to watch the people, little clumps of red and blue and pink and white and saffron, turning aside to go to their own villages, dispersing and growing small by twos and threes across the level plain. Kim felt these things, though he could not give tongue to his feelings, and so contented himself with buying peeled sugar-cane and spitting the pith generously about his path. From time to time the lama took snuff, and at last Kim could endure the silence no longer.

'This is a good land—the land of the South!' said he. 'The air is good; the water is good. Eh?'

'And they are all bound upon the Wheel,' said the lama. 'Bound from life after life. To none of these has the Way been shown.' He shook himself back to this world.

'And now we have walked a weary way,' said Kim. 'Surely we shall soon come to a *parao* (a resting-place). Shall we stay there? Look, the sun is sloping.'

'Who will receive us this evening?'

'That is all one. This country is full of good folk. Besides,'—he sunk his voice beneath a whisper,—'we have money.'

The crowd thickened as they neared the resting-place which marked the end of their day's journey. A line of stalls selling very simple food and tobacco, a stack of firewood, a police-station, a well, a horse-trough, a few trees, and, under them, some trampled ground dotted with the black ashes of old fires, are all that mark a *parao* on the Grand Trunk; if you except the beggars and the crows—both hungry.

By this time the sun was driving broad golden spokes through the lower branches of the mango trees; the parakeets and doves were coming home in their hundreds; the chattering, gray-backed Seven Sisters, talking over the day's adventures, walked back and forth in two and threes almost under the feet of the travellers; and shufflings and scufflings in the branches showed that the bats were ready to go out on the night-picket. Swiftly the light gathered itself together, painted for an instant the faces and the cart-wheels and the bullocks' horns as red as blood. Then the night fell, changing the touch of the air, drawing a low, even haze, like a gossamer veil of blue, across the face of the country, and bringing out, keen and distinct, the smell of wood-smoke and cattle and the good scent of wheaten cakes cooked on ashes. The evening patrol hurried out of the police-station with important coughings and reiterated orders; and a live charcoal ball in the cup of a wayside carter's hookah glowed red while Kim's eye mechanically watched the last flicker of the sun on the brass tweezers.

The life of the *parao* was very like that of the Kashmir Serai on a small scale. Kim dived into the happy Asiatic disorder which, if you only allow time, will bring you everything that a simple man needs.

His wants were few, because, since the lama had no caste scruples, cooked food from the nearest stall would serve; but, for luxury's sake, Kim bought a handful of dung-cakes to build a fire. All about, coming and going round the little flames, men cried for oil, or grain, or sweetmeats, or tobacco, jostling one another while they waited their turn at the well; and under the men's voices you heard from halted, shuttered carts the high squeals and giggles of women whose faces should not be seen in public.

Nowadays, well-educated natives are of opinion that when their womenfolk travel—and they visit a good deal—it is better to take them quickly by rail in a properly screened compartment; and that custom is spreading. But there are always those of the old rock who hold by the use of their forefathers; and, above all, there are always the old women,—more conservative than the men,—who toward the end of their days go a pilgrimage. They, being withered and undesirable, do not, under certain circumstances, object to unveiling. After their long seclusion, during which they have always been in business touch with a thousand outside interests, they love the bustle and stir of the open road, the gatherings at the shrines, and the infinite possibilities of gossip with like-minded dowagers. Very often it suits a long-suffering family that a strong-tongued, iron-willed old lady should disport herself about India in this fashion; for certainly pilgrimage is grateful to the Gods. So all about India, in the most remote places, as in the most public, you find some knot of grizzled servitors in nominal charge of an old lady who is more or less curtained and hid away in a bullock-cart. Such men are staid and discreet, and when a European or a high-caste native is near will net their charge with most elaborate precautions; but in the ordinary haphazard chances of pilgrimage the precautions are not taken. The old lady is, after all, intensely human, and lives to look upon life.

Kim marked down a gaily ornamented *ruth* or family bullock-cart, with a broidered canopy of two domes, like a double-humped camel, which had just been drawn into the *parao*. Eight men made its retinue, and two of the eight were armed with rusty sabres—sure signs that they followed a person of distinction, for the common folk do not bear arms. An increasing cackle of complaints, orders, and jests, and what to a European would have been bad language, came from behind the curtains. Here was evidently a woman used to command.

Kim looked over the retinue critically. Half of them were thin-legged, gray-bearded Ooryas from down country. The other half were duffle-clad, felt-hatted hillmen of the North; and that mixture told its own tale, even if he had not overheard the incessant sparring between the two divisions. The old lady was going south on a visit—probably to a rich relative, most probably to a son-in-law, who had sent up an escort as a mark of respect. The hillmen would be of her own people—Kulu or Kangra folk. It was quite clear that she was not taking her daughter down to be wedded, or the curtains would have been laced home and the guard would have allowed no one near the car. A merry and a high-spirited dame, thought Kim, balancing the dung-cake in one hand, the cooked food in the other, and piloting the lama with a nudging shoulder. Something might be made out of the meeting. The lama would give him no help, but, as a conscientious *chela*, Kim was delighted to beg for two.

He built his fire as close to the cart as he dared, waiting for one of the escort to order him away. The lama dropped wearily to the ground, much as a heavy fruit-eating bat cowers, and returned to his rosary.

'Stand farther off, beggar!' The order was shouted in broken Hindustanee by one of the hillmen.

'Huh! It is only a *pahari*' (a hillman), said Kim over his shoulder. 'Since when have the hill-asses owned all Hindustan?'

The retort was a swift and brilliant sketch of Kim's pedigree for three generations.

'Ah!' Kim's voice was sweeter than ever, as he broke the dung-cake into fit pieces. 'In *my* country we call that the beginning of love-talk.'

A harsh, thin cackle behind the curtains put the hillman on his mettle for a second shot.

'Not so bad—not so bad,' said Kim with calm. 'But have a care, my brother, lest we—*we*, I say—be minded to give a curse or so in return. And our curses have the knack of biting home.'

The Ooryas laughed; the hillman sprang forward threateningly; the lama suddenly raised his head, bringing his huge tam-o'-shanter cap into the full light of Kim's new-started fire.

'What is it?' said he.

The man halted as though struck to stone. 'I—I—am saved from a great sin,' he stammered.

'The foreigner has found him a priest at last,' whispered one of the Ooryas.

'Hai! Why is that beggar-brat not well beaten?' the old woman cried.

The hillman drew back to the cart and whispered something to the curtain. There was dead silence, then a muttering.

'This goes well,' thought Kim, pretending neither to see nor hear.

'When—when—he has eaten'—the hillman fawned on Kim—'it—it is requested that the Holy One will do the honour to talk to one who would speak to him.'

'After he has eaten he will sleep,' Kim returned loftily. He could not quite see what new turn the game had taken, but stood resolute to profit by it. 'Now, I will get him his food.' The last sentence, spoken loudly, ended with a sigh as of faintness.

'I—I myself and the others of my people will look to that—if it is permitted.'

'It is permitted,' said Kim, more loftily than ever. 'Holy One, these people will bring us food.'

'The land is good. All the country of the South is good—a great and terrible world,' mumbled the lama drowsily.

'Let him sleep,' said Kim, 'but look to it that we are well fed when he wakes. He is a very holy man.'

Again one of the Ooryas said something contemptuously.

'He is not a *faquir*. He is not a down-country beggar,' Kim went on severely, addressing the stars. 'He is the most holy of holy men. He is above all castes. I am his *chela*.'

'Come here!' said the flat thin voice behind the curtain; and Kim came, conscious that eyes he could not see were staring at him. One skinny brown finger heavy with rings lay on the edge of the cart, and the talk went this way:

'Who is that one?'

'An exceeding holy one. He comes from far off. He comes from Tibet.'

'Where in Tibet?'

'From behind the snows—from a very far place. He knows the stars; he makes horoscopes; he reads nativities. But he does not do this for money. He does it for kindness and great charity. I am his disciple. I am called also the Friend of the Stars.'

'Thou art no hillman.'

'Ask him. He will tell thee I was sent to him from the stars to show him an end to his pilgrimage.'

'Humph! Consider, brat, that I am an old woman and not altogether a fool. Lamas I know, and to these I give reverence, but thou art no more a lawful *chela* than this my finger is the pole of this waggon. Thou art a casteless Hindu—a bold and unblushing beggar, attached, belike, to the Holy One for the sake of gain.'

'Do we not all work for gain?' Kim changed his tone promptly to match that altered voice. 'I have heard'—this was a bow drawn at a venture—'I have heard——'

'What hast thou heard?' she snapped, rapping with the finger.

'Nothing that I well remember, but some talk in the bazars, which is doubtless a lie, that even Rajahs—small hill Rajahs——'

'But none the less of good Rajput blood.'

'Assuredly of good blood. That these even sell the more comely of their womenfolk for gain. Down south they sell them—to zemindars and such—all of Oudh.'

If there be one thing in the world that the small hill Rajahs deny it is just this charge; but it happens to be one thing that the bazars believe, when they discuss the mysterious slave-traffics of India.[2] The old lady explained to Kim, in a tense, indignant whisper, precisely what manner and fashion of malignant liar he was. Had Kim hinted this when she was a girl, he would have been pommelled to death that same evening by an elephant. This was perfectly true.

'Ahai! I am only a beggar's brat, as the Eye of Beauty has said,' he wailed in extravagant terror.

'Eye of Beauty, forsooth! Who am I that thou shouldst fling beggar-endearments at me?' And yet she laughed at the long-forgotten word. 'Forty years ago that might have been said, and not without truth. Ay, thirty years ago. But it is the fault of this gadding up and down Hind that a king's widow must jostle all the scum of the land, and be made a mock by beggars.'

'Great Queen,' said Kim promptly, for he heard her shaking with indignation, 'I am even what the Great Queen says I am; but none the less is my master holy. He has not yet heard the Great Queen's order that——'

'Order? I order a Holy One—a Teacher of the Law—to come and speak to a woman? Never!'

'Pity my stupidity. I thought it was given as an order——'

'It was not. It was a petition. Does this make all clear?'

A silver coin clicked on the edge of the cart. Kim took it and salaamed profoundly. The old lady recognised that, as the eyes and the ears of the lama, he was to be propitiated.

---

[2]Kim's aspersions against Oudh may be politically inflected. Before annexation by the British in 1856, this fertile northern region had been ruled by patrons of accomplished courtesans; during the Rebellion, it emerged as a center of violent resistance. Through Kim's teasing implication of *zemindars* (local landowners) in human trafficking, Kipling underscores contemporary British concern with "white slavery," even as he bypasses equally notorious controversies over local colonial military regulation of prostitution.

'I am but the Holy One's disciple. When he has eaten perhaps he will come.'

'Oh, villain and shameless rogue!' The jewelled forefinger shook itself at him reprovingly; but he could hear the old lady's chuckle.

'Nay, what is it?' he said, dropping into his most caressing and confidential tone—the one, he well knew, that few could resist. 'Is—is there any need of a son in thy family? Speak freely, for we priests——' That last was a direct plagiarism from a *faquir* by the Taksali Gate.

'We priests! Thou art not yet old enough to——' She checked the joke with another laugh. 'Believe me, now and again, we women, O priest, think of other matters than sons. Moreover, my daughter has borne her man-child.'

'Two arrows in the quiver are better than one; and three are better still.' Kim quoted the proverb with a meditative cough, looking discreetly earthward.

'True—oh, true. But perhaps that will come. Certainly those down-country Brahmins are utterly useless. I sent gifts and monies and gifts again to them, and they prophesied.'

'Ah,' drawled Kim, with infinite contempt, 'they prophesied!' A professional could have done no better.

'And it was not till I remembered my own Gods that my prayers were heard. I chose an auspicious hour, and—perhaps thy Holy One has heard of the Abbot of the Lung-Cho lamassery. It was to him I put the matter, and behold in the due time all came about as I desired. The Brahmin in the house of the father of my daughter's son has since said that it was through *his* prayers—which is a little error that I will explain to him when we reach our journey's end. And so afterwards I go to Buddh Gaya, to make *shraddha* for the father of my children.'

'Thither go we.'

'Doubly auspicious,' chirruped the old lady. 'A second son at least!'

'O Friend of all the World!' The lama had waked, and, simply as a child bewildered in a strange bed, called for Kim.

'I come! I come, Holy One!' He dashed to the fire, where he found the lama already surrounded by dishes of food, the hillmen visibly adoring him and the Southerners looking sourly.

'Go back! Withdraw!' Kim cried. 'Do we eat publicly like dogs?' They finished the meal in silence, each turned a little from the other, and Kim topped it with a native-made cigarette.

'Have I not said an hundred times that the South is a good land? Here is a virtuous and high-born widow of a Hill Rajah on pilgrimage, she says, to Buddh Gaya. She it is sends us those dishes; and when thou art well rested she would speak to thee.'

'Is this also thy work?' The lama dipped deep into his snuff-gourd.

'Who else watched over thee since our wonderful journey began?' Kim's eyes danced in his head as he blew the rank smoke through his nostrils and stretched him on the dusty ground. 'Have I failed to oversee thy comforts, Holy One?'

'A blessing on thee.' The lama inclined his solemn head. 'I have known many men in my so long life, and disciples not a few. But to none among men, if so be thou art woman-born, has my heart gone out as it has to thee—thoughtful, wise, and courteous, but something of a small imp.'

'And I have never seen such a priest as thou.' Kim considered the benevolent yellow face wrinkle by wrinkle. 'It is less than three days since we took road together, and it is as though it were a hundred years.'

'Perhaps in a former life it was permitted that I should have rendered thee some service. May be'—he smiled—'I freed thee from a trap; or, having caught thee on a hook in the days when I was not enlightened, cast thee back into the river.'

'May be,' said Kim quietly. He had heard this sort of speculation again and again, from the mouths of many whom the English would not consider imaginative. 'Now, as regards that woman in the bullock-cart, *I* think she needs a second son for her daughter.'

'That is no part of the Way,' sighed the lama. 'But at least she is from the Hills. Ah, the Hills, and the snow of the Hills!'

He rose and stalked to the cart. Kim would have given his ears to come too, but the lama did not invite him; and the few words he caught were in an unknown tongue, for they spoke some common speech of the mountains. The woman seemed to ask questions which the lama turned over in his mind before answering. Now and again he heard the sing-song cadence of a Chinese quotation. It was a strange picture that Kim watched between drooped eyelids. The lama, very straight and erect, the deep folds of his yellow clothing slashed with black in the light of the *parao* fires precisely as a knotted tree-trunk is slashed with the shadow of the long sun, addressed a tinsel and lacquered *ruth* which burned like a many-coloured jewel in the same uncertain light. The patterns on the gold-worked curtains ran up and down, melting and reforming as the folds shook and quivered to the night wind; and when the talk grew more earnest the jewelled forefinger snapped out little sparks of light between the embroideries. Behind the cart was a wall of uncertain darkness speckled with little flames and alive with half-caught forms and faces and shadows. The voices of early evening had settled down to one soothing hum whose deepest note was the steady chumping of the bullocks above their chopped straw, and whose highest was the tinkle of a Bengali dancing-girl's *sitar*. Most men had eaten and pulled deep at their gurgling, grunting hookahs, which in full blast sound like bull-frogs.

At last the lama returned. A hillman walked behind him with a wadded cotton-quilt and spread it carefully by the fire.

'She deserves ten thousand grandchildren,' thought Kim. 'None the less, but for me, these gifts would not have come.'

'A virtuous woman—and a wise one.' The lama slackened off, joint by joint, like a slow camel. 'The world is full of charity to those who follow the Way.' He flung a fair half of the quilt over Kim.

'And what said she?' Kim rolled up in his share of it.

'She asked me many questions and propounded many problems—the most of which were idle tales which she had heard from devil-serving priests who pretend to follow the Way. Some I answered, and some I said were foolish. Many wear the Robe, but few keep the Way.'

'True. That is true.' Kim used the thoughtful, conciliatory tone of those who wish to draw confidences.

'But by her lights she is most right-minded. She desires greatly that we should go with her to Buddh Gaya; her road being ours, as I understand, for many days' journey to the southward.'

'And?'

'Patience a little. To this I said that my search came before all things. She had heard many foolish legends, but this great truth of my River she had never heard. Such are the priests of the lower hills! She knew the Abbot of Lung-Cho, but she did not know of my River— nor the tale of the Arrow.'

'And?'

'I spoke therefore of the Search, and of the Way, and of matters that were profitable; she desiring only that I should accompany her and make prayer for a second son.'

'Aha! "We women" do *not* think of anything save children,' said Kim sleepily.

'Now, since our roads run together for a while, I do not see that we in any way depart from our Search if so be we accompany her—at least as far as—I have forgotten the name of the city.'

'Ohé!' said Kim, turning and speaking in a sharp whisper to one of the Ooryas a few yards away. 'Where is your master's house?'

'A little behind Saharunpore, among the fruit gardens.' He named the village.

'That was the place,' said the lama. 'So far, at least, we can go with her.'

'Flies go to carrion,' said the Oorya, in an abstracted voice.

'For the sick cow a crow; for the sick man a Brahmin.' Kim breathed the proverb impersonally to the shadow-tops of the trees overhead.

The Oorya grunted and held his peace.

'So then we go with her, Holy One?'

'Is there any reason against? I can still step aside and try all the rivers that the road overpasses. She desires that I should come. She very greatly desires it.'

Kim stifled a laugh in the quilt. When once that imperious old lady had recovered from her natural awe of a lama he thought it probable that she would be worth listening to.

He was nearly asleep when the lama suddenly quoted a proverb: 'The husbands of the talkative have a great reward hereafter.' Then Kim heard him snuff thrice, and dozed off, still laughing.

The diamond-bright dawn woke men and crows and bullocks together. Kim sat up and yawned, shook himself, and thrilled with delight. This was seeing the world in real truth; this was life as he would have it—bustling and shouting, the buckling of belts, and beating of bullocks and creaking of wheels, lighting of fires and cooking of food, and new sights at every turn of the approving eye. The morning mist swept off in a whorl of silver, the parrots shot away to some distant river in shrieking green hosts: all the well-wheels within earshot went to work. India was awake, and Kim was in the middle of it, more awake and more excited than any one, chewing on a twig that he would presently use as a tooth-brush; for he borrowed right- and left-handedly from all the customs of the country he knew and loved. There was no need to worry about food—no need to spend a cowrie at the crowded stalls. He was the disciple of a holy man annexed by a strong-willed old lady. All things would be prepared for them, and when they were respectfully invited so to do they would sit and eat. For the rest,—Kim giggled here as he cleaned his teeth,—his hostess would rather heighten the enjoyment of the road. He inspected her bullocks critically, as they came up grunting and blowing under the yokes. If they went too fast—it was not likely—there would be a pleasant seat for himself along the pole; the lama would sit beside the driver. The escort, of course, would walk. The old lady, equally of course, would talk a great deal, and by what he had heard that conversation would not lack salt. She was already ordering, haranguing, rebuking, and, it must be said, cursing her servants for delays.

'Get her her pipe. In the name of the Gods, get her her pipe and stop her ill-omened mouth,' cried an Oorya, tying up his shapeless bundles of bedding. 'She and the parrots are alike. They screech in the dawn.'

'The lead-bullocks! Hai! Look to the lead-bullocks!' They were backing and wheeling as a grain-cart's axle caught them by the horns. 'Son of an owl, where dost thou go?' This to the grinning carter.

'Ai! Yai! Yai! That within there is the Queen of Delhi going to pray for a son,' the man called back over his high load. 'Room for the Queen of Delhi and her prime minister the gray monkey climbing up his own sword!'[3] Another cart loaded with bark for a down-country tannery followed close behind, and its driver added a few compliments as the *ruth*-bullocks backed and backed again.

From behind the shaking curtains came one volley of invective. It did not last long, but in kind and quality, in blistering, biting appropriateness, it was beyond anything that even Kim had heard. He could see the carter's bare chest collapse with amazement, as the man salaamed reverently to the voice, leaped from the pole, and helped the escort haul their volcano on to the main road. Here the voice told him truthfully what sort of wife he had wedded, and what she was doing in his absence.

'Oh, *shabash*!' murmured Kim, unable to contain himself, as the man slunk away.

'Well done, indeed? It is a shame and a scandal that a poor woman may not go to make a prayer to her gods except she be jostled and insulted by all the refuse of Hindustan—that she must eat *gâli* (abuse) as men eat *ghi*. But I have yet a wag left to my tongue—a word or two well spoken that serves the occasion. And *still* am I without my tobacco! Who is the one-eyed and luckless son of shame that has not yet prepared my pipe?'

It was hastily thrust in by a hillman, and a trickle of thick smoke from each corner of the curtains showed that peace was restored.

If Kim had walked proudly the day before, disciple of a holy man, to-day he paced with tenfold pride in the train of a semi-royal procession, with a recognised place under the patronage of an old lady of charming manners and infinite resource. The escort, their heads tied up native fashion, fell in on either side the cart, shuffling enormous clouds of dust.

The lama and Kim walked a little to one side; Kim chewing his stick of sugar-cane, and making way for no one under the status of a priest. They could hear the old lady's tongue clack as steadily as a rice-husker. She bade the escort tell her what was going on on the

---

[3]A scathing reference to Zinat Mahal (1821–82), favorite wife of the elderly King Bahadur Shah Zafar of Delhi, the last of the Mughal emperors (1775–1862). Though the Queen of Delhi seems to have sided with the British during the 1857 Rebellion, earlier attempts to establish her son as heir had already brought her into conflict with colonial authorities. After the Rebellion, she shared her husband's exile in Rangoon, where she died.

road; and so soon as they were clear of the *parao* she flung back the curtains and peered out, her veil a third across her face. Her men did not eye her directly when she addressed them, and thus the proprieties were more or less observed.

A dark, sallowish District Superintendent of Police, faultlessly uniformed, an Englishman, trotted by on a tired horse, and, seeing from her retinue what manner of person she was, chaffed her.

'O mother,' he cried, 'do they do this in the *zenanas*? Suppose an Englishman came by and saw that thou hadst no nose?'

'What?' she shrilled back. 'Thy own mother has no nose? Why say so, then, on the open road?'

It was a fair counter. The Englishman threw up his hand with the gesture of a man hit at swordplay. She laughed and nodded.

'Is this a face to tempt virtue aside?' She withdrew all her veil and stared at him.

It was by no means lovely, but as the man gathered up his reins he called it a Moon of Paradise, a Disturber of Integrity, and a few other fantastic epithets which doubled her up with mirth.

'That is a *nut-cut* (rogue),' she said. 'All police-constables are *nut-cuts*; but the police-wallahs are the worst. Hai, my son, thou hast never learned all that since thou camest from *Belait* (Europe). Who suckled thee?'

'A *pahareen*—a hillwoman of Dalhousie, my mother. Keep thy beauty under a shade—O Dispenser of Delights,' and he was gone.

'These be the sort'—she took a fine judicial tone, and stuffed her mouth with *pan*. 'These be the sort to oversee justice. They know the land and the customs of the land. The others, all new from Europe, suckled by white women and learning our tongues from books, are worse than the pestilence. They do harm to Kings.' Then she told a long, long tale to the world at large, of an ignorant young policeman who had disturbed some small Hill Rajah, a ninth cousin of her own, in the matter of a trivial land-case, winding up with a quotation from a work by no means devotional.

Then her mood changed, and she bade one of the escort ask whether the lama would walk alongside and discuss matters of religion. So Kim dropped back into the dust and returned to his sugar-cane. For an hour or more the lama's tam-o'-shanter showed like a moon through the haze; and, from all he heard, Kim gathered that the old woman wept. One of the Ooryas half apologised for his rudeness overnight, saying that he had never known his mistress of so bland a temper, and he ascribed it to the presence of the strange priest. Personally, he believed in Brahmins, though, like all natives, he was acutely aware of their cunning and their greed. Still, when Brahmins but irritated with begging demands the mother of his master's wife, and when she sent them away so angry that they cursed the whole retinue (which was the real reason of the second off-side bullock going lame, and of the pole breaking the night before), he was prepared to accept any priest of any other denomination in or out of India. To this Kim assented with wise nods, and bade the Oorya observe that the lama took no money, and that the cost of his and Kim's food would be repaid a hundred times in the good luck that would attend the caravan henceforward. He also told stories of Lahore city, and sang a song or two which made the escort laugh. As a town-mouse well acquainted with the latest songs by the most fashionable composers,—they are women for the most part,— Kim had a distinct advantage over men from a little fruit-village behind Saharunpore, but he let that advantage be inferred.

At noon they turned aside to eat, and the meal was good, plentiful, and well-served on plates of clean leaves, in decency, out of drift of the dust. They gave the scraps to certain beggars, that all requirements might be fulfilled, and sat down to a long, luxurious smoke. The old lady had retreated behind her curtains, but mixed most freely in the talk, her servants arguing with and contradicting her as servants do throughout the East. She compared the cool and the pines of the Kangra and Kulu hills with the dust and the mangoes of the South; she told a tale of some old local Gods at the edge of her husband's territory; she roundly abused the tobacco which she was then smoking, reviled all Brahmins, and speculated without reserve on the coming of many grandsons.

CHAPTER V

Here come I to my own again—
Fed, forgiven, and known again—
Claimed by bone of my bone again,
    And sib to flesh of my flesh!
The fatted calf is dressed for me,
But the husks have greater zest for me . .
I think my pigs will be best for me,
    So I'm off to the styes afresh.
                                The Prodigal Son.[1]

ONCE more the lazy, string-tied, shuffling procession got under way, and she slept till they reached the next halting-stage. It was a very

[1]Revised in *Songs from Books*, these lines open "The Prodigal Son. (Western Version)." Like the hero of biblical parable (Luke 15.11–32), the full poem's speaker is a rich man's son who has returned home destitute. Kipling's prodigal, however, was "sent out" to the land in which he was robbed; and he worked, not merely lived, with the hogs there. Now he is setting off to take up his "job again": "I have learned what pays with hogs / And—I have that knowledge to sell!"

short march, and time lacked an hour to sundown, so Kim cast about for means of amusement.

'But why not sit and rest?' said one of the escort. 'Only the devils and the English walk to and fro without reason.'

'Never make friends with the Devil, a monkey, or a boy. No man knows what they will do next,' said his fellow.

Kim turned a scornful back—he did not want to hear the old story how the Devil played with the boys and repented of it—and walked idly across country.

The lama strode after him. All that day, whenever they passed a stream, he had turned aside to look at it, but in no case had he received any warning that he had found his River. Insensibly too the comfort of speaking to some one in a reasonable tongue, and of being properly considered and respected as her spiritual adviser by a well-born woman, had weaned his thoughts a little from the Search. And further, he was prepared to spend serene years in his quest; having nothing of the white man's impatience, but a great faith.

'Where goest thou?' he called after Kim.

'No whither—it was a small march, and all this'—Kim waved his hands abroad—'is new to me.'

'She is beyond question a wise and a discerning woman. But it is hard to meditate when——'

'All women are thus.' Kim spoke as might have Solomon.

'Before the lamassery was a broad platform,' the lama muttered, looping up the well-worn rosary, 'of stone. On that I have left the marks of my feet—pacing to and fro with these.'

He clicked the beads, and began the '*Om mane pudme hum*' of his devotion; grateful for the cool, the quiet, and the absence of dust.

One thing after another drew Kim's idle eye across the plain. There was no purpose in his wanderings, except that the build of the huts near by seemed new, and he wished to investigate.

They came out on a broad tract of grazing-ground, brown and purple in the afternoon light, with a heavy clump of mangoes in the centre. It struck Kim as curious that no shrine stood in so eligible a spot: the boy was observing as any priest for these things. Far across the plain walked side by side four men, made small by the distance. He looked intently under his curved palms and caught the sheen of brass.

'Soldiers. White soldiers!' said he. 'Let us see.'

'It is always soldiers when thou and I go out alone together. But I have never seen the white soldiers.'

'They do no harm except when they are drunk. Keep behind this tree.'

They stepped behind the thick trunks in the cool dark of the mango-tope. Two little figures halted; the other two came forward uncertainly. They were the advance-party of a regiment on the march, sent out, as usual, to mark the camp. They bore five-foot sticks with fluttering flags, and called to each other as they spread over the flat earth.

At last they entered the mango-grove, walking heavily.

'It's here or hereabouts—officers' tents under the trees, I take it, an' the rest of us can stay outside. Have they marked out for the baggage-waggons behind?'

They cried again to their comrades in the distance, and the rough answer came back faint and mellowed.

'Shove the flag in here, then,' said one.

'What do they prepare?' said the lama, wonder-struck. 'This is a great and terrible world. What is the device on the flag?'

A soldier thrust a stave within a few feet of them, grunted discontentedly, pulled it up again, conferred with his companion, who looked up and down the shaded case of greenery, and returned it.

Kim stared with all his eyes, his breath coming short and sharp between his teeth. The soldiers stamped off into the sunshine.

'O Holy One,' he gasped, 'my horoscope! The drawing in the dust by the priest at Umballa! Remember what he said. First come two—*ferashes*—to make all things ready—in a dark place, as it is always at the beginning of a vision.'

'But this is not vision,' said the lama. 'It is the world's Illusion, and no more.'

'And after them comes the Bull—the Red Bull on the green field. Look! It is he!'

He pointed to the flag that was snap-snapping in the evening breeze not ten feet away. It was no more than an ordinary camp marking-flag; but the regiment, always punctilious in matters of millinery, had charged it with the regimental device, the Red Bull, which is the crest of the Mavericks—the great Red Bull on a background of Irish green.

'I see, and now I remember,' said the lama. 'Certainly it is thy Bull. Certainly, also, the two men came to make all ready.'

'They are soldiers—white soldiers. What said the priest? "The sign over against the Bull is the sign of War and armed men." Holy One, this thing touches my Search.'

'True. It is true.' The lama stared fixedly at the device that flamed like a ruby in the dusk. 'The priest at Umballa said that thine was the sign of War.'

'What is to do now?'

'Wait. Let us wait.'

'Even now the darkness clears,' said Kim. It was only natural that the descending sun should at last strike through the tree-trunks, across the grove, filling it with mealy gold light for a few minutes; but to Kim it was crown of the Umballa Brahmin's prophecy.

'Hark!' said the lama. 'One beats a drum—far off!'

At first the sound, carrying diluted through the still air, resembled the beating of an artery in the head. Soon a sharpness was added.

'Ah! The music,' Kim explained. He knew the sound of a regimental band, but it amazed the lama.

At the far end of the plain a heavy, dusty column crawled in sight. Then the wind brought the tune:—

> *We crave your condescension*
> *To tell you what we know*
> *Of marching in the Mulligan Guards*
> *To Sligo Port below.*

Here broke in the shrill-tongued fifes:—

> *We shouldered arms,*
> *We marched—we marched away*
> *From Phœnix Park*
> *We marched to Dublin Bay.*
> *The drums and the fifes,*
> *Oh, sweetly they did play,*
> *As we marched—marched—marched—with the Mulligan*
> *Guards!*[2]

It was the band of the Mavericks playing the regiment to camp; for the men were route-marching with their baggage. The rippling column swung into the level—carts behind it—divided left and right, ran about like an ant-hill, and . . .

'But this is sorcery!' said the lama.

The plain dotted itself with tents that seemed to rise, all spread, from the carts. Another rush of men invaded the grove, pitched a huge tent in silence, ran up yet eight or nine more by the side of it, unearthed cooking-pots, pans, and bundles, which were taken possession of by a crowd of native servants; and behold the mango-tope turned into an orderly town as they watched!

[2]The comic song "The Mulligan Guards" was composed in 1872 by Americans David Braham and Edward Harrigan, who was half of the vaudeville team of Harrigan and (Tony) Hart. In 1879, they began a 7-year series of musical farces around the song, including *The Mulligan Guard Ball,* which centers on a conflict between two of New York's neighborhood militias, the Irish-American Mulligan Guards and their archenemies, the all-African-American Skidmore Guards. There were no actual Mulligan Guards; the inclusion of the song in *Kim* links the equally fictional Mavericks to stage Irishness.

'Let us go,' said the lama, sinking back afraid, as the fires twinkled and white officers with jingling swords stalked into the mess-tent.

'Stand back in the shadow. No one can see beyond the light of a fire,' said Kim, his eyes still on the flag. He had never before watched the routine of a seasoned regiment pitching camp in thirty minutes.

'Look! look! look!' clucked the lama. 'Yonder comes a priest.'

It was Bennett, the Church of England chaplain of the regiment, limping in dusty black. One of his flock had made some rude remarks about the chaplain's mettle; and to abash him Bennett had marched step by step with the men that day. The black dress, gold cross on the watch-chain, the hairless face, and the soft, black wideawake hat would have marked him as a holy man anywhere in all India. He dropped into a camp-chair by the door of the mess-tent and slid off his boots. Three or four officers gathered round him, laughing and joking over his exploit.

'The talk of white men is wholly lacking in dignity,' said the lama, who judged only by tone. 'But I have considered the countenance of that priest, and I think he is learned. Is it likely that he will understand our talk? I would talk to him of my Search.'

'Never speak to a white man till he is fed,' said Kim, quoting a well-known proverb. 'They will eat now, and—and I do not think they are good to beg from. Let us go back to the resting-place. After we have eaten we will come again. It certainly was a Red Bull—*my* Red Bull.'

They were both noticeably absent-minded when the old lady's retinue set their meal before them; so none broke their reserve, for it is not lucky to annoy guests.

'Now,' said Kim, picking his teeth, 'we will return to that place; but thou, O Holy One, must wait a little way off, because thy feet are heavier than mine and I am anxious to see more of that Red Bull.'

'But how canst thou understand the talk? Walk slowly. The road is dark,' the lama replied uneasily.

Kim put the question aside. 'I marked a place near to the trees,' said he, 'where thou canst sit till I call. Nay,' as the lama made some sort of protest, 'remember this is *my* Search—the Search for my Red Bull. The sign in the stars was not for thee. I know a little of the customs of white soldiers, and I always desire to see some new things.'

'What dost thou not know of this world?' The lama squatted obediently in a little hollow of the ground not a hundred yards from the hump of the mango trees dark against the star-powdered sky.

'Stay till I call.' Kim flitted into the dusk. He knew that in all probability there would be sentries round the camp, and smiled to himself as he heard the thick boots of one. A boy who can dodge over the roofs of Lahore city on a moonlight night, using every little patch and corner of darkness to discomfit his pursuer, is not likely to be checked by a line of well-trained soldiers. He paid them the compliment of crawling between a couple, and, running and halting, crouching and dropping flat, worked his way toward the lighted mess-tent where, close pressed behind the mango tree, he waited till some chance word should give him a returnable lead.[3]

The one thing now in his mind was further information as to the Red Bull. For aught he knew, and Kim's limitations were as curious and sudden as his expansions, the men, the nine hundred thorough devils of his father's prophecy, might pray to the beast after dark, as Hindus pray to the Holy Cow. That at least would be entirely right and logical, and the padre with the gold cross would be therefore the man to consult in the matter. On the other hand, remembering sober-faced padres whom he had avoided in Lahore city, the priest might be an inquisitive nuisance who would bid him learn. But had it not been proven at Umballa that his sign in the high heavens portended war and armed men? Was he not the Friend of the Stars as well as of all the world, crammed to the teeth with dreadful secrets? Lastly,—and firstly as the undercurrent of all his quick thoughts,—this adventure, though he did not know the English word, was a stupendous lark—a delightful continuation of his old flights across the housetops, as well as the fulfilment of sublime prophecy. He lay belly-flat and wriggled towards the mess-tent door, a hand on the amulet round his neck.

It was as he suspected. The Sahibs prayed to their God; for in the centre of the mess-table—its sole ornament when they were on the line of march—stood a golden bull fashioned from old-time loot of the Summer Palace at Pekin—a red-gold bull with lowered head, ramping upon a field of Irish green.[4] To him the Sahibs held out their glasses and cried aloud confusedly.

Now the Reverend Arthur Bennett always left mess after that toast, and being rather tired by his march his movements were more abrupt than usual. Kim, with slightly raised head, was still staring at his totem on the table, when the chaplain stepped on his right shoulder-blade. Kim flinched under the leather, and, rolling sideways, brought down the chaplain, who, ever a man of action, caught him by the throat and nearly choked the life out of him. Kim then kicked him desperately in the stomach. Mr. Bennett gasped and doubled up but without relaxing his grip, rolled over again, and silently hauled Kim to his own tent. The Mavericks were incurable practical jokers;

---

[3] A metaphor from card-playing.

[4] The Mavericks apparently participated in the Second Opium War of 1856–60 (see p. xiii). The "red bull" is probably the ox in the Chinese zodiac.

and it occurred to the Englishman that silence was best till he had made complete inquiry.

'Why, it's a boy!' he said, as he drew his prize under the light of the tent-pole lantern, then shaking him severely cried: 'What were you doing? You're a thief. *Choor? Mallum?*' His Hindustanee was very limited, and the ruffled and disgusted Kim intended to keep to the character laid down for him. As he recovered his breath he was inventing a beautifully plausible tale of his relations to some mess-scullion, and at the same time keeping a keen eye on and a little under the chaplain's left arm-pit. The chance came; he ducked for the doorway, but a long arm shot out and clutched at his neck, snapping the amulet string and closing on the amulet.

'Give it me. O give it me. Is it lost? Give me the papers.'

The words were in English—the tinny, saw-cut English of the native-bred, and the chaplain jumped.

'A scapular,' said he, opening his hand. 'No, some sort of heathen charm. Why—why, do you speak English? Little boys who steal are beaten. You know that?'

'I do not—I did not steal.' Kim danced in agony like a terrier at a lifted stick. 'O give it me. It is my charm. Do not thieve it from me.'

The chaplain took no heed, but, going to the tent door, called aloud. A fattish, clean-shaven man appeared.

'I want your advice, Father Victor,' said Bennett. 'I found this boy in the dark outside the mess-tent. Ordinarily, I should have chastised him and let him go, because I believe him to be a thief. But it seems he talks English, and he attaches some sort of value to a charm round his neck. I thought perhaps you might help me.'

Between himself and the Roman Catholic chaplain of the Irish contingent lay, as Bennett believed, an unbridgeable gulf, but it was noticeable that whenever the Church of England dealt with a human problem she was very likely to call in the Church of Rome. Bennett's official abhorrence of the Scarlet Woman[5] and all her ways was only equalled by his private respect for Father Victor.

'A thief talking English is it? Let's look at his charm. No, it is not a scapular, Bennett.' He held out his hand.

'But have we any right to open it? A sound whipping——'

'I did *not* thieve,' protested Kim. 'You have hit me kicks all over my body. Now give me my charm and I will go away.'

'Not quite so fast; we'll look first,' said Father Victor, leisurely rolling out poor Kimball O'Hara's '*ne varietur*' parchment, his clearance-

---

[5]Roman Catholic Church (a Protestant slur, a synonym for prostitute). The Irish regiment has a chaplain from the Church of England for Protestant soldiers, mostly from Northern Ireland or upper-class English officers, and a Catholic chaplain for most of the Irish soldiers, who would have been working class.

certificate, and Kim's baptismal certificate. On this last O'Hara—
with some confused idea that he was doing wonders for his son—had
scrawled scores of times: '*Look after the boy. Please look after the
boy,*'—signing his name and regimental number in full.

'Powers of Darkness below!' said Father Victor, passing all over
to Mr. Bennett. 'Do you know what these things are?'

'Yes,' said Kim. 'They are mine, and I want to go away.'

'I do not quite understand,' said Mr. Bennett. 'He probably
brought them on purpose. It may be a begging trick of some kind.'

'I never saw a beggar less anxious to stay with his company, then.
There's the makings of a gay mystery here. Ye believe in Providence,
Bennett?'

'I hope so.'

'Well, I believe in miracles, so it comes to the same thing. Powers
of Darkness! Kimball O'Hara! And his son! But then he's a native,
and I saw Kimball married myself to Annie Shott. How long have you
had these things, boy?'

'Ever since I was a little baby.' Father Victor stepped forward
quickly and opened the front of Kim's upper garment. 'You see, Bennett, he's not very black. What's your name?'

'Kim.'

'Or Kimball?'

'Perhaps. Will you let me go away?'

'What else?'

'They call me Kim Rishti ke. That is Kim of the Rishti.'

'What is that—"Rishti"?'

'*Eye*-rishti—that was the regiment—my father's.'

'Irish, oh I see.'

'Yess. That was how my father told me. My father, he has lived.'

'Has lived where?'

'Has lived. Of *course* he is dead—gone-out.'

'Oh. That's your abrupt way of putting it, is it?'

Bennett interrupted. 'It is possible I have done the boy an injustice. He is certainly white, though evidently neglected. I am sure I
must have bruised him. I do not think spirits——'

'Get him a glass of sherry, then, and let him squat on the cot. Now,
Kim,' continued Father Victor, 'no one is going to hurt you. Drink that
down and tell us about yourself. The truth, if you've no objection.'

Kim coughed a little as he put down the empty glass, and considered. This seemed a time for caution and fancy. Small boys who
prowl about camps are generally turned out after a whipping. But he
had received no stripes; the amulet was evidently working in his
favour, and it looked as though the Umballa horoscope and the few

words that he could remember of his father's maunderings fitted in most miraculously. Else why did the fat padre seem so impressed, and why the glass of hot yellow wine from the lean one?

'My father, he is dead in Lahore city since I was very little. The woman, she kept *kabarri* shop near where the hire-carriages are.' Kim began with a plunge, not quite sure how far the truth would serve him.

'Your mother?'

'*No*'—with a gesture of disgust. 'She went out when I was born. My father, he got these papers from the Jadoo-Gher—what do you call that?' (Bennett nodded) 'because he was in—good-standing. What do you call that?' (again Bennett nodded). 'My father told me that. He said too, and also the Brahmin who made the drawing in the dust at Umballa two days ago, *he* said, that I shall find a Red Bull on a green field and that the Bull shall help me.'

'A phenomenal little liar,' muttered Bennett.

'Powers of Darkness below, what a country!' murmured Father Victor. 'Go on, Kim.'

'I did *not* thieve. Besides, I am just now disciple of a very holy man. He is sitting outside. We saw two men come with flags, making the place ready. That is *always* so in a dream, or on account of a—a—prophecy. So I knew it was come true. I saw the Red Bull on the green field, and my father he said: "Nine hundred *pukka* devils and the Colonel riding on a horse will look after you when you find the Red Bull!" I did not know what to do when I saw the Bull, but I went away and I came again when it was dark. I wanted to see the Bull again, and I saw the Bull again with the—the Sahibs praying to it. I think the Bull shall help me. The holy man said so too. He is sitting outside. Will you hurt him, if I call him a shout now? He is very holy. He can witness to all the things I say, and he knows I am not a thief.'

'"Officers praying to a bull!" What in the world do you make of that?' said Bennett. '"Disciple of a holy man!" Is the boy mad?'

'It's O'Hara's boy, sure enough. O'Hara's boy leagued with all the Powers of Darkness. It's very much what his father would have done—if he was drunk. We'd better invite the holy man. He may know something.'

'He does not know anything,' said Kim. 'I will show you him if you come. He is my master. Then afterwards we can go.'

'Powers of Darkness!' was all that Father Victor could say, as Bennett marched off, with a firm hand on Kim's shoulder.

They found the lama where he had dropped.

'The Search is at an end for me,' shouted Kim in the vernacular. 'I have found the Bull, but God knows what comes next. They will not hurt you. Come to the fat priest's tent with this thin man and see the end. It is all new, and they cannot talk Hindi. They are only uncurried donkeys.'

'Then it is not well to make a jest of their ignorance,' the lama returned. 'I am glad if thou art rejoiced, *chela*.'

Dignified and unsuspicious, he strode into the little tent, saluted the Churches as a Churchman, and sat down by the open charcoal brazier. The yellow lining of the tent reflected in the lamp-light made his face red-gold.

Bennett looked at him with the triple-ringed uninterest of the creed that lumps nine-tenths of the world under the title of 'heathen.'

'And what was the end of the search? What gift has the Red Bull brought?' The lama addressed himself to Kim.

'He says, "What are you going to do?"' Bennett was staring uneasily at Father Victor, and Kim, for his own ends, took upon himself the office of interpreter.

'I do not see what concern this *faquir* has with the boy, who is probably his dupe or his confederate,' Bennett began. 'We cannot allow an English boy——Assuming that he is the son of a Mason, the sooner he goes to the Masonic Orphanage the better.'

'Ah! That's your opinion as Secretary to the Regimental Lodge,' said Father Victor; 'but we might as well tell the old man what we are going to do. He doesn't look like a villain.'

'My experience is that one can never fathom the Oriental mind. Now Kimball, I wish you to tell this man what I say—word for word.'

Kim gathered the import of the next few sentences and began thus:

'Holy One, the thin fool who looks like a camel says that I am the son of a Sahib.'

'But how?'

'Oh, it is true. I knew it since my birth, but *he* could only find it out by reading the amulet from my neck and reading all the papers. He thinks that once a Sahib is always a Sahib, and between the two of them they purpose to keep me in this regiment or to send me to a *madrissah* (a school). It has happened before. I have always avoided it. The fat fool is of one mind and the camel-like one of another. But that is no odds. I may spend one night here and perhaps the next. It has happened before. Then I will run away and return to thee.'

'But tell them that thou art my *chela*. Tell them how thou didst come to me when I was faint and bewildered. Tell them of our Search, and they will surely let thee go now.'

'I have already told them. They laugh, and they talk of the police.'

'What are you saying?' asked Mr. Bennett.

'Oah. He only says that if you do not let me go it will stop him in his business—his ur-gent private af-fairs.' This last was a reminiscence of some talk with a Eurasian clerk in the Canal Department, but it only drew a smile, which nettled him. 'And if you *did* know what his business was you would not be in such a beastly hurry to interfere.'

'What is it then?' said Father Victor, not without feeling, as he watched the lama's face.

'There is a River in this country which he wishes to find so verree much. It was put out by an Arrow which——' Kim tapped his foot impatiently as he translated in his own mind from the vernacular to his clumsy English. "Oah, it was made by our Lord God Buddha you know, and if you wash there you are washed away from all your sins and made as white as cotton-wool.' (Kim had heard mission-talk in his time.) 'I am his disciple, and we *must* find that River. It is so verree valuable to us.'

'Say that again,' said Bennett. Kim obeyed, with amplifications.

'But this is gross blasphemy,' cried the Church of England.

'Tck! Tck!' said Father Victor sympathetically. 'I'd give a good deal to be able to talk the vernacular. A river that washes away sin! And how long have you two been looking for it?'

'Oh, many days. Now we wish to go away and look for it again. It is not here, you see.'

'I see,' said Father Victor gravely. 'But he can't go on in that old man's company. It would be different, Kim, if you were not a soldier's son. Tell him that the regiment will take care of you and make you as good a man as your—as good a man as can be. Tell him that if he believes in miracles he must believe that——'

'There is no need to play on his credulity,' Bennett interrupted.

'I'm doing no such thing. He must believe that the boy's coming here—to his own regiment—in search of his Red Bull is in the nature of a miracle. Consider the chances against it, Bennett. This one boy in all India, and our regiment of all others on the line o' march for him to meet with! It's predestined on the face of it. Yes, tell him it's *Kismet*.[6] *Kismet, mallum?* (Do you understand?)'

He turned towards the lama, to whom he might as well have talked of Mesopotamia.

'They say,'—the old man's eye lighted at Kim's speech,—'they say that the meaning of my horoscope is now accomplished, and that being led back—though as thou knowest I went out of curiosity—to these people and their Red Bull I must needs go to a *madrissah* and be turned into a Sahib. Now I make pretence of agreement, for at the worst it will be but a few meals eaten away from thee. Then I will slip away and follow down the road to Saharunpore. Therefore, Holy

[6]Fate, or destiny, in Urdu, Arabic, Turkish, and Persian; not a Tibetan Buddhist concept.

One, keep with that Kulu woman—on no account stray far from her cart till I come again. Past question, my sign is of War and of armed men. See how they have given me wine to drink and set me upon a bed of honour! My father must have been some great person. So if they raise me to honour among them, good. If not, good again. However it goes, I will run back to thee when I am tired. But stay with the Rajputni, or I shall miss thy feet. . . . Oah yess,' said the boy, 'I have told him everything you tell me to say.'

'And I cannot see any need why he should wait,' said Bennett, feeling in his trouser-pocket. 'We can investigate the details later—and I will give him a ru——'

'Give him time. May be he's fond of the lad,' said Father Victor, half-arresting the clergyman's motion.

The lama dragged forth his rosary and pulled his huge hat-brim over his eyes.

'What can he want now?'

'He says'—Kim put up one hand. 'He says: Be quiett. He wants to speak to me by himself. You see you do not know one little word of what he says, and I think if you talk he will perhaps give you very bad curses. When he takes those beads like that, you see he always wants to be quiett.'

The two Englishmen sat overwhelmed, but there was a look in Bennett's eye that promised ill for Kim when he should be relaxed to the religious arm.

'A Sahib and the son of a Sahib——' The lama's voice was harsh with pain. 'But no white man knows the land and the customs of the land as thou knowest. How comes it this is true?'

'What matter, Holy One: but remember it is only for a night or two. Remember, I can change swiftly. It will all be as it was when I first spoke to thee under Zam-Zammah the great gun——'

'As a boy in the dress of white men—when I first went to the Wonder House. And a second time thou wast a Hindu. What shall the third incarnation be?' He chuckled drearily. 'Ah, *chela*, thou hast done a wrong to an old man because my heart went out to thee.'

'And mine to thee. But how could I know that the Red Bull would bring me to this business?'

The lama covered his face afresh, and nervously rattled the rosary. Kim squatted beside him and laid hold upon a fold of his clothing.

'Now it is understood that the boy is a Sahib?' he went on in a muffled tone. 'Such a Sahib as was he who kept the images in the Wonder House.' The lama's experience of white men was limited. He seemed to be repeating a lesson. 'So then it is not seemly that he should do other than as the Sahibs do. He must go back to his own people.'

'For a day and a night and a day,' Kim pleaded.

'No, ye don't!' Father Victor saw Kim edging towards the door, and interposed a strong leg.

'I do not understand the customs of white men. The Priest of the Images in the Wonder House in Lahore was more courteous than the thin one here. This boy will be taken from me. They will make a Sahib of my disciple? Woe to me, how shall I find my River? Have *they* no disciples? Ask.'

'He says he is very sorry that he cannot find the River now any more. He says, Why have you no disciples, and stop bothering him? He wants to be washed of his sins.'

Neither Bennett nor Father Victor found any answer ready.

Said Kim in English, distressed for the lama's agony: 'I think if you will let me go now we will walk away quietly and not steal. We will look for that River like before I was caught. I wish I did not come here to find the Red Bull and all that sort of thing. I do not want it.'

'It's the very best day's work you ever did for yourself, young man,' said Bennett.

'Good heavens, I don't know how to console him,' said Father Victor, watching the lama intently. 'He can't take the boy away with him, and yet he's a good man—I'm sure he's a good man. Bennett, if you give him that rupee he'll curse you root and branch!'

They listened to each other's breathing—three—five full minutes. Then the lama raised his head, and looked forth across them into space and emptiness.

'And I am a follower of the Way,' he said bitterly. 'The sin is mine and the punishment is mine. I made believe to myself—for now I see it was but make-belief—that thou wast sent to me to aid in the Search. So my heart went out to thee for thy charity and thy courtesy and the wisdom of thy little years. But those who follow the Way must permit not the fire of any desire or attachment, for that is all illusion. As says . . .' He quoted an old, old Chinese text, backed it with another, and reinforced these with a third. 'I stepped aside from the Way, my *chela*. It was no fault of thine. I delighted in the sight of life, the new people upon the roads, and in thy joy at seeing these things. I was pleased with thee who should have considered my Search and my Search alone. Now I am sorrowful because thou art taken away and my River is far from me. It is the Law which I have broken!'

'Powers of Darkness below!' said Father Victor, who, wise in the confessional, heard the pain in every sentence.

'I see now that the sign of the Red Bull was a sign for me as well as for thee. All Desire is red—and evil. I will do penance and find my River alone.'

'At least go back to the Kulu woman,' said Kim, 'otherwise thou wilt be lost upon the roads. She will feed thee till I run back to thee.'

The lama waved a hand to show that the matter was finally settled in his mind.

'Now,'—his tone altered as he turned to Kim,—'what will they do with thee? At least I may, acquiring merit, wipe out past ill.'

'Make me a Sahib—so they think. The day after to-morrow I return. Do not grieve.'

'Of what sort? Such a one as this or that man?' He pointed to Father Victor. 'Such an one as those I saw this evening—men wearing swords and stamping heavily?'

'May be.'

'That is not well. These men follow desire and come to emptiness. Thou must not be of their sort.'

'The Umballa priest said that my Star was War,' Kim interjected. 'I will ask these fools—but there is truly no need. I will run away this night, for all I wanted to see the new things.'

Kim put two or three questions in English to Father Victor, translating the replies to the lama.

Then: 'He says, "You take him from me and you cannot say what you will make him." He says, "Tell me before I go, for it is not a small thing to make a child."'

'You will be sent to a school. Later on, we shall see. Kimball, I suppose you'd like to be a soldier?'

'*Gorah-log* (white-folk). No-ah! No-ah!' Kim shook his head violently. There was nothing in his composition to which drill and routine appealed. 'I will not be a soldier.'

'You will be what you're told to be,' said Bennett; 'and you should be grateful that we're going to help you.'

Kim smiled compassionately. If these men lay under the delusion that he would do anything that he did not fancy, so much the better.

Another long silence followed. Bennett fidgeted with impatience, and suggested calling a sentry to evict the *faquir*.

'Do they give or sell learning among the Sahibs? Ask them,' said the lama, and Kim interpreted.

'They say that money is paid to the teacher—but that money the regiment will give. . . . What need? It is only for a night.'

'And—the more money is paid the better learning is given?' The lama disregarded Kim's plans for an early flight. 'It is no wrong to pay for learning; to help the ignorant to wisdom is always a merit.' The rosary clicked furiously as an abacus. Then he faced his oppressors.

'Ask them for how much money do they give a wise and suitable teaching? and in what city is that teaching given?'

'Well,' said Father Victor in English, when Kim had translated, 'that depends. The regiment would pay for you all the time you are at the Military Orphanage; or you might go on the Punjab Masonic Orphanage's list (not that he or you 'ud understand what that means); but the best schooling a boy can get in India is, of course, at St. Xavier's in Partibus at Lucknow.'[7] This took some time to interpret, for Bennett wished to cut it short.

'He wants to know how much?' said Kim placidly.

'Two or three hundred rupees a year.' Father Victor was long past any sense of amazement. Bennett, impatient, did not understand.

'He says: "Write that name and the money upon a paper and give it him." And he says you must write your name below, because he is going to write a letter in some days to you. He says you are a good man. He says the other man is a fool. He is going away.'

The lama rose suddenly. 'I follow my Search,' he cried, and was gone.

'He'll run slap into the sentries,' cried Father Victor, jumping up as the lama stalked out; 'but I can't leave the boy.' Kim made swift motion to follow, but checked himself. There was no sound of challenge outside. The lama had disappeared.

Kim settled himself composedly on the chaplain's cot. At least the lama had promised that he would stay with the Rajput woman from Kulu, and the rest was of the smallest importance. It pleased him that the two padres were so evidently excited. They talked long in undertones, Father Victor urging some scheme on Mr. Bennett, who seemed incredulous. All this was very new and fascinating, but Kim felt sleepy. They called men into the tent—one of them certainly was the Colonel, as his father had prophesied—and they asked him an infinity of questions, chiefly about the woman who looked after him, all of which Kim answered truthfully. They did not seem to think the woman a good guardian.

After all, this was the newest of his experiences. Sooner or later, if he chose, he could escape into great, gray, formless India, beyond tents and padres and colonels. Meantime, if the Sahibs were to be impressed, he would do his best to impress them. He too was a white man.

After much talk that he could not comprehend, they handed him over to a sergeant, who had strict instructions not to let him escape. The regiment would go on to Umballa, and Kim would be sent up,

---

[7]St. Xavier, Spanish Jesuit Apostle of the East Indies, who died in China in 1552, was canonized in 1621. Many Catholic schools in India bear his name; Kipling would have known the one in Bombay. *In partibus* (short for *in partibus infidelium* or "in the land of the unbelievers") refers to an area that has a bishop but is not an actual diocese.

partly at the expense of the Lodge and in part by subscription, to a place called Sanawar.

'It's miraculous past all whooping, Colonel,' said Father Victor, when he had talked without a break for ten minutes. 'His Buddhist friend has levanted after taking my name and address. I can't quite make out whether he'll pay for the boy's education or whether he is preparing some sort of witchcraft on his own account.' Then to Kim: 'You'll live to be grateful to your friend the Red Bull yet. We'll make a man of you at Sanawar—even at the price o' making you a Protestant.'

'Certainly—most certainly,' said Bennett.

'But you will not go to Sanawar,' said Kim.

'But we will go to Sanawar, little man. That's the order of the Commander-in-Chief, who's a trifle more important than O'Hara's son.'

'You will not go to Sanawar. You will go to thee war.'

There was a shout of laughter from the full tent.

'When you know your own regiment a trifle better you won't confuse the line of march with line of battle, Kim. We hope to go to "thee war" sometime.'

'Oah, I know all thatt.' Kim drew his bow again at a venture. If they were not going to the war, at least they did not know what he knew of the talk in the verandah at Umballa.

'I know you are not at thee war now; but I tell *you* that as soon as you get to Umballa you will be sent to the war—the new war. It is a war of eight thousand men, besides the guns.'

'That's explicit. D'you add prophecy to your other gifts? Take him along, Sergeant. Take up a suit for him from the Drums,[8] an' take care he doesn't slip through your fingers. Who says the age of miracles is gone by? I think I'll go to bed. My poor mind's weakening.'

At the far end of the camp, silent as a wild animal, an hour later sat Kim, newly washed all over, in a horrible stuff suit that rasped his arms and legs.

'A most amazin' young bird,' said the sergeant. 'He turns up in charge of a yellow-headed buck-Brahmin priest, with his father's lodge certificates round his neck, talkin' God knows what all of a red bull. The buck-Brahmin evaporates without explanations, an' the bhoy sets cross-legged on the chaplain's bed prophesyin' bloody war to the men at large. Injia's a wild land for a God-fearin' man. I'll just tie his leg to the tent-pole in case he'll go through the roof. What did ye say about the war?'

'Eight thousand men, besides guns,' said Kim. 'Very soon you will see.'

'You're a consolin' little imp. Lie down between the Drums an' go to bye-bye. Those two boys beside ye will watch your slumbers.'

[8]The regiment's drummer boys, who would have been about Kim's age.

CHAPTER VI

Now I remember comrades—
　Old playmates on new seas—
Whenas we traded orpiment
　Among the savages.
Ten thousand leagues to southward,
　And thirty years removed—
They knew not noble Valdez,
　But me they knew and loved.
　　　　　　Song of Diego Valdez.[1]

VERY early in the morning the white tents came down and disappeared as the Mavericks took a side-road to Umballa. It did not skirt the resting-place, and Kim, trudging beside a baggage-cart under fire of comments from soldiers' wives, was not so confident as overnight. He discovered that he was closely watched—Father Victor on the one side, and Mr. Bennett on the other.

In the forenoon the column checked. A camel-orderly handed the Colonel a letter. He read it, and spoke to a Major. Half a mile in the rear, Kim heard a hoarse and joyful clamour rolling down on him through the thick dust. Then some one beat him on the back, crying: 'Tell us how ye knew, ye little limb of Satan? Father dear, see if ye can make him tell.'

A pony ranged alongside, and he was hauled on to the priest's saddle-bow.

'Now, my son, your prophecy of last night has come true. Our orders are to entrain at Umballa for the front to-morrow.'

'What is that?' said Kim, for '*front*' and '*entrain*' were newish words to him.

'We are going to "thee war," as you called it.'

'Of course you are going to thee war. I said last night.'

'Ye did; but, Powers o' Darkness, how did ye know?'

Kim's eyes sparkled. He shut his lips, nodded his head, and looked unspeakable things. The chaplain moved on through the dust, and privates, sergeants, and subalterns called one another's attention to the boy. The Colonel, at the head of the column, stared at him curiously. 'It

---

[1]Blamed for England's defeat of the Spanish Armada in 1588, Admiral Diego Flores de Valdes returned to prison in Spain. In the 14-stanza *Definitive Edition* poem of which these revised lines form stanza 3, the still-powerful Valdez reveals that his youthful, free-roving, desirous self has already been sacrificed to solitary "bondage of great deeds." Orpiment is a rare, yellow-orange mineral: Used in alchemy and as a poison, it is also the source of that bright, dangerous pigment known as "Chinese Yellow" or "King's Yellow."

was probably some bazar rumour,' he said; 'but even then——' He referred to the paper in his hand. 'Hang it all, the thing was only decided within the last forty-eight hours.'

'Are there many more like you in India?' said Father Victor, 'or are you by way o' being a *lusus naturæ?*'

'Now I have told you,' said the boy, 'will you let me go back to my old man? If he has not stayed with that woman from Kulu, I am afraid he will die.'

'By what I saw of him he's as well able to take care of himself as you. No. Ye've brought us luck, an' we're goin' to make a man of you. I'll take ye back to your baggage-cart and ye'll come to me this evening.'

For the rest of the day Kim found himself an object of distinguished consideration among a few hundred white men. The story of his appearance in camp, the discovery of his parentage, and his prophecy, had lost nothing in the telling. A big, shapeless white woman on a pile of bedding asked him mysteriously whether she thought her husband would come back from the war. Kim reflected gravely, and said that he would, and the woman gave him food. In many respects, this big procession that played music at intervals—this crowd that talked and laughed so easily—resembled a festival in Lahore city. So far, there was no sign of hard work, and he resolved to lend the spectacle his patronage. At evening there came out to meet them bands of music, and played the Mavericks into camp near Umballa railway station. That was an interesting night. Men of other regiments came to visit the Mavericks. The Mavericks went visiting on their own account. Their pickets hurried forth to bring them back, met pickets of strange regiments on the same duty; and, after a while, the bugles blew madly for more pickets with officers to control the tumult. The Mavericks had a reputation for liveliness to live up to. But they fell in on the platform next morning in perfect shape and condition; and Kim, left behind with the sick, women, and boys, found himself shouting farewells excitedly as the trains drew away. Life as a Sahib was amusing so far; but he touched it with a very cautious hand. Then they marched him back in charge of a drummer-boy to empty, lime-washed barracks, whose floors were covered with rubbish and string and paper, and whose ceilings gave back his lonely footfall. Native fashion, he curled himself up on a stripped cot and went to sleep. An angry man stumped down the verandah, woke him up, and said he was a schoolmaster. This was enough for Kim, and he retired into his shell. He could just puzzle out the various English Police notices in Lahore city, because they affected his comfort; and among the many guests of the woman who looked after him had been a queer German who painted scenery for the Parsee travelling theatre. He told Kim that he had been 'on the barricades in

Forty-eight,' and therefore—at least that was how it struck Kim—he would teach the boy to write in return for food.[2] Kim had been kicked as far as single letters, but did not think well of them.

'I do not know anything. Go away!' said Kim, scenting evil. Hereupon the man caught him by the ear, dragged him to a room in a far-off wing where a dozen drummer-boys were sitting on forms, and told him to be still if he could do nothing else. This he managed very successfully. The man explained something or other with white lines on a black board for at least half an hour, and Kim continued his interrupted nap. He much disapproved of the present aspect of affairs, for this was the very school and discipline he had spent two-thirds of his young life in avoiding. Suddenly a beautiful idea occurred to him, and he wondered that he had not thought of it before.

The man dismissed them, and first to spring through the verandah into the open sunshine was Kim.

"'Ere you! 'Alt! Stop!' said a high voice at his heels. 'I've got to look after you. My orders are not to let you out of my sight. Where are you goin'?'

It was the drummer-boy who had been hanging round him all the forenoon—a fat and freckled person of about fourteen, and Kim loathed him from the soles of his boots to his cap-ribbons.

'To the bazar—to get sweets—for you,' said Kim, after thought.

'Well, the bazar's out o' bounds. If we go there we'll get a dressing-down. You come back.'

'How near can we go?' Kim did not know what bounds meant, but he wished to be polite—for the present.

"'Ow near? 'Ow far, you mean? We can go as far as that tree down the road.'

'Then I will go there.'

'All right. I ain't goin'. It's too 'ot. I can watch you from 'ere. It's no good your runnin' away. If you did, they'd spot you by your clothes. That's regimental stuff you're wearin'. There ain't a picket in Umballa wouldn't 'ead you back quicker than you started out.'

This did not impress Kim as much as the knowledge that his raiment would tire him out if he tried to run. He slouched to the tree at the corner of a bare road leading towards the bazar, and eyed the natives passing. Most of them were barrack-servants of the lowest caste. Kim hailed a sweeper, who promptly retorted with a piece of unnec-

[2]Lively, eclectic, and often ambitiously staged, popular Parsee performances proved central to the development of 19th-c. Indian theater. Though the most famous 1848 barricades were in Paris, Kim's teacher could easily have fought in Berlin, Dresden, Frankfurt, Vienna, or Prague. A revolutionary turned scene painter might well enjoy teaching a poor market boy to read.

essary insolence, in the natural belief that the European boy could not follow. The low, quick answer undeceived him. Kim put his fettered soul into it, thankful for the late chance to abuse somebody in the tongue he knew best. 'And now, go to the nearest letter-writer in the bazar and tell him to come here. I would write a letter.'

'But—but what manner of white man's son art thou, to need a bazar letter-writer? Is there not a schoolmaster in the barracks?'

'Ay; and Hell is full of the same sort. Do my order, you—you Od! Thy mother was married under a basket! Servant of Lal Beg' (Kim knew the god of the sweepers), 'run on my business or we will talk again.'

The sweeper shuffled off in haste. 'There is a white boy by the barracks waiting under a tree who is not a white boy,' he stammered to the first bazar letter-writer he came across. 'He needs thee.'

'Will he pay?' said that spruce scribe, gathering up his desk and pens and sealing-wax all in order.

'I do not know. He is not like other boys. Go and see. It is well worth.'

Kim danced with impatience when the slim young Kayeth hove in sight. As soon as his voice could carry he cursed him volubly.

'First I will take my pay,' the letter-writer said. 'Bad words have made the price higher. But who art thou, dressed in that fashion, to speak in this fashion?'

'Aha! That is in the letter which thou shalt write. Never was such a tale. But I am in no haste. Another writer will serve me. Umballa city is as full of them as is Lahore.'

'Four annas,' said the writer, sitting down and spreading his cloth in the shade of a deserted barrack-wing.

Mechanically Kim squatted beside him,—squatted as only the natives can,—in spite of the abominable clinging trousers.

The writer regarded him sideways.

'That is the price to ask of Sahibs,' said Kim. 'Now fix me a true one.'

'An anna and a half. How do I know, having written the letter, that thou wilt not run away?'

'I must not go beyond this tree, and there is also the stamp to be considered.'

'I get no commission on the price of the stamp. Once more, what manner of white boy art thou?'

'That shall be said in the letter, which is to Mahbub Ali, the horse-dealer in the Kashmir Serai, at Lahore. He is my friend.'

'Wonder on wonder!' murmured the letter-writer, dipping a reed in the inkstand. 'To be written in Hindi?'

'Assuredly. To Mahbub Ali then. Begin! *I have come down with the old man as far as Umballa in the train. At Umballa I carried the news of the bay mare's pedigree.*' After what he had seen in the garden, he was not going to write of white stallions.

'Slower a little. What has a bay mare to do. . . . Is it Mahbub Ali the great dealer?'

'Who else? I have been in his service. Take more ink. Again. *As the order was, so I did it. We then went on foot towards Benares, but on the third day we found a certain regiment.* Is that down?'

'Ay, *pulton*,' murmured the writer, all ears.

'*I went into their camp and was caught, and by means of the charm about my neck, which thou knowest, it was established that I was the son of some man in the regiment: according to the prophecy of the Red Bull, which thou knowest was common talk of our bazar.*' Kim waited for this shaft to sink into the letter-writer's heart, cleared his throat, and continued: '*A priest clothed me and gave me a new name. . . . One priest, however, was a fool. The clothes are very heavy, but I am a Sahib and my heart is heavy too. They send me to a school and beat me. I do not like the air and water here. Come then and help me, Mahbub Ali, or send me some money, for I have not sufficient to pay the writer who writes this.*'

'"Who writes this." It is my own fault that I was tricked. Thou art as clever as Husain Bux that forged the Treasury stamps at Nucklao. But what a tale! What a tale! Is it true by any chance?'

'It does not profit to tell lies to Mahbub Ali. It is better to help his friends by lending them a stamp. When the money comes I will repay.'

The writer grunted doubtfully, but took a stamp out of his desk, sealed the letter, handed it over to Kim, and departed. Mahbub Ali's was a name of power in Umballa.

'That is the way to win a good account with the Gods,' Kim shouted after him.

'Pay me twice over when the money comes,' the man cried over his shoulder.

'What was you bukkin' to that nigger about?'[3] said the drummer-boy when Kim returned to the verandah. 'I was watchin' you.'

'I was only talkin' to him.'

'You talk the same as a nigger, don't you?'

'No-ah! No-ah! I onlee speak a little. What shall we do now?'

'The bugles 'ill go for dinner in arf a minute. My Gawd! I wish I'd gone up to the front with the regiment. It's awful doin' nothin' but school down 'ere. Don't you 'ate it?'

---

[3]The drummer boy's use of "nigger" underscores both his radical ignorance of India and his incompetence at verbal abuse (see p. 86). By making the boy a native of Liverpool, Kipling evokes the British slave trade (officially ended in 1807). See next page. Later editions shift the boy's home to London.

'Oah yess!'

'I'd run away if I knew where to go to, but, as the men say, in this bloomin' Injia you're only a prisoner at large. You can't desert without bein' took back at once. I'm fair sick of it.'

'You have been in Be—England?'

'W'y, I only come out last troopin' season with my mother. I should think I 'ave been in England. What a ignorant little beggar you are. You was brought up in the gutter, wasn't you?'

'Oah yess. Tell me something about England. My father he came from there.'

Though he would not say so, Kim of course disbelieved every word the drummer-boy spoke about the Liverpool suburb which was his England. It passed the heavy time till dinner—a most unappetising meal served to the boys and a few invalids in a corner of a barrack-room. But that he had written to Mahbub Ali, Kim would have been almost depressed. The indifference of native crowds he was used to; but this strong loneliness among white men preyed on him. He was grateful when, in the course of the afternoon, a big soldier took him over to Father Victor, who lived in another wing across another dusty parade-ground. The priest was reading an English letter written in purple ink. He looked at Kim more curiously than ever.

'An' how do you like it, my son, as far as you've gone? Not much, eh? It must be hard—very hard on a wild animal. Listen now. I've an' amazin' epistle from your friend.'

'Where is he? Is he well? Oah! If he knows to write me letters, it is all right.'

'You're fond of him then?'

'*Of* course I am fond of him. He was fond of me.'

'It seems so by the look of this. He can't write English, can he?'

'Oah no. Not that I know, but *of* course he found a letter-writer who can write English verree well, and so he wrote. I do hope you understand.'

'That accounts for it. D'you know anything about his money affairs?' Kim's face showed that he did not.

'How can I tell?'

'That's what I'm askin'. Now listen if you can make head or tail o' this. We'll skip the first part. . . . It's written from Jagadhir Road. . . . *"Sitting on wayside in grave meditation, trusting to be favoured with your Honour's applause of present step, which recommend your Honour to execute for Almighty God's sake. Education is greatest blessing if of best sorts. Otherwise no earthly use."* Faith, the old man's hit the bull's-eye that time! *"If your Honour condescending giving my boy best educations Xavier"* (I suppose that's St. Xavier in Partibus) *"in terms of our conversation dated in your tent 15th instant"* (a business-like touch there!) *"then Almighty God blessing your Honour's succeedings to third an' fourth generation and"*—now listen!—*"confide in your Honour's humble servant for adequat remuneration per hoondie per annum three hundred rupees a year to one expensive education St. Xavier, Lucknow, and allow small time to forward same per hoondie sent to any part of India as your Honour shall address yourself. This servant of your Honour has presently no place to lay crown of his head, but going to Benares by train on account of persecution of old woman talking so much and unanxious residing Saharunpore in any domestic capacity."* Now what in the world does that mean?'

'She has asked him to be *puro*—her clergyman—at Saharunpore, I think. He would not do that on account of his River. She *did* talk.'

'It's clear to you, is it? It beats me altogether. *"So going to Benares, where will find address and forward rupees for boy who is apple of eye, and for Almighty God's sake execute this education, and your petitioner as in duty bound shall ever awfully pray. Written by Sobrao Satai, Failed Entrance Alahabad University, for Venerable Teshoo Lama the priest of Such-zen looking for a River, address care of Tirthankers' Temple, Benares. P.M.—Please note boy is apple of eye, and rupees shall be sent per hoondie three hundred per annum. For God Almighty's sake."* Now, is that ravin' lunacy or a business proposition? I ask you, because I'm fairly at my wits' end.'

'He says he will give me three hundred rupees a year, so he will give me them.'

'Oh, that's the way you look at it, is it?'

'*Of* course. If he says so!'

The priest whistled; then he addressed Kim as an equal.

'I don't believe it; but we'll see. You were goin' off to-day to the Military Orphanage at Sanawar, where the regiment would keep you till you were old enough to enlist. Ye'd be brought up to the Church of England. Bennett arranged for that. On the other hand, if ye go to St. Xavier's ye'll get a better education an'—an' can have the religion. D'ye see my dilemma?'

Kim saw nothing save a vision of the lama going south in a train with none to beg for him.

'Like most people, I'm going to temporise. If your friend sends the money from Benares—Powers of Darkness below, where's a street-beggar to raise three hundred rupees?—ye'll go down to Lucknow and I'll pay your fare, because I can't touch the subscription-money if I intend, as I do, to make ye a Catholic. If he doesn't, ye'll go to the Military Orphanage at the regiment's expense. I'll allow him three days' grace, though I don't believe it at all. Even then, if he fails in his payments later on . . . but it's beyond me. We can only walk one step at a time in this world, praise God. An' they sent Bennett to the front an' left me behind. He can't expect everything.'

'Oah yess,' said Kim vaguely.

The priest leaned forward. 'I'd give a month's pay to find what's goin' on inside that little round head of yours.'

'There is nothing,' said Kim, and scratched it. He was wondering whether Mahbub Ali would send him as much as a whole rupee. Then he could pay the letter-writer and write letters to the lama at Benares. Perhaps Mahbub Ali would visit him next time he came south with horses. Surely he must know that Kim's delivery of the letter to the officer at Umballa had caused the great war which the men and boys had discussed so loudly over the barrack dinner-tables. But if Mahbub Ali did not know this, it would be very unsafe to tell him so. Mahbub Ali was hard upon boys who knew, or thought they knew, too much.

'Well, till I get further news'—Father Victor's voice interrupted the reverie—'ye can run along and play with the other boys. They'll teach ye something—but I don't think ye'll like it.'

The day dragged to its weary end. When he wished to sleep he was instructed how to fold up his clothes and set out his boots; the other boys deriding. Bugles waked him in the dawn; the schoolmaster caught him after breakfast, thrust a page of meaningless characters under his nose, gave them senseless names, and whacked him without reason. Kim meditated poisoning him with opium borrowed from a barrack-sweeper, but reflected that, as they all ate at one table in public (this was peculiarly revolting to Kim, who preferred to turn his back on the world at meals), the stroke might be dangerous. Then he attempted running off to the village where the priest had tried to drug the lama— the village where the old soldier lived. But far-seeing sentries at every exit headed back the little scarlet figure. Trousers and jacket crippled body and mind alike, so he abandoned the project and fell back, Oriental fashion, on time and chance. Three days of torment passed in the big, echoing white rooms. He walked out of afternoons under escort of the drummer-boy, and all he heard from his companion were the few useless words which seemed to make two-thirds of the white man's abuse. Kim knew and despised them all long ago. The boy resented his silence and lack of interest by beating him, as was only natural. He did not care for any of the bazars which were in bounds. He styled all natives 'niggers'; yet servants and sweepers called him abominable names to his face, and, misled by their deferential attitude, he never understood. This somewhat consoled Kim for the beatings.

On the morning of the fourth day a judgment overtook that drummer. They had gone out together towards Umballa race-course. He returned alone, weeping, with news that young O'Hara, to whom he had been doing nothing in particular, had hailed a scarlet-bearded nigger on horseback; that the nigger had then and there laid into him with a peculiarly adhesive quirt, picked up young O'Hara, and borne him off at full gallop. These tidings came to Father Victor, and he drew down his long upper lip. He was already sufficiently startled by a letter from the Temple of the Tirthankers at Benares, enclosing a native banker's note of hand for three hundred rupees, and an amazing prayer to 'Almighty God.' The lama would have been more annoyed than the priest had he known how the bazar letter-writer had translated his phrase 'to acquire merit.'

'Powers of Darkness below!' Father Victor fumbled with the note. 'An' now he's off with another of his peep-o'-day friends.[4] I don't know whether it will be a greater relief to me to get him back or to have him lost. He's beyond my comprehension. How the Divil—yes, he's the man I mean—can a street-beggar raise money to educate white boys?'

Three miles off, on Umballa race-course, Mahbub Ali, reining a gray Cabuli stallion with Kim in front of him, was saying:

'But, Little Friend of all the World, there is *my* honour and reputation to be considered. All the officer-sahibs in all the regiments, and all Umballa, know Mahbub Ali. Men saw me pick thee up and chastise that boy. We are seen now from far across this plain. How can I take thee away, or account for thy disappearing if I set thee down and let thee run off into the crops? They would put me in jail. Be patient. Once a Sahib, always a Sahib. When thou art a man—who knows—thou wilt be grateful to Mahbub Ali.'

'Take me beyond their sentries where I can change this red. Give me money and I will go to Benares and be with my lama again. I do not want to be a Sahib, and remember I did deliver that message.'

The stallion bounded wildly. Mahbub Ali had incautiously driven home the sharp-edged stirrup. (He was not the new sort of fluent horse-dealer who wears English boots and spurs.) Kim drew his own conclusions from that betrayal.

'That was a small matter. It lay on the straight road to Benares. I and the Sahib have by this time forgotten it. I send so many letters and messages to men who ask questions about horses, I cannot well

[4]Father Victor's reference underscores his preoccupation with his own homeland's history of religious sectarian violence. The late 18th-c. militant Irish Protestant "Peep o' Day Boys" were named for their early morning attacks on Catholic homes.

remember one from the other. Was it some matter of a bay mare that Peters Sahib wished the pedigree of?'

Kim saw the trap at once. If he had said 'bay mare' Mahbub would have known by his very readiness to fall in with the amendment that the boy suspected something. Kim replied therefore:

'Bay mare. No. *I* do not forget my messages thus. It was a white stallion.'

'Ay, so it was. A white Arab stallion. But thou didst write bay mare to me.'

'Who cares to tell truth to a letter-writer?' Kim answered, feeling Mahbub's palm on his heart.

'Hi! Mahbub, you old villain, pull up!' cried a voice, and an Englishman raced alongside on a little polo-pony. 'I've been chasing you half over the country. That Cabuli of yours can go. For sale, I suppose?'

'I have some young stuff coming on made by Heaven for the delicate and difficult polo-game. He has no equal. He——'

'Plays polo and waits at table. Yes. We know all that. What the deuce have you got there?'

'A boy,' said Mahbub gravely. 'He was being beaten by another boy. His father was once a white soldier in the big war.[5] The boy was a child in Lahore city. He played with my horses when he was a babe. Now I think they will make him a soldier. He has been newly caught by his father's regiment that went up to the war last week. But I do not think he wants to be a soldier. I take him for a ride. Tell me where thy barracks are and I will set thee there.'

'Let me go. I can find the barracks alone.'

'And if thou runnest away who will say it is not my fault?'

'He'll run back to his dinner. Where has he to run to?' the Englishman asked.

'He was born in the land. He has friends. He goes where he chooses. He is a *chabuk sawai* (a sharp chap). It needs only to change his clothing, and in a twinkling he would be a low-caste Hindi boy.'

'The deuce he would!' The Englishman looked critically at the boy as Mahbub headed towards the barracks. Kim ground his teeth. Mahbub was mocking him, as faithless Afghans will; for he went on:

'They will send him to a school and put heavy boots on his feet and swaddle him in these clothes. Then he will forget all he knows. Now which of the barracks is thine?'

Kim pointed—he could not speak—to Father Victor's wing, all staring white near by.

[5] Anglo-Afghan War of 1878–80.

'Perhaps he will make a good soldier,' said Mahbub reflectively. 'He will make a good orderly at least. I sent him to deliver a message once from Lahore. A message concerning the pedigree of a white stallion.'

Here was deadly insult on deadlier injury—and the Sahib to whom he had so craftily given that war-waking letter heard it all. Kim beheld Mahbub Ali frying in flame for his treachery, but for himself he saw one long gray vista of barracks, schools, and barracks again. He gazed imploringly at the clear-cut face in which there was no glimmer of recognition; but even at this extremity it never occurred to him to throw himself on the white man's mercy or to denounce the Afghan. And Mahbub stared deliberately at the Englishman, who stared as deliberately at Kim, quivering and tongue-tied.

'My horse is well trained,' said the dealer. 'Others would have kicked, Sahib.'

'Ah,' said the Englishman at last, rubbing his pony's damp withers with his whip-butt. 'Who makes the boy a soldier?'

'He says the regiment that found him, and especially the padre-sahib of that regiment.'

'There is the padre!' Kim choked as bare-headed Father Victor sailed down upon them from the verandah.

'Powers o' Darkness below, O'Hara! How many more mixed friends do you keep in Asia?' he cried, as Kim slid down and stood helplessly before him.

'Good morning, Padre,' the Colonel said cheerily. 'I know you by reputation well enough. Meant to have come over and called before this. I'm Creighton.'

'Of the Ethnological Survey?' said Father Victor. The Colonel nodded. 'Faith I'm glad to meet ye then; an' I owe you some thanks for bringing back the boy.'

'No thanks to me, Padre. Besides, the boy wasn't going away. You don't know old Mahbub Ali'—the horse-dealer sat impassive in the sunlight. 'You will when you have been in the station a month. He sells us all our crocks. That boy is rather a curiosity. Can you tell me anything about him?'

'Can I tell you?' puffed Father Victor. 'You'll be the one man that could help me in my quandaries. Tell you! Powers o' Darkness, I'm bursting to tell some one who knows something o' the native!'

A groom came round the corner. Colonel Creighton raised his voice, speaking in Urdu. 'Very good, Mahbub Ali, but what is the use of telling me all those stories about the pony. Not one pie more than three hundred and fifty rupees will I give.'

'The Sahib is a little hot and angry after riding,' the horse-dealer returned, with the leer of a privileged jester. 'Presently, he will see my horse's points more clearly. I will wait till he has finished his talk with the padre. I will wait under that tree.'

'Confound you!' The Colonel laughed. 'That comes of looking at one of Mahbub's horses. He's a regular old leech, Padre. Wait then, if thou hast so much time to spare, Mahbub. Now I'm at your service, Padre. Where is the boy? Oh, he's gone off to collogue with Mahbub. Queer sort of boy. Might I ask you to send my mare round under cover?'

He dropped into a chair which commanded a clear view of Kim and Mahbub Ali in conference beneath the tree. The padre went indoors for cheroots.

Creighton heard Kim say bitterly: 'Trust a Brahmin before a snake, and a snake before a harlot, and a harlot before an Afghan, Mahbub Ali.'

'That is all one,' the great red beard wagged solemnly. 'Children should not see a carpet on the loom till the pattern is made plain. Believe me, Friend of all the World, I do thee great service. They will not make a soldier of thee.'

'You crafty old sinner,' thought Creighton. 'But you're not far wrong. That boy mustn't be wasted if he is as advertised.'

'Excuse me half a minute,' cried the padre from within, 'but I'm gettin' the documents of the case.'

'If through me the favour of this bold and wise Colonel Sahib comes to thee, and thou art raised to honour, what thanks wilt thou give Mahbub Ali when thou art a man?'

'Nay, nay; I begged thee to let me take the road again, where I should have been safe; and thou hast sold me back to the English. What will they give thee for blood-money?'

'A cheerful young demon!' The Colonel bit his cigar, and turned politely to Father Victor.

'What are the letters that the fat priest is waving before the Colonel? Stand behind the stallion as though looking at my bridle!' said Mahbub Ali.

'A letter from my lama which he wrote from Jagadhir Road, saying that he will pay three hundred rupees by the year for my schooling.'

'Oho! Is old Red Hat of that sort? At which school?'

'God knows. I think in Nucklao.'

'Yes. There is a big school there for the sons of Sahibs—and half-Sahibs. I have seen it when I sell horses there. So the lama also loved the Friend of all the World?'

'Ay; and *he* did not tell lies, or return me to captivity.'

'Small wonder the padre does not know how to unravel the thread. How fast he talks to the Colonel Sahib.' Mahbub Ali chuckled. 'By Allah!'—the keen eyes swept the verandah for an instant—

'thy lama has sent what to me looks like a note of hand. I have had some small dealings in *hoondies*. The Colonel Sahib is looking at it.'

'What good is all this to me?' said Kim wearily. 'Thou wilt go away, and they will return me to those empty rooms where there is no good place to sleep and where the boys beat me.'

'I do not think that. Have patience, child. All Pathans are not faithless—except in horseflesh.'

Five—ten—fifteen minutes passed, Father Victor talking energetically or asking questions which the Colonel answered.

'Now I've told you everything that I know about the boy from beginnin' to end; and it's a blessed relief to me. Did ye ever hear the like?'

'At any rate, the old man has sent the money. Gobind Sahai's notes of hand are good from here to China,' said the Colonel. 'The more one knows about natives the less can one say what they will or won't do.'

'That's consolin'—from the head of the Ethnological Survey.[6] It's this mixture of Red Bulls and Rivers of Healing (poor heathen, God help him!) an' notes of hand and Masonic certificates. Are you a Mason, by any chance?'

'By Jove, I am, now I come to think of it. That's an additional reason,' said the Colonel absently.

'I'm glad ye see a reason in it. But as I said, it's the mixture o' things that's beyond me. An' his prophesyin' to our Colonel sitting on my bed with his little shimmy torn open showing his white skin; an' the prophecy comin' true! They'll cure all that nonsense at St. Xavier's, eh?'

'Sprinkle him with holy water,' the Colonel laughed.

'On my word, I fancy I ought to sometimes. But I'm hoping he'll be brought up as a good Catholic. All that troubles me is what'll happen if the old beggar man——'

'Lama, lama, my dear sir; and some of them are gentlemen in their own country.'

'The lama then, fails to pay next year. He's a fine business head to plan on the spur of the moment, but he's bound to die some day. An' takin' a heathen's money to give a child a Christian education——'

'But he said explicitly what he wanted. As soon as he knew the boy was a white he seems to have made his arrangements accordingly. I'd give a month's pay to hear how he explained it all at the Tirthankers' Temple at Benares. Look here, Padre, I don't pretend to know much about natives, but if he says he'll pay, he'll pay—dead or

[6]Creighton invents this government bureau as a cover for the real work of the Great Game. Although ethnological work was key to the governing of India, there was no official Ethnological Survey. Creighton seems to run two sets of spies: The ethnological side, on which Hurree Chunder Mookerjee works, authenticates every detail of the various peoples of the region for political and military purposes, while the surveying side maps, also for political and military purposes.

alive. I mean his heirs will assume the debt. My advice to you is, send the boy down to Lucknow. If your Anglican chaplain thinks you've stolen a march on him——'

'Bad luck to Bennett! He was sent to the front instead o' me. Doughty certified me medically unfit. I'll excommunicate Doughty if he comes back alive! Surely Bennett ought to be content with——'

'Glory, leaving you the religion. Quite so! As a matter of fact I don't think Bennett will mind. Put the blame on me. I—er—strongly recommend sending the boy to St. Xavier's. He can go down on pass as a soldier's orphan, so the railway fare will be saved. You can buy him an outfit from the regimental subscription. The Lodge will be saved the expense of his education, and that will put the Lodge in a good temper. It's perfectly easy. I've got to go down to Lucknow next week. I'll look after the boy on the way—give him in charge of my servants, and so on.'

'You're a good man.'

'Not in the least. Don't make that mistake. The lama has sent us money for a definite end. We can't very well return it. We shall have to do as he says. Well, that's settled, isn't it? Shall we say that, Tuesday next, you'll hand him over to me at the night train south? That's only three days. He can't do much harm in three days.'

'It's a weight off my mind, but—this thing here?'—he waved the note of hand—'I don't know Gobind Sahai: or his bank, which may be a hole in a wall.'

'*You've* never been a subaltern in debt. I'll cash it if you like, and send you the vouchers in proper order.'

'But with all your own work too! It's askin'——'

'It's not the least trouble indeed. You see, as an ethnologist, the thing's very interesting to me. I'd like to make a note of it for some Government work that I'm doing. The transformation of a regimental badge like your Red Bull into a sort of fetish that the boy follows is very interesting.'

'But I can't thank you enough.'

'There's one thing you can do. All we Ethnological men are as jealous as jackdaws of one another's discoveries. They're of no interest to any one but ourselves, of course, but you know what book-collectors are like. Well, don't say a word, directly or indirectly, about the Asiatic side of the boy's character—his adventures and his prophecy, and so on. I'll worm them out of the boy later on and—you see?'

'I do. Ye'll make a wonderful account of it. Never a word will I say to any one till I see it in print.'

'Thank you. That goes straight to an ethnologist's heart. Well, I must be getting back to my breakfast. Good Heavens! Old Mahbub here still?' He raised his voice, and the horse-dealer came out from under the shadow of the tree. 'Well, what is it?'

'As regards that young horse,' said Mahbub, 'I say that when a colt is born to be a polo-pony, closely following the ball without teaching—when such a colt knows the game by divination—then I say it is a great wrong to break that colt to a heavy cart, Sahib!'

'So do I say also, Mahbub. The colt will be entered for polo only. (These fellows think of nothing in the world but horses, Padre.) I'll see you to-morrow, Mahbub, if you've anything likely for sale.'

The dealer saluted, horseman fashion, with a sweep of the off hand. 'Be patient a little, Friend of all the World,' he whispered to the agonised Kim. 'Thy fortune is made. In a little while thou goest to Nucklao, and—here is something to pay the letter-writer. I shall see thee again, I think, many times,' and he cantered off down the road.

'Listen to me,' said the Colonel from the verandah, speaking in the vernacular. 'In three days thou wilt go with me to Lucknow, see-ing and hearing new things all the while. Therefore sit still for three days and do not run away. Thou wilt go to school at Lucknow.'

'Shall I meet my Holy One there?' Kim whimpered.

'At least Lucknow is nearer to Benares than Umballa. It may be thou wilt go under my protection. Mahbub Ali knows this, and he will be angry if thou returnest to the road now. Remember—much has been told me which I do not forget.'

'I will wait,' said Kim, 'but the boys will beat me.'

Then the bugles blew for dinner.

CHAPTER VII

Unto whose use the pregnant suns are poised
  With idiot moons and stars retracting stars?
Creep thou betweene—thy coming's all unnoised.
  Heaven hath her high as earth her baser wars.
Heir to these tumults, this affright, that fraye
(By Adam's fathers' own sin bound alway);
Peer up, draw out thy horoscope and say
  Which planet mends thy threadbare fate or mars!
SIR JOHN CHRISTIE.[1]

IN the afternoon the red-faced schoolmaster told Kim that he had been 'struck off the strength,'[2] which conveyed no meaning to him till

---

[1]As revised in *Songs from Books,* under the generic title "Chapter Heading," line 6 reads: "(By Adam's, father's, own, sin bound alway)." Sir John Christie has never been identified.

[2]Removed from the regiment.

he was ordered to go away and play. Then he ran to the bazar, and found the young letter-writer to whom he owed a stamp.

'Now I pay,' said Kim royally, 'and now I need another letter to be written.'

'Mahbub Ali is in Umballa,' said the writer jauntily. He was, by virtue of his office, a bureau of general misinformation.

'This is not to Mahbub, but to a priest. Take thy pen and write quickly. *To Teshoo Lama, the holy one from Bhotiyal seeking for a River, who is now in the Temple of the Tirthankers at Benares.* Take more ink! *In three days I am to go down to Nucklao to the school at Nucklao. The name of the school is Xavier. I do not know where that school is, but it is at Nucklao.*'

'But I know Nucklao,' the writer interrupted. 'I know the school.'

'Tell him where it is, and I give half an anna.'

The reed pen scratched busily. 'He cannot mistake.' The man lifted his head. 'Who watches us across the street?'

Kim looked up hurriedly and saw Colonel Creighton in tennis-flannels.

'Oh, that is some Sahib who knows the fat priest in the barracks. He is beckoning me.'

'What dost thou?' said the Colonel, when Kim trotted up.

'I—I am not running away. I send a letter to my Holy One at Benares.'

'I had not thought of that. Hast thou said that I take thee to Luck-now?'

'Nay, I have not. Read the letter, if there be a doubt.'

'Then why hast thou left out my name in writing to that Holy One?' The Colonel smiled a queer smile. Kim took his courage in both hands.

'It was said once to me that it is inexpedient to write the names of strangers concerned in any matter, because by the naming of names many good plans are brought to confusion.'

'Thou hast been well taught,' the Colonel replied, and Kim flushed. 'I have left my cheroot-case in the Padre's verandah. Bring it to my house this even.'

'Where is the house?' said Kim. His quick wit told him that he was being tested in some fashion or another, and he stood on guard.

'Ask any one in the big bazar.' The Colonel walked on.

'He has forgotten his cheroot-case,' said Kim, returning. 'I must bring it to him this evening. That is all my letter except, thrice over, *Come to me! Come to me! Come to me!* Now I will pay for a stamp and put it in the post.' He rose to go, and as an after-thought asked: 'Who is that angry-faced Sahib who lost the cheroot-case?'

'Oh, he is only Creighton Sahib—a very foolish Sahib, who is a Colonel Sahib without a regiment.'

'What is his business?'

'God knows. He is always buying horses which he cannot ride, and asking riddles about the works of God—such as plants and stones and the customs of people. The dealers call him the father of fools, because he is so easily cheated about a horse. Mahbub Ali says he is madder than all other Sahibs.'

'Oh!' said Kim, and departed. His training had given him some small knowledge of character, and he argued that fools are not given information which leads to calling out eight thousand men besides guns. The Commander-in-Chief of all India does not talk, as Kim had heard him talk, to fools. Nor would Mahbub Ali's tone have changed, as it did every time he mentioned the Colonel's name, if the Colonel had been a fool. Consequently—and this set Kim to skipping—there was a mystery somewhere, and Mahbub Ali probably spied for the Colonel much as Kim had spied for Mahbub. And, like the horse-dealer, the Colonel evidently respected people who did not show themselves to be too clever.

He rejoiced that he had not betrayed his knowledge of the Colonel's house; and when, on his return to barracks, he discovered that no cheroot-case had been left behind, he beamed with delight. Here was a man after his own heart—a tortuous and indirect person playing a hidden game. Well, if he could be a fool, so could Kim.

He showed nothing of his mind when Father Victor, for three long mornings, discoursed to him of an entirely new set of gods and godlings—notably of a goddess called Mary, who, he gathered, was one with Bibi Miriam of Mahbub Ali's theology. He betrayed no emotion when, after the lecture, Father Victor dragged him from shop to shop buying articles of outfit, nor when envious drummer-boys kicked him because he was going to a superior school did he complain, but awaited the play of circumstances with an interested soul. Father Victor, good man, took him to the station, put him into an empty second-class next to Colonel Creighton's first, and bade him farewell with genuine feeling.

'They'll make a man o' you, O'Hara, at St. Xavier's—a white man, an', I hope, a good man. They know all about your comin', an' the Colonel will see that ye're not lost or mislaid anywhere on the road. I've given you a notion of religious matters,—at least I hope so,—and you'll remember, when they ask you your religion, that you're a Cath'lic. Better say Roman Cath'lic, tho' I'm not fond of the word.'

Kim lit a rank cigarette—he had been careful to buy a stock in the bazar—and lay down to think. This solitary passage was very different from that joyful down-journey in the third-class with the lama. 'Sahibs get little pleasure of travel,' he reflected. '*Hai mai!* I go from one place to another as it might be a kick-ball. It is my *Kismet*. No man can escape his *Kismet*. But I am to pray to Bibi Miriam, and I am a Sahib'—he looked at his boots ruefully. 'No; I am Kim. This is the great world, and I am only Kim. Who is Kim?' He considered his own identity, a thing he had never done before, till his head swam. He was one insignificant person in all this roaring whirl of India, going southward to he knew not what fate.

Presently the Colonel sent for him, and talked for a long time. So far as Kim could gather, he was to be diligent and enter the Survey of India as a chain-man.[3] If he were very good, and passed the proper examinations, he would be earning thirty rupees a month at seventeen years old, and Colonel Creighton would see that he found suitable employment.

Kim pretended at first to understand perhaps one word in three of this talk. Then the Colonel, seeing his mistake, turned to fluent and picturesque Urdu and Kim was contented. No man could be a fool who knew the language so intimately, who moved so gently and silently, and whose eyes were so different from the dull fat eyes of other Sahibs.

'Yes, and thou must learn how to make pictures of roads and mountains and rivers—to carry these pictures in thy eye till a suitable time comes to set them upon paper. Perhaps some day, when thou art a chain-man, I may say to thee when we are working together: "Go across those hills and see what lies beyond." Then one will say: "There are bad people living in those hills who will slay the chain-man if he be seen to look like a Sahib." What then?'

Kim thought. Would it be safe to return the Colonel's lead?

'I would tell what that other man had said.'

'But if I answered: "I will give thee a hundred rupees for knowledge of what is behind those hills—for a picture of a river and a little news of what the people say in the villages there"?'

'How can I tell? I am only a boy. Wait till I am a man.' Then, seeing the Colonel's brow clouded, he went on: 'But I think I should in a few days earn the hundred rupees.'

'By what road?'

Kim shook his head resolutely. 'If I said how I would earn them, another man might hear and forestall me. It is no good to sell knowledge for nothing.'

'Tell now.' The Colonel held up a rupee. Kim's hand half reached towards it, and dropped.

---

[3]Surveyor's assistant, in charge of the positioning and reading of the measuring chain.

'Nay, sahib; nay. I know the price that will be paid for the answer, but I do not know why the question is asked.'

'Take it for a gift, then,' said Creighton, tossing it over. 'There is a good spirit in thee. Do not let it be blunted at St. Xavier's. There are many boys there who despise the black men.'

'Their mothers were bazar-women,' said Kim. He knew well there is no hatred like that of the half-caste for his brother-in-law.

'True; but thou art a Sahib and the son of a Sahib. Therefore, do not at any time be led to contemn the black men. I have known boys newly entered into the service of the Government who feigned not to understand the talk or the customs of black men. Their pay was cut for ignorance. There is no sin so great as ignorance. Remember this.'

Several times in the course of the long twenty-four hours' run south did the Colonel send for Kim, always developing this latter text.

'We be all on one lead-rope, then,' said Kim at last, 'the Colonel, Mahbub Ali, and I—when I become a chain-man. He will use me as Mahbub Ali employed me, I think. That is good, if it allows me to re-turn to the road again. This clothing grows no easier by wear.'

When they came to the crowded Lucknow station there was no sign of the lama. He swallowed his disappointment, while the Colonel bundled him into a *ticca-garri* with his neat belongings and despatched him alone to St. Xavier's.

'I do not say farewell, because we shall meet again,' he cried. 'Again, and many times, if thou art one of good spirit. But thou art not yet tried.'

'Not when I brought thee'—Kim actually dared to use the *tum* of equals[4]—'a white stallion's pedigree that night?'

'Much is gained by forgetting, little brother,' said the Colonel, with a look that pierced through Kim's shoulder-blades as he scuttled into the carriage.

It took him nearly five minutes to recover. Then he sniffed the new air appreciatively. 'A rich city,' he said. 'Richer than Lahore. How good the bazars must be. Coachman, drive me a little through the bazars here.'

'My order is to take thee to the school.' The driver used the 'thou,' which is rudeness when applied to a white man. In the clearest and most fluent vernacular Kim pointed out his error, climbed on to the box-seat, and, perfect understanding established, drove for a cou-ple of hours up and down, estimating, comparing, and enjoying. There is no city—except Bombay, the queen of all—more beautiful in her garish style than Lucknow, whether you see her from the bridge over the river, or from the top of the Imambara looking down on the

[4]Familiar, as opposed to formal, second-person address.

gilt umbrellas of the Chutter Munzil, and the trees in which the town is bedded. Kings have adorned her with fantastic buildings, endowed her with charities, crammed her with pensioners, and drenched her with blood. She is the centre of all idleness, intrigue, and luxury, and shares with Delhi the claim to talk the only pure Urdu.

'A fair city—a beautiful city.' The driver, as a Lucknow man, was pleased with the compliment, and told Kim many astounding things where an English guide would have talked of the Mutiny.[5]

'Now we will go to the school,' said Kim at last. The great old school of St. Xavier's in Partibus, block on block of low white buildings, stands in vast grounds over against the Gumti River, at some distance from the city.

'What like of folk are they within?' said Kim.

'Young Sahibs—all devils; but to speak truth, and I drive many of them to and fro from the railway station, I have never seen one that had in him the making of a more perfect devil than thou—this young Sahib whom I am now driving.'

Naturally, for he was never trained to consider them in any way improper, Kim had passed the time of day with one or two frivolous ladies at upper windows in a certain street, and naturally, in the exchange of compliments, had acquitted himself well. He was about to acknowledge the driver's last insolence, when his eye—it was growing dusk—caught a figure sitting by one of the white plaster gate-pillars in the long sweep of wall.

'Stop!' he cried. 'Stay here. I do not go to the school at once.'

'But what is to pay me for this coming and recoming?' said the driver petulantly. 'Is the boy mad? Last time it was a dancing-girl. This time it is a priest.'

Kim was in the road headlong, patting the dusty feet beneath the dirty yellow robe.

'I have waited here a day and a half,' the lama's level voice began. 'Nay, I had a disciple with me. He that was my friend at the Temple of the Tirthankers gave me a guide for this journey. I came from Benares in the train, when thy letter was given me. Yes, I am well fed. I need nothing.'

'But why didst thou not stay with the Kulu woman, O Holy One? In what way didst thou get to Benares? My heart has been heavy since we parted.'

'The woman wearied me by constant flux of talk and requiring charms for children. I separated myself from that company, permit-

---

[5]Site of a prolonged siege during the 1857 Rebellion, and then the most violent British reprisals, Lucknow would have interested most British tourists for that aspect of its history.

ting her to acquire merit by gifts. She is at least a woman of open hands, and I made a promise to return to her house if need arose. Then, perceiving myself alone in this great and terrible world, I bethought me of the *te-rain* to Benares, where I knew one abode in the Tirthankers' Temple who was a Seeker, even as I.'

'Ah! Thy River,' said Kim. 'I had forgotten the River.'

'So soon, my *chela*? I have never forgotten it; but when I had left thee it seemed better that I should go to the temple and take counsel, for, look you, India is very large, and it may be that wise men before us, some two or three, have left a record of the place of our River. There is debate in the Temple of the Tirthankers on this matter; some saying one thing, and some another. They are courteous folk.'

'So be it; but what dost thou do now?'

'I acquire merit in that I help thee, my *chela*, to wisdom. The priest of that body of men who serve the Red Bull wrote me that all should be as I desired for thee. I sent the money to suffice for one year, and then I came, as thou seest me, to watch for thee going up into the Gates of Learning. A day and a half have I waited—not because I was led by any affection towards thee—that is no part of the Way—but, as they said at the Tirthankers' Temple, because, money having been paid for learning, it was right that I should oversee the end of the matter. They resolved my doubts most clearly. I had a fear that, perhaps, I came because I wished to see thee—misguided by the red mist of affection. It is not so. . . . Moreover, I am troubled by a dream.'

'But surely, Holy One, thou hast not forgotten the road and all that befell on it. Surely it was a little to see me that thou didst come?'

'The horses are cold, and it is past their feeding-time,' whined the driver.

'Go to Jehannum and abide there with thy reputationless aunt!' Kim snarled over his shoulder. 'I am all alone in this land; I know not where I go nor what shall befall me. My heart was in that letter I sent thee. Except for Mahbub Ali, and he is a Pathan, I have no friend save thee, Holy One. Do not altogether go away.'

'I have considered that also,' the lama replied, in a shaking voice. 'It is manifest that from time to time I shall acquire merit—if before that I have not found my River—by assuring myself that thy feet are set on wisdom. What they will teach thee I do not know, but the priest wrote me that no son of a Sahib in all India will be better taught than thou. So from time to time, therefore, I will come again. Maybe thou wilt be such a Sahib as he who gave me these spectacles'—the lama wiped them elaborately—'in the Wonder House at Lahore. That is my hope, for he was a Fountain of Wisdom—wiser than many abbots. . . . Again, may be thou wilt forget me and our meetings.'

'If I eat thy bread,' cried Kim passionately, 'how shall I ever forget thee?'

'No—no.' He put the boy aside. 'I must go back to Benares. From time to time, now that I know the customs of letter-writers in this land, I will send thee a letter, and from time to time I will come and see thee.'

'But whither shall I send my letters?' wailed Kim, clutching at the robe, all forgetful that he was a Sahib.

'To the Temple of the Tirthankers at Benares. That is the place I have chosen till I find my River. Do not weep; for, look you, all Desire is illusion and a new binding upon the Wheel. Go up to the Gates of Learning. Let me see thee go. . . . Dost thou love me? Then go, or my heart cracks. . . . I will come again. Surely I will come again.'

The lama watched the *ticca-garri* rumble into the compound, and strode off, snuffing between each long stride.

'The Gates of Learning' shut with a clang.

* * *

The country-born and bred boy has his own manners and customs, which do not resemble those of any other land; and his teachers approach him by roads which an English master would not understand. Therefore, you would scarcely be interested in Kim's experiences as a St. Xavier's boy among two or three hundred precocious youths, most of whom had never seen the sea. He suffered the usual penalties for breaking out of bounds when there was cholera in the city. This was before he had learned to write fair English, and so was obliged to find a bazar letter-writer. He was, of course, indicted for smoking and for the use of abuse more full-flavoured than even St. Xavier's had ever heard. He learned to wash himself with the Levitical scrupulosity of the native-born, who in his heart considers the Englishman rather dirty. He played the usual tricks on the patient coolies pulling the punkahs in the sleeping-rooms where the boys thrashed through the hot nights telling tales till the dawn; and quietly he measured himself against his self-reliant mates.

They were sons of subordinate officials in the Railway, Telegraph, and Canal services; of warrant-officers, sometimes retired and sometimes acting as commanders-in-chief to a feudatory Rajah's army; of captains of the Indian Marine, Government pensioners, planters, Presidency shopkeepers, and missionaries. A few were cadets of the old Eurasian houses that have taken strong root in Dhurrumtollah[6]—

---

[6]Part of Calcutta: Popular among the Portuguese, who began to immigrate in the 15th c. Eurasians often had Portuguese surnames such as Pereira, De Souza, and D'Silva.

Pereiras, De Souzas, and D'Silvas. Their parents could well have educated them in England, but they loved the school that had served their own youth, and generation followed sallow-hued generation at St. Xavier's. Their homes ranged from Howrah of the railway people to abandoned cantonments like Monghyr and Chunar; lost tea-gardens Shillong-way; villages where their fathers were large landholders in Oudh or the Deccan; Mission-stations a week from the nearest railway line; seaports a thousand miles south, facing the brazen Indian surf; and cinchona-plantations south of all. The mere story of their adventures, which to them were no adventures, on their road to and from school would have crisped a Western boy's hair. They were used to jogging off alone through a hundred miles of jungle, where there was always the delightful chance of being delayed by tigers; but they would no more have bathed in the English Channel in an English August, than their brothers across the world would have lain still while a leopard snuffed at their palanquin. There were boys of fifteen who had spent a day and a half on an islet in the middle of a flooded river, taking charge, as by right, of a camp of frantic pilgrims returning from a shrine; there were seniors who had requisitioned a chance-met Rajah's elephant, in the name of St. Francis Xavier, when the rains once blotted out the cart-track that led to their father's estate, and had all but lost the huge beast in a quicksand. There was a boy who, he said, and none doubted, had helped his father to beat off with rifles from the verandah a rush of Akas in the days when those head-hunters were bold against lonely plantations.

And every tale was told in the even, passionless voice of the native-born, mixed with quaint reflections, borrowed unconsciously from native foster-mothers, and turns of speech that showed they had been that instant translated from the vernacular. Kim watched, listened, and approved. This was not insipid, single-word talk of drummer-boys. It dealt with a life he knew and in part understood. The atmosphere suited him, and he throve by inches. They gave him a white drill suit as the weather warmed, and he rejoiced in the new-found bodily comforts as he rejoiced to use his sharpened mind over the tasks they set him. His quickness would have delighted an English master; but at St. Xavier's they know the first rush of minds developed by sun and surroundings, as they know the half-collapse that sets in at twenty-two or twenty-three.

None the less he remembered to hold himself lowly. When tales were told of hot nights, Kim did not sweep the board with his reminiscences; for St. Xavier's looks down on boys who 'go native altogether.' One must never forget that one is a Sahib, and that some day, when examinations are passed, one will command natives. Kim made a note of this, for he began to understand where examinations led.[7]

Then came the holidays from August to October—the long holidays imposed by the heat and the rains. Kim was informed that he would go north to some station in the hills behind Umballa, where Father Victor would arrange for him.

'A barrack school?' said Kim, who had asked many questions and thought more.

'Yes, I suppose so,' said the master. 'It will not do you any harm to keep you out of mischief. You can go up with young De Castro as far as Delhi.'

Kim considered it in every possible light. He had been diligent, even as the Colonel advised. A boy's holiday was his own property,—of so much the talk of his companions had advised him,—and a barrack-school would be torment after St. Xavier's. Moreover—this was magic worth anything else—he could write. In three months he had discovered how men can speak to each other without a third party, at the cost of half an anna and a little knowledge. No word had come from the lama, but there remained the Road. Kim yearned for the caress of soft mud squishing up between the toes, as his mouth watered for mutton stewed with butter and cabbages, for rice speckled with strong-scented cardamoms, for the saffron-tinted rice, garlic and onions, and the forbidden greasy sweetmeats of the bazars. They would feed him raw beef on a platter at the barrack school, and he must smoke by stealth. But again, he was a Sahib and was at St. Xavier's, and that pig Mahbub Ali . . . No, he would not test Mahbub's hospitality—and yet . . . He thought it out alone in the dormitory, and came to the conclusion he had been unjust to Mahbub.

The school was empty; nearly all the masters had gone away; Colonel Creighton's railway pass lay in his hand, and Kim puffed himself that he had not spent Colonel Creighton's or Mahbub's money in riotous living. He was still lord of two rupees seven annas. His new bullock-trunk, marked 'K. O'H.,' and bedding-roll lay in the empty sleeping-room. 'Sahibs are always tied to their baggage,' said Kim, nodding at them. 'You will stay here.' He went out into the warm rain, smiling sinfully, and sought a certain house whose outside he had noted down some time before. . . .

'Arré! Dost thou know what manner of women we be in this quarter? O shame!'

[7]See p. 244 for information about the Indian Survey exam.

'Was I born yesterday?' Kim squatted native fashion on the cushions of that upper room. 'A little dye-stuff and three yards of cloth to help out a jest. Is it much to ask?'

'Who is *she*? Thou art full young, as Sahibs go, for this devilry.'

'Oh, she? She is the daughter of a certain schoolmaster of a regiment in the cantonments. He has beaten me twice because I went over their wall in these clothes. Now I would go as a gardener's boy. Old men are very jealous.'

'That is true. Hold thy face still while I dab on the juice.'

'Not too black, *Naikan*. I would not appear to her as a *hubshi* (nigger).'

'Oh, love makes nought of these things. And how old is she?'

'Twelve years, I think,' said the shameless Kim. 'Spread it also on the breast. It may be her father will tear my clothes off me and if I am piebald——' he laughed.

The girl worked busily, dabbing a twist of cloth into a little saucer of brown dye that holds longer than any walnut juice.

'Now send out and get me a cloth for the turban. Woe is me, my head is all unshaved! And he will surely knock off my turban.'

'I am not a barber, but I will make shift. Thou wast born to be a breaker of hearts! All this disguise for one evening? Remember, the stuff does not wash away.' She shook with laughter till her bracelets and anklets jingled. 'But who is to pay me for this? Huneefa herself could not have given thee better stuff.'

'Trust in the Gods, my sister,' said Kim gravely, screwing his face round as the stain dried. 'Besides, hast thou ever helped to paint a Sahib thus before?'

'Never indeed. But a jest is not money.'

'It is worth much more.'

'Child, thou art beyond all dispute the most shameless son of Shaitan that I have ever known to take up a poor girl's time with this play, and then to say: "Is not the jest enough?" Thou wilt go very far in this world.' She gave the dancing-girls' salutation in mockery.

'All one. Make haste and rough-cut my head.' Kim shifted from foot to foot, his eyes ablaze with mirth as he thought of the fat days before him. He gave the girl four annas, and ran down the stairs in the likeness of a low-caste Hindu boy—perfect in every detail. A cookshop was his next point of call, where he feasted in extravagance and greasy luxury.

On Lucknow station platform he watched young De Castro, all covered with prickly-heat, get into a second-class compartment. Kim patronised a third, and was the life and soul of it. He explained to the company that he was assistant to a juggler who had left him behind sick with fever, and that he would pick up his master at Umballa. As the occupants of the carriage changed, he varied this tale, or adorned it with all the shoots of a budding fancy, the more rampant for being held off native speech so long. In all India that night was no human being so joyful as Kim. At Umballa he got out and headed eastward, plashing over the sodden fields to the village where the old soldier lived.

About this time Colonel Creighton at Simla was advised from Lucknow by wire that young O'Hara had disappeared. Mahbub Ali was in town selling horses, and to him the Colonel confided the affair one morning cantering round Annandale race-course.

'Oh, that is nothing,' said the horse-dealer. 'Men are like horses. At certain times they need salt, and if that salt is not in the mangers they will lick it up from the earth. He has gone back to the Road again for a while. The *madrissah* wearied him. I knew it would. Another time, I will take him upon the Road myself. Do not be troubled, Creighton Sahib. It is as though a polo-pony, breaking loose, ran out to learn the game alone.'

'Then he is not dead, think you?'

'Fever might kill him. I do not fear for the boy otherwise. A monkey does not fall among trees.'

Next morning, on the same course, Mahbub's stallion ranged alongside the Colonel.

'It is as I had thought,' said the horse-dealer. 'He has come through Umballa at least, and there he has written a letter to me, having learned in the bazar that I was here.'

'Read,' said the Colonel, with a sigh of relief. It was absurd that a man of his position should take an interest in a little country-bred vagabond; but the Colonel remembered the conversation in the train, and often in the past few months had caught himself thinking of the queer, silent, self-possessed boy. His evasion, of course, was the height of insolence, but it argued some resource and nerve.

Mahbub's eyes twinkled as he reined out into the centre of the cramped little plain, where none could come near unseen.

'"*The Friend of the Stars, who is the Friend of all the World*——"'

'What is this?'

'A name we give him in Lahore city. "*The Friend of all the World takes leave to go to his own places. He will come back upon the appointed day. Let the box and the bedding-roll be sent for; and if there has been a fault, let the Hand of Friendship turn aside the Whip of Calamity.*" There is yet a little more, but——'

'No matter, read.'

'"*Certain things are not known to those who eat with forks. It is better to eat with both hands for a while. Speak soft words to those*

who do not understand this that the return may be propitious." Now
the manner in which that was cast is of course the work of the letter-
writer, but see how wisely the boy has devised the matter of it so that
no hint is given except to those who know!'

'Is this the Hand of Friendship to avert the Whip of Calamity?'
laughed the Colonel.

'See how wise is the boy. He would go back to the Road again, as
I said. Not knowing yet thy trade——'

'I am not quite sure of that,' the Colonel muttered.

'He turns to me to make a peace between you. Is he not wise? He
says he will return. He is but perfecting his knowledge. Think, Sahib!
He has been three months at the school. And he is not mouthed to
that bit. For my part, I rejoice: the pony learns the game.'

'Ay, but another time he must not go alone.'

'Why? He went alone before he came under the Colonel Sahib's
protection. When he comes to the Great Game he must go alone—
alone, and at peril of his head. *Then*, if he spits, or sneezes, or sits
down other than as the people do whom he watches, he may be slain.
Why hinder him now? Remember how the Persians say: The jackal
that lives in the wilds of Mazanderan can only be caught by the
hounds of Mazanderan.'

'True. It is true, Mahbub Ali. And if he comes to no harm, I do
not desire anything better. But it is great insolence on his part.'

'He does not tell me, even, whither he goes,' said Mahbub. 'He is
no fool. When his time is accomplished he will come to me. It is time
the healer of pearls took him in hand. He ripens too quickly—as
Sahibs reckon.'

This prophecy was fulfilled to the letter a month later. Mahbub
had gone down to Umballa to bring up a fresh consignment of horses,
and Kim met him on the Kalka road at dusk riding alone, begged an
alms of him, was sworn at, and replied in English. There was nobody
within earshot to hear Mahbub's gasp of amazement.

'Oho! And where hast thou been?'

'Up and down—down and up.'

'Come under a tree, out of the wet, and tell.'

'I stayed for a while with an old man near Umballa; anon with a
household of my acquaintance in Umballa. With one of these I went as
far as Delhi to the southward. That is a wondrous city. Then I drove a
bullock for a *teli* (an oilman) coming north; but I heard of a great feast
forward in Puttiala, and thither went I in the company of a firework-
maker. It was a great feast' (Kim rubbed his stomach). 'I saw Rajahs,
and elephants with gold and silver trappings; and they lit all the fireworks at once, whereby eleven men were killed, my firework-maker

among them, and I was blown across a tent but took no harm. Then I came back to the *rêl* with a Sikh horseman, to whom I was groom for my bread; and so here.'

'*Shabash!*' said Mahbub Ali.

'But what does the Colonel Sahib say? I do not wish to be beaten.'

'The Hand of Friendship has averted the Whip of Calamity; but another time, when thou takest the Road it will be with me. This is too early.'

'Late enough for me. I have learned to read and to write English a little at the *madrissah*. I shall soon be altogether a Sahib.'

'Hear him!' laughed Mahbub, looking at the little drenched figure dancing in the wet. 'Salaam—Sahib,' and he saluted ironically. 'Well, art tired of the Road, or wilt thou come on to Umballa with me and work back with the horses?'

"I come with thee, Mahbub Ali.'

CHAPTER VIII

> Something I owe to the soil that grew—
> More to the life that fed—
> But most to Allah Who gave me two
> Separate sides to my head.
>
> I would go without shirts or shoes,
> Friends, tobacco or bread
> Sooner than for an instant lose
> Either side of my head.[1]

'THEN in God's Name take blue for red,' said Mahbub, alluding to the Hindu colour of Kim's disreputable turban.

Kim countered with the old proverb, 'I will change my faith and my bedding, but *thou* must pay for it.'

The dealer laughed till he nearly fell from his horse. At a shop on the outskirts of the city the change was made, and Kim stood up, externally at least, a Mohammedan.

Mahbub hired a room over against the railway station, sent for a cooked meal of the finest with almond-curd sweetmeats (*balushai* we call it) and fine-chopped Lucknow tobacco.

---

[1]Revised in *Songs from Books* as the first and final stanzas of "The Two-Sided Man," these lines are spoken by a Muslim who thanks Allah for having rendered him capable of generosity towards believers of other religions. The original *McClure's* installment began instead with lines from the 1890 "Ballad of King's Jest" (see p. 274).

'This is better than some other meat that I ate with the Sikh,' said Kim, grinning as he squatted, 'and assuredly they give no such victuals at my *madrissah*.'

'I have a desire to hear of that same *madrissah*.' Mahbub stuffed himself with great boluses of spiced mutton fried in fat with cabbage and golden-brown onions. 'But tell me first, altogether and truthfully, the manner of thy escape. For, O Friend of all the World,'—he loosed his cracking belt,—'I do not think it is often that a Sahib and the son of a Sahib runs away from there.'

'How should they? They do not know the land. It was nothing,' said Kim, and began his tale. When he came to the disguisement and the interview with the girl in the bazar, Mahbub Ali's gravity went from him. He laughed aloud and beat his hand on his thigh.

'*Shabash! Shabash!* Oh, well done, little one! What will the healer of turquoises say to this? Now, slowly, let us hear what befell afterwards—step by step, omitting nothing.'

Step by step then, Kim told his adventures between coughs as the full-flavoured tobacco caught his lungs.

'I said,' growled Mahbub Ali to himself, 'I *said* it was the pony breaking out to play polo. The fruit is ripe already—except that he must learn his distances and his pacings, and his rods and his compasses. Listen now. I have turned aside the Colonel's whip from thy skin, and that is no small service.'

'True.' Kim puffed serenely. 'That is all true.'

'But it is not to be thought that this running out and in is any way good.'

'It was my holiday, Hajji. I was a slave for many weeks. Why should I not run away when the school was shut? Look, too, how I, living upon my friends or working for my bread, as I did with the Sikh, have saved the Colonel Sahib a great expense.'

Mahbub's lips twitched under his well-pruned Mohammedan moustache.

'What are a few rupees'—the Pathan threw out his open hand carelessly—'to the Colonel Sahib? He spends them for a purpose, not in any way for love of thee.'

'That,' said Kim slowly, 'I knew a very long time ago.'

'Who told?'

'The Colonel Sahib himself. Not in those many words, but plainly enough for one who is not altogether a mud-head. Yea, he told me in the *te-rain* when we went down to Lucknow.'

'Be it so. Then I will tell thee more, Friend of all the World, though in the telling I lend thee my head.'

'It was forfeit to me,' said Kim, with deep relish, 'in Umballa, when thou didst pick me up on the horse after the drummer-boy beat me.'

'Speak a little plainer. All the world may tell lies save thou and I. For equally is thy life forfeit to me if I chose to raise my finger here.'

'And this is known to me also,' said Kim, readjusting the live charcoal-ball on the weed. 'It is a very sure tie between us. Indeed thy hold is surer even than mine; for who would miss a boy beaten to death, or, it may be, thrown into a well by the roadside? Many people here and in Simla and across the passes behind the Hills would, on the other hand, say: 'What has come to Mahbub Ali,' if he were found dead among his horses. Surely too the Colonel Sahib would make inquiries. But again,'—Kim's face puckered with cunning,—'he would not make overlong inquiry, lest people should ask: "What has this Colonel Sahib to do with that horse-dealer?" But I—if I lived——'

'As thou wouldst surely die——'

'It may be; but I say, *if* I lived, I, and I alone, would know that one had come by night, as a common thief perhaps, to Mahbub Ali's bulk-head in the serai, and there had slain him, either before or after that thief had made a full search into his saddle-bags and between the soles of his slippers. Is that news to tell to the Colonel, or would he say to me—(I have not forgotten when he sent me back for a cigar-case that he had *not* left behind him)—"What is Mahbub Ali to me?"'

Up went a gout of heavy smoke. There was a long pause: then Mahbub Ali spoke in admiration: 'And with these things on thy mind, dost thou lie down and rise again among all the Sahibs' little sons at the *madrissah* and meekly take instruction from thy teachers?'

'It is an order,' said Kim blandly. 'Who am I to dispute an order?'

'A most finished son of Eblis,' said Mahbub Ali. 'But what is this tale of the thief and the search?'

'That which I saw,' said Kim, 'the night that my lama and I lay next thy place in the Kashmir Serai. The door was left unlocked, which I think is not thy custom, Mahbub. He came in as one assured that thou wouldst not soon return. My eye was against a knot-hole in the plank. He searched as it were for something—not a rug, not stirrups, nor a bridle, nor brass pots—something little and most carefully hid. Else why did he prick with an iron between the soles of thy slippers?'

'Ha!' Mahubib Ali smiled gently. 'And seeing these things, what tale didst thou fashion to thyself, Well of the Truth?'

'None. I put my hand upon my amulet, which lies always next to my skin, and, remembering the pedigree of a white stallion that I had bitten out of a piece of Mussalmani bread, I went away to Umballa perceiving that a heavy trust was laid upon me. At that hour, had I chosen, thy head was forfeit. It needed only to say to that man, "I have here a paper concerning a horse which I cannot read." And then?' Kim peered at Mahbub under his eyebrows.

'Then thou wouldst have drunk water twice—perhaps thrice, afterwards. I do not think more than thrice,' said Mahbub simply.

'It is true. I thought of that a little, but most I thought that I loved thee, Mahbub. Therefore I went to Umballa, as thou knowest, but (and this thou dost not know) I lay hid in the garden-grass to see what Colonel Creighton Sahib might do upon reading the white stallion's pedigree.'

'And what did he?' for Kim had bitten off the conversation.

'Dost *thou* give news for love, or dost thou sell it?' Kim asked.

'I sell and—I buy.' Mahbub took a four-anna piece out of his belt and held it up.

'Eight!' said Kim, mechanically following the huckster instinct of the East.

Mahbub laughed, and put away the coin. 'It is too easy to deal in that market, Friend of all the World. Tell me for love. Our lives lie in each other's hand.'

'Very good. I saw the Jang-i-Lat Sahib come to a big dinner. I saw him in Creighton Sahib's office. I saw the two read the white stallion's pedigree. I heard the very orders given for the opening of a great war.'

'Hah!' Mahbub nodded with deepest eyes afire. 'The game is well played. That war is done now, and the evil, we hope, nipped before the flower—thanks to me—and thee. What didst thou later?'

'I made the news as it were a hook to catch me victual and honour among the villagers in a village whose priest drugged my lama. But I bore away the old man's purse, and the Brahmin found nothing. So next morning he was angry. Ho! Ho! And I also used the news when I fell into the hands of that white regiment with their Bull!'

'That was foolishness.' Mahbub scowled. 'News is not meant to be thrown about like dung-cakes, but used sparingly—like *bhang*.'

'So I think now, and moreover, it did me no sort of good. But that was very long ago,'—he made as to brush it all away with a thin brown hand,—'and since then, and especially in the nights under the punkah at the *madrissah*, I have thought very greatly.'

'Is it permitted to ask whither the Heaven-born's thought might have led?' said Mahbub, with an elaborate sarcasm, smoothing his scarlet beard.

'It is permitted,' said Kim, and threw back the very tone. 'They say at Nucklao that no Sahib must tell a black man that he has made a fault.'

Mahbub's hand shot into his bosom, for to call a Pathan a 'black man' (*kala admi*) is a blood-insult. Then he remembered and laughed. 'Speak, Sahib: thy black man hears.'

'But,' said Kim, 'I am *not* a Sahib, and I say I made a fault when I cursed thee, Mahbub Ali, on the day at Umballa I thought I was betrayed by a Pathan. I was senseless; for I was but newly caught, and I wished to kill that low-caste drummer-boy. I say now, Hajji, that it was well done; and I see my road all clear before me to a good service. I will stay in the *madrissah* till I am ripe.'

'Well said. Especially are distances and numbers and the manner of using compasses to be learned in that game. One waits in the Hills above to show thee.'

'I will learn their teaching upon a condition—that my time is given to me without question when the *madrissah* is shut. Ask that for me of the Colonel.'

'But why not ask the Colonel in the Sahib's tongue?'

'The Colonel is the servant of the Government. He is sent hither and yon at a word, and must consider his own advancement. (See how much I have already learned at Nucklao!) Moreover, the Colonel I know since three months only. I have known one Mahbub Ali for six years. So! To the *madrissah* I will go. At the *madrissah* I will learn. In the *madrissah* I will be a Sahib. But when the *madrissah* is shut, then must I be free and go among my people. Otherwise I die!'

'And who are thy people, Friend of all the World?'

'This great and beautiful land,' said Kim, waving his paw round the little clay-walled room where the oil-lamp in its niche burned heavily through the tobacco-smoke. 'And, further, I would see my lama again. And further, I need money.'

'That is the need of every one,' said Mahbub ruefully. 'I will give thee eight annas, for much money is not picked out of horses' hooves, and it must suffice for many days. As to all the rest, I am well pleased, and no further talk is needed. Make haste to learn, and in three years, or it may be less, thou wilt be an aid—even to me.'

'Have I been such a hindrance till now?' said Kim, with a boy's giggle.

'Do not give answers,' Mahbub grunted. 'Thou art my new horse-boy. Go and bed among my men. They are near the north end of the station, with the horses.'

'They will beat me to the south end of the station if I come without authority.'

Mahbub felt in his belt, wetted his thumb on a cake of Chinese ink, and dabbed the impression on a piece of soft native paper. From Balkh to Bombay men know that rough-ridged print with the old scar running diagonally across it.

'That is enough to show my headman. I come in the morning.'

'By which road?' said Kim.

'By the road from the City. There is but one, and then we return to Creighton Sahib. I have saved thee a beating.'

'Allah! What is a beating when the very head is loose on the shoulders?'

Kim slid out quietly into the night, walked half round the house, keeping close to the walls, and headed away from the station for a mile or so. Then, fetching a wide compass, he worked back at leisure, for he needed time to invent a story if any of Mahbub's retainers asked questions.

They were camped on a piece of waste ground beside the railway, and, being natives, had not, of course, unloaded the two trucks in which Mahbub's animals stood among a consignment of country-breds bought by the Bombay tram-company. The headman, a broken-down, consumptive-looking Mohammedan, promptly challenged Kim, but was pacified at sight of Mahbub's sign-manual.

'The Hajji has of his favour given me service,' said Kim testily. 'If this be doubted, wait till he comes in the morning. Meantime, a place by the fire.'

Followed the usual aimless babble that every low-caste native must raise on every occasion. It died down, and Kim lay out behind the little knot of Mahbub's followers, almost under the wheels of a horse-truck, a borrowed blanket for covering. Now a bed among brickbats and ballast-refuse on a damp night, between overcrowded horses and unwashed Baltis, would not appeal to many white boys; but Kim was utterly happy. Change of scene, service, and surroundings were the breath of his little nostrils, and thinking of the neat white cots of St. Xavier's all arow under the punkah gave him joy as keen as the repetition of the multiplication-table in English.

'I am very old,' he thought sleepily. 'Every month I become a year more old. I was very young, and a fool to boot, when I took Mahbub's message to Umballa. Even when I was with that white regiment I was very young and small and had no wisdom. But now I learn every day, and in three years the Colonel will take me out of the *madrissah* and let me go upon the Road with Mahbub hunting for horses' pedigrees, or maybe I shall go by myself; or maybe I shall find the lama and go with him. Yes; that is best. To walk again as a *chela* with my lama when he comes back to Benares.' The thoughts came more slowly and disconnectedly. He was plunging into a beautiful dreamland when his ears caught a whisper, thin and sharp, above the monotonous babble round the fire. It came from behind the iron-skinned horse-truck.

'He is not here then?'

'Where should he be but roystering in the City. Who looks for a rat in a frog-pond? Come away. He is not our man.'

'He must not go back beyond the Passes a second time. It is the order.'

'Hire some woman to drug him. It is a few rupees only, and there is no evidence.'

'Except the woman. It must be more certain; and remember the price upon his head.'

'Ay, but the police have a long arm, and we are far from the Border. If it were in Peshawur now!'

'Yes—in Peshawur,' the second voice sneered. 'Peshawur, full of his blood-kin—full of bolt-holes and women behind whose clothes he will hide. Yes, Peshawur or Jehannum would suit us equally well.'

'Then what is the plan?'

'O fool, have I not told it a hundred times. Wait till he comes to lie down, and then one sure shot. The trucks are between us and pursuit. We have but to run back over the lines and go our way. They will not see whence the shot came. Wait here at least till the dawn. What manner of *faquir* art thou to shiver at a little watching?'

'Oho!' thought Kim, behind close-shut eyes. 'Once again it is Mahbub. Indeed a white stallion's pedigree is not a good thing to peddle to Sahibs! Or maybe Mahbub has been selling other news. Now what is to do, Kim? I know not where Mahbub houses, and if he comes here before the dawn they will shoot him. That would be no profit for thee, Kim. And this is not a matter for the police. That would be no profit for Mahbub; and,' he giggled almost aloud, 'I do not remember any lesson at Nucklao which will help me. Allah! Here is Kim and yonder are they. First then, Kim must wake and go away, so that they shall not suspect. A bad dream wakes a man—thus——'

He threw the blanket off his face, and raised himself suddenly with the terrible, bubbling, meaningless yell of the Asiatic roused by nightmare.

'Urr-urr-urr-urr! Ya-la-la-la-la! *Narain!* The *churel!* The *churel!*'

A *churel* is the peculiarly malignant ghost of a woman who has died in child-bed. She haunts lonely roads, her feet are turned backwards on the ankles, and she leads men to torment.

Louder rose Kim's quavering howl, till at last he leaped to his feet and staggered off sleepily, while the camp cursed him for waking them. Some twenty yards farther up the line he lay down again, taking care that the whisperers should hear his grunts and groans as he recomposed himself. After a few minutes he rolled towards the road and stole away into the thick darkness.

He paddled along swiftly till he came to a culvert, and dropped behind it, his chin on a level with the coping-stone. Here he could command all the night-traffic, himself unseen.

Two or three carts passed, jingling out to the suburbs; a coughing policeman and a hurrying foot-passenger or two who sang to keep off evil spirits. Then rapped the shod feet of a horse.

'Ah! This is more like Mahbub,' thought Kim, as the beast shied at the little head above the culvert.

'Ohé, Mahbub Ali,' he whispered, 'have a care!'

The horse was reined back almost on its haunches, and forced towards the culvert.

'Never again,' said Mahbub, 'will I take a shod horse for night-work. They pick up all the bones and nails in the city.' He stooped to lift its forefoot, and that brought his head within a foot of Kim's. 'Down—keep down,' he muttered. 'The night is full of eyes.'

'Two men wait thy coming behind the horse-trucks. They will shoot thee at thy lying down, because there is a price on thy head. I heard, sleeping near the horses.'

'Didst thou see them? . . . Hold still, Sire of Devils!' This furiously to the horse.

'No.'

'Was one dressed belike as a *faquir?*'

'One said to the other, "What manner of a *faquir* art thou, to shiver at a little watching?"'

'Good. Go back to the camp and lie down. I do not die to-night.'

Mahbub wheeled his horse and vanished. Kim tore back down the ditch till he reached a point opposite his second resting-place, slipped across the road like a weasel, and re-coiled himself in the blanket.

'At least Mahbub knows,' he thought contentedly. 'And certainly he spoke as one expecting it. I do not think those two men will profit by to-night's watch.'

An hour passed, and, with the best will in the world to keep awake all night, he slept deeply. Now and again a night train roared along the metals within twenty feet of him; but he had all the Oriental's indifference to mere noise, and it did not even weave a dream through his slumber.

Mahbub was anything but asleep. It annoyed him vehemently that people outside his tribe and unaffected by his casual amours should pursue him for the life. His first and natural impulse was to cross the line lower down, work up again, and, catching his well-wishers from behind, summarily slay them. Here, he reflected with sorrow, another branch of the Government, totally unconnected with Colonel Creighton, might demand explanations which would be hard to supply; and he knew that south the Border a perfectly ridiculous fuss is made about a corpse or so. He had not been troubled in this way since he sent Kim to Umballa with the message, and hoped that suspicion had been finally diverted.

Then a most brilliant notion struck him.

'The English do eternally tell the truth,' he said, 'therefore we of this country are eternally made foolish. By Allah, I will tell the truth to an Englishman! Of what use is the Government police if a poor Kabuli be robbed of his horses in their very trucks. This is as bad as Peshawur! I should lay a complaint at the station. Better still, some young Sahib on the Railway! They are zealous, and if they catch thieves it is remembered to their honour.'

He tied up his horse outside the station, and strode on to the platform.

'Hullo, Mahbub Ali!' said a young Assistant District Traffic Superintendent who was waiting to go down the line—a tall, tow-haired, horsey youth in dingy white linen. 'What are you doing here? Selling weeds—eh?'

'No; I am not troubled for my horses. I come to look for Lutuf Ullah. I have a truck-load up the line. Could any one take them out without the Railway's knowledge?'

''Shouldn't think so, Mahbub. You can claim against us if they do.'

'I have seen two men crouching under the wheels of one of the trucks nearly all the night. *Faquirs* do not steal horses, so I gave them no more thought. I would find Lutuf Ullah, my partner.'

'The deuce you did? And you didn't bother your head about it? 'Pon my word, it's just almost as well that I met you. What were they like, eh?'

'They were only *faquirs*. They will no more than take a little grain perhaps from one of the trucks. There are many up the line. The State will never miss the dole. I came here seeking for my partner, Lutuf Ullah——'

'Never mind your partner. Where are your horse-trucks?'

'A little to this side of the farthest place where they make lamps for the trains.'

'The signal-box. Yes.'

'And upon the rail nearest to the road upon the right-hand side—looking up the line thus. But as regards Lutuf Ullah—a tall man with a broken nose, and a Persian greyhound—Aie!'

The boy had hurried off to wake up a young and enthusiastic policeman; for, as he said, the Railway had suffered much from depredations in the goods-yard. Mahbub Ali chuckled in his dyed beard.

'They will walk in their boots, making a noise, and then they will wonder why there are no *faquirs*. They are very clever boys—Barton Sahib and Young Sahib.'

He waited idly for a few minutes, expecting to see them hurry up the line girt for action. A light engine slid through the station, and he caught a glimpse of young Barton in the cab.

'I did that child an injustice. He is not altogether a fool,' said Mahbub Ali. 'To take a fire-carriage for a thief is a new game!'

When Mahbub Ali came to his camp in the dawn, no one thought it worth while to tell him any news of the night. No one, at least, but one small horse-boy, newly advanced to the great man's service, whom Mahbub called to his tiny tent to assist in some packing.

'It is all known to me,' whispered Kim, bending above the saddle-bags. 'Two Sahibs came up on a *te-rain*. I was running to and fro in the dark on this side of the trucks as the *te-rain* moved up and down slowly. They fell upon two men sitting under this truck—Hajji, what shall I do with this lump of tobacco? Wrap it in paper and put it under the salt-bag? Yes—and struck them down. But one man struck at a Sahib with a *faquir's* buck's horn' (Kim meant the conjoined black-buck horns, which are a *faquir's* sole temporal weapon)—'the blood came. So the other Sahib, first smiting his own man senseless, smote the stabber with a short gun which had rolled from the first man's hand. They all raged as though mad together.'

Mahbub smiled with heavenly resignation. 'No! That is not so much *dewanee* (madness, or a case for the civil court—the word can be punned upon both ways) as *nizamut* (a criminal case). A gun sayest thou? Ten good years in jail.'

'Then they both lay still, but I think they were nearly dead when they were put on the *te-rain*. Their heads moved thus. And there is much blood on the line. Come and see?'

'I have seen blood before. Jail is the sure place—and assuredly they will give false names, and assuredly no man will find them for a long time. They were unfriends of mine. Thy Fate and mine seem on one string. What a tale for the healer of pearls! Now swiftly with the saddle-bags and the cooking-platter. We will take out the horses and away to Simla.'

Swiftly,—as Orientals understand speed,—with long explanations, with abuse and windy talk, carelessly, amid a hundred checks for little things forgotten, the untidy camp broke up and led the half-dozen stiff and fretful horses along the Kalka road in the fresh of the rain-swept dawn. Kim, regarded as Mahbub Ali's favourite by all who wished to stand well with the Pathan, was not called upon to work. They strolled on by the easiest of stages, halting every few hours at a wayside shelter. Very many Sahibs travel along the Kalka road; and, as Mahbub Ali says, every young Sahib must needs esteem himself a judge of a horse, and, though he be over head in debt to the money-lender, must make as if to buy. That was the reason that Sahib after Sahib, rolling along in a stage-carriage, would stop and open talk. Some would even descend from their vehicles and feel the horses' legs; asking inane questions, or, through sheer ignorance of the vernacular, grossly insulting the imperturbable trader.

'When first I dealt with Sahibs, and that was when Colonel Soady Sahib was Governor of Fort Abazai and flooded the Commissioner's camping-ground for spite,'[2] Mahbub confided to Kim as the boy filled his pipe under a tree, 'I did not know how greatly they were fools, and this made me wroth. As thus——' and he told Kim a tale of an expression, misused in all innocence, that doubled Kim up with mirth. 'Now I see, however,'—he exhaled smoke slowly,—'that it is with them as with all men—in certain matters they are wise, and in others most foolish. Very foolish it is to use the wrong word to a stranger; for though the heart may be clean of offence, how is the stranger to know that? He is more like to search truth with a dagger.'

'True. True talk,' said Kim solemnly. 'Fools speak of a cat when a woman is brought to bed, for instance. I have heard them.'

'Therefore, in one situate as thou art, it particularly behoves thee to remember this with both kinds of faces. Among Sahibs, never forgetting thou art a Sahib; among the folk of Hind, always remembering thou art——' he paused, with a puzzled smile.

'What am I? Mussalman, Hindu, Jain, or Buddhist? That is a hard nut.'

'Thou art beyond question an unbeliever, and therefore thou wilt be damned. So says my Law—or I think it does. But thou art also my Little Friend of all the World, and I love thee. So says my heart. This matter of creeds is like horseflesh. The wise man knows horses are good—that there is a profit to be made from all; and for myself—but that I am a good Sunni and hate the men of Tirah[3]—I could believe the same of all the Faiths. Now manifestly a Kattiawar mare taken from the sands of her birthplace and removed to the west of Bengal founders—nor is even a Balkh stallion (and there are no better horses than those of Balkh, were they not so heavy in the shoulder) of any account in the great Northern deserts beside the snow-camels I have

[2]In *Eighteen Years in the Khyber, 1879–1898* (1900), Robert Warburton recounts how, between 1870 and 1872, Col. Soady's recreational cultivation of private crops interfered with local irrigation systems, angering villagers as well as providing the water to flood the campground.

[3]A remote valley near Afghanistan, the Tirah became a battleground in 1897–98 as British colonial forces, famously including Indian-led regiments, fought Orakzai and Afridi clans for control of the Khyber Pass. Predominantly Sunni, the area is also home to a notable Shi'ite population, and torn by longstanding, ongoing religious violence.

seen. Therefore I say in my heart the Faiths are like the horses. Each has merit in its own country.'

'But my lama said altogether a different thing.'

'Oh, he is an old dreamer of dreams from Bhotiyal. My heart is a little angry, Friend of all the World, that thou shouldst see such worth in a man so little known.'

'It is true, Hajji; but that worth do I see; and to him my heart is drawn.'

'And his to thine, I hear. Hearts are like horses. They come and they go against bit or spur. Shout Gul Sher Khan yonder to drive in that bay stallion's pickets more firmly. We do not want a horse-fight at every resting-stage, and the dun and the black will be locked in a little. . . . Now hear me. Is it necessary to the comfort of thy heart to see that lama?'

'It is one part of my bond,' said Kim. 'If I do not see him, and if he is taken from me, I will go out of that *madrissah* in Nucklao and, and—once gone, who is to find me again?'

'It is true. Never was colt held on a lighter heel-rope than thou.' Mahbub nodded his head.

'Do not be afraid.' Kim spoke as though he could have vanished on the moment. 'My lama has said that he will come to see me at the *madrissah*——'

'A beggar and his bowl in the presence of those young Sa——'

'Not all!' Kim cut in with a snort. 'Their eyes are blued and their nails are blackened with low-caste blood, many of them. Sons of *metheeranees*—brothers-in-law to the *bhungi* (sweeper).'

We need not follow the rest of the pedigree; but Kim made his little point clearly and without heat, chewing a piece of sugar-cane the while.

'Friend of all the World,' said Mahbub, pushing over the pipe for the boy to clean, 'I have met many men, women, and boys, and not a few Sahibs. I have never in all my days met such an imp as thou art.'

'And why? When I always tell thee the truth.'

'Perhaps the very reason, for this is a world of danger to honest men.' Mahbub Ali hauled himself off the ground, girt in his belt, and went over to the horses.

'Or sell it?'

There was that in the tone that made Mahbub halt and turn. 'What new devilry?'

'Eight annas, and I will tell,' said Kim, grinning. 'It touches thy peace.'

'O Shaitan!' Mahbub gave the money.

'Rememberest thou the little business of the thieves in the dark, down yonder at Umballa?'

'Seeing they sought my life, I have not altogether forgotten. Why?'

'Rememberest thou the Kashmir Serai?'

'I will twist thy ears in a moment, Sahib.'

'No need—Pathan. Only, the second *faquir*, whom the Sahibs beat senseless, was the man who came to search thy bulkhead at Lahore. I saw his face as they helped him on the engine. The very same man.'

'Why didst thou not tell before?'

'Oh, he will go to jail, and be safe for some years. There is no need to tell more than is necessary at any one time. Besides, I did not then need money for sweetmeats.'

'Allah kerim!' said Mahbub Ali. 'Wilt thou some day sell my head for a few sweetmeats if the fit takes thee?'

* * *

Kim will remember till he dies that long, lazy journey from Umballa, through Kalka and the Pinjore Gardens near by, up to Simla.[4] A sudden spate in the Gugger River swept down one horse (the most valuable, be sure), and nearly drowned Kim among the dancing boulders. Farther up the road the horses were stampeded by a Government elephant, and being in high condition of grass food, it cost a day and a half to get them together again. Then they met Sikandar Khan coming down with a few unsaleable screws,—remnants of his string,—and Mahbub, who has more of horse-coping in his little finger-nail than Sikandar Khan in all his tents, must needs buy two of the worst, and that meant eight hours' laborious diplomacy and untold tobacco. But it was all pure delight—the wandering road, climbing, dipping, and sweeping about the growing spurs; the flush of the morning laid along the distant snows; the branched cacti, tier upon tier on the stony hillsides; the voices of a thousand water-channels; the chatter of the monkeys; the solemn deodars, climbing one after another with down-drooped branches; the vista of the Plains rolled out far beneath them; the incessant twanging of the tonga-horns and the wild rush of the led horses when a tonga swung round a curve; the halts for prayers (Mahbub was very religious in dry-washings and bellowings when time did not press); the evening conferences by the halting-places, when camels and bullocks chewed solemnly together and the stolid drivers told the news of the Road—all these things lifted Kim's heart to song within him.

'But, when the singing and dancing is done,' said Mahbub Ali, 'comes the Colonel Sahib's, and that is not so sweet.'

[4]Greatest of the hill stations at which the British Indian Army and British civilians spent the hot months, Simla (Shimla) is dramatically located on a ridge of the Himalayas. The city, which was known as the "Queen of the Hills," served as summer capital for the imperial government.

'A fair land—a most beautiful land is this of Hind—and the land of the Five Rivers[5] is fairer than all,' Kim half chanted. 'Into it I will go again if Mahbub Ali or the Colonel lift hand or foot against me. Once gone, who shall find me? Look, Hajji, is yonder the city of Simla? Allah, what a city!'

'My father's brother, and he was an old man when Mackerson Sahib's well was new at Peshawur,[6] could recall when there were but two houses in it.'

He led the horses below the main road into the lower Simla bazar—the crowded rabbit-warren that climbs up from the valley to the Town Hall at an angle of forty-five. A man who knows his way there can defy all the police of India's summer capital; so cunningly does verandah communicate with verandah, alley-way with alley-way, and bolt-hole with bolt-hole. Here live those who minister to the wants of the glad city—jhampanis who pull the pretty ladies' rickshaws by night and gamble till the dawn; grocers, oil-sellers, curio-vendors, firewood dealers, priests, pickpockets, and native employees of the Government: here are discussed by courtesans the things which are supposed to be profoundest secrets of the India Council; and here gather all the sub-sub-agents of half the native States. Here, too, Mahbub Ali rented a room, much more securely locked than his bulkhead at Lahore, in the house of a Mohammedan cattle-dealer. It was a place of miracles, too, for there went in at twilight a Mohammedan horse-boy, and there came out an hour later a Eurasian lad—the Lucknow girl's dye was of the best—in badly fitting shop-clothes.

'I have spoken with Creighton Sahib,' quoth Mahbub Ali, 'and a second time has the Hand of Friendship averted the Whip of Calamity. He says that thou hast altogether wasted sixty days upon the Road, and it is too late, therefore, to send thee to any hill-school.'

'I have said that my holidays are my own. I do not go to school twice over. That is one part of my bond.'

'The Colonel Sahib is not yet aware of the contract. Thou art to lodge in Lurgan Sahib's house till it is time to go again to Nucklao.'

'I had sooner lodge with thee, Mahbub.'

'Thou dost not know the honour. Lurgan Sahib himself asked for thee. Thou wilt go up the hill and along the road atop, and there thou must forget for a while that thou hast ever seen or spoken to me,

---

[5]The Punjab.

[6]Linguist, soldier, and distinguished frontier Political Officer, Frederick Mackeson (1807–53) oversaw building projects including a militarily crucial Khyber Pass road. The well in question forms part of a memorial built after he was assassinated by a religious fanatic while serving as Commissioner at Peshawur.

Mahbub Ali, who sells horses to Creighton Sahib, whom thou dost not know. Remember this order.'

Kim nodded. 'Good,' said he, 'and who is Lurgan Sahib? Nay'— he caught Mahbub's sword-keen glance—'indeed I have never heard his name. Is he by chance'—he lowered his voice—'one of us?'

'What talk is this of *us*, Sahib?' Mahbub Ali returned, in the tone he used towards Europeans. 'I am a Pathan; thou art a Sahib and the son of a Sahib. Lurgan Sahib has a shop among the European shops. All Simla knows it. Ask there . . . and, Friend of all the World, he is one to be obeyed to the last wink of his eyelashes. Men say he does magic, but that should not touch thee. Go up the hill and ask. Here begins the Great Game.'

CHAPTER IX

S'doaks was son of Yelth the wise—
Chief of the Raven clan.
Itswoot the Bear had him in care
To make him a medicine-man.

He was quick and quicker to learn—
Bold and bolder to dare:
He danced the dread Kloo-Kwallie Dance
To tickle Itswoot the Bear!
Oregon Legend.[1]

KIM flung himself whole-heartedly upon the next turn of the wheel. He would be a Sahib again for a while. In that idea, so soon as he had reached the broad road under Simla town-hall, he cast about for one to impress. A Hindu child, some ten years old, squatted under a lamp-post.

'Where is Mr. Lurgan's house?' demanded Kim.

'I do not understand English,' was the answer, and Kim shifted his speech accordingly.

'I will show.'

Together they set off through the mysterious dusk, full of the noises of a city below the hillside, and the breath of a cool wind in deodar-

[1]The only *Kim* epigraph uncollected in Kipling's works, these lines have been attributed to Irish playwright Dion Boucicault (Keskar). Whatever their origin, they invoke mythic American Indian coming-of-age rituals of western Washington (formerly the Oregon Territory). Yelth the raven, his son S'Doaks, and Itswoot the bear are traditional Quinault Indian figures: Like the painful, potentially disabling Kloo-kwallie dance, they appear in Walter Shelley Phillips's 1896 *Totem Tales: Indian Stories Told, Gathered in the Pacific Northwest.*

crowned Jakko, shouldering the stars. The house-lights, scattered on every level, made, as it were, a double firmament. Some were fixed, others belonged to the rickshaws of careless, open-spoken English folk, going out to dinner.

'It is here,' said Kim's guide, and halted in a verandah flush with the main road. No door stayed them, but a curtain of beaded reeds that split up the lamp-light beyond.

'He is come,' said the boy, in a voice little louder than a sigh, and vanished. Kim felt sure that the boy had been posted to guide him from the first, but putting a bold face on it, parted the curtain. A black-bearded man, with a green shade over his eyes, sat at a table, and, one by one, with short, white hands, picked up globules of light from a tray before him, threaded them on a glancing silken string, and hummed to himself the while. Kim was conscious that beyond the circle of light the room was full of things that smelt like all the temples of all the East. A whiff of musk, a puff of sandal-wood, and a breath of sickly jessamine-oil caught his opened nostrils.

'I am here,' said Kim at last, speaking in the vernacular: the smells made him forget that he was to be a Sahib.

'Seventy-nine, eighty, eighty-one,' the man counted to himself, stringing pearl after pearl so quickly that Kim could scarcely follow his fingers. He slid off the green shade and looked fixedly at Kim for a full half-minute. The pupils of the eye dilated and closed to pin-pricks, as if at will. There was a *faquir* by the Taksali Gate who had just this gift and made money by it, especially when cursing silly women. Kim stared with interest. His disreputable friend could further twitch his ears, almost like a goat, and Kim was disappointed that this new man could not imitate him.

'Do not be afraid,' said Mr. Lurgan suddenly.

'Why should I fear?'

'Thou wilt sleep here to-night, and stay with me till it is time to go again to Nucklao. It is an order.'

'It is an order,' Kim repeated. 'But where shall I sleep?'

'Here, in this room.' Lurgan Sahib waved his hand towards the darkness behind him.

'So be it,' said Kim composedly. 'Now?'

He nodded and held the lamp above his head. As the light swept them, there leaped out from the walls a collection of Tibetan devil-dance masks, hanging above the fiend-embroidered draperies of those ghastly functions—horned masks, scowling masks, and masks of idiotic terror. In a corner, a Japanese warrior, mailed and plumed, menaced him with a halberd, and a score of lances and *khandas* and *kuttars* gave back the unsteady gleam. But what interested Kim more than all these things—he had seen devil-dance masks at the Lahore Museum—was a glimpse of the soft-eyed Hindu child who had left him in the doorway, sitting cross-legged under the table of pearls with a little smile on his scarlet lips.

'I think that Lurgan Sahib wishes to make me afraid. And I am sure that the devil's brat below the table wishes to see me afraid. This place,' he said aloud, 'is like a Wonder House. Where is my bed?'

Lurgan Sahib pointed to a native quilt in a corner by the loathsome masks, picked up the lamp, and left the room black.

'Was that Lurgan Sahib?' Kim asked as he cuddled down. No answer. He could hear the Hindu boy breathing, however, and, guided by the sound, crawled across the floor, and cuffed into the darkness, crying: 'Give answer, devil! Is this the way to lie to a Sahib?'

From the darkness he fancied he could hear the echo of a chuckle. It could not be his soft-fleshed companion, because he was weeping. So Kim lifted up his voice and called aloud: 'Lurgan Sahib! O Lurgan Sahib! Is it an order that thy servant does not speak to me?'

'It is an order.' The voice came from behind him and he started.

'Very good. But remember,' he muttered, as he resought the quilt, 'I will beat thee in the morning. I do not love Hindus.'

That was no cheerful night; the room being overfull of voices and music. Kim was waked twice by some one calling his name. The second time he set out in search, and ended by bruising his nose against a box that certainly spoke with a human tongue, but in no sort of human accent. It seemed to end in a tin trumpet and to be joined by wires to a smaller box on the floor—so far, at least, as he could judge by touch. And the voice, very hard and whirring, came out of the trumpet. Kim rubbed his nose and grew furious, thinking, as usual, in Hindi.

'This with a beggar from the bazar might be good but—I am a Sahib and the son of a Sahib and, which is twice as much more beside, a student of Nucklao. Yess' (here he turned to English), 'a boy of St. Xavier's. Damn Mr. Lurgan's eyes!—It is some sort of machinery like a sewing-machine. Oh, it is a *great* cheek of him—we are not frightened that way at Lucknow—No!' Then in Hindi: 'But what does *he* gain? He is only a trader—I am in his shop. But Creighton Sahib is a Colonel—and I think Creighton Sahib gave orders that it should be done. *How* I will beat that Hindu in the morning! What is this?'

The trumpet-box was pouring out a string of the most elaborate abuse that even Kim had ever heard, in a high uninterested voice, that for a moment lifted the short hairs of his neck. When the vile thing drew breath, Kim was reassured by the soft, sewing-machine-like whirr.

'*Chûp!*' (be still) he cried, and again he heard a chuckle that decided him. '*Chûp*—or I break your head.'

The box took no heed. Kim wrenched at the tin trumpet and something lifted with a click. He had evidently raised a lid. If there were a devil inside, now was its time for—he sniffed—thus did the sewing-machines of the bazar smell. He would clean that *shaitan*. He slipped off his jacket, and plunged it into the box's mouth. Something long and round bent under the pressure, there was a whirr and the voice stopped—as voices must if you ram a thrice-doubled coat on to the wax cylinder and into the works of an expensive phonograph. Kim finished his slumbers with a serene mind.

In the morning he was aware of Lurgan Sahib looking down on him.

'Oah!' said Kim, firmly resolved to cling to his Sahib-dom. 'There was a box in the night that gave me bad talk. So I stopped it. Was it your box?'

The man held out his hand.

'Shake hands, O'Hara,' he said. 'Yes, it was my box. I keep such things because my friends the Rajahs like them. That one is broken, but it was cheap at the price. Yes, my friends, the Kings, are very fond of toys—and so am I sometimes.'

Kim looked him over out of the corners of his eyes. He was a Sahib in that he wore Sahib's clothes; the accent of his Urdu, the intonation of his English, showed that he was anything but a Sahib. He seemed to understand what moved in Kim's mind ere the boy opened his mouth, and he took no pains to explain himself as did Father Victor or the Lucknow masters. Sweetest of all—he treated Kim as an equal on the Asiatic side.

'I am sorry you cannot beat my boy this morning. He says he will kill you with a knife or poison. He is jealous, so I have put him in the corner and I shall not speak to him to-day. He has just tried to kill me. You must help me with the breakfast. He is almost too jealous to trust, just now.'

Now a genuine imported Sahib from England would have made a great to do over this tale. Lurgan Sahib stated it as simply as Mahbub Ali was used to record his little affairs in the North.

The back verandah of the shop was built out over the sheer hillside, and they looked down into their neighbours' chimney-pots, as is the custom of Simla. But even more than the purely Persian meal cooked by Lurgan Sahib with his own hands, the shop fascinated Kim. The Lahore Museum was larger, but here were more wonders—ghost-daggers and prayer-wheels from Tibet; turquoise and raw amber necklaces; green jade bangles; curiously packed incense-sticks in jars crusted over with raw garnets; the devil-masks of overnight and a wall full of peacock-blue draperies; gilt figures of Buddha, and little portable lacquer altars; Russian samovars with turquoises on the lid; egg-shell china sets in quaint octagonal cane boxes; yellow ivory crucifixes—from Japan of all places in the world, so Lurgan Sahib said; carpets in dusty bales, smelling atrociously, pushed back behind torn and rotten screens of geometrical work; Persian water-jugs for the hands after meals; dull copper incense-burners neither Chinese nor Persian, with friezes of fantastic devils running round them; tarnished silver belts that knotted like raw hide; hair-pins of jade, ivory, and plasma; arms of all sorts and kinds, and a thousand other oddments were cased, or piled, or merely thrown into the room, leaving a clear space only round the rickety deal table, where Lurgan Sahib worked.

'Those things are nothing,' said his host, following Kim's glance. 'I buy them because they are pretty, and sometimes I sell—if I like the buyer's look. My work is on the table—some of it.'

It blazed in the morning light—all red and blue and green flashes, picked out with the vicious blue-white spurt of a diamond here and there. Kim opened his eyes.

'Oh, they are quite well, those stones. It will not hurt them to take the sun. Besides, they are cheap. But with sick stones it is very different.' He piled Kim's plate anew. 'There is no one but *me* can doctor a sick pearl and re-blue turquoises. I grant you opals—any fool can cure an opal—but for a sick pearl there is only me. Suppose I were to die! Then there would be no one. . . . Oh no! *You* cannot do anything with jewels. It will be quite enough if you understand a little about the Turquoise—some day.'

He moved to the end of the verandah to refill the heavy, porous clay water-jug from the filter.

'Do you want drink?'

Kim nodded. Lurgan Sahib, fifteen feet off, laid one hand on the jar. Next instant, it stood at Kim's elbow, full to within half an inch of the brim—the white cloth only showing, by a small wrinkle, where it had slid into place.

'Wah!' said Kim in most utter amazement. 'That is magic.' Lurgan Sahib's smile showed that the compliment had gone home.

'Throw it back.'

'It will break.'

'I say, throw it back.'

Kim pitched it at random. It fell short and crashed into fifty pieces, while the water dripped through the rough verandah boarding.

'I said it would break.'

'All one. Look at it. Look at the largest piece.'

That lay with a sparkle of water in its curve, as it were a star on the floor. Kim looked intently; Lurgan Sahib laid one hand gently on the nape of his neck, stroked it twice or thrice, and whispered: 'Look! It shall come to life again, piece by piece. First the big piece shall join itself to two others on the right and the left—on the right and the left. Look!'

To save his life, Kim could not have turned his head. The light touch held him as in a vice, and his blood tingled pleasantly through him. There was one large piece of the jar where there had been three, and above them the shadowy outline of the entire vessel. He could see the verandah through it, but it was thickening and darkening with each beat of his pulse. Yet the jar—how slowly the thoughts came!—the jar had been smashed before his eyes. Another wave of prickling fire raced down his neck, as Lurgan Sahib moved his hand.

'Look! It is coming into shape,' said Lurgan Sahib.

So far Kim had been thinking in Hindi, but a tremor came on him, and with an effort like that of a swimmer before sharks, who hurls himself half out of the water, his mind leaped up from a darkness that was swallowing it and took refuge in—the multiplication-table in English!

'Look! It is coming into shape,' whispered Lurgan Sahib.

The jar had been smashed—yess, smashed—not the native word, he would not think of that—but smashed—into fifty pieces, and twice three was six, and thrice three was nine, and four times three was twelve. He clung desperately to the repetition. The shadow-outline of the jar cleared like a mist after rubbing eyes. There were the broken shards; there was the spilt water drying in the sun, and through the cracks of the verandah showed, all ribbed, the white house-wall below—and thrice twelve was thirty-six!

'Look! Is it coming into shape?' asked Lurgan Sahib.

'But it *is* smashed—smashed,' he gasped—Lurgan Sahib had been muttering softly for the last half-minute. Kim wrenched his head aside. 'Look! *Dekho!* It is there as it was there.'

'It is there as it was there,' said Lurgan, watching Kim closely while the boy rubbed his neck. 'But you are the first of a many who have ever seen it so.' He wiped his broad forehead.

'Was that more magic?' Kim asked suspiciously. The tingle had gone from his veins; he felt unusually wide awake.

'No, that was not magic. It was only to see if there was—a flaw in a jewel. Sometimes very fine jewels will fly all to pieces if a man holds them in his hand, and knows the proper way. That is why one must be careful before one sets them. Tell me, did you see the shape of the pot?'

'For a little time. It began to grow like a flower from the ground.'

'And then what did you do? I mean, how did you think?'

'Oah! I knew it was broken, and so, I think, that was what I thought—and it *was* broken.'

'Hm! Has any one ever done that same sort of magic to you before?'

'If it was,' said Kim, 'do you think I should let it again? I should run away.'

'And now you are not afraid—eh?'

'Not now.'

Lurgan Sahib looked at him more closely than ever. 'I shall ask Mahbub Ali—not now, but some day later,' he muttered. 'I am pleased with you—yes; and I am pleased with you—no. You are the first that ever saved himself. I wish I knew what it was that . . . But you are right. You should not tell that—not even to me.'

He turned into the dusky gloom of the shop, and sat down at the table, rubbing his hands softly. A small, husky sob came from behind a pile of carpets. It was the Hindu child obediently facing towards the wall: his thin shoulders worked with grief.

'Ah! He is jealous, so jealous. I wonder if he will try to poison me again in my breakfast, and make me cook it twice.'

'*Kubbee—kubbee nahin*,' came the broken answer.

'And whether he will kill this other boy?'

'*Kubbee—kubbee nahin*' (never—never. No!)

'What do *you* think he will do?' He turned suddenly on Kim.

'Oah! I do not know. Let him go, perhaps. Why did he want to poison you?'

'Because he is so fond of me. Suppose you were fond of some one, and you saw some one come, and the man you were fond of was more pleased with him than he was with you, what would you do?'

Kim thought. Lurgan repeated the sentence slowly in the vernacular.

'I should not poison that man,' said Kim reflectively, 'but I should beat that boy—*if* that boy was fond of my man. But first I would ask that boy if it were true.'

'Ah! He thinks every one must be fond of me.'

'Then I think he is a fool.'

'Hearest thou?' said Lurgan Sahib to the shaking shoulders. 'The Sahib's son thinks thou art a little fool. Come out, and next time thy heart is troubled, do not try white arsenic quite so openly. Surely the Devil Dasim was lord of our table-cloth that day! It might have made me ill, child, and then a stranger would have guarded the jewels. Come!'

The child, heavy-eyed with much weeping, crept out from behind the bale and flung himself passionately at Lurgan Sahib's feet, with an extravagance of remorse that impressed even Kim.

'I will look into the ink-pools[2]—I will faithfully guard the jewels! Oh, my father and my mother, send *him* away!' He indicated Kim with a backward jerk of his bare heel.

---

[2] "A pool of ink in the palm of the hand seems to have been used by a medium who was able to accelerate self-hypnotism and second sight by staring at it" (Brigadier Alec Mason, Kipling Society's Online Reader's Guide, <http://www.kipling.org/uk>). In Kipling's "The Finest Story in the World," Bengali law student Grish Chunder suggests using this technique.

'Not yet—not yet. In a little while he will go away again. But now he is at school—at a new *madrissah*—and thou shalt be his teacher. Play the Play of the Jewels against him. I will keep tally.'

The child dried his tears at once, and dashed to the back of the shop, whence he returned with a copper tray.

'Give me!' he said to Lurgan Sahib. 'Let them come from thy hand, for he may say that I knew them before.'

'Gently—gently,' the man replied, and from a drawer under the table dealt a half handful of clattering trifles into the tray.

'Now,' said the child, waving an old newspaper. 'Look on them as long as thou wilt, stranger. Count and, if need be, handle. One look is enough for *me*.' He turned his back proudly.

'But what is the game?'

'When thou hast counted and handled and art sure that thou canst remember them all, I cover them with this paper, and thou must tell over the tally to Lurgan Sahib. *I* will write mine.'

'Oah!' The instinct of competition waked in his breast. He bent over the tray. There were but fifteen stones on it. 'That is easy,' he said after a minute. The child slipped the paper over the winking jewels and scribbled in a native account-book.

'There are under that paper five blue stones—one big, one smaller, and three small,' said Kim, all in haste. 'There are four green stones, and one with a hole in it; there is one yellow stone that I can see through, and one like a pipe-stem. There are two red stones, and—and—I made the count fifteen, but two I have forgotten. No! Give me time. One was of ivory, little and brownish; and—and—give me time . . .'

'One—two'—Lurgan Sahib counted him out up to ten. Kim shook his head.

'Hear my count!' the child burst in, trilling with laughter. 'First, are two flawed sapphires—one of two ruttees and one of four as I should judge. The four-ruttee sapphire is chipped at the edge. There is one Turkestan turquoise, plain with black veins, and there are two inscribed—one with a Name of God in gilt, and the other being cracked across, for it came out of an old ring, I cannot read. We have now all five blue stones. Four flawed emeralds there are, but one is drilled in two places, and one is a little carven——'

'Their weights?' said Lurgan Sahib impassively.

'Three—five—five—and four ruttees as I judge it. There is one piece of old greenish pipe amber, and a cut topaz from Europe. There is one ruby of Burma, of two ruttees, without a flaw, and there is a balas-ruby, flawed, of two ruttees. There is a carved ivory from China representing a rat sucking an egg; and there is last—ah ha!—a ball of crystal as big as a bean set in a gold leaf.'

He clapped his hands at the close.

'He is thy master,' said Lurgan Sahib, smiling.

'Huh! He knew the names of the stones,' said Kim, flushing. 'Try again! With common things such as he and I both know.'

They heaped the tray again with odds and ends gathered from the shop, and even the kitchen, and every time the child won, till Kim marvelled.

'Bind my eyes—let me feel once with my fingers, and even *then* I will leave thee open-eyed behind,' he challenged.

Kim stamped with vexation when the lad made his boast good.

'If it were men—or horses' he said, 'I could do better. This playing with tweezers and knives and scissors is too little.'

'Learn first—teach later,' said Lurgan Sahib. 'Is he thy master?'

'Truly. But how is it done?'

'By doing it many times over till it is done perfectly—for it is worth doing.'

The Hindu boy, in highest feather, actually patted Kim on the back.

'Do not despair,' he said. 'I myself will teach thee.'

'And I will see that thou art well taught,' said Lurgan Sahib, still speaking in the vernacular, 'for except my boy here—it was foolish of him to buy so much white arsenic when, if he had asked, I could have given it—except my boy here I have not in a long time met with one better worth teaching. And there are ten days more ere thou canst return to Lucknao where they teach nothing—at the long price. We shall, I think, be friends.'

They were a most mad ten days, but Kim enjoyed himself too much to reflect on their craziness. In the morning they played the Jewel Game—sometimes with veritable stones, sometimes with piles of swords and daggers, sometimes with photographs of natives. Through the afternoons he and the Hindu boy would mount guard in the shop, sitting dumb behind a carpet-bale or a screen and watching Mr. Lurgan's many and very curious visitors. There were small Rajahs, escorts coughing in the verandah, who came to buy curiosities—such as phonographs and mechanical toys. There were ladies in search of necklaces, and men, it seemed to Kim—but his mind may have been vitiated by early training—in search of the ladies; natives from independent and feudatory courts whose ostensible business was the repair of broken necklaces—rivers of light poured out upon the table—but whose true end seemed to be to raise money for angry Maharanees or young Rajahs. There were Babus to whom Lurgan Sahib talked with austerity and authority, but at the end of each interview he gave them money in coined silver and currency notes.

There were occasional gatherings of long-coated theatrical natives who discussed metaphysics in English and Bengali, to Mr. Lurgan's great edification. He was always interested in religions. At the end of the day, Kim and the Hindu boy—whose name varied at Lurgan's pleasure—were expected to give a detailed account of all that they had seen and heard—their view of each man's character, as shown in his face, talk, and manner, and their notions of his real errand. After dinner, Lurgan Sahib's fancy turned more to what might be called dressing-up, in which game he took a most informing interest. He could paint faces to a marvel; with a brush-dab here and a line there changing them past recognition. The shop was full of all manner of dresses and turbans, and Kim was apparelled variously as a young Mohammedan of good family, an oilman, and once—which was a joyous evening—as the son of an Oudh landholder in the fullest of full dress. Lurgan Sahib had a hawk's eye to detect the least flaw in the make-up; and lying on a worn teak-wood couch, would explain by the half-hour together how such and such a caste talked, or walked, or coughed, or spat, or sneezed, and, since 'hows' matter little in this world, the 'why' of everything. The Hindu child played this game clumsily. That little mind, keen as an icicle where tally of jewels was concerned, could not temper itself to enter another's soul; but a demon in Kim woke up and sang with joy as he put on the changing dresses, and changed speech and gesture therewith.

Carried away by enthusiasm, he volunteered to show Lurgan Sahib one evening how the disciples of a certain caste of *faquir*, old Lahore acquaintances, begged doles by the roadside; and what sort of language he would use to an Englishman, to a Punjabi farmer going to a fair, and to a woman without a veil. Lurgan Sahib laughed immensely, and begged Kim to stay as he was, immobile for half an hour—cross-legged, ash-smeared, and wild-eyed, in the back room. At the end of that time entered a hulking, obese Babu whose stockinged legs shook with fat, and Kim opened on him with a shower of wayside chaff. Lurgan Sahib—this annoyed Kim—watched the Babu and not the play.

'I think,' said the Babu heavily, lighting a cigarette, 'I am of opeenion that it is most extraordinary and effeecient performance. Except that you had told me I should have opined that—that—that you were pulling my legs. How soon can he become approximately effeecient chain-man? Because *then* I shall indent for him.'

'That is what he must learn at Lucknow.'

'Then order him to be jolly dam-quick. Good-night, Lurgan.' The Babu swung out with the gait of a bogged cow.

When they were telling over the day's list of visitors, Lurgan Sahib asked Kim who he thought the man might be.

'God knows!' said Kim cheerily. The tone might almost have deceived Mahbub Ali, but it failed entirely with the healer of sick pearls.

'That is true. God, He knows; but I wish to know what you think.'

Kim glanced sideways at his companion, whose eye had a way of compelling truth.

'I—I think he will want me when I come from the school, but'—confidentially, as Lurgan Sahib nodded approval—'I do not understand how *he* can wear many dresses and talk many tongues.'

'Thou wilt understand many things later. He is a writer of tales for a certain Colonel. His honour is great only in Simla, and it is noticeable that he has no name, but only a number and a letter—that is a custom among us.'

'And is there a price upon his head too—as upon Mah—all the others?'

'Not yet; but if a boy rose up who is now sitting here and went—look, the door is open!—as far as a certain house with a red-painted verandah, behind that which was the old theatre in the Lower Bazar, and whispered through the shutters: "Hurree Chunder Mookerjee bore the bad news of last month," that boy might take away a belt full of rupees.'

'How many?' said Kim promptly.

'Five hundred—a thousand—as many as he might ask for.'

'Good. And how long might such a boy live after the news was told?' He smiled merrily at Lurgan Sahib's very beard.

'Ah! That is to be well thought of. Perhaps if he were very clever, he might live out the day—but not the night. By no means the night.'

'Then what is the Babu's pay if so much is put upon his head?'

'Eighty—perhaps a hundred—perhaps a hundred and fifty rupees; but the pay is the least part of the work. From time to time, God causes men to be born—and thou art one of them—who have a lust to go abroad at the risk of their lives and discover news—to-day it may be of far-off things, to-morrow of some hidden mountain, and the next day of some near-by men who have done a foolishness against the State. These souls are very few; and of these few, not more than ten are of the best. Among these ten I count the Babu, and that is curious. How great therefore and desirable must be a business that brazens the heart of a Bengali!'

'True. But the days go slowly for me. I am yet a boy, and it is only within two months I learned to write Angrezi. Even now I cannot read it well. And there are yet years and years and long years before I can be even a chain-man.'

'Have patience, Friend of all the World'—Kim started at the title. 'Would I had a few of the years that so irk thee. I have proved thee in several small ways. This will not be forgotten when I make my report to the Colonel Sahib.' Then, changing suddenly into English with a deep laugh:—

'By Jove! O'Hara, I think there is a great deal in you; but you must not become proud and you must not talk. You must go back to Lucknow and be a good little boy and mind your book, as the English say, and perhaps, next holidays if you care, you can come back to me!' Kim's face fell. 'Oh, I mean *if* you like. I know where you want to go.'

Four days later a seat was booked for Kim and his small trunk at the rear of a Kalka tonga. His companion was the whale-like Babu, who, with a fringed shawl wrapped round his head, and his fat open-work-stockinged left leg tucked under him, shivered and grunted in the morning chill.

'How comes it that this man is one of *us?*' thought Kim, considering the jelly-back as they jolted down the road; and the reflection threw him into most pleasant day-dreams. Lurgan Sahib had given him five rupees—a splendid sum—as well as the assurance of his protection if he worked. Unlike Mahbub, Lurgan Sahib had spoken most explicitly of the reward that would follow obedience, and Kim was content. If only, like the Babu, he could enjoy the dignity of a letter and a number—and a price upon his head! Some day he would be all that and more. Some day he might be almost as great as Mahbub Ali! The housetops of his search should be half India; he would follow Kings and ministers, as in the old days he had followed *vakils* and lawyers' touts across Lahore city for Mahbub Ali's sake. Meantime, there was the present, and not at all unpleasant, fact of St. Xavier's immediately before him. There would be new boys to condescend to, and there would be tales of holiday adventures to hear. Young Martin, son of the tea-planter at Manipur, had boasted that he would go to war, with a rifle, against the head-hunters. That might be, but it was certain young Martin had not been blown half across the fore-court of a Patiala palace by an explosion of fireworks; nor had he. . . . Kim fell to telling himself the story of his own adventures through the last three months. He could paralyse St. Xavier's—even the biggest boys who shaved—with the recital, were that permitted. But it was, of course, out of the question. There would be a price upon his head in good time, as Lurgan Sahib had assured him; and if he talked foolishly now, not only would that price never be set, but Colonel Creighton would cast him off—and he would be left to the wrath of Lurgan Sahib and Mahbub Ali—for the short space of life that would remain to him.

'So I should lose Delhi for the sake of a fish,' was his proverbial philosophy. It behoved him to forget his holidays (there would always remain the fun of inventing imaginary adventures) and, as Lurgan Sahib had said, to work.

Of all the boys hurrying back to St. Xavier's, from Sukkur in the sands to Galle beneath the palms, none was so filled with virtue as Kimball O'Hara, jiggetting down to Umballa behind Hurree Chunder Mookerjee, whose name on the books of one section of the Ethnological Survey was R.17.

And if additional spur were needed, the Babu supplied it. After a huge meal at Kalka, he spoke uninterruptedly. Was Kim going to school? Then he, an M.A. of Calcutta University, would explain the advantages of education. There were marks to be gained by due attention to Latin and Wordsworth's *Excursion* (all this was Greek to Kim). French, too, was vital, and the best was to be picked up in Chandernagore, a few miles from Calcutta. Also a man might go far, as he himself had done, by strict attention to plays called *Lear* and *Julius Cæsar*, both much in demand by examiners. *Lear* was not so full of historical allusions as *Julius Cæsar*; the book cost four annas, but could be bought second-hand in Bow Bazar for two. Still more important than Wordsworth, or the eminent authors, Burke and Hare,[3] was the art and science of mensuration. A boy who had passed his examination in these branches—for which, by the way, there were no cram-books— could, by merely marching over a country with a compass and a level and a straight eye, carry away a picture of that country which might be sold for large sums in coined silver. But as it was occasionally inexpedient to carry about measuring-chains, a boy would do well to know the precise length of his own foot-pace, so that when he was deprived of what Hurree Chunder called 'adventitious aids' he might still tread his distances. To keep count of thousands of paces, Hurree Chunder's experience had shown him nothing more valuable than a rosary of eighty-one or a hundred and eight beads, for 'it was divisible and subdivisible into many multiples and sub-multiples.' Through the volleying drifts of English, Kim caught the general trend of the talk, and it interested him very much. Here was a new craft that a man could tuck away in his head; and by the look of the large wide world unfolding itself before him, it seemed that the more a man knew the better for him.

Said the Babu when he had talked for an hour and a half, 'I hope some day to enjoy your offeecial acquaintance. *Ad interim*, if I may be pardoned that expression, I shall give you this betel-box which is

---

[3]Culmination of a series of jokes at the expense of Hurree Babu's education. He may mean Edmund Burke, the Irish politician and writer, and Augustus Hare, an English travel writer; but any English reader would think of William Burke and William Hare, early-19th-c. grave robbers and murderers who sold their victims' bodies for dissection.

highly valuable article and cost me two rupees only four years ago.' It was a cheap, heart-shaped brass thing with three compartments for carrying the eternal betel-nut, lime and *pan*-leaf; but it was filled with little tabloid-bottles. 'That is reward of merit for your performance in character of that holy man. You see, you are so young you think you will last for ever and not take care of your body. It is great nuisance to go sick in the middle of business. I am fond of drugs myself, and they are handy to cure poor people too. These are good departmental drugs—quinine and so on. I give it you for souvenir. Now good-bye. I have urgent private business here by the roadside.'

He slipped out noiselessly as a cat, on the Umballa road, hailed a passing ekka and jingled away, while Kim, tongue-tied, twiddled the brass betel-box in his hands.

* * *

The record of a boy's education interests few save his parents, and, as you know, Kim was an orphan. It is written in the books of St. Xavier in Partibus that a report of Kim's progress was forwarded at the end of each term to Colonel Creighton and to Father Victor, from whose hands duly came the money for his schooling. It is further recorded in the same books that he showed a great aptitude for mathematical studies as well as map-making, and carried away a prize (*The Life of Lord Lawrence*, tree-calf,[4] two vols., nine rupees, eight annas) for proficiency therein; and the same term played in St. Xavier's eleven[5] against the Allyghur Mohammedan College, his age being fourteen years and ten months. He was also re-vaccinated (from which we may assume that there had been another epidemic of small-pox at Lucknow) about the same time. Pencil notes on the edge of an old muster-roll record that he was punished several times for 'conversing with improper persons,' and it seems that he was once sentenced to heavy pains for 'absenting himself for a day in the company of a street beggar.' That was when he got over the gate and pleaded with the lama through a whole day down the banks of the Goomtee to accompany him on the road next holidays—for one month—for a little week; and the lama set his face as a flint against it, averring that the time had not yet come. Kim's business, said the old man as they ate cakes together, was to get all the wisdom of the Sahibs and then he would see. The hand of friendship must in some way have averted the whip of calamity, for six weeks later Kim seems to have passed an examination in elementary surveying 'with great credit,' his

---

[4]Bound in calfskin with a motif of trees. Lawrence was Governor-General of India, 1864–69.

[5]Cricket team (eleven players on a field at a time).

age being fifteen years and eight months. From this date the record is silent. His name does not appear in the year's batch of those who entered for the subordinate Survey of India, but against it stand the words 'removed on appointment.'

Several times in those three years, cast up at the Temple of the Tirthankers in Benares the lama, a little thinner and a shade yellower, if that were possible, but gentle and untainted as ever. Sometimes it was from the South that he came—from south of Tuticorin, whence the wonderful fire-boats go to Ceylon where are priests who know Pali; sometimes it was from the wet green West and the thousand cotton-factory chimneys that ring Bombay; and once from the North, where he had doubled back eight hundred miles to talk a day with the Keeper of the Images in the Wonder House. He would stride to his cell in the cool, cut marble—the priests of the Temple were good to the old man—wash off the dust of travel, make prayer, and depart for Lucknow, well accustomed now to the ways of the rail, in a third-class carriage. Returning, it was noticeable, as his friend the Seeker pointed out to the head-priest, that he ceased for a while to mourn the loss of his River, or to draw wondrous pictures of the Wheel of Life, but preferred to talk of the beauty and wisdom of a certain mysterious *chela* whom no man of the temple had ever seen. Yes, he had followed the traces of the Blessed Feet throughout all India. (The curator has still in his possession a most marvellous account of his wanderings and meditations.) There remained nothing more in life but to find the River of The Arrow. Yet it was shown to him in dreams that it was a matter not to be undertaken with any hope of success unless that seeker had with him the one *chela* appointed to bring the event to a happy issue, and versed in great wisdom—such wisdom as white-haired Keepers of Images possess. For example, (here came out the snuff-gourd, and the kindly Jain priests made haste to be silent):—

'Long and long ago, when Devadatta was King of Benares—let all listen to the *Jâtaka!*[6]—an elephant was captured for a time by the king's hunters and, ere he broke free, beringed with a grievous leg-iron. This he strove to remove with hate and frenzy in his heart, and hurrying up and down the forests, besought his brother-elephants to wrench it asunder. One by one, with their strong trunks, they tried and failed. At the last they gave it as their opinion that the ring was not to be broken by any bestial power. And in a thicket, new-born, wet with the moisture of birth, lay a day-old calf of the herd whose mother had

---

[6]Sacred scriptures, containing "birth stories" of the Gautama Buddha, Jâtaka tales could have reached English-speaking readers through translations by the British scholar T. W. Rhys Davids. In *Something of Myself*, Kipling writes of his sorrow at having had to cut a longer account of the lama's stories.

died. The fettered elephant, forgetting his own agony, said: "If I do not help this suckling it will perish under our feet." So he stood above the young thing, making his legs buttresses against the uneasily moving herd; and he begged milk of a virtuous cow, and the calf throve, and the ringed elephant was the calf's guide and defence. Now the days of an elephant—let all listen to the *Jâtaka!*—are thirty-five years to his full strength, and through thirty-five Rains the ringed elephant befriended the younger, and all the while the fetter ate into the flesh.

'Then one day the young elephant saw the half-buried iron, and turning to the elder said: "What is this?" "It is even my sorrow," said he who had befriended him. Then that other put out his trunk and in the twinkling of an eyelash abolished the ring, saying: "The appointed time has come." So the virtuous elephant who had waited temperately and done kind acts was relieved, at the appointed time, by the very calf whom he had turned aside to cherish—let all listen to the *Jâtaka!*—for the Elephant was Ananda, and the Calf that broke the ring was none other than The Lord Himself. . . .'

Then he would shake his head benignly, and over the ever-clicking rosary point out how free that elephant calf was from the sin of pride. He was as humble as a *chela* who, seeing his master sitting in the dust outside the Gates of Learning, overleapt the gates (though they were locked) and took his master to his heart in the presence of the proud-stomached city. Rich would be the reward of such a master and such a *chela* when the time came for them to seek freedom together!

So did the lama speak, coming and going across India as softly as a bat. A sharp-tongued old woman in a house among the fruit-trees behind Saharunpore honoured him as the woman honoured the prophet,[7] but his chamber was by no means upon the wall. In an apartment of the forecourt overlooked by cooing doves he would sit, while she laid aside her useless veil and chattered of spirits and fiends of Kulu, of grandchildren unborn, and of the free-tongued brat who had talked to her in the resting-place. Once, too, he strayed alone from the Grand Trunk Road below Umballa to the very village whose priest had tried to drug him; but the kind heaven that guards lamas sent him at twilight through the crops, absorbed and unsuspicious, to the ressaldar's door. Here was like to have been a grave misunderstanding, for the old soldier asked him why the Friend of the Stars had gone that way only six days before.

'That may not be,' said the lama. 'He has gone back to his own people.'

'He sat in that corner telling a hundred merry tales five nights ago,' his host insisted. 'True, he vanished somewhat suddenly in the

---

[7]"Elisha passed to Shunem, where was a great woman; and she constrained him to eat bread" (2 Kings 4.8–10).

dawn after foolish talk with my grand-daughter. He grows apace, but he is the same Friend of the Stars as brought me true word of the war. Have ye parted?'

'Yes—and No,' the lama replied. 'We—we have not altogether parted, but the time is not ripe that we should take the Road together. He acquires wisdom in another place. We must wait.'

'All one—but if it were not the boy how did he come to speak so continually of thee?'

'And what said he?' asked the lama eagerly.

'Sweet words—an hundred thousand—that thou art his father and mother and such all. Pity that he does not take the Queen's service. He is fearless.'

This news amazed the lama, who did not then know how religiously Kim kept to the contract made with Mahbub Ali, and perforce ratified by Colonel Creighton. . . .

'There is no holding the young pony from the game,' said the horse-dealer when the Colonel pointed out that vagabonding over India in holiday time was absurd. 'If permission be refused to go and come as he chooses, he will make light of the refusal. Then who is to catch him? Colonel Sahib, only once in a thousand years is a horse born so well fitted for the game as this our colt. And we need men.'

CHAPTER X

Your tiercel's too long at hack, Sire. He's no eyass
But a passage-hawk that footed ere we caught him,
Dangerously free o' the air. Faith! were he mine
(As mine's the glove he binds to for his tirings)
I'd fly him with a make-hawk. He's in yarak
Plumed to the very point—so manned so weathered . . .
Give him the firmament God made him for,
And what shall take the air of him?—*Old Play.*[1]

LURGAN SAHIB did not use as direct speech, but his advice tallied with Mahbub's; and the upshot was good for Kim. He knew better now

---

[1]The "old play" is Kipling's unfinished *Gow's Watch*, from which the epigraph is slightly revised. Spoken as if by a trainer to the owner of a young raptor (*tiercel*), these lines argue that the bird in question has been left too long "at hack": that is, free to return at will for *tirings* (tough training scraps) from his trainer's glove. No mere downy nestling (*eyass*), this is a "passage hawk" who had already caught prey (*footed*) and learned a dangerous taste for free flight before being captured. Now full grown, accustomed to humans (*manned*), and trained to open-air obedience (*weathered*), the bird is primed to hunt (*in yarak*). Best, then, to send him out in company with a training companion, or "make hawk."

than to leave Lucknow city in native garb, and if Mahbub were any-where within reach of a letter, it was to Mahbub's camp he headed, and made his change under the Pathan's wary eye. Could the little Survey paint-box that he used for map-tinting in term-time have found a tongue to tell of holiday doings, he might have been expelled. Once Mahbub and he went together as far as the beautiful city of Bombay, with three truck-loads of tram-horses, and Mahbub nearly melted when Kim proposed a sail in a dhow across the Indian Ocean to buy Gulf Arabs, which he understood from a hanger-on of the dealer Abdul Rahman, fetched better prices than mere Kabulis.

He dipped his hand into the dish with that great trader when Mahbub and a few co-religionists were invited to a big Haj dinner. They came back by way of Karachi by sea, when Kim took his first experience of sea-sickness sitting on the fore-hatch of a coasting-steamer, well persuaded he had been poisoned. The Babu's famous drug-box proved useless, though Kim had restocked it at Bombay. Mahbub had business at Quetta, and there Kim, as Mahbub admit-ted, earned his keep, and perhaps a little over, by spending four curi-ous days as scullion in the house of a fat Commissariat sergeant, from whose office-box, in an auspicious moment, he removed a little vel-lum ledger which he copied out—it seemed to deal entirely with cat-tle and camel sales—by moonlight, lying behind an outhouse, all through one hot night. Then he returned the ledger to its place, and, at Mahbub's word, left that service unpaid, rejoining him six miles down the road, the clean copy in his bosom.

'That soldier is a small fish,' Mahbub Ali explained, 'but in time we shall catch the larger one. He only sells oxen at two prices—one for himself and one for the Government—which I do not think is a sin.'

'Why could not I take away the little book and be done with it?'

'Then he would have been frightened, and he would have told his master. Then we should miss, perhaps, a great number of new rifles which seek their way up from Quetta to the North. The Game is so large that one sees but a little at a time.'

'Oho!' said Kim, and held his tongue. That was in the monsoon holidays, after he had taken the prize for mathematics. The Christ-mas holidays he spent—deducting ten days for private amusements—with Lurgan Sahib, where he sat for the most part in front of a roaring wood-fire—Jakko-road was four feet deep in snow that year—and—the small Hindu had gone away to be married—helped Lurgan to thread pearls. He made Kim learn whole chapters of the the Koran by heart, till he could deliver them with the very roll and cadence of a mullah. Moreover, he told Kim the names and properties of many native drugs, as well as the runes proper to recite when you administer them. And in the evenings he wrote charms on parchment—elaborate pentagrams crowned with the names of devils—Murra, and Awan the Companion of Kings—all fantastically written in the corners. More to the point, he advised Kim as to the care of his own body, the cure of fever-fits, and simple remedies of the Road. A week before it was time to go down, Colonel Creighton Sahib—this was unfair—sent Kim a written examination-paper that concerned itself solely with rods and chains and links and angles.

Next holidays he was out with Mahbub, and here, by the way, he nearly died of thirst, plodding through the sand on a camel to the mysterious city of Bikaneer, where the wells are four hundred feet deep, and lined throughout with camel-bone. It was not an amusing trip from Kim's point of view, because—in defiance of the contract—the Colonel ordered him to make a map of that wild, walled city; and since Mohammedan horse-boys and pipe-tenders are not expected to drag Survey-chains round the capital of an independent native state, Kim was forced to pace all his distances by means of a bead rosary. He used the compass for bearings as occasion served—after dark chiefly, when the camels had been fed—and by the help of his little Survey paint-box of six colour-cakes and three brushes, he achieved something not remotely unlike the city of Jeysalmir. Mahbub laughed a great deal, and advised him to make up a written report as well; and in the back of the big account-book that lay under the flap of Mahbub's pet saddle Kim fell to work.

'It must hold everything that thou hast seen or touched or considered. Write as though the Jung-i-Lat Sahib himself had come by stealth with a vast army outsetting to war.'

'How great an army?'

'Oh, half a lakh of men.'

'Folly! Remember how few and bad were the wells in the sand. Not a thousand thirsty men could come near by here.'

'Then write that down—also all the old breaches in the walls—and whence the firewood is cut—and what is the temper and disposition of the King. I stay here till all my horses are sold. I will hire a room by the gateway, and thou shalt be my accountant. There is a good lock to the door.'

The report in its unmistakable St. Xavier's running script, and the brown, yellow, and lake-daubed map, was on hand a few years ago (a careless clerk filed it with the rough notes of E.23's second Seistan survey), but by now the pencil characters must be almost illegible. Kim translated it, sweating under the light of an oil-lamp, to Mahbub, the second day of their return-journey. The Pathan rose and stooped over his dappled saddle-bags.

'I knew it would be worthy a dress of honour, and so I made one ready,' he said smiling. 'Were I Amir of Afghanistan (and some day we may see him), I would fill thy mouth with gold.' He laid the garments formally at Kim's feet. There was a gold-embroidered Peshawur turban-cap, rising to a cone, and a big turban-cloth ending in a broad fringe of gold. There was a Delhi embroidered waistcoat to slip over a milky white shirt, fastening to the right, ample and flowing; green pyjamas with twisted silk waist-string; and that nothing might be lacking, russia-leather slippers, smelling divinely, with arrogantly curled tips.

'Upon a Wednesday, and in the morning, to put on new clothes is auspicious,' said Mahbub solemnly. 'But we must not forget the wicked folk in the world. So!'

He capped all the splendour, that was taking Kim's delighted breath away, with a mother-of-pearl, nickel-plated, self-extracting .450 revolver.

'I had thought of a smaller bore, but reflected that this takes Government bullets. A man can always come by those—especially across the Border. Stand up and let me look.' He clapped Kim on the shoulder. 'May you never be tired, Pathan![2] Oh, the hearts to be broken! Oh, the eyes under the eyelashes, looking sideways!'

Kim turned about, pointed his toes, stretched, and felt mechanically for the moustache that was just beginning. Then he stooped towards Mahbub's feet to make proper acknowledgment with fluttering, quick-patting hands; his heart too full for words. Mahbub forestalled and embraced him.

'My son,' said he, 'what need of words between us? But is not the little gun a delight? All six cartridges come out at one twist. It is borne in the bosom next the skin, which, as it were, keeps it oiled. Never put it elsewhere, and please God, thou shalt some day kill a man with it.'

'*Hai mai!*' said Kim ruefully. 'If a Sahib kills a man he is hung in the jail.'

'True: but one pace beyond the Border, men are wiser. Put it away; but fill it first. Of what use is a gun unfed?'

'When I go back to the *madrissah* I must return it. They do not allow little guns. Thou wilt keep it for me?'

'Son, I am wearied of that *madrissah*, where they take the best years of a man to teach him what he can only learn upon the Road. The folly of the Sahibs has neither top nor bottom. No matter. Maybe thy written report shall save thee further bondage; and God He knows we need men more and more in the Game.'

[2]Traditional Afghan greeting.

They marched, jaw-bound against blowing sand, across the salt desert to Jodhpore, where Mahbub and his handsome nephew Habib-Ullah did much trading; and then sorrowfully, in European clothes, which he was fast outgrowing, Kim went second-class to St. Xavier's. Three weeks later, Colonel Creighton, pricing Tibetan ghost-daggers at Lurgan's shop, faced Mahbub Ali openly mutinous. Lurgan Sahib operated as support in reserve.

'The pony is made—finished—mouthed and paced, Sahib! From now on, day by day, he will lose his manners if he is kept at tricks. Drop the rein on his back and let go,' said the horse-dealer. 'We need him.'

'But he is so young, Mahbub—not more than sixteen—is he?'

'When I was fifteen, I had shot my man and begot my man, Sahib.'

'You impenitent old heathen.' Creighton turned to Lurgan. The black beard nodded assent to the wisdom of the Afghan's dyed scarlet.

'*I* should have used him long ago,' said Lurgan. 'The younger the better. That is why I always have my really valuable jewels watched by a child. You sent him to me to try. I tried him in every way: he is the only boy I could not make to see things.'

'In the crystal—in the ink-pool?' demanded Mahbub.

'No. Under my hand, as I told you. That has never happened before. It means that he is strong enough—but you think it skittles, Colonel Creighton—to make any one do anything he wants. And that is three years ago. I have taught him a good deal since, Colonel Creighton. I think you waste him now.'

'Hmm! Maybe you're right. But, as you know, there is no Survey work for him at present.'

'Let him out—let him go,' Mahbub interrupted. 'Who expects any colt to carry heavy weight at first? Let him run with the caravans like our white camel-colts—for luck. I would take him myself, but——'

'There is a little business where he would be most useful—in the South,' said Lurgan, with peculiar suavity, dropping his heavy blued eyelids.

'E.23 has that in hand,' said Creighton quickly. 'He must not go down there. Besides, he knows no Turki.'

'Only tell him the shape and the smell of the letters we want and he will bring them back,' Lurgan insisted.

'No. That is a man's job,' said Creighton.

It was a wry-necked matter of unauthorised and incendiary correspondence between a person who claimed to be the ultimate authority in all matters of the Mohammedan religion throughout the world, and a younger member of a royal house who had been brought to book for kidnapping women within British territory. The Moslem Archbishop had been emphatic and over-arrogant; the young prince was merely sulky at the curtailment of his privileges, but there was no need he should continue a correspondence which might some day compromise him. One letter indeed had been procured, but the finder was later found dead by the roadside in the habit of an Arab trader, as E.23, taking up the work, duly reported.

These facts, and a few others not to be published, made both Mahbub and Creighton shake their heads.

'Let him go out with his Red Lama,' said the horse-dealer with visible effort. 'He is fond of the old man. He can learn his paces by the rosary at least.'

'I have had some dealings with the old man—by letter,' said Colonel Creighton, smiling to himself. 'Whither goes he?'

'Up and down the land, as he has these three years. He seeks a River of Healing. God's curse upon all——' Mahbub checked himself. 'He beds down at the Temple of the Tirthankers or at Buddh Gaya when he is in from the Road. Then he goes to see the boy at the *madrissah* as we know, for the boy was punished for it twice or thrice. He is quite mad, but a peaceful man. I have met him. The Babu also has had dealings with him. We have watched him for three years. Red Lamas are not so common in Hind that one loses track.'

'Babus are very curious,' said Lurgan meditatively. 'Do you know what Hurree Babu really wants? He wants to be made a member of the Royal Society by taking ethnological notes.[3] I tell you, I tell him about the lama everything that Mahbub and the boy have told me. Hurree Babu goes down to Benares—at his own expense, I think.'

'*I* don't,' said Creighton briefly. He had paid Hurree's travelling expenses, out of a most lively curiosity to learn what the lama might be.

'And he applies to the lama for information on lamaism, and devil dances, and spells and charms, several times in these few years. Holy Virgin! I could have told him all that yee-ars ago. I think Hurree Babu is getting too old for the Road. He likes better to collect manners and customs information. Yes, he wants to be an F.R.S.'

'Hurree thinks well of the boy, doesn't he?'

'Oh, very indeed—we have had some pleasant evenings at my little place—but I think it would be waste to throw him away with Hurree on the Ethnological side.'

'Not for a first experience. How does that strike you, Mahbub? Let the boy run with the lama for six months. After that we can see. He will get experience.'

[3]Extant since 1660, The Royal Society of London for Improving Natural Knowledge, or Royal Society, is the United Kingdom, Commonwealth, and Republic of Ireland's national academy of science. Election as a Fellow of the Royal Society (FRS) is an extraordinary lifetime honor.

'He has it already, Sahib—as a fish controls the water he swims in; but for every reason it will be well to loose him from the school.'

'Very good, then,' said Creighton, half to himself. 'He can go with the lama, and if Hurree Babu cares to keep an eye on them so much the better. He won't lead the boy into any danger as Mahbub would. Curious—his wish to be an F.R.S. Very human, too. He *is* best on the Ethnological side—Hurree.'

No money and no preferment would have drawn Creighton from his work on the Indian Survey, but deep in his heart also lay the ambition to write "F.R.S." after his name. Honours of a sort he knew could be obtained by ingenuity and the help of friends, but, to the best of his belief, nothing save work—papers representing a life of it—took a man into the Society which he had bombarded for years with monographs on strange Asiatic cults and unknown customs. Nine men out of ten would flee from a Royal Society soirée in extremity of boredom; but Creighton was the tenth, and at times his soul yearned for the crowded rooms in easy London where silver-haired, bald-headed gentlemen who know nothing of the Army move among spectroscopic experiments, the lesser plants of the frozen tundras, electric flight-measuring machines, and apparatus for slicing into fractional millimetres the left eye of the female mosquito. By all right and reason, it was the Royal Geographical that should have appealed to him, but men are as chancy as children in their choice of playthings. So Creighton smiled, and thought the better of Hurree Babu, moved by like desire.

He dropped the ghost-dagger and looked up at Mahbub.

'How soon can we get the colt from the stable?' said the horse-dealer, reading his eyes.

'Hmm. If I withdraw him by order now—what will he do, think you? I have never before assisted at the teaching of such an one.'

'He will come to me,' said Mahbub promptly. 'Lurgan Sahib and I will prepare him for the Road.'

'So be it, then. For six months he shall run at his choice: but who will be his sponsor?'

Lurgan slightly inclined his head. 'He will not tell anything, if that is what you are afraid of, Colonel Creighton.'

'It's only a boy, after all.'

'Ye-es; but first, he has nothing to tell; and secondly, he knows what would happen. Also, he is very fond of Mahbub, and of me a little.'

'Will he draw pay?' demanded the practical horse-dealer.

'Food and water allowance only. Twenty rupees a month.'

One advantage of the Secret Service is that it has no worrying audit. The service is ludicrously starved, of course, but the funds are administered by a few men who do not call for vouchers or present itemised accounts. Mahbub's eyes lighted with almost a Sikh's love of money. Even Lurgan's impassive face changed. He considered the years to come when Kim would have been entered and made to the Great Game that never ceases day and night, throughout India. He foresaw honour and credit in the mouths of a chosen few, coming to him from his pupil. Lurgan Sahib had made E.23 what E.23 was, out of a bewildered, impertinent, lying, little North-West Province man.

But the joy of these masters was pale and smoky beside the joy of Kim when St. Xavier's Head called him aside, with word that Colonel Creighton had sent for him.

'I understand, O'Hara, that he has found you a place as an assistant chain-man in the Canal Department: that comes of taking up mathematics. It is great luck for you, for you are only seventeen; but of course you understand that you do not become *pukka* (permanent) till you have passed the autumn examination. So you must not think you are going out into the world to enjoy yourself, or that your fortune is made. There is a great deal of hard work before you. Only, if you succeed in becoming *pukka*, you can rise, you know, to four hundred and fifty a month.' Whereat the Principal gave him much good advice as to his conduct, and his manners, and his morals; and others, his elders, who had not been wafted into billets, talked, as only Anglo-Indian lads can, of favouritism and corruption. Indeed, young Cazalet, whose father was a pensioner at Chunar, hinted very broadly that Colonel Creighton's interest in Kim was directly paternal; and Kim, instead of retaliating, did not even use language. He was thinking of the immense fun to come, of Mahbub's letter of the day before, all neatly written in English, making appointment for that afternoon in a house the very name of which would have crisped the Principal's hair with horror. . . .

Said Kim to Mahbub in Lucknow railway station that evening, above the luggage-scales—'I feared lest, at the last, the roof would fall upon me and cheat me. Is it indeed all finished, O my father?'

Mahbub snapped his fingers to show the utterness of that end, and his eyes blazed like red coals.

'Then where is the pistol that I may wear it?'

'Softly! A half-year, to run without heel-ropes. I begged that much from Colonel Creighton Sahib. At twenty rupees a month. Old Red Hat knows that thou art coming.'

'I will pay thee *dustoorie* (commission) on my pay for three months,' said Kim gravely. 'Yea, two rupees a month. But first we must get rid of these.' He plucked his thin linen trousers and dragged at his collar. 'I have brought with me all that I need on the Road. My trunk has gone up to Lurgan Sahib's.'

'Who sends his salaams to thee—Sahib.'

'Lurgan Sahib is a very clever man. But what dost thou do?'

'I go North again, upon the Great Game. What else? Is thy mind still set on following old Red Hat?'

'Do not forget he made me that I am—though he did not know it. Year by year, he sent the money that taught me.'

'I would have done as much—had it struck my thick head,' Mahbub growled. 'Come away. The lamps are lit now, and none will mark thee in the bazar. We go to Huneefa's house.'

On the way thither, Mahbub gave him much the same sort of advice as his mother gave to Lemuel, and curiously enough, Mahbub was exact to point out how Huneefa and her likes destroyed kings.[4]

'And I remember,' he quoted maliciously, 'one who said, "Trust a snake before a harlot and a harlot before a Pathan, Mahbub Ali." Now, excepting as to Pathans, of whom I am one, all that is true. Most true is it in the Great Game, for it is by means of women that all plans come to ruin and we lie out in dawning with our throats cut. So it happened to such a one,'—he gave the reddest particulars.

'Then why——?' Kim paused before a filthy staircase that climbed to the warm darkness of an upper chamber, in the ward that is behind Azim Ullah's tobacco-shop. Those who know it call it The Bird-cage—it is so full of whisperings and whistlings and chirrupings.

The room, with its dirty cushions and half-smoked hookahs, smelt abominably of stale tobacco. In one corner lay a huge and shapeless woman clad in greenish gauzes, and decked, brow, nose, ear, neck, wrist, arm, waist, and ankle with heavy native jewellery. When she turned it was like the clashing of copper pots. A lean cat in the balcony outside the window mewed hungrily. Kim checked, bewildered, at the door-curtain.

'Is that the new stuff, Mahbub?' said Huneefa lazily, scarce troubling to remove the mouthpiece from her lips. 'O Buktanoos!'—like most of her kind, she swore by the Djinns—'O Buktanoos! He is very good to look upon.'

'That is part of the selling of the horse,' Mahbub explained to Kim, who laughed.

'I have heard that talk since my Sixth Day,' he replied, squatting by the light. 'Whither does it lead?'

'To protection. To-night we change thy colour. This sleeping under roofs has blanched thee like an almond. But Huneefa has the secret of a colour that catches. No painting of a day or two. Also, we fortify thee against the chances of the Road. That is *my* gift to thee, my son. Take out all metals on thee and lay them here. Make ready, Huneefa.'

---

[4]In Proverbs 31.1–9, King Lemuel's mother counsels him to avoid strong drink, lest he "forget the law." "Give not thy strength unto women," she advises, "nor thy ways to that which destroyeth kings."

Kim dragged forth his compass, Survey paint-box, and the new-filled medicine-box. They had all accompanied his travels, and boy-like he valued them immensely.

The woman rose slowly and moved with her hands a little spread before her. Then Kim saw that she was blind. 'No, no,' she muttered, 'the Pathan speaks truth—my colour does not go in a week or a month, and those whom I protect are under strong guard.'

'When one is far off and alone, it would not be well to grow blotched and leprous of a sudden,' said Mahbub. 'When thou wast with me I could oversee the matter. Besides, a Pathan is a fair-skin. Strip to the waist now and look how thou art whitened.' Huneefa felt her way back from an inner room. 'It is no matter, she cannot see.' He took a pewter bowl from her ringed hand.

The dye-stuff showed blue and gummy. Kim experimented on the back of his wrist, with a dab of cotton-wool; but Huneefa heard him.

'No, no,' she cried, 'the thing is not done thus, but with the proper ceremonies. The colouring is the least part. I give thee the full protection of the Road.'

'*Jadoo?*' (magic), said Kim, with a half start. He did not like the white, sightless eyes. Mahbub's hand on his neck bowed him to the floor, nose within an inch of the boards.

'Be still. No harm comes to thee, my son. I am thy sacrifice!'[5]

He could not see what the woman was about, but heard the clish-clash of her jewellery for many minutes. A match lit up the darkness; he caught the well-known purr and fizzle of grains of incense. Then the room filled with smoke—heavy, aromatic, and stupefying. Through growing drowse he heard the names of devils—of Zulbazan, Son of Eblis, who lives in bazars and *paraos*, making all the sudden lewd wickedness of wayside halts; of Dulhan, invisible about mosques, the dweller among the slippers of the Faithful, who hinders folk from their prayers; and Musboot, Lord of lies and panic. Huneefa, now whispering in his ear, now talking as from an immense distance, touched him with horrible soft fingers, but Mahbub's grip never shifted from his neck till, relaxing with a sigh, the boy lost his senses.

'Allah! How he fought! We should never have done it but for the drugs. That was his White blood, I take it,' said Mahbub testily. 'Go on with the *dawut* (invocation). Give him full Protection.'

'*O Hearer! Thou that hearest with ears, be present. Listen, O Hearer!*' Huneefa moaned, her dead eyes turned to the west. The dark room filled with moanings and snortings.

From the outer balcony, a ponderous figure raised a round bullet head and coughed nervously.

[5]Traditional honorific response.

'Do not interrupt this ventriloquial necromanciss, my friend,' it said in English. 'I opine that it is very disturbing to you, but no enlightened observer is jolly well upset.'

'. . . *I will lay a plot for their ruin! O Prophet, bear with the unbelievers. Let them alone awhile!*' Huneefa's face, turned to the northward, worked horribly, and it was as though voices from the ceiling answered her.

Hurree Babu returned to his note-book, balanced on the windowsill, but his hand shook. Huneefa, in some sort of drugged ecstasy, wrenched herself to and fro as she sat cross-legged by Kim's still head, and called upon devil after devil, in the ancient order of the ritual, binding them to avoid the boy's every action.

'*With Him are the keys of the Secret Things! None knoweth them beside Himself. He knoweth that which is in the dry land and in the sea!*' Again broke out the unearthly whistling responses.

'I—I apprehend it is not at all malignant in its operation?' said the Babu, watching the throat-muscles quiver and jerk as Huneefa spoke with tongues. 'It—it is not likely that she has killed the boy? If so, I decline to be witness at the trial. . . . What was the last hypothetical devil mentioned?'

'Babuji,'[6] said Mahbub in the vernacular. 'I have no regard for the devils of Hind, but the Sons of Eblis are far otherwise, and whether they be *jumalee* (well-affected) or *jullalee* (terrible) they love not Kafirs.'

'Then you think I had better go?' said Hurree Babu, half rising. 'They are, of course, dematerialised phenomena. Spencer says——'[7]

Huneefa's crisis passed, as these things must, in a paroxysm of howling, with a touch of froth at the lips. She lay spent and motionless beside Kim, and the crazy voices ceased.

'Wah! That work is done. May the boy be better for it; and Huneefa is surely a mistress of *dawut*. Help haul her aside, Babu. Do not be afraid.'

'How am I to fear the absolutely non-existent?' said Hurree Babu, talking English to reassure himself. It is an awful thing still to dread the magic that you contemptuously investigate—to collect folk-lore for the Royal Society with a lively belief in all Powers of Darkness.

---

[6]The suffix "ji" signals affection and respect.

[7]Hurree Babu's ongoing self-definition as a "Herbert Spencerian," which first surfaces here as an attempt to dismiss the supernatural, aligns him with a disparate, conflicted community of readers. Widely read by Indian intellectuals, including radical Indian nationalists, British liberal sociologist, political theorist, and psychologist Herbert Spencer (1820–1903) elaborated a "social Darwinism" linked to evolutionary justifications for imperialism and scientific racism, even as he asserted liberal principles of national and individual self-rule and voiced doubts as to the future of British imperial control in India.

Mahbub chuckled. He had been out with Hurree on the Road ere now. 'Let us finish the colouring,' said he. 'The boy is well protected if—if the Lords of the Air have ears to hear. I am a *sufi* (free-thinker), but when one can get blind-sides of a woman, a stallion, or a devil, why go round to invite a kick? Set him upon the way, Babu, and see that old Red Hat does not lead him beyond our reach. I must get back to my horses.'

'All raight,' said Hurree Babu. 'He is at present a curious spectacle.'

* * *

About third cock-crow, Kim woke after a sleep of thousands of years. Huneefa, in her corner, snored heavily, but Mahbub was gone.

'I hope you were not frightened,' said an oily voice at his elbow. 'I superintended entire operation, which was most interesting from ethnological point of view. It was high-class *dawut*.'

'Huh!' said Kim, recognising Hurree Babu, who smiled ingratiatingly.

'And also I had honour to bring down from Lurgan your present costume. I am not in the habit offeecially of carrying such gauds to subordinates, but'—he giggled—'your case is noted as exceptional on the books. I hope Mr. Lurgan will note my action.'

Kim yawned and stretched himself. It was good to turn and twist within loose clothes once again.

'What is this?' He looked curiously at the heavy duffle-stuff loaded with the scents of the far North.

'Oho! That is inconspicuous dress of *chela* attached to service of lamaistic lama. *Complete* in every particular,' said Hurree Babu, rolling into the balcony to clean his teeth at a goglet. 'I am of opeenion it is not your old gentleman's precise religion, but rather sub-variant of same. I have contributed rejected notes to *Asiatic Quarterly Review*[8] on these subjects. Now it is curious that the old gentleman himself is totally devoid of religiosity. He is not a dam particular.'

'Do you know him?'

Hurree Babu held up his hand to show he was engaged in the prescribed rites that accompany tooth-cleaning and such things among decently bred Bengalis. Then he recited in English an Arya-Somaj prayer of a theistical nature,[9] and stuffed his mouth with *pan* and betel.

[8]Renamed *The Imperial and Asiatic Quarterly Review* in 1891, this periodical was published in England by the Oriental Institute.

[9]Founded by Dayanand Sarasvati (1824–83) in the mid-1870s, the Arya-Somaj was an eclectic and evangelical monotheistic Hindu socio-religious movement that proposed to purify India by restoring ancient Vedic scriptures and values. Strongly associated with Indian nationalism, the movement urged radical reform of the caste system, rejected idolatry, and called for abolition of child marriage and compulsory widowhood.

'Oah yes. I have met him several times at Benares, and also at Buddh Gaya, to interrogate him on religious points and devil-worship. He is pure agnostic—same as me.'

Huneefa stirred in her sleep, and Hurree Babu jumped nervously to the copper incense-burner, all black and discoloured in morning-light, rubbed a finger in the accumulated lampblack, and drew it diagonally across his face.

'Who has died in thy house?' asked Kim in the vernacular.

'None. But she may have the Evil Eye—that sorceress,' the Babu replied.

'What dost thou do now, then?'

'I will set thee on thy way to Benares, if thou goest thither, and tell thee what must be known by Us.'

'I go. At what hour runs the *te-rain*?' He rose to his feet, looked round the desolate chamber and at the yellow-wax face of Huneefa as the low sun stole across the floor. 'Is there money to be paid that witch?'

'No. She has charmed thee against all devils and all dangers—in the name of her devils. It was Mahbub's desire.' In English: 'He is highly obsolete, *I* think, to indulge in such supersteetion. Why, it is all ventri*lo*quy. Belly-speak—eh?'

Kim snapped his fingers mechanically to avert whatever evil—Mahbub, he knew, meditated none—might have crept in through Huneefa's ministrations; and Hurree giggled once more. But as he crossed the room he was careful not to step in Huneefa's blotched, squat shadow on the boards. Witches—when their time is on them—can lay hold of the heels of a man's soul if he does that.

'Now you must well listen,' said the Babu when they were in the fresh air. 'Part of these ceremonies which we witnessed they include supply of effeecient amulet to those of our Department. If you feel in your neck you will find one small silver amulet, verree cheap. That is *ours*. Do you understand?'

'Oah yes, *hawa-dilli*' (a heart-lifter), said Kim, feeling at his neck.

'Huneefa she makes them for two rupees twelve annas with—oh, all sorts of exorcisms. They are quite common, except they are partially black enamel, and there is a paper inside each one full of names of local saints and such things. *Thatt* is Huneefa's look-out, you see? Huneefa makes them onlee for us, but in case she does not, when we get them we put in, before issue, one small piece of turquoise. Mr. Lurgan, he gives them. There is no other source of supply; but it was me invented all this. It is strictly unoffeecial of course, but convenient for subordinates. Colonel Creighton he does not know. He is European. The turquoise is wrapped in the paper. . . . Yes, that is road to railway station. . . . Now suppose you go with the lama, or with me, I hope, some day, or with

Mahbub. Suppose we get into a dam-tight place. I am a fearful man—most fearful—but I tell you I have been in dam-tight places more than hairs on my head. You say: "I am Son of the Charm." Verree good.'

'I do not understand quite. We must not be heard talking English here.'

'That is all raight. I am only Babu showing off my English to you. All we Babus talk English to show off,' said Hurree, flinging his shoulder-cloth jauntily. 'As I was about to say, "Son of the Charm" means that you may be member of the *Sat Bhai*—the Seven Brothers, which is Hindi *and* Tantric. It is popularly supposed to be extinct society, but I have written notes to show it is still extant. You see it is all my invention. Verree good. *Sat Bhai* has many members, and perhaps before they jolly-well-cut-your-throat they may give you just a chance for life.[10] That is useful, anyhow. And moreover, these foolish natives—if they are not too excited—they always stop to think before they kill a man who says he belongs to any speecific organisation. You see? You say then when you are in tight place, "I am Son of the Charm," and you get—perhaps—ah—your second wind. That is only in extreme instances, or to open negotiations with a stranger. Can you quite see? Verree good. But suppose now, I, or any one of the Department, come to you dressed quite different. You would not know me at all unless I choose, I bet you. Some day I will prove it. I come as Ladakhi trader—oh anything—and I say to you: "You want to buy precious stones?" You say: "Do I look like a man who buys precious stones?" Then I say: "Even verree poor man can buy a turquoise or *tarkeean*."'

'That is *kichree*—vegetable curry,' said Kim.

'Of course it is. You say: "Let me see the *tarkeean*." Then I say: "It was cooked by a woman, and perhaps it is bad for your caste." Then you say: "There is no caste when men go to—look for *tarkeean*." You stop a little between those words, "to—look." That is thee whole secret. The little stop before the words.'

Kim repeated the test-sentence.

'That is all right. Then I will show you my turquoise if there is time, and then you know who I am, and then we exchange views and documents and those-all things. And so it is with any other man of us. We talk sometimes about turquoises and sometimes about *tarkeean*, but always with that little stop in the words. It is verree easy. First, "Son of the Charm," if you are in a tight place. Perhaps that may help

[10]Literally, a babbling thrush that flocks in groups of seven; the phrase *Sat Bhai* had already been used to name a secret society in Kipling's story "Miss Youghal's Sais." Though historical precedent for the name exists (confederating Hill Rajahs adopt it in Walter Hamilton's *East-India Gazetteer of 1828*, for example), Hurree's choice seems to be an inside joke. The Royal Order of the Sat Bhai was a well-known Masonic group with dubious claims to Hindu origin.

you—perhaps not. Then what I have told you about the *tarkeean*, if you want to transact offeecial business with a strange man. Of course, at present, you have no offeecial business. You are—ah ha!—supernumerary on probation. Quite unique specimen. If you were Asiatic of birth you might be employed right off; but this half-year of leave is to make you de-Englishised, you see? The lama, he expects you, because I have demi-offeecially informed him you have passed all your examinations, and will soon obtain Government appointment. Oh ho! You are on acting-allowance you see: so if you are called upon to help Sons of the Charm mind you jolly well try. Now I shall say good-bye, my dear fellow, and I hope you—ah—will come out top-side all raight.'

Hurree Babu stepped back a pace or two into the crowd at the entrance of Lucknow station and—was gone. Kim drew a deep breath and hugged himself all over. The nickel-plated revolver he could feel in the bosom of his sad-coloured robe, the amulet was on his neck; begging-gourd, rosary, and ghost-dagger (Mr. Lurgan had forgotten nothing) were all to hand, with medicine, paint-box, and compass, and in a worn old purse-belt embroidered with porcupine quill-patterns lay a month's pay. Kings could be no richer. He bought sweetmeats in a leaf-cup from a Hindu trader, and ate them with glad rapture till a policeman ordered him off the steps.

CHAPTER XI

Give the man who is not made
    To his trade
Swords to fling and catch again,
Coins to ring and snatch again,
Men to harm and cure again,
Snakes to charm and lure again—
He'll be hurt by his own blade,
By his serpents disobeyed,
By his clumsiness bewrayed,
By the people mocked to scorn—
    So 'tis not with juggler born.
Pinch of dust or withered flower,
    Chance-flung fruit or borrowed staff,
Serve his need and shore his power,
    Bind the spell, or loose the laugh!
        But a man who, etc., Op. 15.[1]

---

[1]Slightly revised, these lines conclude "The Juggler's Song" in *Songs from Books*. In the full poem, the speaker boasts of his skill as the expression of innate gifts: "Tell me how my tricks are done—" he challenges: "Tell me how the mango grows?"

FOLLOWED a sudden natural reaction.

'Now am I alone—all alone,' he thought. 'In all India is no one so alone as I! If I die to-day, who shall bring the news—and to whom? If I live and God is good, there will be a price upon my head, for I am a Son of the Charm—I, Kim.'

A very few white people, but many Asiatics, can throw themselves into a mazement as it were by repeating their own names over and over again to themselves, letting the mind go free upon speculation as to what is called personal identity. When one grows older, the power, usually, departs, but while it lasts it may descend upon a man at any moment.

'Who is Kim—Kim—Kim?'

He squatted in a corner of the clanging waiting-room, rapt from all other thoughts; hands folded in lap, and pupils contracted to pin-points. In a minute—in another half second—he felt he would arrive at the solution of the tremendous puzzle; but here, as always happens, his mind dropped away from those heights with the rush of a wounded bird, and passing his hand before his eyes, he shook his head.

A long-haired Hindu *bairagi* (holy man), who had just bought a ticket, halted before him at that moment and stared intently.

'I also have lost it,' he said sadly. 'It is one of the Gates to the Way, but for me it has been shut many years.'

'What is the talk?' said Kim, abashed.

'Thou wast wondering there in thy spirit what manner of thing thy soul might be. The seizure came of a sudden. *I* know. Who should know but I? Whither goest thou?'

'Toward Kashi' (Benares).

'There are no Gods there. I have proved them. I go to Prayag (Allahabad) for the fifth time—seeking the road to Enlightenment. Of what faith art thou?'

'I too am a Seeker,' said Kim, using one of the lama's pet words. 'Though'—he forgot his Northern dress for the moment—'though Allah alone knoweth what I seek.'

The old fellow slipped the *bairagi's* crutch under his armpit and sat down on a patch of ruddy leopard's skin as Kim rose at the call for the Benares train.

'Go in hope, little brother,' he said. 'It is a long road to the feet of the One; but thither do we all travel.'

Kim did not feel so lonely after this, and ere he had sat out twenty miles in the crowded compartment, was cheering his neighbours with a string of most wonderful yarns about his own and his master's magical gifts.

Benares struck him as a peculiarly filthy city, though it was pleasant to find how his cloth was respected. At least one-third of the population prays eternally to some group or other of the many million deities, and so revere every sort of holy man. Kim was guided to the Temple of the Tirthankers, about a mile outside the city, near Sarnath, by a chance-met Punjabi farmer—a Kamboh from Jullundur-way who had appealed in vain to every God of his homestead to cure his small son, and was trying Benares as a last resort.

'Thou art from the North?' he asked, shouldering through the press of the narrow, stinking streets much like his own pet bull at home.

'Ay, I know the Punjab. My mother was a Pahareen, but my father came from Amritzar—by Jandiala,' said Kim, oiling his ready tongue for the needs of the Road.

'Jandiala—Jullundur? Oho! Then we be neighbours in some sort, as it were.' He nodded tenderly to the wailing child in his arms. 'Whom dost thou serve?'

'A most holy man at the Temple of the Tirthankers.'

'They are all most holy and—most greedy,' said the Jat with bitterness. 'I have walked the pillars and trodden the temples till my feet are flayed, and the child is no whit better. And the mother being sick too. . . . Hush, then, little one. . . . We changed his name when the fever came. We put him into girl's clothes. There was nothing we did not do, except—I said to his mother when she bundled me off to Benares—she should have come with me—I *said* Sakhi Sarwar Sultan[2] would serve us best. We know His generosity, but these down-country Gods are strangers.'

The child turned on the cushion of the huge corded arms and looked at Kim through heavy eyelids.

'And was it all worthless?' Kim asked, with easy interest.

'All worthless—all worthless,' said the child, lips cracking with fever.

'The Gods have given him a good mind, at least,' said the father proudly. 'To think he should have listened so cleverly. Yonder is thy temple. Now I am a poor man,—many priests have dealt with me,—but my son is my son, and if a gift to thy master can cure him—I am at my very wits' end.'

Kim considered for a while, tingling with pride. Three years ago he would have made prompt profit on the situation and gone his way without a thought; but now, the very respect the Jat paid him proved that he was a man. Moreover, he had tasted fever once or twice already, and knew enough to recognise starvation when he saw it.

[2]There is a famous Muslim shrine to the 12th-c. Syed Ahmad Sultan, popularly known as Sakhi Sarwar, at his burial place in the foothills of the Suleman Mountains in the Punjab. The shrine includes a Hindu temple and a monument to Baba Nanak, the Sikh Guru.

'Call him forth and I will give him a bond on my best yoke, so that the child is cured.'

Kim halted at the carved outer door of the temple. A white-clad Oswal banker from Ajmir, his sins of usury new wiped out, asked him what he did.

'I am *chela* to Teshoo Lama, an Holy One from Bhotiyal—within there. He bade me come. I wait. Tell him.'

'Do not forget the child,' cried the importunate Jat over his shoulder, and then bellowed in Punjabi: 'O Holy One—O disciple of the Holy One—O Gods above all the Worlds—behold affliction sitting at the gate!' That cry is so common in Benares that the passers never turned their heads.

The Oswal, at peace with mankind, carried the message into the darkness behind him, and the easy, uncounted Eastern minutes slid by; for the lama was asleep in his cell, and no priest would wake him. When the click of his rosary again broke the hush of the inner court where the calm images of the Arhats stand, a novice whispered, 'Thy *chela* is here,' and the old man strode forth, forgetting the end of that prayer.

Hardly had the tall figure shown in the door-way than the Jat ran before him, and, lifting up the child, cried: 'Look upon this, Holy One; and if the Gods will, he lives—he lives!'

He fumbled in his waist-belt and drew out a small silver coin.

'What is now?' The lama's eyes turned to Kim. It was noticeable he spoke far clearer Urdu than long ago, under Zam-Zammah; but the father would allow no private talk.

'It is no more than a fever,' said Kim. 'The child is not well fed.'

'He sickens at everything, and his mother is not here.'

'If it be permitted, I may cure, Holy One.'

'What! Have they made thee a healer? Wait here,' said the lama, and he sat down by the Jat upon the lowest step of the temple, while Kim, looking out of the corner of his eyes, slowly opened the little betel-box. He had dreamed dreams at school of returning to the lama as a Sahib—of chaffing the old man before he revealed himself—boy's dreams all. There was more drama in this abstracted, brow-puckered search through the tabloid-bottles, with a pause here and there for thought and a muttered invocation between whiles. Quinine he had in tablets, and dark brown meat-lozenges—beef most probably, but that was not *his* business. The little thing would not eat, but it sucked at a lozenge greedily, and said it liked the salt taste.

'Take then these six.' Kim handed them to the man. 'Praise the Gods, and boil three in milk; other three in water. After he has drunk the milk give him this (it was the half of a quinine pill), and wrap him warm. Give him the water of the other three, and the other half of this white pill when he wakes. Meantime, here is another brown medicine that he may suck at on the way home.'

'Gods, what wisdom!' said the Kamboh, snatching.

It was as much as Kim could remember of his own treatment in a bout of autumn malaria—if you except the patter that he added to impress the lama.

'Now go! Come again in the morning.'

'But the price—the price,' said the Jat, and threw back his sturdy shoulders. 'My son is my son. Now that he will be whole again, how shall I go back to his mother and say I took help by the wayside and did not even give a bowl of curds in return?'

'They are alike, these Jats,' said Kim softly. 'The Jat stood on his dunghill and the King's elephants went by. "O driver," said he, "what will you sell those little donkeys for?"'

The Jat burst into a roar of laughter, stifled with apologies to the lama. 'It is the saying of my own country—the very talk of it. So are we Jats all. I will come to-morrow with the child; and the blessing of the Gods of the Homesteads—who are good little Gods—be on you both. . . . Now, son, we grow strong again. Do not spit it out, little Princeling! King of my Heart, do not spit it out, and we shall be strong men, wrestlers and club-wielders, by morning.'

He moved away, crooning and mumbling. The lama turned to Kim, and all the loving old soul of him looked out through his narrow eyes.

'To heal the sick is to acquire merit; but first one gets knowledge. That was wisely done, O Friend of all the World.'

'I was made wise by thee, Holy One,' said Kim, forgetting the little play just ended; forgetting St. Xavier's; forgetting his white blood; forgetting even the Great Game as he stooped, Mohammedan fashion, to touch his master's feet in the dust of the Jain temple. 'My teaching I owe to thee. I have eaten thy bread three years. My time is finished. I am loosed from the schools. I come to thee.'

'Herein is my reward. Enter! Enter! And is all well?' They passed to the inner court, where the afternoon sun sloped golden across. 'Stand that I may see. So!' He peered critically. 'It is no longer a child, but a man, ripened in wisdom, walking as a physician. I did well—I did well when I gave thee up to the armed men on that black night. Dost thou remember our first day under Zam-Zammah?'

'Ay,' said Kim. 'Dost thou remember when I leapt off the carriage the first day I went to——'

'The Gates of Learning? Truly. And the day that we ate the cakes together at the back of the river by Nucklao. Aha! Many times hast thou begged for me, but that day I begged for thee.'

'Good reason,' quoth Kim. 'I was then a scholar in the Gates of Learning, and attired as a Sahib. Do not forget, Holy One,' he went on playfully, 'I am still a Sahib—by thy favour.'

'True. And a Sahib in most high esteem. Come to my cell, *chela*.'

'How is that known to thee?'

The lama smiled. 'First by means of letters from the kindly priest whom we met in the camp of armed men; but he is now gone to his own country, and I sent the money to his brother.' Colonel Creighton, who had succeeded to the trusteeship when Father Victor went to England with the Mavericks, was hardly the chaplain's brother. 'But I do not well understand Sahibs' letters. They must be interpreted to me. I chose a surer way. Many times when I returned from my Search to this temple, which has always been a nest to me, there came one seeking Enlightenment—a man from Leh—that had been, he said, a Hindu, but wearied of all those Gods.' The lama pointed to the Arhats.

'A fat man?' said Kim, a twinkle in his eye.

'Very fat; but I perceived in a little his mind was wholly given up to useless things—such as devils and charms and the form and fashion of our tea-drinkings in the monasteries, and by what road we initiated the novices. A man abounding in questions; but he was a friend of thine, *chela*. He told me that thou wast on the road to much honour as a scribe. And I see thou art a physician.'

'Yes, that am I—a scribe, when I am a Sahib, but it is set aside when I come as thy disciple. I have accomplished the years appointed for a Sahib.'

'As it were a novice?' said the lama, nodding his head. 'Art thou freed from the schools? I would not have thee unripe.'

'I am all free. In due time I take service under the Government as a scribe——'

'Not as a warrior. That is well.'

'But first I come to wander—with thee. Therefore I am here. Who begs for thee, these days?' he went on quickly. The ice was thin.

'Very often I beg myself; but, as thou knowest, I am seldom here, except when I come to look again at my disciple. From one end to another of Hind have I travelled afoot and in the *te-rain*. A great and a wonderful land! But here, when I put in, is as though I were in my own Bhotiyal.'

He looked round the little clean cell complacently. A low cushion gave him a seat, on which he had disposed himself in the cross-legged attitude of the Bodhisat emerging from meditation; a black teakwood table, not twenty inches high, set with copper tea-cups, was before him. In one corner stood a tiny altar, also of heavily carved teak, bearing a copper-gilt image of the seated Buddha and fronted by a lamp, an incense-holder, and a pair of copper flower-pots.

'The Keeper of the Images in the Wonder House acquired merit by giving me these a year since,' he said, following Kim's eye. 'When one is far from one's own land such things carry remembrance; and we must reverence the Lord for that He showed the Way. See!' he pointed to a curiously-built mound of coloured rice crowned with a fantastic metal ornament. 'When I was abbot in my own place—before I came to better knowledge—I made that offering daily. It is the Sacrifice of the Universe to the Lord. Thus do we of Bhotiyal offer all the world daily to the Excellent Law. And I do it even now, though I know that the Excellent One is beyond all pinchings and pattings.' He snuffed from his gourd.

'It is well done, Holy One,' Kim murmured, sinking at ease on the cushions, very happy and rather tired.

'And also,' the old man chuckled, 'I write pictures of the Wheel of Life.[3] Three days to a picture. I was busied on it—or it may be I shut my eyes a little—when they brought word of thee. It is good to have thee here: I will show thee my art—not for pride's sake, but because thou must learn. The Sahibs have not *all* this world's wisdom.'

He drew from under the table a sheet of strangely scented yellow Chinese paper, the brushes, and slab of India ink. In cleanest, severest outline he had traced the Great Wheel with its six spokes, whose centre is the conjoined Hog, Snake, and Dove (Ignorance, Anger, and Lust), and whose compartments are all the heavens and hells, and all the chances of human life. Men say that the Bodhisat Himself first drew it with grains of rice upon dust, to teach His disciples the cause of things. Many ages have crystallised it into a most wonderful convention crowded with hundreds of little figures whose every line carries a meaning. Few can translate the picture-parable; there are not twenty in all the world who can draw it surely without a copy: of those who can both draw and expound are but three.

'I have a little learned to draw,' said Kim. 'But this is a marvel beyond marvels.'

'I have written it for many years,' said the lama. 'Time was when I could write it all between one lamp-lighting and the next. I will teach thee the art—after due preparation; and I will show thee the meaning of the Wheel.'

'We take the Road, then?'

'The Road and our Search. I was but waiting for thee. It was made plain to me in a hundred dreams—notably one that came upon the night of the day that the Gates of Learning first shut—that without thee I should never find my River. Again and again, as thou knowest, I put this from me, fearing an illusion. Therefore I would not take thee with me

[3]See p. 157.

L. A. Waddell
The Wheel of Life: Picturing the Buddhist Theory of the Universe.

that day at Lucknow, when we ate the cakes. I would not take thee till the time was ripe and auspicious. From the Hills to the Sea, from the Sea to the Hills have I gone, but it was vain. Then I remembered the *Jâtaka.*'

He told Kim the story of the elephant with the leg-iron, as he had told it so often to the Jain priests.

'Further testimony is not needed,' he ended serenely. 'Thou wast sent for an aid. That aid removed, my Search came to naught. Therefore we will go out again together, and our Search is sure.'

'Whither go we?'

'What matters, Friend of all the World? The Search, I say, is sure. If need be, the River will break from the ground before us. I acquired merit when I sent thee to the Gates of Learning, and gave thee the jewel that is Wisdom. Thou didst return, I saw even now, a follower of Sakyamuni, the Physician, whose altars are many in Bhotiyal. It is sufficient. We are together, and all things are as they were—Friend of all the World—Friend of the Stars—my *chela!*'

Then they talked of matters secular; but it was noticeable that the lama never demanded any details of life at St. Xavier's, nor showed the faintest curiosity as to the manners and customs of Sahibs. His mind moved all in the past, and he revived every step of their wonderful first journey together, rubbing his hands and chuckling, till it pleased him to curl himself up into sudden sleep of old age.

Kim watched the last dusty sunshine fade out of the court, and played with his ghost-dagger and rosary. The clamour of Benares, oldest of all earth's cities awake before the Gods, day and night, beat round the walls as the sea's roar round a breakwater. Now and again, a Jain priest crossed the court, with some small offering to the images, and swept the path about him lest by chance he should take the life of a living thing. A lamp twinkled, and there followed the sound of a prayer. Kim watched the stars as they rose one after another in the still, sticky dark, till he fell asleep at the foot of the altar. That night he dreamed in Hindustanee, with never an English word. . . .

'Holy One, there is the child to whom we gave the medicine,' he said, about three o'clock in the morning, when the lama, also waking from dreams, would have fared forth on pilgrimage. 'The Jat will be here at the light.'

'I am well answered. In my haste I would have done a wrong.' He sat down on the cushions and returned to his rosary. 'Surely old folk are as children,' he said pathetically. 'They desire a matter—behold, it must be done at once, or they fret and weep! Many times when I was upon the Road I have been ready to stamp with my feet at the hindrance of an ox-cart in the way, or a mere cloud of dust. It was not so when I was a man—a long time ago. None the less it is wrongful——'

'But thou art indeed old, Holy One.'

'The thing was done. A Cause was put out into the world, and, old or young, sick or sound, knowing or unknowing, who can rein in the effect of that Cause? Does the Wheel hang still if a child spin it— or a drunkard? *Chela*, this is a great and a terrible world.'

'I think it good,' Kim yawned. 'What is there to eat? I have not eaten since yesterday even.'

'I had forgotten thy need. Yonder is good Bhotiyal tea and cold rice.'

'We cannot walk far on such stuff.' Kim felt all the European's lust for flesh-meat, which is not accessible in a Jain temple. Yet, instead of going out at once with the begging-bowl, he stayed his stom-

ach on slabs of cold rice till the full dawn. It brought the farmer, voluble, stuttering with gratitude.

'In the night the fever broke and the sweat came,' he cried. 'Feel
here—his skin is fresh and new! He esteemed the salt lozenges, and
took milk with greed.' He drew the cloth from the child's face, and it
smiled sleepily at Kim. A little knot of Jain priests, silent but all-ob-
servant, gathered by the temple door. They knew, and Kim knew that
they knew, how the old lama had met his disciple. Being courteous
folk, they had not obtruded themselves overnight by presence, word,
or gesture. Wherefore Kim repaid them as the sun rose.

'Thank the Gods of the Jains, brother,' he said, not knowing how
those Gods were named. 'The fever is indeed broken.'

'Look! See!' The lama beamed in the background upon his hosts
of three years. 'Was there ever such a *chela*? He follows our Lord the
Healer.'

Now the Jains officially recognise all the Gods of the Hindu creed,
as well as the Lingam and the Snake. They wear the Brahminical
thread;[4] they adhere to every claim of Hindu caste-law. But, because
they knew and loved the lama, because he was an old man, because he
sought the Way, because he was their guest, and because he collogued
long of nights with the head-priest—as free-thinking a metaphysician
as ever split one hair into seventy—they murmured assent.

'Remember,'—Kim bent over the child,—'this trouble may come
again.'

'Not if thou hast the proper spell,' said the father.

'But in a little while we go away.'

'True,' said the lama to all the Jains. 'We go now together upon
the Search whereof I have often spoken. I waited till my *chela* was
ripe. Behold him! We go North. Never again shall I look upon this
place of my rest, O people of good will.'

'But I am not a beggar.' The cultivator rose to his feet, clutching
the child.

'Be still. Do not trouble the Holy One,' a priest cried.

'Go,' Kim whispered. 'Meet us again under the big railway bridge,
and for the sake of all the Gods of our Punjab, bring food—curry, pulse,
cakes fried in fat, and sweetmeats. Specially sweetmeats. Be swift!'

The pallor of hunger suited Kim very well as he stood, tall and
slim, in his sad-coloured, sweeping robes, one hand on his rosary and
the other in the attitude of benediction, faithfully copied from the
lama. An English observer might have said that he looked rather like

---

[4]This cotton thread represents the second birth of the "twice born," marking them as
both in this life and in eternity simultaneously.

the young saint of a stained-glass window, whereas he was but a growing lad faint with emptiness.

Long and formal were the farewells, thrice ended and thrice renewed. The Seeker—he who had invited the lama to that haven from far-away Tibet, a silver-faced, hairless ascetic—took no part in it, but meditated, as always, alone among the images. The others were very human; pressing small comforts upon the old man,—a betel-box, a fine new iron pencase, a food-bag, and such like,—warning him against the dangers of the world without, and prophesying a happy end to the Search. Meantime Kim, lonelier than ever, squatted on the steps, and swore to himself in the language of St. Xavier's.

'But it is my own fault,' he concluded. 'With Mahbub, I ate Mahbub's bread, or Lurgan Sahib's. At St. Xavier's, three meals a day. Here I must jolly well look out for myself. Besides, I am not in good training. *How* I could eat a plate of beef now! . . . Is it finished, Holy One?'

The lama, both hands raised, intoned a final blessing in ornate Chinese. 'I must lean on thy shoulder,' said he, as the temple-gates closed. 'We grow stiff, I think.'

The weight of a six-foot man is not light to steady through miles of crowded streets, and Kim, loaded down with bundles and packages for the way, was glad to reach the shadow of the railway bridge.

'Here we eat,' he said resolutely, as the Kamboh, blue-robed and smiling, hove in sight, a basket in one hand and the child on the other.

'Fall to, Holy Ones!' he cried from fifty yards. (They were by the shoal under the first bridge-span, out of sight of hungry priests.) 'Rice and good curry, cakes all warm and well scented with *hing* (asafœtida), curds and sugar. King of my fields,' this to the small son, 'let us show these holy men that we Jats of Jullundur can pay a service. . . . I had heard the Jains would eat nothing that they had not cooked, but truly'—he looked away politely over the broad river—'where there is no eye there is no caste.'

'And we,' said Kim, turning his back and heaping a leaf-platter for the lama, 'are beyond all castes.'

They gorged themselves on the good food in silence. Not till he had licked the last of the sticky sweet-stuff from his little finger did Kim note that the Kamboh too was girt for travel.

'If our roads lie together,' he said roughly, 'I go with thee. One does not often find a worker of miracles, and the child is still weak. But *I* am not altogether a reed.' He picked up his *lathi*—a five-foot male-bamboo ringed with bands of polished iron—and flourished it in the air. 'The Jats are called quarrelsome, but that is not true. Except when we are crossed, we are like our own buffaloes.'

'So be it,' said Kim. 'A good stick is a good reason.'

The lama gazed placidly up-stream, where in long, smudged per-spective the ceaseless columns of smoke go up from the burning-ghats by the river. Now and again, despite all municipal regulations, the fragment of a half-burned body bobbed by on the full current.

'But for thee,' said the Kamboh, drawing the child into his hairy breast, 'I might to-day have gone thither—with this one. The priests tell us that Benares is holy—which none doubt—and desirable to die in. But I do not know their Gods, and they ask for money; and when one has done one worship a shaved-head vows it is of none effect ex-cept one do another. Wash here! Wash there! Pour, drink, lave, and scatter flowers—but always pay the priests. No, the Punjab for me, and the soil of the Jullundur-*doab* for the best soil in it.'

'I have said many times—in the temple I think—that if need be, the River will open at our feet. We will therefore go North,' said the lama, rising. 'I remember a pleasant place, set about with fruit-trees, where one can walk in meditation—and the air is cooler there. It comes from the Hills and the snow of the Hills.'

'What is the name?' said Kim.

'How should I know? Didst thou not—no, that was after the Army rose out of the earth and took thee away. I abode there in meditation in a room against the dovecot—except when she talked eternally.'

'Oho! the woman from Kulu. That is by Saharunpore.' Kim laughed.

'How does the spirit move thy master? Does he go afoot, for the sake of past sins?' the Jat demanded cautiously. 'It is a far cry to Delhi.'

'No,' said Kim. 'I will beg a *tikkut* for the *te-rain*.' One does not own to the possession of money in India.

'Then in the name of the Gods, let us take the fire-carriage. My son is best in his mother's arms. The Government has brought on us many taxes, but it gives us one good thing—the *te-rain* that joins friends and unites the anxious. A wonderful matter is the *te-rain*.'

They all piled into it a couple of hours later, and slept through the heat of the day. The Kamboh plied Kim with ten thousand questions as to the lama's walk and work in life, and received some curious an-swers. Kim was content to be where he was, to look out upon the flat North-Western landscape, and to talk to the changing mob of fellow-passengers. Even to-day, tickets and ticket-clipping are dark oppres-sion to Indian rustics. They do not understand why, when they have paid for a magic piece of paper, strangers should punch great pieces out of the charm. So, long and furious are the debates between trav-ellers and Eurasian ticket-collectors. Kim assisted at two or three with grave advice, meant to darken council and to show off his wis-dom before the lama and the admiring Kamboh. But at Somna Road the Fates sent him a matter to think upon.[5] There tumbled into the compartment, as the train was moving off, a mean, lean little person—a Mahratta, so far as Kim could judge by the cock of the tight turban. His face was cut, his muslin upper-garment was badly torn, and one leg was bandaged. He told them that a country-cart had upset and nearly slain him: he was going to Delhi, where his son lived. Kim watched him closely. If, as he asserted, he had been rolled over and over on the earth, there should have been signs of gravel-rash on the skin. But all his injuries seemed clean cuts, and a mere fall from a cart could not cast a man into such extremity of terror. As, with shaking fingers, he knotted up the torn cloth about his neck he laid bare an amulet of the kind called a keeper-up of the heart. Now, amulets are common enough, but they are not generally strung on square-plaited copper wire, and still fewer amulets bear black enamel on silver. There were none except the Kamboh and the lama in the compartment, which, luckily, was of an old type with solid ends. Kim made as to scratch in his bosom, and thereby lifted his own amulet. The Mahratta's face changed altogether at the sight, and he disposed the amulet fairly on his breast.

'Yes,' he went on to the Kamboh, 'I was in haste, and the cart, driven by a bastard, bound its wheel in a water-cut, and besides the harm done to me there was lost a full dish of *tarkeean*. I was not a Son of the Charm (a lucky man) that day.'

'That was a great loss,' said the Kamboh, withdrawing interest. His experience of Benares had made him suspicious.

'Who cooked it?' said Kim.

'A woman.' The Mahratta raised his eyes.

'But all women can cook *tarkeean*,' said the Kamboh. 'It is a good curry, as I know.'

'Oh yes, it is a good curry,' said the Mahratta.

'And cheap,' said Kim. 'But what about caste?'

'Oh, there is no caste where men go to—look for *tarkeean*,' the Mahratta replied, in the prescribed cadence. 'Of whose service art thou?'

'Of the service of this Holy One.' Kim pointed to the happy, drowsy lama, who woke with a jerk at the well-loved word.

'Ah, he was sent from Heaven to aid me. He is called the Friend of all the World. He is also called the Friend of the Stars. He walks as a physician—his time being ripe. Great is his wisdom.'

'And a Son of the Charm,' said Kim under his breath, as the Kamboh made haste to prepare a pipe lest the Mahratta should beg.

'And who is *that*?' the Mahratta asked, glancing sideways nervously.

[5]See the version of the scene that follows in Kipling's MS (p. 263).

'One whose child I—we have cured, who lies under great debt to us.—Sit by the window, man from Jullundur. Here is a sick one.'

'Humph! *I* have no desire to mix with chance-met wastrels. *My* ears are not long. *I* am not a woman wishing to overhear secrets.' The Jat slid himself heavily into a far corner.

'Art thou anything of a healer? I am ten leagues deep in calamity,' cried the Mahratta, picking up the cue.

'The man is cut and bruised all over. I go about to cure him,' Kim retorted. 'None interfered between thy babe and me.'

'I am rebuked,' said the Kamboh meekly. 'I am thy debtor for the life of my son. Thou art a miracle-worker—— I know it.'

'Show me the cuts.' Kim bent over the Mahratta's neck, his heart nearly choking him; for this was the Great Game with a vengeance. 'Now, tell thy tale swiftly, brother, while I say a charm.'

'I come from the South, where my work lay. One of us they slew by the roadside. Hast thou heard?' Kim shook his head. He, of course, knew nothing of E.23's predecessor, slain down South in the habit of an Arab trader. 'Having found a certain letter which I was sent to seek, I came away. I escaped from the city and ran to Mhow. So sure was I that none knew, I did not change my face. At Mhow a woman brought charge against me of theft of jewellery in that city which I had left. Then I saw the cry was out against me. I ran from Mhow by night, bribing the police, who had been bribed to hand me over without question to my enemies in the South. Then I lay in old Chitor city a week, a penitent in a temple, but I could not get rid of the letter which was my charge. I buried it under the Queen's Stone, at Chitor, in the place known to us all.'

Kim did not know, but not for worlds would he have broken the thread.

'At Chitor, look you, I was all in Kings' country; for Kotah to the east is beyond the Queen's law, and east again lie Jeypur and Gwalior.[6] Neither love spies, and there is no justice. I was hunted like a wet jackal; but I broke through at Bandakui, where I heard there was a charge against me of murder in the city I had left—of the murder of a boy. They have both the corpse and the witnesses waiting.'

'But cannot the Government protect?'

'We of the Game are beyond protection. If we die, we die. Our names are blotted from the book. That is all. At Bandakui, where lives one of us, I thought to slip the scent by changing my face, and so made me a Mahratta. Then I came to Agra, and would have turned back to Chitor to recover the letter. So sure I was I had slipped them.

[6]Native States, as opposed to British territories, and so beyond the British ("Queen's") law.

Therefore I did not send a *tar* (telegram) to any one saying where the letter lay. I wished the credit of it all.'

Kim nodded. He understood that feeling well.

'But at Agra, walking in the streets, a man cried a debt against me, and approaching with many witnesses, would hale me to the courts then and there. Oh, they are clever in the South! He recognised me as his agent for cotton. May he burn in Hell for it!'

'And wast thou?'

'O fool! I was the man they sought for the matter of the letter! I ran into the Fleshers' Ward and came out by the House of the Jew, who feared a riot and pushed me forth. I came afoot to Somna Road—I had only money for my *tikkut* to Delhi—and there, while I lay in a ditch with a fever, one sprang out of the bushes and beat me and cut me and searched me from head to foot. Within earshot of the *te-rain* it was!'

'Why did he not slay thee out of hand?'

'They are not so foolish. If I am taken in Delhi at the instance of lawyers, upon a proven charge of murder, my body is handed over to the State that desires it. I go back guarded, and then—I die slowly for an example to the rest of us. The South is not my country. I run in circles—like a goat with one eye. I have not eaten for two days. I am marked'—he touched the filthy bandage on his leg—'so that they will know me at Delhi.'

'Thou art safe in the *te-rain*, at least.'

'Live a year at the Great Game and tell me that again! The wires will be out against me at Delhi, describing every tear and rag upon me. Twenty—a hundred, if need be—will have seen me slay that boy. And thou art useless!'

Kim knew enough of native methods of attack not to doubt that the case would be deadly complete—even to the corpse. The Mahratta twitched his fingers with pain from time to time. The Kamboh in his corner glared sullenly; the lama was busy over his beads; and Kim, fumbling doctor-fashion at the man's neck, thought out his plan between invocations.

'Hast thou a charm to change my shape? Else I am dead. Five—ten minutes alone, if I had not been so pressed, and I might——'

'Is he cured yet, miracle-worker?' said the Kamboh jealously. 'Thou hast chanted long enough.'

'Nay. There is no cure for his hurts, as I see, except he sit for three days in the habit of a *bairagi*.' This is a common penance, often imposed on a fat trader by his spiritual teacher.

'One priest always goes about to make another priest,' was the retort. Like most grossly superstitious folk, the Kamboh could not keep his tongue from deriding his Church.

'Will thy son be a priest, then? It is time he took more of my quinine.'

'We Jats are all buffaloes,' said the Kamboh, softening anew.

Kim rubbed a finger-tip of bitterness on the child's trusting little lips. 'I have asked for nothing,' he said sternly to the father, 'except food. Dost thou grudge me that? I go to heal another man. Have I thy leave—Prince?'

Up flew the man's huge paws in supplication. 'Nay—nay. Do not mock me thus.'

'It pleases me to cure this sick one. Thou shalt acquire merit by aiding. What colour ash is there in thy pipe-bowl? White. That is auspicious. Was there raw turmeric among thy food-stuffs?'

'I—I——'

'Open thy bundle!'

It was the usual collection of small oddments: bits of cloth, quack medicines, cheap fairings, a clothful of *atta*,—grayish, rough-ground native flour,—twists of down-country tobacco, tawdry pipe-stems, and a packet of curry-stuff, all wrapped in a quilt. Kim turned it over with the air of a wise warlock, muttering a Mohammedan invocation.

'This is wisdom I learned from the Sahibs,' he whispered to the lama; and here, when one thinks of his training at Lurgan's, he spoke no more than the truth. 'There is a great evil in this man's fortune, as shown by the stars, which—which troubles him. Shall I take it away?'

'Friend of the Stars, thou hast done well in all things. Let it be at thy pleasure. Is it another healing?'

'Quick! Be quick!' gasped the Mahratta. 'The train may stop.'

'A healing against the shadow of death,' said Kim, mixing the Kamboh's flour with the mingled charcoal and tobacco ash in the red-earth bowl of the pipe. E.23, without a word, slipped off his turban and shook down his long black hair.

'That is my food—priest,' the Jat growled.

'A buffalo in the temple! Hast thou dared to look even thus far?' said Kim. 'I must do mysteries before fools; but have a care for thy eyes. Is there a film before them already? I save the babe, and for return thou—oh, shameless!' The man flinched at the direct gaze, for Kim was wholly in earnest. 'Shall I curse thee, or shall I——' He picked up the outer cloth of the bundle and threw it over the bowed head. 'Dare so much as to think a wish to see, and—and—even I cannot save thee. Sit! Be dumb!'

'I am blind—dumb. Forbear to curse! Co—come child; we will play a game of hiding. Do not, for my sake, look from under the cloth.'

'I see hope,' said E.23. 'What is thy scheme?'

'This comes next,' said Kim, plucking the thin body-shirt. E.23 hesitated, with all a North-West man's dislike of baring his body.

'What is caste to a cut throat?' said Kim, rending it to the waist. 'We must make thee a yellow Saddhu all over. Strip—strip swiftly, and shake thy hair over thy eyes while I scatter the ash. Now, a caste-mark on thy forehead.' He drew from his bosom the little Survey paint-box and a cake of crimson lake.

'Art thou only a beginner?' said E.23, labouring literally for the dear life, as he slid out of his body-wrappings and stood clear in the loin-cloth while Kim splashed in a noble caste-mark on the ash-smeared brow.

'But two days entered to the Game, brother,' Kim replied. 'Smear more ash on the bosom.'

'Hast thou met—a physician of sick pearls?' He switched out his long, tight-rolled turban-cloth and, with swiftest hands, rolled it over and under about his loins into the intricate devices of a Saddhu's cincture.

'Hah! Dost thou know his touch, then? He was my teacher for a while. We must bar thy legs. Ash cures wounds. Smear it again.'

'I was his pride once, but thou art almost better. The Gods are kind to us! Give me *that*.'

It was a tin box of opium pills among the rubbish of the Jat's bundle. E.23 gulped down a half handful. 'They are good against hunger, fear, and chill. And they make the eyes red too,' he explained. 'Now I shall have heart to play the Game. We lack only a Saddhu's tongs. What of the old clothes?'

Kim rolled them small, and stuffed them into the slack folds of his tunic. With a yellow-ochre paint cake he smeared the legs and the breast, great streaks against the background of flour, ash, and turmeric.

'The blood on them is enough to hang thee, brother.'

'May be; but no need to throw them out of the window. . . . It is finished.' His voice thrilled with a boy's pure delight in the Game. 'Turn and look, O Jat!'

'The Gods protect us,' said the hooded Kamboh, emerging like a buffalo from the reeds. 'But—whither went the Mahratta? What hast thou done?'

Kim had been trained by Lurgan Sahib; and E.23, by virtue of his business, was no bad actor. In place of the tremulous, shrinking trader there lolled against the corner an all but naked, ash-smeared, ochre-barred, dusty-haired Saddhu, his swollen eyes—opium takes quick effect on an empty stomach—luminous with insolence and bestial lust, his legs crossed under him, Kim's brown rosary round his neck, and a scant yard of worn, flowered chintz on his shoulders. The child buried his face in his amazed father's arms.

'Look up, Princeling! We travel with warlocks, but they will not hurt thee. Oh, do not cry. . . . What is the sense of curing a child one day and killing him with fright the next?'

'The child will be fortunate all his life. He has seen a great healing. When I was a child I made clay men and horses.'

'I have made them too. Sír Banás, he comes in the night and makes them all alive at the back of our kitchen-midden,' piped the child.

'And so thou art not frightened at anything. Eh, Prince?'

'I was frightened because my father was frightened. I felt his arms shake.'

'Oh, chicken-man,' said Kim, and even the abashed Jat laughed. 'I have done a healing on this poor trader. He must forsake his gains and his account-books, and sit by the wayside three nights to overcome the malignity of his enemies. The Stars are against him.'

'The fewer money-lenders the better say I; but, Saddhu or no Saddhu, he should pay for my stuff on his shoulders.'

'So? But that is thy child on thy shoulder—given over to the burning-ghat not two days ago. There remains one thing more. I did this charm in thy presence because need was great. I changed his shape and his soul. None the less, if, by any chance, O man from Jullundur, thou rememberest what thou hast seen, either among the elders sitting under the village tree, or in thy own house, or in company of thy priest when he blesses thy cattle, a murrain will come among the buffaloes, and a fire in thy thatch, and rats in the corn-bin, and the curse of our Gods upon thy fields that they may be barren before thy feet and after thy ploughshare.' This was part of an old curse picked up from a *faquir* by the Taksali Gate in the days of Kim's innocence. It lost nothing by repetition.

'Cease, Holy One! In mercy, cease!' cried the Jat. 'Do not curse the household. I saw nothing! I heard nothing! I am thy cow!' and he made to grab at Kim's bare foot beating rhythmically on the carriage floor.

'But since thou hast been permitted to aid me in the matter of a pinch of flour and a little opium and such trifles as I have honoured by using in my art, so will the Gods return a blessing,' and he gave it at length, to the man's immense relief. It was one that he had learned from Lurgan Sahib.

The lama stared through his spectacles as he had not stared at the business of disguisement.

'Friend of the Stars,' he said at last, 'thou hast acquired great wisdom. Beware that it do not give birth to pride. No man having the Law before his eyes speaks hastily of any matter which he has seen or encountered.'

'No—no—no indeed,' cried the farmer, fearful lest the master should be minded to improve on the pupil. E.23, with relaxed mouth, gave himself up to the opium that is meat, tobacco, and medicine to the spent Asiatic.

So, in a silence of awe and great miscomprehension, they slid into Delhi about lamp-lighting time.

CHAPTER XII

Who hath desired the Sea—the sight of salt-water unbounded?
The heave and the halt and the hurl and the crash of the comber
    wind-hounded?
The sleek-barrelled swell before storm—gray, foamless, enormous,
    and growing?
Stark calm on the lap of the Line—or the crazy-eyed hurricane
    blowing?
His Sea in no showing the same—his Sea and the same 'neath
    all showing—
        His Sea that his being fulfils?
So and no otherwise—so and no otherwise Hill-men desire
    their Hills![1]

'I HAVE found my heart again,' said E.23, under cover of the platform's tumult. 'Hunger and fear make men dazed, or I might have thought of this escape before. I was right. They come to hunt for me. Thou hast saved my head.'

A group of yellow-trousered Punjab policemen, headed by a hot and perspiring young Englishman, parted the crowd about the carriages. Behind them, inconspicuous as a cat, ambled a small fat person who looked like a lawyer's tout.

'See the young Sahib reading from a paper. My description is in his hand,' said E.23. 'They go carriage by carriage, like fisher-folk netting a pool.'

When the procession reached their compartment, E.23 was counting his beads with a steady jerk of the wrist; while Kim jeered at him for being so drugged as to have lost the ringed fire-tongs which are the Saddhu's distinguishing mark. The lama, deep in meditation, stared straight before him; and the farmer, glancing furtively, gathered up his belongings.

'Nothing here but a parcel of holy-bolies,' said the Englishman aloud, and passed on amid a ripple of uneasiness; for native police mean extortion to the native all India over.

'The trouble now,' whispered E.23, 'lies in sending a wire as to the place where I hid that letter I was sent to find. I cannot go to the *tar*-office in this guise.'

'Is it not enough I have saved thy neck?'

'Not if the work be left unfinished. Did never the healer of sick pearls tell thee so? Comes another Sahib! Ah!'

---

[1]The complete "Sea and the Hills" in *The Five Nations* (1903), replaces "that his being fulfills" (l.6), with the erotic "as she slackens or thrills," also changing "Hill men" (l.7) to "hillmen." A *comber* is a long wave that has peaked, breaking into foam; the *Line*, the equator.

This was a tallish, sallowish District Superintendent of Police,— belt, helmet, polished spurs and all,—strutting and twirling his dark moustache.

'What fools are these Police Sahibs!' said Kim genially.

E.23 glanced up under his eyelids. 'It is well said,' he muttered in a changed voice. 'I go to drink water. Keep my place.'

He blundered out almost into the Englishman's arms, and was bad-worded in clumsy Urdu.

'*Tum mut?* You drunk? You mustn't bang about as though Delhi station belonged to you, my friend.'

E.23, not moving a muscle of his countenance, answered with a stream of the filthiest abuse, at which Kim naturally rejoiced. It reminded him of the drummer-boys and the barrack-sweepers at Umballa in the terrible time of his first schooling.

'My good fool,' the Englishman drawled. '*Nickle-jao!* Go back to your carriage.'

Step by step, withdrawing deferentially, and dropping his voice, the yellow Saddhu clomb back to the carriage, cursing the D.S.P. to remotest posterity by—here Kim almost jumped—by the curse of the Queen's Stone, by the writing under the Queen's Stone, and by an assortment of Gods with wholly new names.

'I don't know what you're saying,'—the Englishman flushed angrily,—'but it's some piece of blasted impertinence. Come out of that!'

E.23, affecting to misunderstand, gravely produced his ticket, which the Englishman wrenched angrily from his hand.

'Oh *zoolum!* What oppression!' growled the Jat from his corner. 'All for the sake of a jest too.' He had been grinning at the freedom of the Saddhu's tongue. 'Thy charms do not work well to-day, Holy One!'

The Saddhu followed the policeman, fawning and supplicating. The ruck of passengers, busy with their babies and their bundles, had not noticed the affair. Kim slipped out behind him; for it flashed through his head that he had heard this angry, stupid Sahib discoursing loud personalities to an old lady near Umballa three years ago.

'It is well,' the Saddhu whispered, jammed in the calling, shouting, bewildered press—a Persian greyhound between his feet and a cageful of yelling hawks under charge of a Rajput falconer in the small of his back. 'He has gone now to send word of the letter which I hid. They told me he was in Peshawur. I might have known that he is like the crocodile—always at the other ford. He has saved me from present calamity, but I owe my life to thee.'

'Is he also one of Us?' Kim ducked under a Mewar camel-driver's greasy armpit and cannoned off a covey of jabbering Sikh matrons.

'Not less than the greatest. We are both fortunate! I will make report to him of what thou hast done. I am safe under his protection.'

He bored through the edge of the crowd, besieging the carriages, and squatted by the bench near the telegraph-office.

'Return, or they take thy place! Have no fear for the work, brother—or my life. Thou hast given me breathing-space, and Strickland Sahib has pulled me to land.[2] We may work together at the Game yet. Farewell!'

Kim hurried to his carriage: elated, bewildered, but a little nettled in that he had no key to the secrets about him.

'I am only a beginner at the Game, that is sure. *I* could not have leaped into safety as did the Saddhu. He knew it was darkest under the lamp. *I* could not have thought to tell news under pretence of cursing . . . and how clever was the Sahib! No matter, I saved the life of one. . . . Where is the Kamboh gone, Holy One?' he whispered, as he took his seat in the now crowded compartment.

'A fear gripped him,' the lama replied, with a touch of tender malice. 'He saw thee change the Mahratta to a Saddhu in the twinkling of an eye, as a protection against evil. That shook him. Then he saw the Saddhu fall sheer into the hands of the *polis*—all the effect of thy art. Then he gathered up his son and fled; for he said that thou didst change a quiet trader into an impudent bandier of words with the Sahibs, and he feared a like fate. Where is the Saddhu?'

'With the *polis*,' said Kim. . . . 'Yet I saved the Kamboh's child.'

The lama snuffed blandly.

'Ah, *chela*, see how thou art overtaken! Thou didst cure the Kamboh's child solely to acquire merit. But thou didst put a spell on the Mahratta with prideful workings—I watched thee—and with sidelong glances to bewilder an old old man and a foolish farmer: whence calamity and suspicion.'

Kim controlled himself with an effort beyond his years. Not more than any other youngster did he like to eat dirt or to be misjudged, but he saw himself in a cleft stick. The train rolled out of Delhi into the night.

'It is true,' he murmured. 'Where I have offended thee I have done wrong.'

'It is more, *chela*. Thou hast loosed an Act upon the world, and as a stone thrown into a pool so spread the consequences thou canst not tell how far.'

This ignorance was well both for Kim's vanity and for the lama's peace of mind, when we think that there was then being handed in at

---

[2]Suckled by a hillwoman, gifted in disguise, and wise both in the ways of Indian culture and the workings of colonial government, the native-born Strickland has already won the woman of Kulu's praise as "the sort to oversee justice" (see chap. 4). Strickland appears in several Kipling short stories; see "Mark of the Beast," p. 286.

Simla a code-wire reporting the arrival of E.23 at Delhi, and, more important, the whereabouts of a letter he had been commissioned to—abstract. Incidentally, an over-zealous policeman had arrested, on charge of murder done in a far southern State, a horribly indignant Ajmir cotton-broker, who was explaining himself to a Mr. Strickland on Delhi platform, while E.23 was paddling through byways into the locked heart of Delhi city. In two hours several telegrams had reached the angry minister of a southern State reporting that all trace of a somewhat bruised Mahratta had been lost; and by the time the leisurely train halted at Saharunpore the last ripple of the stone Kim had helped to heave was lapping against the steps of a mosque in faraway Roum—where it disturbed a pious man at prayers.

The lama made his in ample form near the dewy bougainvillea-trellis near the platform, cheered by the clear sunshine and the presence of his disciple. 'We will put these things behind us,' he said, indicating the brazen engine and the gleaming track. 'The jolting of the *te-rain*—though a wonderful thing—has turned my bones to water. We will use clean air henceforward.'

'Let us go to the Kulu woman's house.' Kim stepped forth cheerily under the bundles. Early morning Saharunpore-way is clean and well scented. He thought of the other mornings at St. Xavier's, and it topped his already thrice-heaped contentment.

'Where is this new haste born from? Wise men do not run about like chickens in the sun. We have come hundreds upon hundreds of *kos* already, and, till now, I have scarcely been alone with thee an instant. How canst thou receive instruction all jostled of crowds? How can I, whelmed by a flux of talk, meditate upon the Way?'

'Her tongue grows no shorter with the years, then?' The disciple smiled.

'Nor her desire for charms. I remember once when I spoke of the Wheel of Life'—the lama fumbled in his bosom for his latest copy—'she was only curious about the devils that besiege children. She shall acquire merit by entertaining us—in a little while—at an after-occasion—softly, softly. Now we will wander loose-foot, waiting upon the Chain of Things.[3] The Search is sure.'

So they travelled very easily across and among the broad bloomful fruit-gardens—by way of Aminabad, Sahaigunge, Akrola of the Ford, and little Phulesa—the line of the Sewaliks always to the north, and behind them again the snows. After long, sweet sleep under the dry stars came the lordly, leisurely passage through a waking vil-

[3]Kipling's metaphor for the Law of Karma, by which good actions bring one closer to enlightenment (nirvana) and bad actions take one farther away. The lama believes that this law will eventually result in his finding the River of the Arrow.

lage—begging-bowl held forth in silence, but eyes roving in defiance of the Law from sky's edge to sky's edge. Then would Kim return soft-footed through the soft dust to his master under the shadow of a mango tree or the thinner shade of a white Doon *siris*, to eat and drink at ease. At mid-day, after talk and a little wayfaring, they slept; meeting the world refreshed when the air was cooler. Night found them adventuring into new territory—some chosen village spied three hours before across the fat land, and much discussed upon the road.

There they told their tale,—a new one each evening so far as Kim was concerned,—and there were they made welcome, either by priest or headman, after the custom of the kindly East.

When the shadows shortened and the lama leaned more heavily upon Kim, there was always the Wheel of Life to draw forth, to hold flat under wiped stones, and with a long straw to expound cycle by cycle. Here sat the Gods on high—and they were dreams of dreams. Here was our Heaven and the world of the demi-Gods—horsemen fighting among the hills. Here were the agonies done upon the beasts, souls ascending or descending the ladder and therefore not to be interfered with. Here were the Hells, hot and cold, and the abodes of tormented ghosts. Let the *chela* study the troubles that come from over-eating—bloated stomach and burning bowels. Obediently then, with bowed head and brown finger alert to follow the pointer, did the *chela* study; but when they came to the Human World, busy and profitless, that is just above the Hells, his mind was distracted; for by the roadside trundled the very Wheel itself, eating, drinking, trading, marrying, and quarrelling—all warmly alive. Often the lama made the living pictures the matter of his text, bidding Kim—too ready—note how the flesh takes a thousand thousand shapes, desirable or detestable as men reckon, but in truth of no account either way; and how the stupid spirit, bond-slave to the Hog, the Dove, and the Serpent—lusting after betel-nut, a new yoke of oxen, women, or the favour of kings—is bound to follow the body through all the Heavens and all the Hells, and strictly round again. Sometimes a woman or a poor man, watching the ritual—it was nothing less—when the great yellow chart was unfolded, would throw a few flowers or a handful of cowries upon its edge. It sufficed these humble ones they had met a Holy One who might be moved to remember them in his prayers.

'Cure them if they are sick,' said the lama, when Kim's sporting instincts woke. 'Cure them if they have fever, but by no means work charms. Remember what befell the Mahratta.'

'Then all Doing is evil?' Kim replied, lying out under a big tree at the fork of the Doon road, watching the little ants run over his hand.

'To abstain from action is well—except to acquire merit.'

'At the Gates of Learning we were taught that to abstain from action was unbefitting a Sahib. And I am a Sahib.'

'Friend of all the World,'—the lama looked directly at Kim,—'I am an old man—pleased with shows as are children. To those who follow the Way there is neither black nor white, Hind nor Bhotiyal. We be all souls seeking escape. No matter what thy wisdom learned among Sahibs, when we come to my River thou wilt be freed from all illusion—at my side. Hai! my bones ache for that River, as they ached in the *terain*; but my spirit sits above my bones, waiting. The Search is sure!'

'I am answered. It is permitted to ask a question?'

The lama inclined his stately head.

'I ate thy bread for three years—as thou knowest. Holy One, whence came——'?

'There is much wealth, as men count it, in Bhotiyal,' the lama returned with composure. 'In my own place I have the illusion of honour. I ask for that I need. I am not concerned with the account. That is for my monastery. Ai! The black high seats in the monastery, and the novices all in order!'

And he told stories, tracing with a finger in the dust, of the immense and sumptuous ritual of avalanche-guarded cathedrals; of processions and devil-dances; of the changing of monks and nuns into swine; of holy cities fifteen thousand feet in the air; of intrigue between monastery and monastery; of voices among the hills, and of that mysterious mirage that dances on dry snow. He spoke even of Lhassa and of the Dalai Lama, whom he had seen and adored.

Each long, perfect day rose behind Kim for a barrier to cut him off from his race and his mother-tongue. He slipped back to thinking and dreaming in the vernacular, and mechanically followed the lama's ceremonial observances at eating, drinking, and the like. The old man's mind turned more and more to his monastery as his eyes turned to the steadfast snows. His River troubled him nothing. Now and again, indeed, he would gaze long and long at a tuft or a twig, expecting, he said, the earth to cleave and deliver its blessing; but he was content to be with his disciple, at ease in the temperate wind that comes down from the Doon. This was not Ceylon, nor Buddh Gaya, nor Bombay, nor some grass-tangled ruins that he seemed to have stumbled upon two years ago. He spoke of those places as a scholar removed from vanity, as a Seeker walking in humility, as an old man, wise and temperate, illumining knowledge with brilliant insight. Bit by bit, disconnectedly, each tale called up by some wayside thing, he spoke of all his wanderings up and down Hind; till Kim, who had loved him without reason, now loved him for fifty good reasons. So they enjoyed themselves in high felicity, abstaining, as the Rule demands, from evil words, covetous desires; not over-eating, not lying on high beds, nor wearing rich clothes. Their stomach told them the time, and the people brought them their food, as the saying is. They were lords of the villages of Aminabad, Sahaigunge, Akrola of the Ford, and little Phulesa, where Kim gave the soulless woman a blessing.

But news travels fast in India, and too soon shuffled across the crop-land, bearing a basket of fruits with a box of Kabul grapes and gilt oranges, a white-whiskered servitor—a lean, dry Oorya—begging them to bring the honour of their presence to his mistress, distressed in her mind that the lama had neglected her so long.

'Now do I remember'—the lama spoke as though it were a wholly new proposition. 'She is virtuous, but an inordinate talker.'

Kim was sitting on the edge of a cow's manger, telling stories to a village smith's children.

'She will only ask for another son for her daughter. I have not forgotten her,' he said. 'Let her acquire merit. Send word that we will come.'

They covered eleven miles through the fields in two days, and were overwhelmed with attentions at the end; for the old lady held a fine tradition of hospitality, to which she forced her son-in-law, who was under the thumb of his women-folk and bought peace by borrowing of the money-lender. Age had not weakened her tongue or her memory, and from a discreetly barred upper window, in the hearing of not less than a dozen servants, she paid Kim compliments that would have flung European audiences into unclean dismay.

'But thou art still the shameless beggar-brat of the *parao*,' she shrilled. 'I have not forgotten thee. Wash ye and eat. The father of my daughter's son is gone away awhile. So we poor women are dumb and useless.'

For proof, she harangued the entire household unsparingly till food and drink were brought; and in the evening—the smoke-scented evening, copper-dun and turquoise across the fields—it pleased her to order her palanquin to be set down in the untidy fore-court by smoky torch-light; and there, behind not too closely drawn curtains, she gossiped.

'Had the Holy One come alone, I should have received him otherwise; but with this rogue, who can be too careful?'

'Maharanee,' said Kim, choosing as always the amplest title, 'is it my fault that none other than a Sahib—a *polis*-sahib—called the Maharanee whose face he——'

'Chitt! That was on the pilgrimage. When we travel—thou knowest the proverb.'

'Called the Maharanee a Breaker of Hearts and a Dispenser of Delights?'

'To remember that! It was true. So he did. That was in the time of the bloom of my beauty.' She chuckled like a contented parrot above the sugar lump. 'Now tell me of thy goings and comings—as much as may be without shame. How many maids, and whose wives, hang upon thy eyelashes? Ye hail from Benares? I would have gone there again this year, but my daughter—we have only two sons. Phaii! Such is the effect of these low plains. Now in Kulu men are elephants. But I would ask thy Holy One—stand aside, rogue—a charm against most lamentable windy colics that in mango-time overtake my daughter's eldest. Two years back he gave me a powerful spell.'

'Oh, Holy One!' said Kim, bubbling with mirth at the lama's rueful face.

'It is true. I gave her one against wind.'

'Teeth—teeth—teeth,' snapped the old woman.

'Cure them when they are sick,' Kim quoted relishingly, 'but by no means work charms. Remember what befell the Mahratta.'

'That was two Rains ago; she wearied me with her continual importunity.' The lama groaned as the Unjust Judge had groaned before him.[4] 'Thus it comes—take note, my *chela*—that even those who would follow the Way are thrust aside by idle women. Three days through, when the child was sick, she talked to me.'

'Arré! and to whom else should I talk? The boy's mother knew nothing, and the father—in the nights of the cold weather it was— "Pray to the Gods," said he, forsooth, and turning over, snored!'

'I gave her the charm. What is an old man to do?'

'"To abstain from action is well—except when we acquire merit."'

'Ah, *chela*, if thou desertest me, I am all alone.'

'He found his milk-teeth easily at any rate,' said the old lady. 'But all priests are alike.'

Kim coughed severely. Being young, he did not approve of her flippancy. 'To importune the wise out of season is to invite calamity.'

'There is a talking *mynah*'—the thrust came back with the well-remembered snap of the jewelled forefinger—'over the stables which has picked up the very tone of the family-priest. Maybe I forget honour to my guests, but if ye had seen *him* double his fists into his belly, which was like a half-grown gourd, and cry: "Here is the pain!" ye would forgive. I am half minded to take the *hakim's* medicine. He sells it cheap, and certainly it makes him fat as Shiv's own bull. *He* does not deny remedies, but I doubted for the child because of the inauspicious colour of the bottles.'

[4]Worn down by tireless pleading, the biblical unjust judge finally accedes: "Though I fear not God, nor regard man; / Yet because this widow troubleth me, I will avenge her, lest by her continual coming she weary me" (Luke 18.4–5).

The lama, under the cover of the monologue, had faded out into the darkness towards the room prepared.

'Thou hast angered him, belike,' said Kim.

'Not he. He is wearied, and I forgot, being a grandmother. (None but a grandmother should ever oversee a child. Mothers are only fit for bearing.) To-morrow, when he sees how my daughter's son is grown, he will write the charm. Then, too, he can judge of the new *hakim's* drugs.'

'Who is the *hakim*, Maharanee?'

'A wanderer, as thou art, but a most sober Bengali from Dacca— a master of medicine. He relieved me of an oppression after meat by means of a small pill that wrought like a devil unchained. He travels about now, vending preparations of great value. He has even papers, printed in Angrezi, telling what things he has done for weak-backed men and slack women. He has been here four days; but hearing ye were coming (*hakims* and priests are snake and tiger the world over) he has, as I take it, gone to cover.'

While she drew breath after this volley, the ancient servant, sitting unrebuked on the edge of the torch-light, muttered: 'This house is a cattle-pound, as it were, for all charlatans and—priests. Let the boy stop eating mangoes . . . but who can argue with a grandmother?' He raised his voice respectfully: 'Sahiba, the *hakim* sleeps after his meat. He is in the quarters behind the dovecot.'

Kim bristled like an expectant terrier. To outface and down-talk a Calcutta-taught Bengali, a voluble Dacca drug-vendor, would be a good game. It was not seemly that the lama, and incidentally himself, should be thrown aside for such an one. He knew those curious bastard English advertisements at the backs of native newspapers. St. Xavier's boys sometimes brought them in by stealth to snigger over among their mates; for the language of the grateful patient recounting his symptoms is most simple and revealing. The Oorya, not unanxious to play off one parasite against the other, slunk away towards the dovecot.

'Yes,' said Kim, with measured scorn. 'Their stock-in-trade is a little coloured water and a very great shamelessness. Their prey are broken-down kings and overfed Bengalis. Their profit is in children— who are not born.'

The old lady chuckled. 'Do not be envious. Charms are better, eh? *I* never gainsaid it. See that thy Holy One writes me a good amulet by the morning.'

'None but the ignorant deny'—a thick, heavy voice boomed through the darkness, as a figure came to rest squatting—'None but the ignorant deny the value of charms. None but the ignorant deny the value of medicines.'

'A rat found a piece of turmeric. Said he: "I will open a grocer's shop,"' Kim retorted.

Battle was fairly joined now, and they heard the old lady stiffen to attention.

'The priest's son knows the names of his nurse and three Gods. Says he: "Hear me, or I will curse you by the three million Great Ones."' Decidedly this invisible had an arrow or two in his quiver. He went on: 'I am but a teacher of the alphabet. I have learned all the wisdom of the Sahibs.'

'The Sahibs never grow old. They dance and they play like children when they are grandfathers. A strong-backed breed,' piped the voice inside the palanquin.

'I have, too, our drugs which loosen humours of the head in hot and angry men. *Siná* well compounded when the moon stands in the proper House; yellow earths I have—*arplan* from China that makes a man renew his youth and astonish his household; saffron from Kashmir, and the best salep of Kabul. Many people have died before——'

'That I surely believe,' said Kim.

'They knew the value of my drugs. I do not give *my* sick the mere ink in which a charm is written, but hot and rending drugs which descend and wrestle with the evil.'

'Very mightily they do so,' sighed the old lady.

The voice launched into an immense tale of misfortune and bankruptcy, studded with plentiful petitions to the Government. 'But for my fate, which overrules all, I had been now in Government employ. I bear a degree from the great school at Calcutta—whither, maybe, the son of this house shall go.'

'He shall indeed. If our neighbour's brat can in a few years be made an F.A.' (First Arts—she used the English word, of which she had heard so often), 'how much more shall children clever as some that I know bear away prizes at rich Calcutta.'

'Never,' said the voice, 'have I seen such a child! Born in an auspicious hour, and—but for that colic which, alas! turning into black cholers, may carry him off like a pigeon—destined to many years, he is enviable.'

'*Hai mai!*' said the old lady. 'To praise children is inauspicious, or I could listen to this talk. But the back of the house is unguarded, and even in this soft air men think themselves to be men and women we know. . . . The child's father is away too, and I must be *chowkedar* (watchman) in my old age. Up! Up! Take up the palanquin. Let the *hakim* and the young priest settle between them whether charms or medicine most avail. Ho! worthless people, fetch tobacco for the guests, and—round the homestead go I!'

The palanquin reeled off, followed by straggling torches and a horde of dogs. Twenty villages knew the Sahiba—her failings, her tongue, and her large charity. Twenty villages cheated her after immemorial custom, but no man would have stolen or robbed within her jurisdiction for any gift under Heaven. None the less, she made great parade of her formal inspections, the riot of which could be heard half-way to Mussoorie.

Kim relaxed, as one augur must when he meets another. The *hakim*, still squatting, slid over his hookah with a friendly foot, and Kim pulled at the good weed. The hangers-on expected grave professional debate, and perhaps a little free doctoring.

'To discuss medicine before the ignorant is of one piece with teaching the peacock to sing,' said the *hakim*.

'True courtesy,' Kim echoed, 'is very often inattention.'

These, be it understood, were company-manners, designed to impress.

'Hi! I have an ulcer on my leg,' cried a scullion. 'Look at it!'

'Get hence! Remove!' said the *hakim*. 'Is it the habit of the place to pester honoured guests? Ye crowd in like buffaloes.'

'If the Sahiba knew——' Kim began.

'Ai! Ai! Come away. They are meat for our mistress. When her young Shaitan's colics are cured perhaps we poor people may be suffered to——'

'The mistress fed thy wife when thou wast in jail for breaking the money-lender's head. Who speaks against her?' The old servitor curled his white moustaches savagely in the young moonlight. '*I* am responsible for the honour of this house. Go!' and he drove the underlings before him.

Said the *hakim*, hardly more than shaping the words with his lips: 'How do you do, Mr. O'Hara? I am jolly glad to see you again.'

Kim's hand clenched about the pipe-stem. Anywhere on the open road, perhaps, he would not have been astonished; but here, in this quiet backwater of life, he was not prepared for Hurree Babu. It annoyed him, too, that he had been hoodwinked.

'Ah ha! I told you at Lucknow—*resurgam*—I shall rise again and you shall not know me. How much did you bet—eh?'

He chewed leisurely upon a few cardamom seeds, but he breathed uneasily.

'But why come here, Babuji?'

'Ah! *Thatt* is the question, as Shakespeare hath said. I come to congratulate you on your extraordinary effeecient performance at Delhi. Oah! I tell you we are all proud of you. It was verree neat and handy. Our mutual friend, he is old friend of mine. He has been in some dam-tight places. Now he will be in some more. He told me; I tell Mr. Lurgan; and he is pleased you graduate so nicely. All the Department is pleased.'

For the first time in his life, Kim thrilled to the clean pride (it can be a deadly pitfall, none the less) of Departmental praise—ensnaring praise from an equal of work appreciated by fellow-workers. Earth has nothing on the same plane to compare with it. But, cried the Oriental in him, Babus do not travel far to retail compliments.

'Tell thy tale, Babu,' he said authoritatively.

'Oah, it is nothing. Onlee I was at Simla when the wire came in about what our mutual friend said he had hidden, and old Creighton——' He looked to see how Kim would take this piece of audacity.

'The Colonel Sahib,' the boy from St. Xavier's corrected.

'*Of* course. He found me at a loose string, and I had to go down to Chitor to find that beastly letter. I do not like the South—too much railway travel; but I drew good travelling allowance. Ha! Ha! I meet our mutual at Delhi on the way back. He lies quiett just now, and says Saddhu-disguise suits him to the ground. Well, there I hear what you have done so well, so quickly, upon the instantaneous spur of the moment. I tell our mutual friend you take the bally bun, by Jove! It was splendid. I come to tell you so.'

'Umm!'

The frogs were busy in the ditches, and the moon slid to her setting. Some happy servant had gone out to commune with the night and to beat upon a drum. Kim's next sentence was in the vernacular.

'How didst thou follow us?'

'Oah. Thatt was nothing. I know from our mutual friend you go to Saharunpore. So I come on. Red lamas are not inconspicuous persons. I buy myself my drug-box, and I am very good doctor really. I go to Akrola by the Ford, and hear all about you, and I talk here and talk there. All the common people know what you do. I know when the hospitable old lady sent the *dooli*. They have great recollections of the old lama's visits here. I know old ladies cannot keep their hands from medicines. So I am a doctor, and—you hear my talk? *I* think it is verree good. My word, Mister O'Hara, they know about you and the lama for fifty miles—the common people. So I come. Do you mind?'

'Babuji,' said Kim, looking up at the broad, grinning face, 'I am a Sahib.'

'My dear Mister O'Hara——'

'And I hope to play the Great Game.'

'You are subordinate to me departmentally at present.'

'Then why talk like an ape in a tree? Men do not come after one from Simla and change their dress, for the sake of a few sweet words. I am not a child. Talk Hindi and let us get to the yolk of the egg. Thou

art here—speaking not one word of truth in ten. Why art thou here?
Give a straight answer.'

'That is so verree disconcerting of the European, Mister O'Hara.
You should know a heap better at your time of life.'

'But I want to know,' said Kim, laughing. 'If it is the Game, I may
help. How can I do anything if you *bukh* (babble) all round the shop.'

Hurree Babu reached for the pipe, and sucked it till it guggled again.

'Now I will speak vernacular. You sit tight, Mister O'Hara. . . . . .
It concerns the pedigree of a white stallion.'

'Still? That was finished long ago.'

'When every one is dead the Great Game is finished. Not before.
Listen to me till the end. There were Five Kings who prepared a sudden war three years ago, when thou wast given the stallion's pedigree
by Mahbub Ali. Upon them, because of that news, and ere they were
ready, fell our Army.'

'Ay—eight thousand men with guns. I remember that night.'

'But the war was not pushed. That is the Government custom.
The troops were recalled because the Government believed the Five
Kings were cowed; and it is not cheap to feed men among the high
Passes. Hilás and Bunár—Rajahs with guns—undertook for a price
to guard the passes against all coming from the North. They
protested both fear and friendship.' He broke off with a giggle into
English: 'Of course, I tell you this unoffeecially to elucidate political
situation, Mister O'Hara. Offeecially, I am debarred from criticising
any action of superior. Now I go on.—This pleased the Government,
anxious to avoid expense, and a bond was made for so many rupees
a month that Hilás and Bunár should guard the Passes as soon as the
State's troops were withdrawn. At that time—it was after we two
met—I, who had been selling tea in Leh,[5] became a clerk of accounts
in the Army. When the troops were withdrawn, I was left behind to
pay the coolies who made new roads in the Hills. This road-making
was part of the bond between Bunár, Hilás, and the Government.'

'So; and then?'

'I tell you, it was jolly beastly cold up there too, after summer,' said
Hurree Babu confidentially. 'I was afraid these Bunár men would cut
my throat every night for thee pay-chest. My native sepoy-guard, they
laughed at me! By Jove! I was such a fearful man. Nevar mind thatt. I go

---

[5]Traditionally a place of peaceful coexistence between Buddhists and Muslims, Leh
stood in a strategically important position in what is now Kashmir. In 1889 and the
early 90s, British officer and explorer Francis Younghusband and his Russian counterpart, Captain Bronislav Gromchevsky, maneuvered for influence in this area on behalf
of their respective governments. Hurree has been working in the key region for the
Great Game.

on colloquially. . . . I send word many times that these two Kings were sold to the North; and Mahbub Ali, who was yet farther north, amply confirmed it. Nothing was done. Only my feet were frozen, and a toe dropped off. I sent word that the roads for which I was paying money to the diggers were being made for the feet of strangers and enemies.'

'For?'

'For the Russians. The thing was an open jest among the coolies. Then I was called down to tell what I knew by speech of tongue. Mahbub came South too. See the end! Over the Passes this year after snow-melting'—he shivered afresh—'come two strangers under cover of shooting wild goats. They bear guns, but they bear also chains and levels and compasses.'

'Oho! The thing gets clearer.'

'They are well received by Hilás and Bunár. They make great promises; they speak as the mouthpiece of a Kaisar with gifts. Up the valleys, down the valleys go they, saying, "Here is a place to build a breastwork; here can ye pitch a fort. Here can ye hold the road against an army"—the very roads for which I paid out the rupees monthly. The Government knows, but does nothing. The three other Kings, who were *not* paid for guarding the passes, tell them by runner of the bad faith of Bunár and Hilás. When all the evil is done, look you—when these two strangers with the levels and the compasses make the Five Kings to believe that a great army will sweep the Passes to-morrow or the next day—Hill-people are all fools—comes the order to me, Hurree Babu, "Go North and see what those strangers do." I say to Creighton Sahib, "This is not a lawsuit, that we go about to collect evidence."' He returned to his English with a jerk: '"By Jove," I said, "why the dooce do you not issue demi-offeecial orders to some brave man to poison them, for an example? It is, if you permit the observation, most reprehensible laxity on your part." And Colonel Creighton, he laughed at me! It is all your beastly English pride. You think no one dare conspire! That is all tommy-rott.'

Kim smoked slowly, revolving the business, so far as he understood it, in his quick mind.

'Then thou goest forth to follow the strangers?'

'No; to meet them. They are coming in to Simla to send down their horns and heads to be dressed at Calcutta. They are exclusively sporting gentlemen, and they are allowed special faceelities by the Government. Of course, we always do that. It is our British pride.'

'Then what is to fear from them?'

'By Jove, they are not black people. I can do all sorts of things with black people, of course. They are Russians, and highly unscrupulous people. I—I do not want to consort with them without a witness.'

'Will they kill thee?'

'Oah, that is nothing. I am good enough Herbert Spencerian, I trust, to meet little thing like death, which is all in my fate, you know. But—but they may beat me.'

'Why?'

Hurree Babu snapped his fingers with irritation. 'Of *course* I shall affeeliate myself to their camp in supernumerary capacity as perhaps interpreter, or person mentally impotent and hungree, or some such thing. And then I must pick up what I can, I suppose. That is as easy for me as playing Mister Doctor to the old lady. Onlee—onlee—you see, Mister O'Hara, I am unfortunately Asiatic, which is serious detriment in some respects. And *all*so I am Bengali—a fearful man.'

'God made the Hare and the Bengali. What shame?' said Kim, quoting the proverb.

'It was process of Evolution, *I* think, from Primal Necessity, but the fact remains in all its *cui bono*.[6] I am, oh, awfully fearful!—I remember once they wanted to cut off my head on the road to Lhassa. (No, I have never reached to Lhassa.) I sat down and cried, Mister O'Hara, anticipating Chinese tortures. I do not suppose these two gentlemen will torture me, but I like to provide for possible contingency with European assistance in emergency.' He coughed and spat out the cardamoms. 'It is purely unoffeecial indent, to which you can say "No, Babu." If you have no pressing engagement with your old man—perhaps you might divert him; perhaps I can seduce his fancies—I should like you to keep in Departmental touch with me till I find those sporting coves. I have great opeenion of you since I met my friend at Delhi. And also I will embody your name in my offeecial report when matter is finally adjudicated. It will be a great feather in your cap. That is why I come really.'

'Humph! The end of the tale, I think, is true; but what of the forepart?'

'About the Five Kings? Oah! there is ever so much truth in it. A lots more than you would suppose,' said Hurree earnestly. 'You come—eh? I go from here straight into the Doon. It is verree verdant and painted meads. I shall go to Mussoorie—to good old Munsoorie Pahar, as the gentlemen and ladies say. Then by Rampur into Chini. That is the only way they can come. I do not like waiting in the cold, but we must wait for them. I want to walk with them to Simla. You see, one Russian is a Frenchman, and I know my French pretty well. I have friends in Chandernagore.'

---

[6]Latin: Literally, "To whom the good?"—"For whose benefit?" Hurree Babu's point seems clear, though his use of Latin is grammatically unorthodox.

'*He* would certainly rejoice to see the Hills again,' said Kim meditatively. 'All his speech these ten days past has been of little else. If we go together——'

'Oah! We can be quite strangers on the road, if your lama prefers. I shall just be four or five miles ahead. There is no hurry for Hurree. That is an Europe pun, ha! ha! and you come after. There is plenty of time; they will plot and survey and map of course. I shall go tomorrow, and you the next day, if you choose. Eh? You go think on it till morning. By Jove, it is near morning now.' He yawned ponderously, and with never a civil word lumbered off to his sleeping-place. But Kim slept little, and his thoughts ran in Hindustanee:

'Well is the Game called great! I was four days a scullion at Quetta, waiting on the wife of the man whose book I stole. And that was part of the Great Game! From the South—God knows how far—came up the Mahratta, playing the Great Game in fear of his life. Now I shall go far and far into the North playing the Great Game. Truly, it runs like a shuttle throughout all Hind. And my share and my joy'—he smiled to the darkness—'I owe to the lama here. Also to Mahbub Ali—also to Creighton Sahib, but chiefly to the Holy One. He is right—a great and a wonderful world—and I am Kim—Kim—Kim—alone—one person—in the middle of it all. But I will see these strangers with their levels and chains . . .'

'What was the upshot of last night's babble?' said the lama, after his orisons.

'There came a strolling seller of drugs—a hanger-on of the Sahiba's. Him I abolished by arguments and prayers, proving that our charms are worthier than his coloured waters.'

'Alas! my charms. Is the virtuous woman still bent upon a new one?'

'Very strictly.'

'Then it must be written, or she will deafen me with her clamour.' He fumbled at his pencase.

'In the Plains,' said Kim, 'are always too many people. In the Hills, as I understand, there are fewer.'

'Oh! the Hills, and the snow upon the Hills.' The lama tore off a tiny square of paper fit to go in an amulet. 'But what dost thou know of the Hills?'

'They are very close.' Kim thrust open the door and looked at the long, peaceful line of the Himalayas flushed in morning-gold. 'Except in the dress of a Sahib, I have never set foot among them.'

The lama snuffed the wind wistfully.

'If we go north,'—Kim put the question to the waking sunrise,—'would not much mid-day heat be avoided by walking among the lower hills at least? . . . Is the charm made, Holy One?'

'I have written the names of seven silly devils—not one of whom is worth a grain of dust in the eye. Thus do foolish women drag us from the Way!'

Hurree Babu came out from behind the dovecot, washing his teeth with ostentatious ritual. Full-fleshed, heavy-haunched, bull-necked, and deep-voiced, he did not look like 'a fearful man.' Kim signed almost imperceptibly that matters were in good train, and when the morning toilet was over Hurree Babu, in flowery speech, came to do honour to the lama. They ate, of course, apart, and afterwards the old lady, more or less veiled behind a window, returned to the vital business of green-mango colics in the young. The lama's knowledge of medicine was of course sympathetic only. He believed that the dung of a black horse, mixed with sulphur, and carried in a snake-skin, was a sound remedy for cholera; but the symbolism interested him far more than the science. Hurree Babu deferred to these views with enchanting politeness, so that the lama called him a courteous physician. Hurree Babu replied that he was no more than an inexpert dabbler in the mysteries; but at least—he thanked the Gods therefor—he knew when he sat in the presence of a master. He himself had been taught by the Sahibs, who do not consider expense, in the lordly halls of Calcutta; but, as he was ever first to acknowledge, there lay a wisdom behind earthly wisdom—the high and lonely lore of meditation. Kim looked on with envy. The Hurree Babu of his knowledge—oily, effusive, and nervous—was gone; gone too was the brazen drug-vendor of overnight. There remained—polished, polite, attentive—a sober, learned son of experience and adversity, gathering wisdom from the lama's lips. The old lady confided to Kim that these rare levels were beyond her. She liked charms with plenty of ink that one could wash off in water, swallow, and be done with. Else what was the use of the Gods? She liked men and women, and she spoke of them—of kinglets she had known in the past; of her own youth and beauty; of the depredations of leopards and the eccentricities of love Asiatic; of the incidence of taxation, rack-renting, funeral ceremonies, her son-in-law (this by allusion, easy to be followed), the care of the young, and the age's lack of decency. And Kim, as interested in the life of this world as she soon to leave it, squatted with his feet under the hem of his robe, drinking all in, while the lama demolished one after another every theory of body-curing put forward by Hurree Babu.

At noon the Babu strapped up his brass-bound drug-box, took his patent-leather shoes of ceremony in one hand, a gay blue and white umbrella in the other, and set off northwards to the Doon, where, he said, he was in demand among the lesser kings of those parts.

'We will go in the cool of the evening, *chela*,' said the lama. 'That doctor, learned in physic and courtesy, affirms that the people among these lower hills are devout, generous, and much in need of a teacher. In a very short time—so says the *hakim*—we come to cool air and the smell of pines.'

'Ye go to the Hills. And by Kulu-road? Oh, thrice happy!' shrilled the old lady. 'But that I am a little pressed with the care of the homestead I would take palanquin . . . but that would be shameless, and my reputation would be cracked. Ho! Ho! I know the road—every march of the road I know. Ye will find charity throughout—it is not denied to the well-looking. I will give orders for provision. A servant to set you forth upon your journey? No. . . . Then I will at least cook ye good food.'

'What a woman is the Sahiba!' said the white-bearded Oorya, when a tumult rose by the kitchen quarters. 'She has never forgotten a friend: she has never forgotten an enemy in all her years. And her cookery—wah!' He rubbed his slim stomach.

There were cakes, there were sweetmeats, there was cold fowl stewed to rags with rice and prunes—enough to burden Kim like a mule.

'I am old and useless,' she said. 'None now love me—and none respect—but there are few to compare with me when I call on the Gods and squat to my cooking-pots. Come again, O people of good will. Holy One and disciple, come again. The room is always prepared; the welcome is always ready. . . . See the women do follow thy *chela* too openly. *I* know the women of Kulu. Take heed, *chela*, lest he run away when he smells his Hills again. . . . Hai! Do not tilt the rice-bag upside down. . . . Bless the household, Holy One, and forgive thy servant her stupidities.'

She wiped her red old eyes on a corner of her veil, and clucked throatily.

'Women talk,' said the lama at last, 'but that is a woman's infirmity. I gave her a charm. She is upon the Wheel and wholly given over to the shows of this life, but none the less, *chela*, she is virtuous, kindly, hospitable—of a whole and zealous heart. Who shall say she does not acquire merit?'

'Not I, Holy One,' said Kim, reslinging the bountiful provision on his shoulders. 'In my mind—behind my eyes—I have tried to picture such an one altogether freed from the Wheel—desiring nothing, causing nothing—a nun, as it were.'

'And, O imp?' The lama almost laughed aloud.

'I cannot make the picture.'

'Nor I. But there are many, many millions of lives before her. She will get wisdom a little, it may be, in each one.'

'And will she forget how to make stews with saffron upon that road?'

'Thy mind is set on things unworthy. But she has skill. I am refreshed all over. When we reach the lower hills I shall be yet stronger. The *hakim* spoke truly to me this morn when he said a breath from the snows blows away twenty years from the life of a man. We will go up into the Hills—the high hills—up to the sound of snow-water and the sound of the trees—for a little while. The *hakim* said that at any time we may return to the Plains, for we do no more than skirt the pleasant places. The *hakim* is full of learning; but he is in no way proud. I spoke to him—when thou wast talking to the Sahiba—of a certain dizziness that lays hold upon the back of my neck in the night, and he said it rose from excessive heat—to be cured by cool air. Upon consideration, I marvelled that I had not thought of such a simple remedy.'

'Didst thou tell him of thy Search?' said Kim, a little jealously. He preferred to sway the lama by his own speech—not through the wiles of Hurree Babu.

'Assuredly. I told him of my dream, and of the manner by which I had acquired merit by causing thee to be taught wisdom.'

'Thou didst not say I was a Sahib?'

'What need? I have told thee many times we be but two souls seeking escape. He said—and he is just herein—that the River of Healing will break forth even as I dreamed—at my feet if need be. Having found the Way, seest thou, that shall free me from the Wheel, need I trouble to find a way about the mere fields of earth—which are illusion? That were senseless. I have my dreams, night upon night repeated; I have the *Jâtaka*; and I have thee, Friend of all the World. It was written in thy horoscope that a Red Bull on a green field—I have not forgotten—should bring thee to honour. Who but I saw that prophecy accomplished? Indeed, I was the instrument. Thou shalt find me my River, being in return the instrument. The Search is sure!'

He set his ivory-yellow face, serene and untroubled, towards the beckoning Hills; his shadow shouldering far before him in the dust.

CHAPTER XIII

Who hath desired the Sea—the immense and contemptuous
surges?
The shudder, the stumble, the swerve ere the star-stabbing
bowsprit emerges—
The orderly clouds of the trade and the ridged roaring
sapphire thereunder—
Unheralded cliff-lurking flaws and the head-sails' low-
volleying thunder?

His Sea in no wonder the same—his Sea and the same in
 each wonder
    His Sea that his being fulfils?
So and no otherwise—so and no otherwise hillmen desire
 their Hills!¹

'WHO goes to the Hills goes to his mother.'

They had crossed the Sewaliks and the half-tropical Doon, left Mussoorie[2] behind them, and headed north along the narrow hill-roads. Day after day they struck deeper into the huddled mountains, and day after day Kim watched the lama return to a man's strength. Among the terraces of the Doon he had leaned on the boy's shoulder, ready to profit by wayside halts. Under the great ramp to Mussoorie he drew himself together as an old hunter faces a well-remembered bank, and where he should have sunk exhausted swung his long draperies about him, drew a deep double-lungful of the diamond air, and walked as only a hillman can. Kim, plains-bred and plains-fed, sweated and panted astonished. 'This is *my* country,' said the lama. 'Beside Such-zen, this is flatter than a rice-field;' and with steady, driving strokes from the loins he strode upwards. But it was on the steep downhill marches, three thousand feet in three hours, that he went utterly away from Kim, whose back ached with holding back, and whose big toe was nigh cut off by his grass sandal-string. Through the speckled shadow of the great deodar-forests; through oak feathered and plumed with ferns; birch, ilex, rhododendron, and pine, out on to the bare hillsides' slippery sunburnt grass, and back into the woodlands' coolth again, till oak gave way to bamboo and palm of the valley, he swung untiring.

Glancing back in the twilight at the huge ridges behind him and the faint, thin line of the road whereby they had come, he would lay out, with a hillman's generous breadth of vision, fresh marches for the morrow; or, halting in the neck of some uplifted pass that gave on Spiti and Kulu, would stretch out his hands yearningly towards the high snows of the horizon. In the dawns they flared windy-red above

---

[1] Like the previous chapter's epigraph, these lines enter *The Five Nations* in altered form. Again, the reference to fulfillment in line 6 disappears, now replaced by "His Sea as she rages or stills." The original *McClure's* chapter's epigraph read as follows: "His own greediness killed the tiger; but the hunter got the Government reward just the same.— Native Proverb."

[2] Colonial hill station in the high ranges above the broad Doon Valley, which stretches between the Siwalik Mountains and the Himalayas. Kim and the lama are moving through a landscape of stunning contrasts and great religious significance. In stark opposition to the fertile Kulu Valley, the Spiti Valley, soon to be mentioned, is famously remote, wild territory. Kedarnath and Badrinath, depicted here as mountain kings, are also sacred sites of pilgrimage.

stark blue, as Kedarnath and Badrinath—kings of that wilderness—took the first sunlight. All day long they lay like molten silver under the sun, and at evening put on their jewels again. At first they breathed temperately upon the travellers, winds good to meet when one crawled over some gigantic hog-back; but in a few days, at a height of nine or ten thousand feet, those breezes bit; and Kim kindly allowed a village of hillmen to acquire merit by giving him a rough blanket-coat. The lama was mildly surprised that any one should object to the knife-edged breezes which had cut the years off his shoulders.

'These are but the lower hills, *chela*. There is no cold till we come to the true Hills.'

'Air and water are good, and the people are devout enough, but the food is very bad,' Kim growled; 'and we walk as though we were mad—or English. It freezes at night, too.'

'A little, maybe; but only enough to make old bones rejoice in the sun. We must not always delight in the soft beds and rich food.'

'We might at the least keep to the road.'

Kim had all a plains-man's affection for the well-trodden track, not six feet wide, that snaked among the mountains; but the lama, being Tibetan, could not refrain from short cuts over spurs and the rims of gravel-strewn slopes. As he explained to his limping disciple, a man bred among mountains can prophesy the course of a mountain-road, and though low-lying clouds might be a hindrance to a short-cutting stranger, they made no earthly difference to a thoughtful man. Thus, after long hours of what would be reckoned very fair mountaineering in civilised countries, they would pant over a saddle-back, sidle past a few landslips, and drop through forest at an angle of forty-five on to the road again. Along their track lay the villages of the hill-folk—mud and earth huts, timbers now and then rudely carved with an axe—clinging like swallows' nests against the steeps, huddled on tiny flats half-way down a three-thousand-foot glissade; jammed into a corner between cliffs that funnelled and focused every wandering blast; or, for the sake of summer pasture, cowering down on a neck that in winter would be ten feet deep in snow. And the people—the sallow, greasy, duffle-clad people, with short bare legs and faces almost Esquimaux—would flock out and adore. The Plains—kindly and gentle—had treated the lama as a holy man among holy men. But the Hills worshipped him as one in the confidence of all the devils. Theirs was an almost obliterated Buddhism, overlaid with a nature-worship fantastic as their own landscapes, elaborate as the terracing of their tiny fields; but they recognised the big hat, the clicking rosary, and the rare Chinese texts for great authority; and they respected the man under the hat.

'We saw thee come down over the black Breasts of Eua,' said a Betah who gave them cheese, sour milk, and stone-hard bread one evening. 'We do not use that often—except when calving cows stray in summer. There is a sudden wind among those stones that casts men down on the stillest day. But what should such folk care for the Devil of Eua!'

Then did Kim, aching in every fibre, dizzy with looking down, footsore with cramping desperate toes into inadequate crannies, take joy in the day's march—such joy as a boy of St. Xavier's who had won the quarter-mile on the flat might take in the praises of his friends. The hills sweated the *ghi* and sugar suet off his bones; the dry air, taken sobbingly at the head of cruel passes, firmed and built out his upper ribs; and the tilted levels put new hard muscles into calf and thigh.

They meditated often on the Wheel of Life—the more so since, as the lama said, they were freed from its visible temptations. Except the gray eagle and an occasional far-seen bear grubbing and rooting on the hillside, the vision of a furious painted leopard met at dawn in a still valley devouring a goat, and now and again a bright-coloured bird, they were alone with the winds and the grass singing under the wind. The women of the smoky huts over whose roofs the two walked as they descended the mountains, were unlovely and unclean, wives of many husbands, and afflicted with goitre. The men were wood-cutters when they were not farmers—meek, and of an incredible simplicity. But that suitable discourse might not fail, Fate sent them, overtaking and overtaken upon the road, the courteous Dacca physician, who paid for his food in ointments good for goitre and councils that restore peace between men and women. He seemed to know these hills as well as he knew the hill dialects, and gave the lama the lie of the land towards Ladakh and Tibet. He said they could return to the Plains at any moment. Meantime, for such as loved mountains, yonder road might amuse. This was not all revealed in a breath, but at evening encounters on the stone threshing-floors, when, patients disposed of, the doctor would smoke and the lama snuff, while Kim watched the wee cows grazing on the house-tops, or threw his soul after his eye across the deep blue gulfs between range and range. And there were talks apart in the dark woods, when the doctor would seek herbs, and Kim, as budding physician, must accompany him.

'You see, Mister O'Hara, I do not know what the deuce-an'-all I shall do when I find our sporting friends; but if you will kindly keep within sight of my umbrella, which is fine fixed point for cadastral survey, I feel much better.'

Kim looked out across the jungle of peaks. 'This is not my country, *hakim*. Easier, I think, to find one louse in a bearskin.'

'Oah, thatt is my strong points. There is no hurry for Hurree. They were at Leh not so long ago. They said they had come down from the Kara Korum with their heads and horns and all. I am onlee afraid they will have sent back all their letters and compromising things from Leh into Russian territoree. Of course they will walk away as far to the East as possible—just to show that they were never among the Western States. You do not know the Hills?' He scratched with a twig on the earth. 'Look! They should have come in by Srinagar or Abbottabad. *Thatt* is their short road—down the river by Bunji and Astor. But they have made mischief in the West. So'—he drew a furrow from left to right—'they march and they march away East to Leh (ah! it is cold there), and down the Indus to Han-lé (I know that road), and then down, you see, to Bushahr and Chini valley. That is ascertained by process of elimination, and also by asking questions from people that I cure so well. Our friends have been a long time playing about and producing impressions. So they are well known from far off. You will see me catch them somewhere in Chini valley. Please keep your eye on the umbrella.'

It nodded like a wind-blown harebell down the valleys and round the mountain sides, and in due time the lama and Kim, who steered by compass, would overhaul it, vending ointments and powders at eventide. 'We came by such and such a way!' The lama would throw a careless finger backward at the ridges, and the umbrella would expend itself in compliments.

They crossed a snowy pass in cold moonlight, when the lama, mildly chaffing Kim, went through up to his knees, like a Bactrian camel—the snow-bred, shag-haired sort that come into the Kashmir Serai. They dipped across beds of light snow and snow-powdered shale, where they took refuge from a gale in a camp of Tibetans hurrying down tiny sheep, each laden with a bag of borax. They came out upon grassy shoulders still snow-speckled, and through forest, to grass anew. For all their marchings, Kedarnath and Badrinath were not impressed; and it was only after days of travel that Kim, uplifted upon some insignificant ten-thousand-foot hummock, could see that a shoulder-knot or horn of the two great lords had—ever so slightly—changed outline.

At last they entered a world within a world—a valley of leagues where the high hills were fashioned of the mere rubble and refuse from off the knees of the mountains. Here one day's march carried them no farther, it seemed, than a dreamer's clogged pace bears him in a nightmare. They skirted a shoulder painfully for hours, and, behold, it was but an outlying boss in an outlying buttress of the main pile! A rounded meadow revealed itself, when they had reached it, for a vast tableland running far into the valley. Three days later, it was a dim fold in the earth to southward.

'Surely the Gods live here,' said Kim, beaten down by the silence and the appalling sweep and dispersal of the cloud-shadows after rain. 'This is no place for men!'

'Long and long ago,' said the lama, as to himself, 'it was asked of the Lord whether the world were everlasting. To this the Excellent One returned no answer. . . . When I was in Ceylon, a wise Seeker confirmed that from the gospel which is written in Pali. Certainly, since we know the way to Freedom, the question were unprofitable, but—look, and know illusion, *chela!* These are the true Hills! They are like my hills by Such-zen. Never were such hills!'

Above them, still enormously above them, earth towered away towards the snow-line, where from east to west across hundreds of miles, ruled as with a ruler, the last of the bold birches stopped. Above that, in scarps and blocks upheaved, the rocks strove to fight their heads above the white smother. Above these again, changeless since the world's beginning, but changing to every mood of sun and cloud, lay out the eternal snow. They could see blots and blurs on its face where storm and wandering wullie-wa got up to dance. Below them, as they stood, the forest slid away in a sheet of blue-green for mile upon mile; below the forest was a village in its sprinkle of ter-raced fields and steep grazing-grounds; below the village they knew, though a thunderstorm worried and growled there for the moment, a pitch of twelve or fifteen hundred feet gave to the moist valley where the streams gather that are the mothers of young Sutluj.

As usual, the lama had led Kim by cow-track and byroad, far from the main route along which Hurree Babu, that 'fearful man,' had bucketed three days before through a storm to which nine Englishmen out of ten would have given full right of way. Hurree was no game-shot,—the snick of a trigger made him change colour,—but, as he him-self would have said, he was 'fairly effeecient stalker,' and he had raked the huge valley with a pair of cheap binoculars to some purpose. Moreover, the white of worn canvas tents against green carries far. Hurree Babu had seen all he wanted to see when he sat on the thresh-ing-floor of Ziglaur, twenty miles away as the eagle flies, and forty by road—that is to say, two small dots which one day were just below the snow-line, and the next had moved downward perhaps six inches on the hillside. Once cleaned out and set to the work, his fat bare legs could cover a surprising amount of ground, and this was the reason why, while Kim and the lama lay in a leaky hut at Ziglaur till the storm should be overpassed, an oily, wet, but always smiling Bengali, talking the best of English with the vilest of phrases, was ingratiating himself with two sodden and rather rheumatic foreigners. He had arrived, revolving many wild schemes, on the heels of a thunderstorm which had split a pine over against their camp, and so convinced a dozen or two forcibly impressed baggage-coolies the day was inauspicious for farther travel that with one accord they had thrown down their loads and jibbed. They were subjects of a Hill-Rajah who farmed out their services, as is the custom, for his private gain; and, to add to their personal distresses, the strange Sahibs had already threatened them with rifles. The most of them knew rifles and Sahibs of old: they were trackers and *shikarris* of the Northern valleys, keen after bear and wild goat; but they had never been thus treated in their lives. So the forest took them to her bosom, and, for all oaths and clamour, refused to restore. There was no need to feign madness or—the Babu had thought of another means of securing a welcome. He wrung out his wet clothes, slipped on his patent-leather shoes, opened the blue and white umbrella, and with mincing gait and a heart beating against his tonsils appeared as 'agent for His Royal Highness, the Rajah of Rampur, gentlemen. What can I do for you, please?'

The gentlemen were delighted. One was visibly French, the other Russian, but they spoke English not much inferior to the Babu's. They begged his kind offices. Their native servants had gone sick at Leh. They had hurried on because they were anxious to bring the spoils of the chase to Simla ere the skins grew moth-eaten. They bore a general letter of introduction (the Babu salaamed to it orientally) to all Government officials. No, they had not met any other shooting-parties *en route*. They did for themselves. They had plenty of supplies. They only wished to push on as soon as might be. At this he waylaid a cowering hillman among the trees, and after three minutes' talk and a little silver (one cannot be economical upon State service, though Hurree's heart bled at the waste) the eleven coolies and the three hangers-on reappeared. At least the Babu would be a witness to oppression.

'My royal master, he will be much annoyed, but these people are onlee common people and grossly ignorant. If your honours will kindly overlook unfortunate affair, I shall be much pleased. In a little while rain will stop and we can then proceed. You have been shooting, eh? That is fine performance!'

He skipped nimbly from one *kilta* to the next, making pretence to adjust each conical basket. The Englishman is not, as a rule, familiar with the Asiatic, but he would not strike across the wrist a kindly Babu who had accidentally upset a *kilta* with a red oilskin top. On the other hand, he would not press drink upon a Babu were he never so friendly, nor would he invite him to meat. The strangers did all these things, and asked many questions,—about women mostly,—to which Hurree returned gay and unstudied answers. They gave him a glass of whitish fluid like to gin, and then more; and in a little time his gravity departed from him. He became thickly treasonous, and spoke in terms of sweeping indecency of a Government which had forced upon him a white man's education and neglected to supply him with a white man's salary. He babbled tales of oppression and wrong till the tears ran down his cheeks for the miseries of his land. Then he staggered off, singing love-songs of Lower Bengal, and collapsed upon a wet tree-trunk. Never was so unfortunate a product of English rule in India more unhappily thrust upon aliens.

'They are all just of that pattern,' said one sportsman to the other in French. 'When we get into India proper thou wilt see. I should like to visit his Rajah. One might speak the good word there. It is possible that he has heard of us and wishes to signify his goodwill.'

'We have not time. We must get into Simla as soon as may be,' his companion replied. 'For my own part, I wish our reports had been sent back from Hilás, or even Leh.'

'The English post is better and safer. Remember we are given all facilities—and name of God!—they give them to us too! Is it unbelievable stupidity?'

'It is pride—pride that deserves and will receive punishment.'

'Yes! To fight a fellow-Continental in our game is something. There is a risk attached, but these people—bah! It is too easy.'

'Pride—all pride, my friend.'

'Now what the deuce is good of Chandernagore being so close to Calcutta and all,' said Hurree, snoring open-mouthed on the sodden moss, 'if I cannot understand their French. They talk so par*ticu*larly fast! It would have been much better to cut their beastly throats.'

When he presented himself again he was racked with a headache—penitent, and volubly afraid that in his drunkenness he might have been indiscreet. He loved the British Government—it was the source of all prosperity and honour, and his master at Rampur held the very same opinion. Upon this the men began to deride him and to quote past words, till step by step, with deprecating smirks, oily grins, and leers of infinite cunning, the poor Babu was beaten out of his defences and forced to speak—truth. When Lurgan was told the tale later, he mourned aloud that he could not have been in the place of the stubborn, inattentive coolies, who with grass mats over their heads and the raindrops puddling in their footprints, waited on the weather. All the Sahibs of their acquaintance—rough-clad men joyously returning year after year to their chosen gullies—had servants and cooks and orderlies, very often hillmen. These Sahibs travelled without any retinue.

Therefore they were poor Sahibs, and ignorant; for no Sahib in his senses would follow a Bengali's advice. But the Bengali, appearing from somewhere, had given them money, and would make shift with their dialect. Used to comprehensive ill-treatment from their own colour, they suspected a trap somewhere, and stood by to run if occasion offered.

Then through the new-washed air, steaming with delicious earth-smells, the Babu led the way down the slopes—walking ahead of the coolies in pride; walking behind the foreigners in humility. His thoughts were many and various. The least of them would have interested his companions beyond words. But he was an agreeable guide, ever keen to point out the beauties of his royal master's domain. He peopled the hills with anything they had a mind to slay—thar, ibex, or markhor, and bears by Elisha's allowance.[3] He discoursed of botany and ethnology with unimpeachable inaccuracy, and his store of local legends—he had been a trusted agent of the State for fifteen years, remember—was inexhaustible.

'Decidedly this fellow is an original,' said the taller of the two foreigners. 'He is like the nightmare of a Viennese courier.'

'He represents *in petto* India in transition—the monstrous hybridism of East and West,' the Russian replied. 'It is *we* who can deal with Orientals.'

'He has lost his own country and has not acquired any other. But he has a most complete hatred of his conquerors. Listen. He confides to me last night,' etc.

Under the striped umbrella Hurree Babu was straining ear and brain to follow the quick-poured French, and keeping both eyes on a *kilta* full of maps and documents—an extra large one with a double red oilskin cover. He did not wish to steal anything. He only desired to know what to steal, and, incidentally, how to get away when he had stolen it. He thanked all the Gods of Hindustan, and Herbert Spencer, that there remained some valuables to steal.

On the second day the road rose steeply to a grass spur above the forest; and it was here, about sunset, that they came across an aged lama—but they called him a bonze—sitting cross-legged above a mysterious chart held down by stones, which he was explaining to a young man, evidently a neophyte, of singular, though unwashen, beauty. The striped umbrella had been sighted half a march away, and Kim had suggested a halt till it came up to them.

'Ha!' said Hurree Babu, resourceful as Puss-in-Boots. 'That is eminent local holy man. Probably subject of my royal master.'

'What is he doing? It is very curious.'

'He is expounding holy picture—*all* hand-worked.'

[3]Thar, ibex, and markhor are types of goats. See 2 Kings 2.23–24: "And there came forth two she bears out of the wood."

The two men stood bare-headed in the wash of the afternoon sun-light low across the gold-coloured grass. The sullen coolies, glad of the check, halted and slid down their loads.

'Look!' said the Frenchman. 'It is like a picture for the birth of a religion—the first teacher and the first disciple. Is he a Buddhist?'

'Of some debased kind,' the other answered. 'There are no true Buddhists among the Hills. But look at the folds of the drapery. Look at his eyes—how insolent! Why does this make one feel that we are so young a people?' The speaker struck passionately at a tall weed. 'We have nowhere left our mark yet. Nowhere! *That*, do you understand, is what disquiets me.' He scowled at the placid face, and the monu-mental calm of the pose.

'Have patience. We shall make your mark together—we and you young people. Meantime, draw his picture.'

The Babu advanced loftily; his back out of all keeping with his deferential speech, or his wink towards Kim.

'Holy One, these be Sahibs. My medicines cured one of a flux, and I go into Simla to oversee his recovery. They wish to see thy picture——'

'To heal the sick is always good. This is the Wheel of Life,' said the lama, 'the same I showed thee in the hut at Ziglaur when the rain fell.'

'And to hear thee expound it.'

The lama's eyes lighted at the prospect of new listeners. 'To ex-pound the Most Excellent Way is good. Have they any knowledge of Hindi, such as had the Keeper of Images?'

'A little, maybe.'

Hereat, simply as a child engrossed with a new game, the lama threw back his head and began the full-throated invocation of the Doctor of Divinity ere he opens the full doctrine. The strangers leaned on their alpenstocks and listened. Kim, squatting humbly, watched the red sun-light on their faces, and the blend and parting of their long shadows. They wore un-English leggings and curious girt-in belts that reminded him hazily of the pictures in a book at St. Xavier's library: *The Adventures of a Young Naturalist in Mexico* was its name. Yes, they looked very like the wonderful M. Sumichrast of that tale,[4] and very unlike the 'highly unscrupulous folk' of Hurree Babu's imagining. The coolies, earth-coloured and mute, crouched reverently some twenty or thirty yards away, and the Babu, the slack of his thin gear snapping like a marking-flag in the chill breeze, stood by with an air of happy proprietorship.

'These are the men,' Hurree whispered, as the ritual went on and the two whites followed the grass blade sweeping from Hell to

[4]Translated, edited, and adapted from the French of Lucien Biart by Parker Gillmore, *Adventures* appeared in 1871. Swiss naturalist François Sumichrast (1828–82), who also wrote on the natural history of Mexico, appears in the book's illustrations.

Heaven and back again. 'All their books are in the large *kilta* with the reddish top,—books and reports and maps,—and I have seen a King's letter that either Hilás or Bunár has written. They guard it most carefully. They have sent nothing back from Hilás or Leh. That is sure.'

'Who is with them?'

'Only the *beegar*-coolies. They have no servants. They are so close they cook their own food.'

'But what am I to do?'

'Wait and see. Only if any chance comes to me thou wilt know where to seek for the papers.'

'This were better in Mahbub Ali's hands than a Bengali's,' said Kim scornfully.

'There are more ways of getting to a sweetheart than butting down a wall.'

'See here the Hell appointed for avarice and greed. Flanked upon the one side by Desire and on the other by Weariness.' The lama warmed to his work, and one of the strangers sketched him in the quick-fading light.

'That is enough,' the man said at last brusquely. 'I cannot understand him, but I want that picture. He is a better artist than I. Ask him if he will sell it.'

'He says "No, sar,"' the Babu replied. The lama, of course, would no more have parted with his chart to a casual wayfarer than an archbishop would pawn the holy vessels of a cathedral. All Tibet is full of cheap reproductions of the Wheel; but the lama was an artist, as well as a wealthy abbot in his own place.

'Perhaps in three days, or four, or ten, if I perceive that the Sahib is a Seeker and of good understanding, I may myself draw him another. But *this* was used for the initiation of a novice. Tell him so, *hakim*.'

'He wishes it now—for money.'

The lama shook his head slowly and began to fold up the Wheel. The Russian, on his side, saw no more than an unclean old man haggling over a dirty piece of paper. He drew out a handful of rupees, and snatched half-jestingly at the chart, which tore in the lama's grip. A low murmur of horror went up from the coolies—some of whom were Spiti men and, by their lights, good Buddhists. The lama rose at the insult; his hand went to the heavy iron pencase that is the priest's weapon, and the Babu danced in agony.

'Now you see—you see why I wanted witnesses. They are highly unscrupulous people. Oh Sar! Sar! You must *not* hit holy man!'

'*Chela!* He has defiled the Written Word!'

It was too late. Before Kim could ward him off, the Russian struck the old man full on the face. Next instant he was rolling over and over down hill with Kim at his throat. The blow had waked every un-known Irish devil in the boy's blood, and the sudden fall of his enemy did the rest. The lama dropped to his knees, half-stunned; the coolies under their loads fled up the hill as fast as plainsmen run across the level. They had seen sacrilege unspeakable, and it behoved them to get away before the Gods and devils of the hills took vengeance. The Frenchman ran towards the lama, fumbling at his revolver with some notion of making him a hostage for his companion. A shower of cut-ting stones—hillmen are very straight shots—drove him away, and a coolie from Ao-chung snatched the lama into the stampede. All came about as swiftly as the sudden mountain-darkness.

'They have taken the baggage and all the guns,' yelled the French-man, firing blindly into the twilight.

'All right, Sar! All right! Don't shoot. I go to rescue,' and Hurree, pounding down the slope, cast himself bodily upon the delighted and astonished Kim, who was banging his breathless foe's head against a boulder.

'Go back to the coolies,' whispered the Babu in his ear. 'They have the baggage. The papers are in the *kilta* with the red top, but look through all. Take their papers, and specially the *murasla* (King's letter). Go! The other man comes!'

Kim tore uphill. A revolver-bullet rang on a rock by his side, and he cowered partridge-wise.

'If you shoot,' shouted Hurree, 'they will descend and annihilate us. I have rescued the gentleman, Sar. This is par*tic*ularly dangerous.'

'By Jove!' Kim was thinking hard in English. 'This is dam-tight place, but *I* think it is self-defence.' He felt in his bosom for Mahbub's gift, and uncertainly—save for a few practice shots in the Bikaner desert, he had never used the little gun—pulled trigger.

'What did I say, Sar!' The Babu seemed to be in tears. 'Come down here and assist to resuscitate. We are all up a tree, I tell you.'

The shots ceased. There was a sound of stumbling feet, and Kim hurried upward through the gloom, swearing like a cat—or a country-bred.

'Did they wound thee, *chela*?' called the lama above him.

'No. And thou?' He dived into a clump of stunted firs.

'Unhurt. Come away. We go with these folk to Shamlegh-under-the-Snow.'

'But not before we have done justice,' a voice cried. 'I have got the Sahibs' guns—all four. Let us go down.'

'He struck the Holy One—we saw it! Our cattle will be barren—our wives will cease to bear! The snows will slide upon us as we go home. . . . On top of all other oppression too!'

The little fir-clump filled with clamouring coolies—panic-stricken, and in their terror capable of anything. The man from Ao-chung clicked the breech-bolt of his gun impatiently, and made as to go down hill.

'Wait a little, Holy One; they cannot go far: wait till I return.'

'It is this person who has suffered wrong,' said the lama, his hand over his brow.

'For that very reason,' was the reply.

'If this person overlooks it, your hands are clean. Moreover, ye acquire merit by obedience.'

'Wait, and we will all go to Shamlegh together,' the man insisted.

For a moment, for just so long as it needs to stuff a cartridge into a breech-loader, the lama hesitated. Then he rose to his feet, and laid a finger on the man's shoulder.

'Hast thou heard? *I* say there shall be no killing—I who was Abbot of Such-zen. Is it any lust of thine to be re-born as a rat, or a snake under the eaves—a worm in the belly of the most mean beast? Is it thy wish to——'

The man from Ao-chung fell to his knees, for the voice boomed like a Tibetan devil-gong.

'Ai! ai!' cried the Spiti men. 'Do not curse us—do not curse him. It was but his zeal, Holy One! . . . Put down the rifle, fool!'

'Anger on anger! Evil on evil! There will be no killing. Let the priest-beaters go in bondage to their own acts. Just and sure is the Wheel, swerving not a hair! They will be born many times—in torment.' His head drooped, and he leaned heavily on Kim's shoulder.

'I have come near to great evil, *chela*,' he whispered in that dead hush under the pines. 'I was tempted to loose the bullet; and truly, in Tibet there would have been a heavy and a slow death for them. . . . He struck me across the face . . . upon the flesh . . .' He slid to the ground, breathing heavily, and Kim could hear the over-driven heart bump and check.

'Have they hurt him to the death?' said the Ao-chung man, while the others stood mute.

Kim knelt over the body in deadly fear. 'Nay,' he cried passionately, 'this is only a weakness.' Then he remembered that he was a white man, with a white man's camp-fittings at his service. 'Open the *kiltas*! The Sahibs may have a medicine.'

'Oho! Then I know it,' said the Ao-chung man with a laugh. 'Not for five years was I Yankling Sahib's *shikarri* without knowing that medicine. I too have tasted it. Behold!'

He drew from his breast a bottle of cheap whisky—such as is sold to explorers at Leh—and cleverly forced a little between the lama's teeth.

'So I did when Yankling Sahib twisted his foot beyond Astor. Aha! I have already looked into their baskets—but we will make fair division at Shamlegh. Give him a little more. It is good medicine. Feel! His heart goes better now. Lay his head down and rub a little on the chest. If he had waited quietly while I accounted for the Sahibs this would never have come. But perhaps the Sahibs may chase us here. Then it would not be wrong to shoot them with their own guns, heh?'

'One is paid, I think, already,' said Kim between his teeth. 'I kicked him in the groin as we went down hill. Would I had killed him!'

'It is well to be brave when one does not live in Rampur,' said one whose hut lay within a few miles of the Rajah's rickety palace. 'If we get a bad name among the Sahibs, none will employ us as *shikarris* any more.'

'Oh, but these are not Angrezi Sahibs—not merry-minded men like Fostum Sahib or Yankling Sahib. They are foreigners—they cannot speak Angrezi as do Sahibs.'

Here the lama coughed and sat up, groping for the rosary.

'There shall be no killing,' he murmured. 'Just is the Wheel! Evil on evil——'

'Nay, Holy One. We are all here.' The Ao-chung man timidly patted his feet. 'Except by thy order, no one shall be slain. Rest awhile. We will make a little camp here, and later, as the moon rises, we go to Shamlegh-under-the-Snow.'

'After a blow,' said a Spiti man sententiously, 'it is best to sleep.'

'There is, as it were, a dizziness at the back of my neck, and a pinching in it. Let me lay my head on thy lap, *chela*. I am an old man, but not free from passion. . . . We must think of the Cause of Things.'

'Give him a blanket. We dare not light a fire lest the Sahibs see.'

'Better get away to Shamlegh. None will follow us to Shamlegh.'

This was the nervous Rampur man.

'I have been Fostum Sahib's *shikarri*, and I am Yankling Sahib's *shikarri*. I should have been with Yankling Sahib now but for this cursed *beegar* (the *corvée*). Let two men watch below with the guns lest the Sahibs do more foolishness. *I* shall not leave this Holy One.'

They sat down a little apart from the lama, and, after listening awhile, passed round a water-pipe whose receiver was an old Day and Martin blacking-bottle. The glow of the red charcoal as it went from hand to hand lit up the narrow, blinking eyes, the high Chinese cheek-bones, and the bull-throats that melted away into the dark duffle folds round the shoulders. They looked like kobolds from some magic mine—gnomes of the hills in conclave. And while they talked, the voices of the snow-waters round them diminished one by one as the night-frost choked and clogged the runnels.

'How he stood up against us!' said a Spiti man admiring. 'I remember an old ibex, out Ladakh-way, that Dupont Sahib missed on a shoulder-shot, seven seasons back, standing up just like him. Dupont Sahib was a good *shikarri*.'

'Not as good as Yankling Sahib.' The Ao-chung man took a pull at the whisky-bottle and passed it over. 'Now hear me—unless any other man thinks he knows more.'

The challenge was not taken up.

'We go to Shamlegh when the moon rises. There we will fairly divide the baggage between us. I am content with this new little rifle and all its cartridges.'

'Are the bears only bad on thy holding?' said a mate, sucking at the pipe.

'No; but musk-pods are worth six rupees apiece now, and thy women can have the canvas of the tents and some of the cooking-gear. We will do all that at Shamlegh before dawn. Then we all go our ways, remembering that we have never seen or taken service with these Sahibs, who may, indeed, say that we have stolen their baggage.'

'That is well for thee, but what will our Rajah say?'

'Who is to tell him? Those Sahibs, who cannot speak our talk, or the Babu, who for his own ends gave us money? Will *he* lead an army against us? What evidence will remain? That we do not need we shall throw on Shamlegh midden, where no man has yet set foot.'

'Who is at Shamlegh this summer?' The place was only a grazing centre of three or four huts.

'The Woman of Shamlegh. *She* has no love for Sahibs, as we know. The others can be pleased with little presents; and here is enough for us all.' He patted the fat sides of the nearest basket.

'But—but——'

'I have said they are not true Sahibs. All their skins and heads were bought in the bazar at Leh. *I* know the marks. I showed them to ye last march.'

'True. They were all bought skins and heads. Some had even the moth in them.'

That was a shrewd argument, and the Ao-chung man knew his fellows.

'If the worst comes to the worst, I shall tell Yankling Sahib, who is a man of a merry mind, and he will laugh. We are not doing any wrong to any Sahibs whom we know. *They* are priest-beaters. They frightened us. We fled! Who knows where we dropped the baggage? Do ye think Yankling Sahib will permit down-country police to wander all over the hills, disturbing his game? It is a far cry from Simla to Chini, and farther from Shamlegh to Shamlegh-midden.'

'So be it, but I carry the big *kilta*. The basket with the red top that the Sahibs pack themselves every morning.'

'Thus it is proved,' said the Shamlegh man adroitly, 'that they are Sahibs of no account. Who ever heard of Fostum Sahib, or Yankling Sahib, or even the little Peel Sahib that sits up of nights to shoot serow—I say, who ever heard of these Sahibs coming into the hills without a down-country cook, and a bearer, and—and all manner of well-paid, high-handed and oppressive folk in their tail? How can they make trouble? What of the *kilta?*'

'Nothing, but that it is full of the Written Word—books and papers in which they wrote, and strange instruments, as of worship.'

'Shamlegh midden will take them all.'

'True! But how if we insult the Sahibs' Gods thereby? I do not like to handle the Written Word in that fashion. And their brass idols are beyond my comprehension. It is no plunder for simple hill-folk.'

'The old man still sleeps. Hst! We will ask his *chela*.' The Ao-chung man refreshed himself, and swelled with pride of leadership.

'We have here,' he whispered, 'a *kilta* whose nature we do not know.'

'But I do,' said Kim cautiously. The lama drew breath in natural, easy sleep, and Kim had been thinking of Hurree's last words. As a player of the Great Game, he was disposed just then to reverence the Babu. 'It is a *kilta* with a red top full of very wonderful things, not to be handled by fools.'

'I said it; I said it,' cried the bearer of that burden. 'Thinkest thou it will betray us?'

'Not if it be given to me. I will draw out its magic. Otherwise it will do great harm.'

'A priest always takes his share.' Whisky was demoralising the Ao-chung man.

'It is no matter to me,' Kim answered, with the craft of his mother-country. 'Share it among you, and see what comes!'

'Not I. I was only jesting. Give the order. There is more than enough for us all. We go our way from Shamlegh in the dawn.'

They arranged and re-arranged their artless little plans for another hour, while Kim shivered with cold and pride. The humour of the situation tickled the Irish and the Oriental in his soul. Here were the emissaries of the dread Power of the North, very possibly as great in their own land as Mahbub or Colonel Creighton, suddenly smitten helpless. One of them, he privately knew, would be lame for a time. They had made promises to Kings. To-night they lay out somewhere below him, chartless, foodless, tentless, gunless—except for Hurree Babu, guideless. And this collapse of their Great Game (Kim wondered to whom they would report it), this panicky bolt into the night, had come about through no craft of Hurree's or contrivance of Kim's, but simply, beautifully, and inevitably as the capture of Mahbub's *faquir*-friends by the zealous young policeman at Umballa.

'They are there—with nothing; and, by Jove, it is cold! I am here with all their things. Oh, they will be angry! I am sorry for Hurree Babu.'

Kim might have saved his pity, for though at that moment the Bengali suffered acutely in the flesh, his soul was puffed and lofty. A mile down the hill, on the edge of the pine-forest, two half-frozen men—one powerfully sick at intervals—were varying mutual recriminations with the most poignant abuse of the Babu, who seemed distraught with terror. They demanded a plan of action. He explained that they were very lucky to be alive; that their coolies, if not then stalking them, had passed beyond recall; that the Rajah, his master, was ninety miles away, and, so far from lending them money and a retinue for the Simla journey, would surely cast them into prison if he heard that they had hit a priest. He enlarged on this sin and its consequences till they bade him change the subject. Their one hope, said he, was unostentatious flight from village to village till they reached civilisation; and, for the hundredth time dissolved in tears, he demanded of the high stars why the Sahibs 'had beaten holy man.'

Ten steps would have taken Hurree into the creaking gloom utterly beyond their reach—to the shelter and food of the nearest village, where glib-tongued doctors were scarce. But he preferred to endure cold, belly-pinch, bad words, and occasional blows in the company of his honoured employers. Crouched against a tree-trunk, he sniffed dolefully.

'And have you thought,' said the uninjured man hotly, 'what sort of spectacle we shall present wandering through these hills among these aborigines?'

Hurree Babu had thought of little else for some hours, but the remark was not to his address.

'We cannot wander! I can hardly walk,' groaned Kim's victim.

'Perhaps the holy man will be merciful in loving-kindness, Sar, otherwise——'

'I promise myself a peculiar pleasure in emptying my revolver into that young bonze when next we meet,' was the unchristian answer.

'Revolvers! Vengeance! Bonzes!' Hurree crouched lower. The war was breaking out afresh. 'Have you no consideration for our loss? The baggage! The baggage!' He could hear the speaker literally dancing on the grass. 'Everything we bore! Everything we have secured! Our gains! Eight months' work! Do you know what that means? "Decidedly it is we who can deal with Orientals!" Oh, you have done well.'

They fell to it in several tongues, and Hurree smiled. Kim was with the *kiltas*, and in the *kiltas* lay eight months of good diplomacy.

There was no means of communicating with the boy, but he could be trusted. For the rest, he could so stage-manage the journey through the hills that Hilás, Bunár, and four hundred miles of hill-roads should tell the tale for a generation. Men who cannot control their own coolies are little respected in the Hills, and the hillman has a very keen sense of humour.

'If I had done it myself,' thought Hurree, 'it would not have been better; and, by Jove, now I think of it, of course I arranged it myself. How quick I have been! Just when I ran down hill I thought it! Thee outrage was accidental, but onlee me could have worked it—ah—for all it was dam well worth. Consider the moral effect upon these ignorant peoples! No treaties—no papers—no written documents at all—and *me* to interpret for them. How I shall laugh with the Colonel! I wish I had their papers also: but you cannot occupy two places in space simultaneously. Thatt is axiomatic.'

CHAPTER XIV

My brother kneels (so saith Kabir)
To stone and brass in heathen-wise,
But in my brother's voice I hear
My own unanswered agonies.
His God is as his Fates assign—
His prayer is all the world's—and mine.
KABIR.[1]

AT moonrise the cautious coolies got under way. The lama, refreshed by his sleep and the spirit, needed no more than Kim's shoulder to bear him along—a silent, swift-striding man. They held the shale-sprinkled grass for an hour, swept round the shoulder of an immortal cliff, and climbed into a new country entirely blocked off from all sight of Chini valley. A huge pasture-ground ran up fan-shaped to the living snow. At its base was perhaps half an acre of flat land, on which stood a few soil and timber huts. Behind them—for, hill-fashion, they

[1]Poet, mystic, and religious reformer, 15th-c. weaver Kabir passionately invoked the unity of divinity and humanity. Attacking the injustices of caste while seeking to build on what he saw as the shared truths of Muslim and Hindu traditions, Kabir became legendary for his celebrations of truthfulness, compassion, and independent individual love of God. "Associate and mix with all, and take the names of all," he is said to have advised: "Say to everyone, yes sir, yes sir. Abide in your own abode." Translating these lines in 1896, Jogendra Nath Bhattacharya reported that there was "hardly a town in India where strolling beggars" might not "be found singing songs of Kabir in original, or as translated in the local dialects" (*Hindu Castes and Sects*). Kipling, who composed another Kabir poem for the *Second Jungle Book*, chose a slightly revised version of this epigraph, retitled "A Song of Kabir," to close his 1912 *Songs from Books*.

were perched on the edge of all things—the ground fell sheer two thousand feet to Shamlegh midden, where never yet man has set foot.

The men made no motion to divide the plunder till they had seen the lama bedded down in the best room of the place, with Kim shampooing his feet, Mohammedan fashion.

'We will send food,' said the Ao-chung man, 'and the red-topped *kilta*. By dawn there will be none to give evidence, one way or the other. If anything is not needed in the *kilta*—see here!'

He pointed through the window—opening into space that was filled with moonlight reflected from the snow—and threw out an empty whisky-bottle.

'No need to listen for the fall. This is the world's end,' he said, and swung off. The lama looked forth, a hand on either sill, with eyes that shone like yellow opals. From the enormous pit before him white peaks lifted themselves yearning to the moonlight. The rest was as the darkness of interstellar space.

'These,' he said slowly, 'are indeed my Hills. Thus should a man abide, perched above the world, separated from delights, considering vast matters.'

'Yes; if he has a *chela* to prepare tea for him, and to fold a blanket for his head, and to chase out calving cows.'

A smoky lamp burned in a niche, but the full moonlight beat it down; and by the mixed light, stooping above the food-bag and cups, Kim moved like a tall ghost.

'Ai! But now I have let the blood cool my head still beats and drums, and there is a cord round the back of my neck.'

'No wonder. It was a strong blow. May he who dealt it——'

'But for my own passions there would have been no evil.'

'What evil? Thou hast saved the Sahibs from death they deserved a hundred times.'

'The lesson is not well learnt, *chela*.' The lama came to rest on a folded blanket, as Kim went forward with his evening routine. 'The blow was but a shadow upon a shadow. Evil in itself—my legs weary apace these latter days!—it met evil in me—anger, rage, and a lust to return evil. These wrought in my blood, woke tumult in my stomach, and dazzled my ears.' Here he drank scalding block-tea ceremonially, taking the hot cup from Kim's hand. 'Had I been passionless, the evil blow would have done only bodily evil—a scar, or a bruise—which is illusion. But my mind was *not* abstracted, for rushed in straight-way a lust to let the Spiti men kill. In fighting that lust, my soul was torn and wrenched beyond a thousand blows. Not till I had repeated the Blessings (he meant the Buddhist Beatitudes) did I achieve calm. But the evil planted in me by that moment's carelessness works out to its end. Just is the Wheel, swerving not a hair! Learn the lesson, *chela*.'

'It is too high for me,' Kim muttered. 'I am still all shaken. I am glad I hurt the man.'

'I felt that sleeping upon thy knees, in the wood below. It disquieted me in my dreams—the evil in thy soul working through to mine. Yet on the other hand'—he loosed his rosary—'I have acquired merit by saving two lives—the lives of those that wronged me. Now I must see into the Cause of Things. The boat of my soul staggers.'

'Sleep, and be strong. That is wisest.'

'I meditate: there is a need greater than thou knowest.'

Till the dawn, hour after hour, as the moonlight paled on the high peaks, and that which had been belted blackness on the sides of the far hills showed as tender green forest, the lama stared fixedly at the wall. From time to time he groaned. Outside the barred door, where discomfited kine came to ask for their old stable, Shamlegh and the coolies gave itself up to plunder and riotous living. The Ao-chung man was their leader, and once they had opened the Sahibs' tinned foods and found that they were very good they dared not turn back. Shamlegh kitchen-midden took the dunnage.

When Kim, after a night of bad dreams, stole forth to brush his teeth in the morning chill, a fair-coloured woman with turquoise-studded head-gear drew him aside.

'The others have gone. They left thee this *kilta* as the promise was. I do not love Sahibs, but thou wilt make us a charm in return for it. We do not wish little Shamlegh to get a bad name on account of the—accident. I am the Woman of Shamlegh.' She looked him over with bold, bright eyes, unlike the usual furtive glance of hillwomen.

'Assuredly. But it must be done in secret.'

She raised the heavy *kilta* like a toy and slung it into her own hut.

'Out and bar the door! Let none come near till it is finished.'

'But afterwards—we may talk?'

Kim tilted the *kilta* on the floor—a cascade of Survey-instruments, books, diaries, letters, maps, and queerly scented native correspondence. At the very bottom was an embroidered bag covering a sealed, gilded, and illuminated document such as one King sends to another. Kim caught his breath with delight, and reviewed the situation from a Sahib's point of view.

'The books I do not want. Besides, they are logarithms—Survey, I suppose.' He laid them aside. 'The letters I do not understand, but Colonel Creighton will. They must all be kept. The maps—they draw better maps than me—*of* course. All the native letters—oho!—and particularly the *murasla*.' He sniffed the embroidered bag. 'That must be from Hilás or Bunár, and Hurree Babu spoke truth. By Jove! It is a fine haul. I wish Hurree could know. . . . The rest must go out of the window.' He fingered a superb prismatic compass and the shiny top of a theodolite. But after all, a Sahib cannot very well steal, and the things might be inconvenient evidence later. He sorted out every scrap of manuscript, every map, and the native letters. They made one softish slab. The three locked ferril-backed books, with five worn pocket-books, he put aside.

'The letters and the *murasla* I must carry inside my coat and under my belt, and the hand-written books I must put into the food-bag. It will be very heavy. No. I do not think there is anything more. If there is, the coolies have thrown it down the *khud*, so *thatt* is all right. Now you go too.' He repacked the *kilta* with all he meant to lose, and hove it up on to the window-sill. A thousand feet below lay a long, lazy, round-shouldered bank of mist, as yet untouched by the morning sun. A thousand feet below that was an hundred-year-old pine-forest. He could see the green tops looking like a bed of moss when a wind-eddy thinned the cloud.

'No! I don't think any one will go after *you!*'

The wheeling basket vomited its contents as it dropped. The theodolite hit a jutting cliff-ledge and exploded like a shell; the books, inkstands, paint-boxes, compasses, and rulers showed for a few seconds like a swarm of bees. Then they vanished; and, though Kim, hanging half out of window, strained his young ears, never a sound came up from the gulf.

'Five hundred—a thousand rupees could not buy them,' he thought sorrowfully. 'It was verree wasteful, but I have all their other stuff—everything they did—I hope. Now how the deuce am I to tell Hurree Babu, and *whatt* the deuce am I to do? And my old man is sick. I must tie up the letters in oilcloth. That is something to do first—else they will get all sweated. . . . And I am all alone!' He bound them into a neat packet, swedging down the stiff, sticky oilcloth at the corners, for his roving life had made him as methodical as an old hunter in matters of the road. Then with double care he packed away the books at the bottom of the food-bag.

The woman rapped at the door.

'But thou hast made no charm,' she said, looking about.

'There is no need.' Kim had completely overlooked the necessity for a little patter-talk. The woman laughed at his confusion irreverently.

'None—for thee. Thou canst cast a spell by the mere winking of an eye. But think of us poor people when thou art gone! They were all too drunk last night to hear a woman. Thou art not drunk?'

'I am a priest.' Kim had recovered himself, and, the woman being aught but unlovely, thought best to stand on his office.

'I warned them that the Sahibs will be angry and will make an inquisition and a report to the Rajah. There is also the Babu with them. Clerks have long tongues.'

'Is that all thy trouble?' The plan rose fully formed in Kim's mind, and he smiled ravishingly.

'Not all,' quoth the woman, putting out a hard brown hand all covered with turquoises set in silver.

'I can finish that in a breath,' he went on quickly. 'The Babu is the very *hakim* (thou hast heard of him?) who was wandering among the hills by Ziglaur. I know him.'

'He will tell for the sake of a reward. Sahibs cannot distinguish one hillman from another, but Babus have eyes for men—and women.'

'Carry a word to him from me.'

'There is nothing I would not do for thee.'

He accepted the compliment calmly, as men must in lands where women make the love, tore a leaf from a note-book, and with a patent indelible pencil wrote in gross Shikast—the script that bad little boys use when they write dirt on walls: '*I have everything that they have written: their pictures of the country, and many letters. Especially the* murasla. *Tell me what to do. I am at Shamlegh-under-the-Snow. The old man is sick.*'

'Take this to him. It will altogether shut his mouth. He cannot have gone far.'

'Indeed no. They are still in the forest across the spur. Our children went to watch them when the light came, and have cried the news as they moved.'

Kim looked his astonishment; but from the edge of the sheep-pasture floated a shrill, kite-like trill. A child tending cattle had picked it up from a brother or sister on the far side of the slope that commanded Chini valley.

'My husbands are also out there gathering wood.' She drew a handful of walnuts from her bosom, split one neatly, and began to eat. Kim affected blank ignorance.

'Dost thou not know the meaning of the walnut—priest?' she said coyly, and handed him the half-shells.

'Well thought of.' He slipped the piece of paper between them quickly. 'Hast thou a little wax to close them on this letter?'

The woman sighed aloud, and Kim relented.

'There is no payment till service has been rendered. Carry this to the Babu, and say it was sent by the Son of the Charm.'

'Ai! Truly! Truly! By a magician—who is like a Sahib.'

'Nay, Son of the Charm: and ask if there be any answer.'

'But if he offer a rudeness? I—I am afraid.'

Kim laughed. 'He is, I have no doubt, very tired and very hungry. The Hills make cold bed-fellows. Hai, my'—it was on the tip of his tongue to say Mother, but he turned it to Sister—'thou art a wise and witty woman. By this time all the villages know what has befallen the Sahibs—eh?'

'True. News was at Ziglaur by midnight, and by to-morrow should be at Kotgarh. The villages are both afraid and angry.'

'No need. Tell the villages to feed the Sahibs and pass them on, in peace. We must get them quietly away from our valleys. To steal is one thing—to kill another. The Babu will understand, and there will be no after-complaints. Be swift. I must tend my master when he wakes.'

'So be it. After service—thou has said?—comes the reward. I am the Woman of Shamlegh, and I hold from the Rajah. I am no common bearer of babes. Shamlegh is thine: hoof and horn and hide, milk and butter. Take or leave.'

She turned resolutely uphill, her silver necklaces clicking on her broad breast, to meet the morning sun fifteen hundred feet above them. This time Kim thought in the vernacular as he waxed down the oilskin edges of the packets.

'How can a man follow the Way or the Great Game when he is eternally pestered by women? There was that girl at Akrola by the Ford; and there was the scullion's wife behind the dovecot—not counting the others—and now comes this one! When I was a child it was well enough, but now I am a man and they will not regard me as a man. Walnuts indeed! Ho! ho! It is almonds in the Plains!'[2]

He went out to levy on the village—not with a begging-bowl, which might do for down-country, but in the manner of a prince. Shamlegh's summer population is only three families—four women and eight or nine men. They were all full of tinned meats—and mixed drinks, from ammoniated quinine to white vodka—for they had taken their full share in the overnight loot. The neat Continental tents had been cut up and shared long ago, and there were patent aluminium sauce-pans abroad.

But they considered the lama's presence a perfect safeguard against all consequences, and impenitently brought Kim of their best—even to a drink of *chang*—the barley-beer that comes from Ladakh-way. Then they thawed out in the sun, and sat with their legs hanging over infinite abysses, chattering, laughing, and smoking. They judged India and its Government solely from their experience of wandering Sahibs who had employed them or their friends as *shikarris*. Kim heard tales of shots missed upon ibex, serow, or markhor, by Sahibs twenty years in their graves—every detail lighted from behind like twigs on tree-tops

[2]A teasing reference to sexual anatomy.

seen against lightning. They told him of their little diseases, and, more important, the diseases of their tiny, sure-footed cattle; of trips as far as Kotgarh, where the strange missionaries live, and beyond even to marvellous Simla, where the streets are paved with silver, and any one, look you, can get service with the Sahibs, who ride about in two-wheeled carts and spend money with a spade. Presently, grave and aloof, walking very heavily, the lama joined himself to the chatter under the eaves, and they gave him great room. The thin air refreshed him, and he sat on the edge of precipices with the best of them, and, when talk languished, flung pebbles into the void. Thirty miles away, as the eagle flies, lay the next range, seamed and channelled and pitted with little patches of brush—forests, each a day's dark march. Behind the village, Shamlegh hill itself cut off all view to southward. It was like sitting in a swallow's nest under the eaves of the roof of the world.

From time to time the lama stretched out his hand, and with a little, low-voiced prompting would point out the road to Spiti and north across the Parungla.

'Beyond, where the hills lie thickest, lies De-ch'en (he meant Hanlé), 'the great Monastery. s'Tag-stan-ras-ch'en built it, and of him there runs this tale.' Whereupon he told it: a fantastic piled narrative of bewitchment and miracles that set Shamlegh agasping. Turning west a little, he speered for the green hills of Kulu, and sought Kailung under the glaciers. 'For thither came I in the old, old days. From Leh I came, over the Baralachi.'

'Yes, yes; we know it,' said the far-faring people of Shamlegh.

'And I slept two nights with the priests of Kailung. These are the hills of my delight! Shadows blessed above all other shadows! There my eyes opened on this world; there my eyes were opened to this world; there I found Enlightenment; and there I girt my loins for my Search. Out of the Hills I came—the high Hills and the strong winds. Oh, just is the Wheel!' He blessed them in detail—the great glaciers, the naked rocks, the piled moraines and tumbled shale; dry upland, hidden salt-lake, age-old timber and fruitful water-shot valley one after the other, as a dying man blesses his folk, and Kim marvelled at his passion.

'Yes—yes. There is no place like our Hills,' said the people of Shamlegh. And they fell to wondering how a man could live in the hot terrible Plains where the cattle run as big as elephants, unfit to plough on a hillside; where village touches village, they had heard, for a hundred miles; where folk went about stealing in gangs, and what the robbers spared the Police carried utterly away.

So the still forenoon wore through, and at the end of it Kim's messenger dropped from the steep pasture as unbreathed as when she had set out.

'I sent a word to the *hakim*,' Kim explained, while she made reverence.

'He joined himself to the idolaters? Nay, I remember he did a healing upon one of them. He has acquired merit, though the healed employed his strength for evil. Just is the Wheel! What of the *hakim*?'

'I feared that thou hadst been bruised and—and I knew he was wise.' Kim took the waxed walnut-shell and read in English on the back of his note: *Your favour received. Cannot get away from present company at present, but shall take them into Simla. After which, hope to rejoin you. Inexpedient to follow angry gentlemen. Return by same road you came, and will overtake. Highly gratified about correspondence due to my forethought.* He says, Holy One, that he will escape from the idolaters, and will return to us. Shall we wait awhile at Shamlegh, then?'

The lama looked long and lovingly upon the hills and shook his head.

'That may not be, *chela*. From my bones outward I do desire it, but it is forbidden. I have seen the Cause of Things.'

'Why? When the Hills gave thee back thy strength day by day? Remember we were weak and fainting down below there in the Doon.'

I became strong to do evil and to forget. A brawler and a swashbuckler upon the hillsides was I.' Kim bit back a smile. 'Just and perfect is the Wheel, swerving not a hair. When I was a man—a long time ago—I did pilgrimage to Guru Ch'wan among the poplars' (he pointed *Bhotan*-wards), 'where they keep the Sacred Horse.'

'Quiet, be quiet!' said Shamlegh, all arow. 'He speaks of Jam-lin-nin-k'or, the Horse That Can Go Round The World In a Day.'

'I speak to my *chela* only,' said the lama, in gentle reproof, and they scattered like frost on south eaves of a morning. 'I did not seek truth in those days, but the talk of doctrine. All illusion! I drank the beer and ate the bread of Guru Ch'wan. Next day one said: "We go out to fight Sangor Gutok down the valley to discover (mark again how Lust is tied to Anger!) which abbot shall bear rule in the valley, and take the profit of the prayers they print at Sangor Gutok." I went, and we fought a day.'

'But how, Holy One?'

'With our long pencases as I could have shown. . . . I say, we fought under the poplars, both abbots and all the monks, and one laid open my forehead to the bone. See!' He tilted back his cap and showed a puckered silvery scar. 'Just and perfect is the Wheel! Yesterday the scar itched, and after fifty years I recalled how it was dealt and the face of him who dealt it; dwelling a little in illusion. Followed that which thou didst see—strife and stupidity. Just is the Wheel! The idolater's blow fell upon the scar. Then I was shaken in my soul: my soul was darkened, and the boat of my soul rocked upon the waters of illusion. Not till I came to Shamlegh could I meditate upon the

Cause of Things, or trace the running grass-roots of Evil. I strove all the long night.'

'But, Holy One, thou art innocent of all evil. May I be thy sacrifice!'

Kim was genuinely distressed at the old man's sorrow, and Mahbub Ali's phrase slipped out unawares.

'In the dawn,' he went on more gravely, ready rosary clicking between the slow sentences, 'came enlightenment. It is here. . . . I am an old man . . . hill-bred, hill-fed, never to sit down among my hills. Three years I travelled through Hind, but—can earth be stronger than Mother Earth? My stupid body yearned to the Hills and the snow of the Hills, from below there. I said, and it is true, my Search is sure. So, at the Kulu woman's house I turned hillward, over-persuaded by myself. There is no blame to the *hakim*. He—following Desire—foretold that the Hills would make me strong. They strengthened me to do evil, to forget my Search. I delighted in life and the lust of life. I desired strong slopes to climb. I cast about to find them. I measured the strength of my body, which is evil, against the high hills. I made a mock of thee when thy breath came short under Jamnotri. I jested when thou wouldst not face the snow of the pass.'

'But what harm? I *was* afraid. It was just. I am not a hillman; and I loved thee for thy new strength.'

'More than once I remember,' he rested his cheek dolefully on his hand, 'I sought thy praise and the *hakim's* for the mere strength of my legs. Thus evil followed evil till the cup was full. Just is the Wheel! All Hind for three years did me all honour. From the Fountain of Wisdom in the Wonder House to'—he smiled—'a little child playing by a big gun—the world prepared my road. And why?'

'Because we loved thee. It is only the fever of the blow. I myself am still sick and shaken.'

'No! It was because I was upon the Way—tuned as are *si-nen* (cymbals) to the purpose of the Law. I departed from that ordinance. The tune was broken: followed the punishment. In my own hills, on the edge of my own country, in the very place of my evil desire, comes the buffet—here!' (He touched his brow.) 'As a novice is beaten when he misplaces the cups, so am I beaten, who was Abbot of Such-zen. No word, look you, but a blow, *chela*.'

'But the Sahibs did not know thee, Holy One?'

'We were well matched. Ignorance and Lust met Ignorance and Lust upon the road, and they begat Anger. The blow was a sign to me, who am no better than a strayed yak, that my place is not here. Who can read the Cause of an act is half-way to Freedom! "Back to the path," says the Blow. "The Hills are not for thee. Thou canst not choose Freedom and go in bondage to the delight of life."'

'If we had never met that thrice-cursed Russian!'

'Our Lord Himself cannot make the Wheel swing backward. And for my merit that I had acquired I gain yet another sign.' He put his hand in his bosom, and drew forth the Wheel of Life. 'Look! I considered this after I had meditated. There remains untorn by the idolater no more than the breadth of my finger-nail.'

'I see.'

'So much, then, is the span of my life in this body. I have served the Wheel all my days. Now the Wheel serves me. But for the merit I have acquired in guiding thee upon the Way, there would have been added to me yet another life ere I had found my River. Is it plain, *chela?*'

Kim stared at the brutally disfigured chart. From left to right diagonally the rent ran—from the Eleventh House where Desire gives birth to the Child (as it is drawn by Tibetans)—across the human and animal worlds, to the Fifth House—the empty House of the Senses. The logic was unanswerable.

'Before our Lord won enlightenment,' the lama folded all away with reverence, 'He was tempted. I too have been tempted, but it is finished. The Arrow fell in the Plains—not in the Hills. Therefore, what make we here?'

'Shall we at least wait for the *hakim?*'

'I know how long I live in this body. What can a *hakim* do?'

'But thou art all sick and shaken. Thou canst not walk.'

'How can I be sick if I see Freedom?' He rose unsteadily to his feet.

'Then I must get food from the village. Oh, the weary Road!' Kim felt that he too needed rest.

'That is lawful. Let us eat and go. The Arrow fell in Plains . . . but I yielded to Desire. Make ready, *chela.*'

Kim turned to the woman with the turquoise head-gear who had been idly pitching pebbles over the cliff. She smiled very kindly.

'I found him like a strayed buffalo in a cornfield—the Babu; snorting and sneezing with cold. He was so hungry that he forgot his dignity and gave me sweet words. The Sahibs have nothing.' She flung out an empty palm. 'One is very sick about the stomach. Thy work?'

Kim nodded, with a bright eye.

'I spoke to the Bengali first—and to the people of a nearby village after. The Sahibs will be given food as they need it—nor will the people ask money. The plunder is already distributed. That Babu makes lying speeches to the Sahibs. Why does he not leave them?'

'Out of the greatness of his heart.'

''Was never a Bengali yet had one bigger than a dried walnut. But it is no matter. . . . Now as to walnuts. After service comes reward. I have said the village is thine.'

'It is my loss,' Kim began. 'Even now I had planned desirable things in my heart which'—there is no need to go through the compliments proper to these occasions. He sighed deeply . . . 'But my master, led by a vision——'

'Huh! What can old eyes see except a full begging-bowl?'

'——turns from this village to the Plains again.'

'Bid him stay.'

Kim shook his head. 'I know my Holy One, and his rage if he be crossed,' he replied impressively. 'His curses shake the Hills.'

'Pity they did not save him from a broken head! I heard that thou wast the tiger-hearted one who smote the Sahib. Let him dream a little longer. Stay!'

'Hillwoman,' said Kim, with austerity that could not harden the outlines of his young oval face, 'these matters are too high for thee.'

'The Gods be good to us! Since when have men and women been other than men and women?'

'A priest is a priest. He says he will go upon this hour. I am his *chela*, and I go with him. We need food for the Road. He is an honoured guest in all the villages, but'—he broke into a pure boy's grin— 'the food here is good. Give me some.'

'What if I do not give it thee? I am the woman of this village.'

'Then I curse thee—a little—not greatly, but enough to remember.' He could not help smiling.

'Thou hast cursed me already by the down-dropped eyelash and the uplifted chin. Curses? What should I care for mere words?' She clenched her hands upon her bosom. . . . 'But I would not have thee to go in anger, thinking hardly of me—a gatherer of cow-dung and grass at Shamlegh, but still a woman of substance.'

'I think nothing,' said Kim, 'but that I am grieved to go, for I am very tired, and that we need food. Here is the bag.'

The woman snatched it angrily. 'I was foolish,' said she. 'Who is thy woman in the Plains? Fair or black? I was fair once. Laughest thou? Once, long ago, if thou canst believe, a Sahib looked on me with favour. Once, long ago, I wore European clothes at the Mission-house yonder.' She pointed towards Kotgarh. 'Once, long ago, I was *Ker-listi-an* and spoke English—as the Sahibs speak it. Yes. My Sahib said he would return and wed me—yes, wed me. He went away—I had nursed him when he was sick—but he never returned. Then I saw that the Gods of Kerlistians lied, and I went back to my own people . . . I have never set eyes on a Sahib since. (Do not laugh at me. The fit is past, little priestling.) Thy face and thy walk and thy fashion of speech put me in mind of my Sahib, though thou art only a wandering mendicant to whom I give a dole. Curse me? Thou canst neither curse nor bless!' She set her hands on her hips and laughed bitterly. 'Thy Gods are lies; thy works are lies; thy words are lies. There are no Gods under all the heavens. I know it. . . . But for awhile I thought it was my Sahib come back, and he was my God. Yes, once I made music on a *pianno* in the Mission-house at Kotgarh. Now I give alms to priests who are *heatthen*.' She wound up with the English word, and tied the mouth of the brimming bag.

'I wait for thee, *chela*,' said the lama, leaning against the door-post.

The woman swept the tall figure with her eyes. 'He walk! He cannot cover half a mile. Whither would old bones go?'

At this Kim, already perplexed by the lama's collapse and foreseeing the weight of the bag, fairly lost his temper.

'What is it to thee, woman of ill-omen, where he goes?'

'Nothing—but something to thee, priest with a Sahib's face. Wilt thou carry him on thy shoulders?'

'I go to the Plains. None must hinder my return. I have wrestled with my soul till I am strengthless. The stupid body is spent, and we are far from the Plains.'

'Behold!' she said simply, and drew aside to let Kim see his own utter helplessness. 'Curse me. May be it will give him strength. Make a charm! Call on thy great God. Thou art a priest.' She turned away.

The lama had squatted limply, still holding by the door-post. One cannot strike down an old man that he recovers again like a boy in a night. Weakness bowed him to the earth, but his eyes that hung on Kim were alive and imploring.

'It is all well,' said Kim. 'It is the thin air that weakens thee. In a little while we go! It is the mountain-sickness. I too am a little sick at stomach,' . . . and he knelt and comforted with such poor words as came first to his lips. Then the woman returned, more erect than ever.

'Thy Gods useless, heh? Try mine. *I* am the Woman of Shamlegh.' She hailed hoarsely, and there came out of a cow-pen her two husbands and three others with a *dooli*, the rude native litter of the Hills, that they use for carrying the sick and for visits of state. 'These cattle,' she did not condescend to look at them, 'are thine for so long as thou shalt need.'

'But we will not go Simla-way. We will not go near the Sahibs,' cried the first husband.

'They will not run away as the others did, nor will they steal baggage. Two I know for weaklings. Stand to the rear-pole, Sonoo and Taree.' They obeyed swiftly. 'Lower now, and lift in that holy man. I will see to the village and your virtuous wives till ye return.'

'When will that be?'

'Ask the priests. Do not pester me. Lay the food-bag at the foot, it balances better so.'

'Oh, Holy One, thy Hills are kinder than our Plains!' cried Kim, relieved, as the lama tottered to the litter. 'It is a very king's bed—a place of honour and ease. And we owe it to————'

'A woman of ill-omen. I need thy blessings as much as I do thy curses. It is *my* order and none of thine. Lift and away! Here! Hast thou money for the road?'

She beckoned Kim to her hut, and stooped above a battered English cash-box under her cot.

'I do not need anything,' said Kim, angered where he should have been grateful. I am already rudely loaded with favours.'

She looked up with a curious smile and laid a hand on his shoulder. 'At least, thank me. I am foul-faced and a hillwoman, but, as thy talk goes, I have acquired merit. Shall I show thee how the Sahibs render thanks?' and her hard eyes softened.

'I am but a wandering priest,' said Kim, his eyes lighting in answer. 'Thou needest neither my blessings nor my curses.'

'Nay. But for one little moment—thou canst overtake the *dooli* in ten strides—*if* thou wast a Sahib, shall I show thee what thou wouldst do?'

'How if I guess, though?' said Kim, and putting his arm round her waist, he kissed her on the cheek, adding in English: 'Thank you ver-ree much, my dear.'

Kissing is practically unknown among Asiatics, which may have been the reason that she leaned back with wide-open eyes and a face of panic.

'Next time,' Kim went on, 'you must not be so sure of your heathen priests. Now I say good-bye.' He held out his hand English-fashion. She took it mechanically. 'Good-bye, my dear.'

'Good-bye, and—and'—she was remembering her English words one by one—'you will come back again? Good-bye, and—thee God bless you.'[3]

Half an hour later, as the creaking litter jolted up the hill path that leads south-easterly from Shamlegh, Kim saw a tiny figure at the hut door waving a white rag.

'She has acquired merit beyond all others,' said the lama. 'For to set a man upon the way to Freedom is half as great as though she had herself found it.'

'Umm,' said Kim thoughtfully, considering the past. 'It may be that I have acquired merit also. . . . At least she did not treat me like a child.' He hitched the front of his robe, where lay the slab of documents and maps, restowed the precious food-bag at the lama's feet, laid his hand on the litter edge, and buckled down to the slow pace of the grunting husbands.

[3]See "Lispeth," p. 281.

'These also acquire merit,' said the lama, after three miles.

'More than that, they shall be paid in silver,' quoth Kim. The Woman of Shamlegh had given it to him; and it was only fair, he argued, that her men should earn it back again.

CHAPTER XV

I'd not give room for an Emperor—
I'd hold my road for a King.
To the Triple Crown I'd not bow down—
But this is a different thing!
I'll not fight with the Powers of Air—
Sentries pass him through!
Drawbridge let fall—He's the Lord of us all—
The Dreamer whose dream came true!
The Siege of the Fairies.[1]

Two hundred miles north of Chini, on the blue shale of Ladakh, lies Yankling Sahib, the merry-minded man, spy-glassing wrathfully across the ridges for some sign of his pet tracker—a man from Ao-chung. But that renegade, with a new Männlicher rifle and two hundred cartridges, is elsewhere, shooting musk-deer for the market, and Yankling Sahib will learn next season how very ill he has been.

Up the valleys of Bushahr—the far-beholding eagles of the Himalayas swerve at his new blue-and-white gored umbrella—hurries a Bengali, once fat and well-looking, now lean and weather-worn. He has received the thanks of two foreigners of distinction, piloted not unskilfully to Mashobra tunnel which leads to the great and gay capital of India. It was not his fault that, blanketed by wet mists, he conveyed them past the telegraph-station and European colony of Kotgarh. It was not his fault, but that of the Gods, of whom he discoursed so engagingly, that he led them into the borders of Nahan, where the Rajah of that state mistook them for deserting British soldiery. Hurree Babu explained the greatness and glory, in their own country, of his companions, till the drowsy kinglet smiled. He explained it to every one who asked—many times—aloud—variously. He begged food, arranged accommodation, proved a skilful leech for an injury of the groin—such a blow as one may receive rolling down a rock-covered hillside in the dark—and in all things indispensable. The reason of his friend-

---

[1]Slightly altered, these lines appear as third and final stanza of "The Fairies' Siege" in *Songs from Books.* Through a series of orders to surrender, the poem's military speaker reiterates the futility of opposing the "unseen" weapons of the "Herald of God." The "Triple Crown" is the tiara of the Roman Catholic pope.

liness did him credit. With millions of fellow-serfs, he had learned to look upon Russia as the great deliverer from the North.[2] He was a fearful man. He had been afraid that he could not save his illustrious employers from the anger of an excited peasantry. He himself would just as lief hit a holy man as not, but. . . . He was deeply grateful and sincerely rejoiced that he had done his 'little possible' towards bringing their venture to—barring the lost baggage—a successful issue. He had forgotten the blows; denied that any blows had been dealt that unseemly first night under the pines. He asked neither pension nor retaining fee, but, if they deemed him worthy, would they write him a testimonial? It might be useful to him later, if others, their friends, came over the Passes. He begged them to remember him in their future greatnesses, for he 'opined subtly' that he, even he, Mohendro Lal Dutt, M.A. of Calcutta,[3] had 'done the state some service.'

They gave him a certificate praising his courtesy, helpfulness, and unerring skill as a guide. He put it in his waist-belt and sobbed with emotion; they had endured so many dangers together. He led them at high noon along crowded Simla Mall to the Alliance Bank of Simla where they wished to establish their identity. Thence he vanished like a dawn-cloud on Jakko.

Behold him, too fine drawn to sweat, too pressed to vaunt the drugs in his little brass-bound box, ascending Shamlegh slope, a just man made perfect. Watch him, all Babudom laid aside, smoking at noon on a cot, while a woman with turquoise-studded head-gear points south-easterly across the bare grass. Litters, she says, do not travel as fast as single men, but his birds should now be in the Plains. The holy man would not stay though Lispeth pressed him. The Babu groans heavily, girds up his huge loins, and is off again. He does not care to travel after dusk; but his days' marches—there is none to enter them in a book—would astonish folk who mock at his race. Kindly villagers, remembering the Dacca drug-vendor of two months ago, give him shelter against evil spirits of the wood. He dreams of Bengali Gods, University textbooks of education, and the Royal Society, London, England. Next dawn the bobbing blue-and-white umbrella goes forward.

---

[2]A jab: Although Russia abolished serfdom in 1861, the peasants were still oppressed.

[3]Hurree Babu's assumed name may allude to a series of well-known 19th-c. Bengali literary figures including poet, translator, and dramatist Michael Madhusudan Dutt (1824–73); editor Govin Chunder Dutt (1828–84), who compiled a groundbreaking Indo-Anglian poetry anthology entitled *The Dutt Family Album*; and his daughter Toru Dutt, (1856–77), a poet, translator, and novelist whose work joined Kipling's in E. C. Stedman's 1895 *Victorian Anthology*. The alias may also invoke an influential critic of imperial policies who had become president of the Indian National Congress in 1899—the distinguished poet, novelist, civil servant, translator, and political and economic thinker Romesh Chunder Dutt (1848–1909).

On the edge of the Doon, Mussoorie well behind them and the Plains spread out in golden dust before, rests a worn litter in which—all the Hills know it—lies a sick lama who seeks a River for his healing. Villages have almost come to blows over the honour of bearing it, for not only has the lama given them blessings, but his disciple good money—full one-third Sahibs' prices. Twelve miles a day has the *dooli* travelled, as the greasy, rubbed pole-ends show, and by roads that few Sahibs use. Over the Nilang Pass in storm when the driven snow-dust filled every fold of the impassive lama's drapery; between the black horns of Raieng where they heard the whistle of the wild goats through the clouds; pitching and strained on the shale below; hard-held between shoulder and clenched jaw when they rounded the hideous curves of the Cut Road under Bhagirati; swinging and creaking to the steady jog-trot of the descent into the Valley of the Waters; pressed along the steamy levels of that locked valley; up, up and out again, to meet the roaring gusts of Kedarnath; set down of mid-days in the dun-gloom of kindly oak-forests; passed from village to village in dawn-chill, when even devotees may be forgiven for swearing at impatient holy men; or by torchlight, when the least fearful think of ghosts—the *dooli* has reached her last stage. The little hill-folk sweat in the modified heat of the lower Sewaliks, and gather round the priests for their blessing and their wage.

'Ye have acquired merit,' says the lama. 'Merit greater than your knowing. And ye will return to the Hills,' he sighs.

'Surely. The high hills as soon as may be.' The bearer rubs his shoulder, drinks water, spits it out again, and readjusts his grass sandal. Kim—his face is drawn and tired—pays very small silver from his belt, heaves out the food-bag, crams an oilskin packet—they are holy writings—into his bosom, and helps the lama to his feet. The peace has come again into the old man's eyes, and he does not look for the hills to fall down and crush him as he did that terrible night when they were delayed by the flooded river.

The men pick up the *dooli* and swing out of sight between the scrub clumps.

The lama raises a hand toward the rampart of the Himalayas. 'Not with you, O blessed among all hills, fell the Arrow of Our Lord! And never shall I breathe your air again!'

'But thou art ten times the stronger man in this good air,' says Kim, for to his wearied soul appeal the well-cropped, kindly plains. 'Here, or hereabouts, fell the Arrow, yes. We will go very softly, perhaps a *kos* a day, for the Search is sure. But the bag weighs heavy.'

'Ay, our Search is sure. I have come out of great temptation.'

* * *

It was never more than a couple of miles a day now, and Kim's shoulders bore all the weight of it—the burden of an old man, the burden of the heavy food-bag with the locked books, the load of the writings on his heart, and the details of the daily routine. He begged in the dawn, set blankets for the lama's meditation, held the weary head on his lap through the noonday heats, fanning away the flies till his wrist ached, begged again in the evenings, and rubbed the lama's feet, who rewarded him with promise of Freedom—to-day, to-morrow, or, at furthest, the next day.

'Never was such a *chela*. I doubt at times whether Ananda more faithfully nursed Our Lord. And thou art a Sahib? When I was a man—a long time ago—I forgot that. Now I look upon thee often, and every time I remember that thou art a Sahib. It is strange.'

'Thou hast said there is neither black nor white. Why plague me with this talk, Holy One? Let me rub the other foot. It vexes me. I am *not* a Sahib. I am thy *chela*, and my head is heavy on my shoulders.'

'Patience a little! We reach Freedom together. Then thou and I, upon the far bank of the River, will look back upon our lives as in the Hills we saw our day's marches laid out behind us. Perhaps I was once a Sahib.'

''Was never a Sahib like thee, I swear it.'

'I am certain the Keeper of the Images in the Wonder House was in past life a very wise abbot. But even his spectacles do not make my eyes see. There fall shadows when I would look steadily. No matter— we know the tricks of the poor stupid carcass—shadow changing to another shadow. I am bound by the illusion of Time and Space. How far came we to-day in the flesh?'

'Perhaps half a *kos*.' Three quarters of a mile, and it was a weary march.

'Half a *kos*. Ha! I went ten thousand thousand in the spirit. How we are all lapped and swathed and swaddled in these senseless things.' He looked at his thin blue-veined hand that found the beads so heavy. '*Chela*, hast thou never a wish to leave me?'

Kim thought of the oilskin packet and the books in the food-bag. If some one duly authorised would only take delivery of them the Great Game might play itself for aught he then cared. He was tired and hot in his head, and a cough that came from the stomach worried him.

'No,' he said almost sternly. 'I am not a dog or a snake to bite when I have learned to love.'

'Thou art too tender for me.'

'Not that either. I have moved in one matter without consulting thee. I have sent a message to the Kulu woman by that woman who gave us the goat's milk this morn, saying that thou wast a little feeble and would need a litter. I beat myself in my mind that I did not do it when we entered the Doon. We stay in this place till the litter returns.'

'I am content. She is a woman with a heart of gold, as thou sayest, but a talker—something of a talker.'

'She will not weary thee. I have looked to that also. Holy One, my heart is very heavy for my many carelessnesses towards thee.' An hysterical catch rose in his throat. 'I have walked thee too far; I have not picked good food always for thee; I have not considered the heat; I have talked to people on the road and left thee alone. . . . I have—I have . . . *Hai mai!* But I love thee . . . and it is all too late. . . . I was a child. . . . Oh why was I not a man! . . .' Overborne by strain, fatigue, and the weight beyond his years, Kim broke down and sobbed at the lama's feet.

'What a to-do is here,' said the old man gently. 'Thou hast never stepped a hair's breadth from the Way of Obedience. Neglect me? Child, I have lived on thy strength as an old tree lives on the lime of a new wall. Day by day, since Shamlegh down, I have stolen strength from thee. *Therefore*, not through any sin of thine, art thou weakened. It is the Body—the silly, stupid Body—that speaks now. Not the assured Soul. Be comforted! Know at least the devils that thou fightest. They are earth-born—children of illusion. We will go to the woman from Kulu. She shall acquire merit in housing us, and specially in tending me. Thou shalt run free till strength returns. I had forgotten the stupid Body. If there be any blame, I bear it. But we are too close to the gates of deliverance to weigh blame. I could praise thee, but what need? In a little—in a very little—we shall sit beyond all needs.'

And so he petted and comforted Kim with wise saws and grave texts on that little understood beast, our Body, who, being but a delusion, insists on posing as the Soul, to the darkening of the Way, and the immense multiplication of unnecessary devils.

'Hai! hai! Let us talk of the woman from Kulu. Think you she will ask another charm for her grandsons? When I was a young man, a very long time ago, I was plagued with these vapours, and some others, and I went to an abbot—a very holy man and a seeker after truth, though then I knew it not. Sit up and listen, child of my soul! My tale was told. Said he to me, "*Chela* know this. There are many lies in the world, and not a few liars, but there are no liars like our bodies, except it be the sensations of our bodies." Considering this I was comforted, and of his great favour he suffered me to drink tea in his presence. Suffer me now to drink tea, for I am thirsty.'

With a laugh above his tears, Kim kissed the lama's feet, and went about tea-making.

'Thou leanest on me in the body, Holy One, but I lean on thee for some other things. Dost know it?'

'I have guessed maybe,' and the lama's eyes twinkled. 'We must change that.'

So, when with scufflings and scrapings and a hot air of importance, paddled up nothing less than the Sahiba's pet palanquin sent twenty miles, with that same grizzled old Oorya servant in charge, and when they reached the disorderly order of the long white rambling house behind Saharunpore, the lama took his own measures.

Said the Sahiba cheerily from an upper window, after compliments: 'What is the good of an old woman's advice to an old man? I told thee—I *told* thee, Holy One, to keep an eye upon the *chela*. How didst thou do it? Never answer me! *I* know. He has been running among the women. Look at his eyes—hollow and sunk—and the Betraying Line from the nose down! He has been sifted out! Fie! Fie! And a priest, too!'

Kim looked up over-weary to smile, shaking his head in denial.

'Do not jest,' said the lama. 'That time is done. We are here upon great matters. A sickness of soul took me in the Hills, and him a sickness of the body. Since then I have lived upon his strength—eating him.'

'Children together—young and old,' she sniffed, but forbore to make any new jokes. 'May this present hospitality restore ye. Hold awhile and I will come to gossip of the high good hills.'

At evening time—her son-in-law was returned, so she did not need to go on inspection round the farm—she won to the meat of the matter, explained low-voicedly by the lama. The two old heads nodded wisely together. Kim had reeled to a room with a cot in it, and was dozing soddenly. The lama had forbidden him to set blankets or get food.

'I know—I know. Who but I?' she cackled. 'We who go down to the burning-ghats clutch at the hands of those coming up from the River of Life with full water-jars—yes, brimming water-jars. I did the boy wrong. He lent thee his strength? It is true that the old eat the young daily. 'Stands now we must restore him.'

'Thou hast many times acquired merit——'

'*My* merit. What is it? Old bag of bones making curries for men who do not ask "Who cooked this?" Now if it were stored up for my grandson——'

'He that had the belly-pain?'

'To think the Holy One remembers *that!* I must tell his mother. It is most singular honour! "He that had the belly-pain"—straightway the Holy One remembered. She will be proud.'

'My *chela* is to me as is a son to the unenlightened.'

'Say grandson, rather. Mothers have not the wisdom of our years. If a child cries they say the heavens are falling. Now a grandmother is far enough separated from the pain of bearing and pleasure of giving the breast to consider whether a cry is wickedness pure or the wind. And since thou speakest once again of wind, when last the Holy One was here, maybe I offended in pressing for charms.'

'Sister,' said the lama, using that form of address a Buddhist monk may sometimes employ towards a nun, 'if charms comfort thee——'

'They are better than ten thousand doctors.'

'I say, if they comfort thee, I who was Abbot of Such-zen, will make as many as thou mayest desire. I have never seen thy face——'

'*That* even the monkeys who steal our loquats count for a gain. Hee! hee!'

'But as he who sleeps there said,' he nodded at the shut door of the guest-chamber across the forecourt, 'thou hast a heart of gold. . . . And he is in the spirit my very "grandson" to me.'

'Good! I am the Holy One's cow.' This was pure Hinduism, but the lama never heeded. 'I am old. I have borne sons in the body. Oh once I could please men! Now I can cure them.' He heard her armlets tinkle as though she bared arms for action. 'I will take over the boy and dose him, and stuff him, and make him all whole. Hai! hai! We old people know something yet.'

Wherefore when Kim, aching in every bone, opened his eyes, and would go to the cook-house to get his master's food, he found strong coercion about him, and a veiled old figure at the door, flanked by the grizzled manservant, who told him precisely the very things that he was on no account to do.

'Thou must have—thou shalt have nothing. What? A locked box in which to keep holy books? Oh, that is another matter. Heavens forbid I should come between a priest and his prayers! It shall be brought, and thou shalt keep the key.'

They pushed the coffer under his cot, and Kim shut away Mahbub's pistol, the oilskin packet of letters, and the locked books and diaries, with a groan of relief. For some absurd reason their weight on his shoulders was nothing to their weight on his poor mind. His neck ached under it of nights.

'Thine is a sickness uncommon in youth these days: since young folk have given up tending their betters. The remedy is sleep, and certain drugs,' said the Sahiba; and he was glad to give himself up to the blankness that half menaced and half soothed him.

She brewed drinks, in some mysterious Asiatic equivalent to the still-room—drenches that smelt pestilently and tasted worse. She stood over Kim till they went down, and inquired exhaustively after they had come up. She laid a taboo upon the forecourt, and enforced it by means of an armed man. It is true he was seventy odd, that his scabbarded sword ceased at the hilt; but he represented the authority of the Sahiba, and loaded wains, chattering servants, calves, dogs, hens, and the like, fetched a wide compass by those parts. Best of all, when the body was cleared, she cut out from the mass of poor relations that crowded the back of the buildings—household dogs, we name them—a cousin's widow, skilled in what Europeans, who know nothing about it, call massage. And the two of them, laying him east and west, that the mysterious earth-currents which thrill the clay of our bodies might help and not hinder, took him to pieces all one long afternoon—bone by bone, muscle by muscle, ligament by ligament, and lastly, nerve by nerve. Kneaded to irresponsible pulp, half hypnotised by the perpetual flick and readjustment of the uneasy *chudders* that veiled their eyes, Kim slid ten thousand miles into slumber—thirty-six hours of it—sleep that soaked like rain after drought.

Then she fed him, and the house spun to her clamour. She caused fowls to be slain; she sent for vegetables, and the sober, slow-thinking gardener, nigh as old as she, sweated for it; she took spices, and milk, and onion, with little fish from the brooks—anon limes for sherbets, quails of the pit, then chicken-livers upon a skewer, with sliced ginger between.

'I have seen something of this world,' she said over the crowded trays, 'and there are but two sorts of women in it—those who take the strength out of a man and those who put it back. Once I was that one, and now I am this. Nay—do not play the priestling with me. Mine was but a jest. If it does not hold good now, it will when thou takest the road again. Cousin'—this to the poor relation, never wearied of extolling her patroness's charity—'he is getting a bloom on the skin of a new-curried horse. Our work is like polishing jewels to be thrown to a dance-girl—eh?'

Kim sat up and smiled. The terrible weakness had dropped from him like an old shoe. His tongue itched for free speech again, and but a week back the lightest word clogged it like ashes. The pain in his neck (he must have caught it from the lama) had gone with the heavy dengue-aches and the evil taste in the mouth. The two old women, a little, but not much more careful about their veils now, clucked as merrily as the hens that had entered picking through the open door.

'Where is my Holy One?' he demanded.

'Hear him! Thy Holy One is well,' she snapped viciously. 'Though that is none of *his* merit. Knew I a charm to make him wise, I'd sell my jewels and buy it. To refuse good food that I cooked myself—and go roving into the fields for two nights on an empty belly—and to tumble into a brook at the end of it—call you *that* holiness? Then, when he has nearly broken what thou hast left of my heart with anxiety he tells me that he has acquired merit. Oh how like are all men! No, that was not it—he tells me that he is freed from all sin. *I* could have told him that before he wetted himself all over. He is well now—this happened a week ago—but burn me such holiness! A babe of three would do better. Do not fret thyself for the Holy One. He keeps both eyes on thee when he is not wading our brooks.'

'I do not remember to have seen him. I remember that the days and nights passed like bars of white and black, opening and shutting. I was not sick: I was only tired.'

'A lethargy that comes by right some few score years later. But it is all done now.'

'Maharanee,' Kim began, but led by the look in her eye, changed it to the title of plain love—'Mother, I owe my life to thee. How shall I make thanks? Ten thousand blessings upon thy house and——'

'The house be unblessed.' (It is impossible to give exactly the old lady's word.) 'Thank the Gods as a priest if thou wilt, but thank me if thou carest as a son. Heavens above! Have I shifted thee and lifted thee and slapped and twisted thy ten toes to find texts flung at my head? Somewhere a mother must have borne thee to break her heart. What used thou to her—son?'

'I had no mother, my mother,' said Kim. 'She died, they tell me, when I was young.'

'*Hai mai!* Then none can say I have robbed her of any right if—when thou takest the road again and this house is but one of a thousand used for shelter and forgotten, after an easy-flung blessing. No matter. I need no blessings, but—but——' She stamped her foot at the poor relation: 'Take up the trays to the house. What is the good of stale food in the room, oh woman of ill-omen?'

'I ha—have borne a son in my time too, but he died,' whimpered the bowed sister-figure behind the *chudder*. 'Thou knowest he died! I only waited for the order to take away the tray.'

'It is I that am the woman of ill-omen,' cried the old lady penitently. 'We that go down to the *chattris* (the big umbrellas above the burning-ghats where the priests take their last dues) clutch hard at the bearers of the *chattis* (water-jars—young folk full of the pride of life, she meant; but the pun is clumsy). When one cannot dance in the festival one must e'en look out of the window, and grandmothering takes all a woman's time. Thy master gives me all the charms I now desire for my daughter's eldest, by reason—is it?—that he is wholly free from sin. The *hakim* is brought very low these days. He goes about poisoning my servants for lack of their betters.'

'What *hakim*, mother?'

'That very Dacca man who gave me the pill which rent me in three pieces. He cast up like a strayed camel a week ago, vowing that he and thou had been blood-brothers together up Kulu-way, and feigning great anxiety for thy health. He was very thin and hungry, so I gave orders to have him stuffed too—him and his anxiety!'

'I would see him if he is here.'

'He eats five times a day, and lances boils for my hinds to save himself from an apoplexy. He is so full of anxiety for thy health that he sticks to the cook-house door and stays himself with scraps. He will keep. We shall never get rid of him.'

'Send him here, mother'—the twinkle returned to Kim's eye for a flash—'and I will try.'

'I'll send him, but to chase him off is an ill turn. At least he had the sense to fish the Holy One out of the brook; thus, as the Holy One did *not* say, acquiring merit.'

'He is a very wise *hakim*. Send him, mother.'

'Priest praising priest? A miracle! If he is any friend of thine (ye squabbled at your last meeting) I'll hale him here with horse-ropes and—and give him a caste-dinner afterwards,[4] my son. . . . Get up and see the world! This lying abed is the mother of seventy devils . . . my son! my son!'

She trotted forth to raise a typhoon off the cook-house, and almost on her shadow rolled in the Babu, robed as to the shoulders like a Roman emperor, jowled like Titus, bare-headed, with new patent-leather shoes, in highest condition of fat, exuding joy and salutations.

'By Jove, Mister O'Hara, but I *am* jolly glad to see you. I will kindly shut the door. It is a pity you are sick. Are you very sick?'

'The papers—the papers from the *kilta*. The maps and the *murasla!*' He held out the key impatiently; for the present need on his soul was to get rid of the loot.

'You are quite right. That is correct departmental view to take. You have got everything?'

'All that was handwritten in the *kilta* I took. The rest I threw down the hill.' He could hear the key's grate in the lock, the sticky pull of the slow-rending oil-cloth, and a quick shuffling of papers. He had been annoyed out of all reason by the knowledge that they lay below him through the sick idle days—a burden incommunicable. For that reason the blood tingled through his body, when Hurree, skipping elephantinely, shook hands again.

'This is fine! This is finest! Mister O'Hara! You have—ha! ha!—swiped the whole bag of tricks—locks, stocks, and barrels. They told me it was eights months' work gone up the spouts! By Jove, how they

---

[4] A ceremonial and festive dinner; the woman of Kulu, who reveres a Buddhist lama, prepares a Hindu dinner for Hurree, a man she may believe to be a Muslim.

beat me! . . . Look, here is the letter from Hilás!' He intoned a line or two of Court Persian, which is the language of authorised and unauthorised diplomacy. 'Mister Rajah Sahib has just about put his foot in the holes. He will have to explain offeecially how the deuce-an'-all he is writing love-letters to the Czar. And they are very cunning maps . . . and there is three or four Prime Ministers of these parts implicated by the correspondence. By Gad, Sar! The British Government will change the succession in Hilás and Bunár, and nominate new heirs to the throne. "Trea-son most base" . . . but you do not understand? Eh?'

'Are they in thy hands?' said Kim. It was all he cared for.

'Just you jolly well bet yourself they are.' He stowed the entire trove about his body, as only Orientals can. 'They are going up to the office, too. The old lady thinks I am permanent fixture here, but I shall go away with these straight off—immediately. Mr. Lurgan will be proud man. You are offeecially subordinate to me, but I shall embody your name in my verbal report. It is a pity we are not allowed written reports. We Bengalis excel in thee exact science.' He tossed back the key and showed the box empty.

'Good. That is good. I was very tired. My Holy One was sick, too. And did he fall into——'

'Oah yess. I am his good friend, I tell you. He was behaving very strange when I came down after you, and I thought perhaps he might have the papers. I followed him on his meditations, and to discuss ethnological points also. You see, I am verree small person here nowadays, in comparison with all his charms. By Jove, O'Hara, do you know, he is afflicted with infirmity of fits. Yess, I tell you. Cataleptic, too, if not also epileptic. I found him in such a state under a tree *in articulo mortem*,[5] and he jumped up and walked into a brook and he was nearly drowned but for me. I pulled him out.'

'Because I was not there!' said Kim. 'He might have died.'

'Yes, he might have died, but he is dry now, and asserts he has undergone transfiguration.' The Babu tapped his forehead knowingly. 'I took notes of his statements for Royal Society—*in posse*.[6] You must make haste and be quite well and come back to Simla, and I will tell you all my tale at Lurgan's. It was splendid. The bottoms of their trousers were *quite* torn, and old Nahan Rajah, he thought they were European soldiers deserting.'

'Oh, the Russians? How long were they with thee?'

---

[5]At the moment of death. This should be *in articulo mortis*. Here, as elsewhere, Hurree Baboo misuses Latin.

[6]Latin: "Within the realm of possibility," or "just in case": that is, in case the Royal Society should be interested in publishing his notes.

'One was a Frenchman. Oh, days and days and days! Now all the hill-people believe all Russians are all beggars. By Jove! they had not one dam-thing that I did not get them. And I told the common people—oah, *such* tales and anecdotes! I will tell you at old Lurgan's when you come up. We will have—ah—a night out! It is feather in both our caps! Yess, and they gave me a certificate. That is creaming joke. You should have seen them at the Alliance Bank identifying themselves! And thank Almighty God you got their papers so well! You do not laugh verree much, but you shall laugh when you are well. Now I will go straight to the railway and get out. You shall have all sorts of credits for your game. When do you come along? We are very proud of you though you gave us great frights. And especially Mahbub.'

'Ay, Mahbub. And where is he?'

'Selling horses in this vi-cinity, of course.'

'Here! Why? Speak slowly. There is a thickness in my head still.'

The Babu looked shyly down his nose. 'Well, you see, I am fearful man, and I do not like responsibility. You were sick, you see, and I did not know where deuce-an'-all the papers were, and if so, how many. So when I had come down here I slipped in private wire to Mahbub— he was at Meerut for races—and I tell him how case stands. He comes up with his men and he consorts with the lama, and then he calls me a fool, and is very rude——'

'But wherefore—wherefore?'

'That is what *I* ask. I only suggest that if any one steals the papers I should like some good strong, brave men to rob them back again. You see they are vitally important, and Mahbub Ali he did not know where you were.'

'Mahbub Ali to rob the Sahiba's house? Thou art mad, Babu,' said Kim with indignation.

'I wanted the papers. Suppose she had stole them? It was only practical suggestion, *I* think. You are not pleased, eh?'

A native proverb—unquotable—showed the blackness of Kim's disapproval.

'Well,'—Hurree shrugged his shoulders,—'there is no accounting for thee taste. Mahbub was angry too. He has sold horses all about here, and he says old lady is *pukka* (thorough) old lady and would not condescend to such ungentlemanly things. *I* do not care. I have got the papers, and I was very glad of moral support from Mahbub. I tell you I am fearful man, but, somehow or other, the more fearful I am the more dam-tight places I get into. So I was glad you came with me to Chini, and I am glad Mahbub was close by. The old lady she is sometimes very rude to me and my beautiful pills.'

'Allah be merciful,' said Kim on his elbow, rejoicing. 'What a beast of wonder is a Babu! And that man walked alone—if he did walk—with robbed and angry foreigners!'

'Oah, thatt was nothing, after they had done beating me; but if I lost the papers it was pretty jolly serious. Mahbub he nearly beat me too, and he went and consorted with the lama no end. I shall stick to ethnological investigations henceforwards. Now good-bye, Mister O'Hara. I can catch 4.25 P.M. to Umballa if I am quick. It will be good times when we all tell thee tale up at Mister Lurgan's. I shall report you offeecially better. Good-bye, my dear fallow, and when next you are under thee emotions please do not use the Mohammedan terms with the Tibet dress.'

He shook hands twice—a Babu to his boot-heels—and opened the door. With the fall of the sunlight upon his still triumphant face he returned to the humble Dacca quack.

'He robbed them,' thought Kim, forgetting his own share in the game. 'He tricked them. He lied to them like a Bengali. They give him a *chit* (a testimonial). He makes them a mock at the risk of his life—*I* never would have gone down to them after the pistol-shots—and then he says he is a fearful man. . . . And he *is* a fearful man. I must get into the world again.'

At first his legs bent like bad pipe-stems, and the flood and rush of the sunlit air dazzled him. He squatted by the white wall, the mind rummaging among the incidents of the long *dooli* journey, the lama's weaknesses, and, now that the stimulus of talk was removed, his own self-pity, of which, like the sick, he had great store. The unnerved brain edged away from all the outside, as a raw horse, once rowelled, sidles from the spur. It was enough, amply enough, that the spoil of the *kilta* was away—off his hands—out of his possession. He tried to think of the lama,—to wonder why he had tumbled into a brook,—but the bigness of the world, seen between the forecourt gates, swept linked thought aside. Then he looked upon the trees and the broad fields, with the thatched huts hidden among crops—looked with strange eyes unable to take up the size and proportion and use of things—stared for a still half-hour. All that while he felt, though he could not put it into words, that his soul was out of gear with its surroundings—a cog-wheel unconnected with any machinery, just like the idle cog-wheel of a cheap Beheea sugar-crusher laid by in a corner. The breezes fanned over him, the parrots shrieked at him, the noises of the populated house behind—squabbles, orders, and reproofs—hit on dead ears.

'I am Kim. I am Kim. And what is Kim?' His soul repeated it again and again.

He did not want to cry,—had never felt less like crying in his life,—but of a sudden easy, stupid tears trickled down his nose, and with an almost audible click he felt the wheels of his being lock up anew on the world without. Things that rode meaningless on the eyeball an instant before slid into proper proportion. Roads were meant to be walked upon, houses to be lived in, cattle to be driven, fields to be tilled, and men and women to be talked to. They were all real and true—solidly planted upon the feet—perfectly comprehensible—clay of his clay, neither more nor less. He shook himself like a dog with a flea in his ear, and rambled out of the gate. Said the Sahiba, to whom watchful eyes reported this move: 'Let him go. I have done my share. Mother Earth must do the rest. When the Holy One comes back from meditation, tell him.'

There stood an empty bullock-cart on a little knoll half a mile away, with a young banian tree behind—a look-out, as it were, above some new-ploughed levels; and his eyelids, bathed in soft air, grew heavy as he neared it. The ground was good clean dust—no new herbage that, living, is half-way to death already, but the hopeful dust that holds the seed of all life. He felt it between his toes, patted it with his palms, and joint by joint, sighing luxuriously, laid him down full length along in the shadow of the wooden-pinned cart. And Mother Earth was as faithful as the Sahiba. She breathed through him to restore the poise he had lost lying so long on a cot cut off from her good currents. His head lay powerless upon her breast, and his opened hands surrendered to her strength. The many-rooted tree above him, and even the dead man-handled wood beside, knew what he sought, as he himself did not know. Hour upon hour he lay deeper than sleep.

Towards evening, when the dust of returning kine made all the horizons smoke, came the lama and Mahbub Ali, both afoot, walking cautiously, for the house had told them where he had gone.

'Allah! What a fool's trick to play in open country,' muttered the horse-dealer. 'He could be shot a hundred times—but this is not the Border.'

'And,' said the lama, repeating a many-times-told tale, 'never was such a *chela*. Temperate, kindly, wise, of ungrudging disposition, a merry heart upon the road, never forgetting, learned, truthful, courteous. Great is his reward!'

'I know the boy—as I have said.'

'And he was all those things?'

'Some of them—but I have not yet found a Red Hat's charm for making him overly truthful. He has certainly been well nursed.'

'The Sahiba is a heart of gold,' said the lama earnestly. 'She looks upon him as her son.'

'Hmph! Half Hind seems that-way disposed. I only wished to see that the boy had come to no harm and was a free agent. As thou knowest, he and I were old friends in the first days of your pilgrimage together.'

'That is a bond between us.' The lama sat down. 'We are at the end of the pilgrimage.'

'No thanks to thee thine was not cut off for good and all a week back. I heard what the Sahiba said to thee when we bore thee up on the cot.' Mahbub laughed, and tugged his new-dyed beard.

'I was meditating upon other matters that tide. It was the *hakim* from Dacca broke my meditations.'

'Otherwise'—this was in Pashtu for decency's sake—'thou wouldst have ended thy meditations upon the sultry side of Hell—being an unbeliever and an idolator for all thy child's simplicity. But now, Red Hat, what is to be done?'

'This very night,'—the words came slowly, vibrating with triumph,—'this very night he will be as free as I am from all taint of sin—assured as I am when he quits this body of Freedom from the Wheel of Things. I have a sign,' he laid his hand above the torn chart in his bosom, 'that my time is short; but I shall have safe-guarded him throughout the years. Remember, I have reached Knowledge, as I told thee only three nights back.'

'It must be true, as the Tirah priest said when I stole his cousin's wife, that I am a *sufi* (a free-thinker); for here I sit,' said Mahbub to himself, drinking in blasphemy unthinkable. ' . . . I remember the tale. On that, then, he goes to *Jannatu l' Adn* (the Gardens of Eden). But how? Wilt thou slay him or drown him in that wonderful river from which the Babu dragged thee?'

'I was dragged from no river,' said the lama simply. 'Thou hast forgotten what befell. I found it by Knowledge.'

'Oh, aye. True,' stammered Mahbub, divided between high indignation and enormous mirth. 'I had forgotten the exact run of what happened. Thou didst find it knowingly.'

'And to say that I would take life is—not a sin, but a madness simple. My *chela* aided me to the River. It is his right to be cleansed from sin—with me.'

'Ay, he needs cleansing. But afterwards, old man—afterwards?'

'What matter under all the heavens? He is sure of Nibban—enlightened—as I am.'

'Well said. I had a fear he might mount Mohammed's Horse and fly away.'

'Nay—he must go forth as a teacher.'

'Aha! Now I see! That is the right gait for the colt. Certainly he must go forth as a teacher. He is somewhat urgently needed as a scribe by the State, for instance.'

'To that end he was prepared. I acquired merit in that I gave alms for his sake. A good deed does not die. He aided me in my Search. I aided him in his. Just is the Wheel, O horse-seller from the North. Let him be a teacher; let him be a scribe—what matter? He will have attained Freedom at the end. The rest is illusion.'

'What matter? When I must have him with me beyond Balkh in six months! I come up with ten lame horses and three strong-backed men—thanks to that chicken of a Babu—to break a sick boy by force out of an old trot's house. It seems that I stand by while a young Sahib is hoisted into Allah knows what of an idolater's heaven by means of old Red Hat. And I am reckoned something of a player of the Game myself! But the madman is fond of the boy; and I must be very reasonably mad too.'

'What is the prayer?' said the lama, as the rough Pashtu rumbled into the red beard.

'No matter at all; but now I understand that the boy, sure of Paradise, can yet enter Government service, my mind is easier. I must get to my horses. It grows dark. Do not wake him. I have no wish to hear him call thee master.'

'But he *is* my disciple. What else?'

'He has told me.' Mahbub choked down his touch of spleen and rose laughing. 'I am not altogether of thy faith, Red Hat—if so small a matter concern thee.'

'It is nothing,' said the lama.

'I thought not. Therefore it will not move thee sinless, new-washed and three parts drowned to boot, when I call thee a good man—a very good man. We have talked together some four or five evenings now, and for all I am a horse-coper I can still, as the saying is, see holiness beyond the legs of a horse. Yea, can see, too, how our Friend of all the World put his hand in thine at the first. Use him well, and suffer him to return to the world as a teacher, when thou hast—bathed his legs, if that be the proper medicine for the colt.'

'Why not follow the Way thyself, and so accompany the boy?'

Mahbub stared stupefied at the magnificent insolence of the demand, which across the Border he would have paid with more than a blow. Then the humour of it touched his worldly soul.

'Softly—softly—one foot at a time, as the lame gelding went over the Umballa jumps. I may come to Paradise later—I have workings that way—great motions—and I owe them to thy simplicity. Thou hast never lied?'

'What need?'

'Oh Allah, hear him! "What need" in this Thy world! Nor ever harmed a man?'

'Once—with a pencase—before I was wise.'

'So? I think the better of thee. Thy teachings are good. Thou hast turned one man that I know from the path of strife.' He laughed immensely. 'He came here open-minded to commit a *dacoity* (a house-robbery with violence). Yes, to cut, rob, kill, and carry off what he desired.'

'A great foolishness!'

'Oh! black shame too. So he thought after he had seen thee—and a few others, male and female. So he abandoned it; and now he goes to beat a big fat Babu man.'

'I do not understand.'

'Allah forbid it! Some men are strong in knowledge, Red Hat. Thy strength is stronger still. Keep it—I think thou wilt. If the boy be not a good servant, pull his ears off.'

With a hitch of his broad Bokhariot belt the Pathan swaggered off into the gloaming, and the lama came down from his clouds so far as to look at the broad back.

'That person lacks courtesy, and is deceived by the shadow of appearances. But he spoke well of my *chela*, who now enters upon his reward. Let me make the prayer! . . . Wake, O fortunate above all born of women. Wake! It is found!'

Kim came up from those deep wells, and the lama attended his yawning pleasure; duly snapping fingers to head off evil spirits.

'I have slept a hundred years. Where——? Holy One, hast *thou* been here long? I went out to look for thee, but'—he laughed drowsily—'I slept by the way. I am all well now. Hast thou eaten? Let us go to the house. It is many days since I tended thee. And the Sahiba fed thee well? Who shampooed thy legs? What of the weaknesses—the belly and the neck, and the beating in the ears?'

'Gone—all gone. Dost thou not know?'

'I know nothing, but that I have not seen thee in a monkey's age. Know what?'

'Strange the knowledge did not reach out to thee, when all my thoughts were theeward.'

'I cannot see the face, but the voice is like a gong. Has the Sahiba made a young man of thee by her cookery?'

He peered at the cross-legged figure, outlined jet-black against the lemon-coloured drift of light. So does the stone Bodhisat sit who looks down upon the patent self-registering turnstiles of the Lahore Museum.

The lama held his peace. Except for the click of the rosary and a faint *clop-clop* of Mahbub's retreating feet, the soft, smoky silence of evening in India wrapped them close.

'Hear me! I bring news.'

'But let us——'

Out shot the long yellow hand compelling silence. Kim tucked his feet under his robe-edge obediently.

'Hear me! I bring news! The Search is finished. Comes now the Reward. . . . Thus. When we were among the Hills, I lived on thy strength till the young branch bowed and nigh broke. When we came out of the Hills, I was troubled for thee and for other matters which I held in my heart. The boat of my soul lacked direction; I could not see into the Cause of Things. So I gave thee over to the virtuous woman altogether. I took no food. I drank no water. Still I saw not the Way. They pressed food upon me and cried at my shut door. So I removed myself to a hollow under a tree. I took no food. I took no water. I sat in meditation two days and two nights, abstracting my mind; in-breathing and outbreathing in the required manner. . . . Upon the second night—so great was my reward—the wise Soul loosed itself from the silly Body and went free. This I have never before attained, though I have stood on the threshold of it. Consider, for it is a marvel!'

'A marvel indeed. Two days and two nights without food! Where was the Sahiba?' said Kim under his breath.

'Yea, my Soul went free, and, wheeling like an eagle, saw indeed that there was no Teshoo Lama nor any other soul. As a drop draws to water, so my soul drew near to the Great Soul which is beyond all things. At that point, exalted in contemplation, I saw all Hind, from Ceylon in the sea to the Hills, and my own Painted Rocks at Such-zen; I saw every camp and village, to the least, where we have ever rested. I saw them at one time and in one place; for they were within the Soul. By this I knew the Soul had passed beyond the illusion of Time and Space and of Things. By this I knew that I was free. I saw thee lying in thy cot, and I saw thee falling downhill under the idol-ater—at one time, in one place, in my Soul, which, as I say, had touched the Great Soul. Also I saw the stupid body of Teshoo Lama lying down, and the *hakim* from Dacca kneeled beside, shouting in its ear. Then my Soul was all alone, and I saw nothing, for I was all things, having reached the Great Soul. And I meditated a thousand thousand years, passionless, well aware of the Causes of all Things. Then a voice cried: "What shall come to the boy if thou art dead?" and I was shaken back and forth in myself with pity for thee; and I said: "I will return to my *chela*, lest he miss the Way." Upon this my Soul, which is the soul of Teshoo Lama, withdrew itself from the Great Soul with strivings and yearnings and retchings and agonies not to be told. As the egg from the fish, as the fish from the water, as the water from the cloud, as the cloud from the thick air; so put forth, so leaped out, so drew away, so fumed up the soul of Teshoo Lama from the Great Soul. Then a voice cried: "The River! Take heed to the River!" and I looked down upon all the world, which was as I had seen it before—one in time, one in place—and I saw plainly the River of the Arrow at my feet. At that hour my Soul was hampered by some evil or other whereof I was not wholly cleansed, and it lay upon my arms and coiled round my waist; but I put it aside, and I cast forth as an eagle in my flight for the very place of the River. I pushed aside world upon world for thy sake. I saw the River below me—the River of the Arrow—and, descending, the waters of it closed over me; and behold I was again in the body of Teshoo Lama, but free from sin, and the *hakim* from Dacca bore up my head in the waters of the River. It is here! It is behind the mango-tope here—even here!'

'Allah Kerim! Oh, well that the Babu was by! Wast thou very wet?'

'Why should I regard? I remember the *hakim* was concerned for the body of Teshoo Lama. He haled it out of the holy water in his hands, and there came afterwards thy horse-seller from the North with a cot and men, and they put the body on the cot and bore it up to the Sahiba's house.'

'What said the Sahiba?'

'I was meditating in that body, and did not hear. So thus the Search is ended. For the merit that I have acquired, the River of the Arrow is here. It broke forth at our feet, as I have said. I have found it. Son of my Soul, I have wrenched my Soul back from the Threshold of Freedom to free thee from all sin—as I am free, and sinless. Just is the Wheel! Certain is our deliverance. Come!'

He crossed his hands on his lap and smiled, as a man may who has won Salvation for himself and his beloved.

THE END

John Lockwood Kipling
The End of the Search

Set shortly after Kim feels the "wheels of his being lock up anew on the world without,"
J. L. Kipling's final bas-relief takes as background that "many-rooted" young tree under
which Kim surrenders to the healing strength of Mother Earth. At center, serenely
grounding the composition, Teshoo Lama meditates before an empty bullock-cart. The
cart seems very much of this world; yet its wheel frames the lama's head, unmistakably invoking Buddhist sacred iconography. To the right, a silhouetted Mahbub Ali stares out of
the frame. Is Kim, reclining ambiguously in the foreground, looking inward—or outward?

Glossary

In addressing terms with complex, often disputed and shifting meanings, we have focused primarily on the task of locating Kipling's novel within the context of late-century Anglo-Indian culture. We have been grateful to consult George Clifford Whitworth's *Anglo-Indian Dictionary* (1885); Edward Balfour's *Cyclopedia of India* (1885); Henry Yule and A. C. Burnell's *Hobson-Jobson*, ed. William Crooke (2nd edition, 1903); and Sharad Keskar's notes to *Kim* in the New Readers' Guide to the works of Rudyard Kipling (http://www.kipling.org.uk/book-mart_fra.htm).

Akali: Literally eternal or immortal; armed order of Sikh devotees.

Akas (Aka Khels): Members of an Afridi clan involved in ongoing conflicts with the British.

Ananda: Buddha's devoted attendant and disciple.

Angrezi: English.

Anna: Unit of Indian currency established under British rule: 1/16th of a rupee.

Arhats: Buddhist saints or sages; monks who attained full enlightenment. Tibetan Arhat painting shows strong Chinese influences.

Arplan: Aphrodisiac, rejuvenating drug (Keskar).

Arré: Equivalent to "Listen!"

Babu (Baboo): Originally a term of respect; used slightingly by the British for educated Bengalis, many of whom worked as managers or clerks.

Baltis: Muslims from Baltistan, north of Lahore.

Betah: "Son"; applied to boys within a given village clan (Keskar).

Bhang: Intoxicating preparation, usually a drink, made from hemp leaves and flowers.

Bhisti: Water carrier.

Bhotiyal: Tibet and Nepal.

Block tea (tea-bricks): Compressed, molded leaves and stems; sometimes used as currency. Tibetans' consumption of Chinese rather than Indian block tea frustrated British colonial traders.

Bibi Miriam: Lady Mary (Virgin Mary).

Būt-parast: (pl. Būt-parasti) Islamic term for idol-worshipper.

Bodhisat: In Buddhism, one who aspires toward perfect enlightenment, both of oneself and others; sometimes used for Siddhartha Gautama before he attained Buddhahood. A bodhisattva is one who, having attained enlightenment, chooses to defer going on to nirvana in order to help others who are still suffering.

Bukkin: Chatter.

Bunnias (Banyas): Hindu merchants, shopkeepers, men of business.

Burning-ghats: Riverbank sections, built up with steps down to the water; used as Hindu cremation grounds.

Chudders: Large cloth sheets, often used as shawls.

Choor: Thief.

Chumars: Low-caste workers in hides and leathers.

Cinchona: Tree whose bark was used in treating malaria.

Coolies: Hired porters, carriers, physical laborers.

Cowrie: White shell used as very small unit of currency.

Dasim: In Islam, the son of Eblis and demon of discord.

Dawut: Islamic practice of exorcism, performed through invocations.

Deodar: Indian cedar; a Himalayan tree sacred to Buddhists and Hindus.

Dewas (Devas): Shining ones; here, something like angels.

Dogra: Located in Jammu, the Punjab, and the Kashmir, Dogras served in famous British fighting regiments.

Dooli: Bamboo stretcher; light litter carried on the shoulders.

Doon siris: Type of acacia tree native to the Doon Valley.

Dunnage: Scraps; packing materials.

Ekka: Small, light, seatless carriage, drawn by a single horse.

Eblis (Iblis; Shaytan; Shaitan): Fallen, demonic tempter; Islamic counterpart to the Jewish and Christian Satan.

Faquirs (Faqirs, Fakirs): Initially, Islamic ascetics devoted to poverty and living from charity; later extended to Hindu holy men. Faquirs' association with miraculous feats led Westerners to use the term for itinerant magicians.

Ferashes: Servants; especially those who pitch tents and spread carpets.

Ferril-backed: Equipped with an iron lock (Keskar).

Ghi: Clarified butter.

Goglet: Small porous bottle used to store and cool water.

Gunga: Ganges, the holy river of the Hindus.

Haj: Pilgrimage to Mecca.

Hajji (Hadji): Title given to Muslims who have made the pilgrimage to Mecca; also a general term of respect.

Hakim: Physician.

Half-caste: Person of mixed European and Indian descent.

Hind: Short for Hindustan, or land of the Hindus; British term for India.

Hoondi: Banker's draft or bill of exchange.

Jain: Member of a large and ancient Indian religious group. Known for its unswerving commitment to *Ahimsa*—the refusal to take life in any form, for whatever reason—Jainism values ascetic discipline as a means of attaining freedom from bondage of rebirth.

Jakko: Mountain near Simla.

Jat: Member of a large ethnic group located mostly in the Punjab. Many Jats were Sikhs.

Jehannum: Hell.

Jhampanis: Men who pulled or pushed open sedan chairs (jhampans) favored by the British.

Kaisar: Emperor.

Kamboh: Member of a Punjabi ethnic group, classified by the British as an "agricultural tribe."

Kabarri: Junk; secondhand goods.

Kafir: Arabic: an infidel or nonbeliever; also natives of Kafiristan.

Kayeth (Kayastha, Kayasth): Member of a Hindu caste of scribes; many attained relatively powerful posts in the British colonial service.

Kentish Fire: Vehement, synchronized clapping, named for public meetings held in Kent, England in 1828–29 to oppose the extension of civil rights to Roman Catholics, and associated with Protestant conservative audiences throughout the century.

Khalsa: Literally, "pure"; an order of Sikh saint-soldiers.

Khanda: Double-edged sword with strong spiritual and iconographic significance for Sikhs.

Khud: Deep drop; precipice.

Kilta: Large wicker or leather basket carried on one's back.

Kos: Imprecise unit of distance, about two miles.

Kuttar: Distinctively shaped, powerful punch dagger used in hand-to-hand combat.

Lakh: Unit of 100,000.

Lala: Hindu title of respect.

Lama: Buddhist religious superior. Kim's lama, Teshoo Lama, is an abbot.

Landau: Horse-drawn four-wheeled carriage.

Lingam: Sacred phallic symbol of Shiva, whose powers include destruction and re-creation.

Lotus: Flower sacred to Buddhism.

***Lusus naturae*:** Latin: freak of nature.

Maharaj: "Great ruler"; honorific form of address.

Maharanees (Maharanis): Queens; a courtesy title.

Mahratta (Maratha): In the broadest, most literal sense, a person from Maharashtra, in western and central India. The Mahrattan Empire's military dominance, which held until 1818, ended after three wars against the British.

Mallum: "Do you know?"; "Understand?"

Mehteranees: Low-caste female street sweepers.

Mian: Title of respect.

Mullah: Learned man; in Islam, a teacher of religious law.

Naikan: Female dancer; euphemism for courtesan or prostitute.

Nickle-jao: "Get out!"

Nirvana: For Hinduism and Buddhism, the highest bliss; the passing-over into another existence, released from suffering and desire.

Nol-kol: A type of vegetable; also known as kohlrabi.

Nucklao: Lucknow.

Od: Member of a Hindu caste of itinerant construction laborers.

Ooryas: People from Orissa, in Eastern India.

Pahareen: Hill woman.

Palanquin: Enclosed sedan chair or litter carried on the shoulders with poles.

Pali: Ancient language, derived from Sanskrit; central to Buddhist sacred texts.

Pan: Chewing mixture of areca nut, lime, and other ingredients, wrapped in betel leaf.

Parao: Resting place; campsite.

Parsee (Parsi): Descendants of the Zoroastrians who fled from Persia to India after the invasion of the Muslim Arabs.

Pashtu: Language of Pathans.

Pathan (Pashtun): Within British India, an Afghani or descendent of Afghanis; in Afghanistan, a member of a distinct, Sunni ethnic group.

Pice: A quarter anna; a very small coin.

Picket: Sentry.

Plasma: Slightly translucent green chalcedony, carved to create gems since ancient times.

Pukka: Genuine; first class; thoroughgoing; permanent.

Pundit (Pandit): Hindu priest or scholar; any expert. Also a British Indian Survey title for trained Indian surveyors.

Punjab: Province in northwestern India; from "five rivers," after the tributaries of the Indus.

Punkah: Framed cloth ceiling fan, worked by pulling a rope.

Quirt: Riding whip with a braided rawhide lash.

Rajahs: Kings or princes.

Rêl: Rail; railway.

Rissaldar (Ressaldar): Indian cavalry commander in the Anglo-Indian Army.

Roum (Rum): Constantinople; now Istanbul, Turkey.

Ruck: Crowd.

Rupee: Standard Anglo-Indian monetary unit.

Ruttees (Rattees): Seeds used as goldsmiths' weights.

Saddhu: Hindu holy man, sage, ascetic; sometimes extended to all holy mendicants.

Sahib: "Master" or "sir"; colonial Indian term for Europeans.

Salaam: "Peace"; salutation, especially Muslim; usually accompanied by a deep, ceremonious bow.

Salep: Medicine, food, or flavoring made from orchid tubers.

Sansis (Sansias): Among those targeted under the colonial government's now-notorious 1871 "Criminal Tribes Amendment," Sansia groups were known for traveling with their families and animals, including dogs.

Sepoy: Indian infantry soldier trained and employed by the British Army.

Serai: Short for "caravanserai"; an inn. "Serai" can also mean "palace"; hence the name Kashmir Serai or, as it is actually known, Sultan Serai, for the square in Old Lahore.

Seven Sisters: Small Indian birds, also known as babblers.

Sewaliks: Foothills of the Himalayas.

Shaitan (Shaytan): Islamic counterpart to Satan.

Shikarris (Shikaris): Game hunters; often guides.

Shabash: "Well done!"

Shraddah: Ceremony in honor of the dead.

Sikh: Literally, "learners" or disciples; followers of Sikhism, a religion of 15th-c. Punjabi origin, influenced both by Hinduism and Islam. Committed both to meditation and military discipline, Sikhs believe in the unity of God and reject the religious claims of caste.

Sinà: The body, especially the chest; also, drugs to clear lungs and bronchial tubes (Keskar).

Sirkar (Sarkar): Government.

Speered: Scots: asked; investigated; enquired.

Stupas: Large shrines housing relics, including relics of the Buddha.

Swedging: Manufacturing or repair process of forcing cold metal into a small space.

Tar-office: Telegraph office.

Theodolite: Surveying instrument; a tripod attached to a small telescope.

Ticca-garri: Hired carriage.

Tirthankars: Aescetics; Jain priests.

Tonga: Small, strong horse-drawn country carriage.

Tope: Grove; sacred or commemorative cairn or mound.

Tum mut: Hindi: "You mustn't" or "Don't" (Keskar).

Urdu: Indian language; a variety of Hindustani, strongly influenced by Arabic and Persian. Originally spoken at the Mughal courts; now the national language of Pakistan.

Vakils: Persons with authority to act for others; representatives or agents; attorneys.

Viharas: Buddhist monasteries; secluded spaces dedicated to Buddhist religious life.

Zenana: Secluded women's quarters within a household.

Zoolum: Tyranny, oppression.

CONTEXTS

Imperialism: British India and Beyond

By 1900, the British Empire was at its height, with holdings in Africa, Asia, Australia, the Americas, and beyond. India was the "jewel in the crown" of the Empire, and just over its border, the Anglo-Afghan War of 1878-80 had consolidated the power of Afghan rulers friendly to British interests. In the Great Game with Russia for control of the subcontinent, Britain covertly surveyed and mapped the regions beyond its colonial borders—a project for which Kim is trained, along official lines documented below. Border tensions also played out in works like those excerpted here: government documents, studies by Indian intellectuals, travel writing, and journalism, including that of the young Kipling.

As "unofficial Poet Laureate of Empire," Kipling would eventually shape popular conceptions of conflicts far beyond India's borders, as Sir Hugh Clifford's memoirs show (p. 247). *Kim* registers these charged political contexts. Published in *McClure's Magazine* during the Second Anglo-Boer War—in which Britain refused to deploy its Indian troops against the white Boers for fear of black Africans taking up arms—it appeared alongside reports of the Boxer Uprising, a violent attempt to end Western influence in China. In the twentieth century, *Kim* took new forms within shifting imperial controversies. In 1950, a Cold War Kim battles Russians in an MGM film, after Hurree Chunder Mookerjee dies. In 1971, a children's matinee rerelease advertises Kim as a rebel against the tyranny of English schools, rather than an Indian-born spy-in-training. Over a century after its first publication, *Kim* remains a magnetic site for controversies about power, empire, and imperialism.

Rudyard Kipling

These articles reporting the situation with Russia at the northern Afghan border, and critiquing Britain's insularity, come from Kipling's scrapbooks of his own journalism at the University of Sussex.

from *the Civil and Military Gazette*

3 September 1886   We publish elsewhere today some translations from the *Novoe Vremya*,[1] which should be interesting to those who have any concern in the movements of the Divine Figure.[2] The *Novoe Vremya* has been allowed to speak its mind pretty plainly; and, in the matter of the Afghan Frontier claims, advocates delay – always delay. Neither Russia nor England "will go beyond a war of words this time," and if Lord Salisbury[3] puts forward "absurd pretensions," it were better, our amiable contemporary thinks, to lay the question aside until it solves itself by the turn of events. What the turn will be, everyone knows only too well. The English nation sees for the most part as far as Brighton or Scarborough. Waiting till England is absorbed in some domestic questions, Russia will, as she has so often done before, quietly absorb the disputed point, express her extreme sorrow at having given any offense, muzzle half a dozen too free spoken journals for a month or two, and strengthen herself in her new possession. Between the kingdom that knows what it wants, and presses forward to its end, and a people, whose foreign policy is conducted by snatches, the end can hardly be doubtful.

22 January 1887   Nature is unkind to the Russian who labours for the civilization of Central Asia. In Tashkend,[4] the city which, he says, he has so vastly improved, a great earthquake in November has completely destroyed several houses, cracked the city walls and most of the houses in the Russian quarter; besides, sadly disturbing the Russian officers at parade service. The loss is supposed to be heavy; but we could have borne the information more cheerfully had a few miles of the Central Asian railway been swallowed up.

---

[1] *"New Times"*: an important Russian political and literary newspaper, published from 1868 to 1917.

[2] The czar.

[3] Robert Gascoyne-Cecil, England's prime minister from June 1885 to January 1886; July 1886 to August 1892; and June 1895 to July 1902.

[4] Present-day capital of Uzbekistan, this Silk Road city was a center for British and Russian espionage during the period of the Great Game.

1 February 1887   The Central Asian Trading Company – the Russian one be it understood – sent a caravan of Russian goods into Thibet last autumn. This was as a feeler to open up Russian communication with Thibet; and, from information received, the caravan was a distinctive improvement on our own "Mission." According to latest news, it has crossed Kashgaria comfortably, and by this time should be in Thibet. The company intend starting a depot for Russian goods anywhere in the country – perhaps at "holy Lhassa"[5]– as it has started them at Merve, Askabad, Meshed, and Kushan. In these four towns, Russian trade is developing in a satisfactory manner. The Company has received, as a gift from the Amir of Bokhara, a piece of land near the Oxus, close to the Charjui railway station.

Muhammad Mafiz Ali, of Kakori, Lucknow District, Late Manager, Raj Singahi, Kheri

> *Written in 1886, during the period of the events of* Kim, *by an Indian civil servant located in a city famous for Urdu literature, this work is dedicated to "M.A. McConaghey, Esq., C.S., Commissioner, Lucknow Division, whose many amiable qualities, more especially, whose urbanity, and high-mindedness in keeping unreserved intercourse with the natives, and whose almost paternal sympathies with them, have endeared him to the natives of Oudh." Sir Syed (or Saiyid) Ahmed Khan, whose praise Ali reprints (see below), was perhaps the most influential Muslim Indian politician of his time. An educator and Islamic reformer whose loyalties lay with the British, he founded the Muhammedan Anglo-Oriental College (later the Aligarh Muslim University), spoke out against the Indian National Congress, and supported both the British raj and Muslim unity. He was knighted in 1888.*

The Truth about Russia and England from a Native's Point of View

The sudden occupation of Panjdeh[1] and the adjacent territory by the Russians last spring awoke the Indian people for the first time to a sense of the approach of a great and powerful neighbour. . . . A general curiosity was aroused in every quarter to learn anything and every-

---

[5]Holy city of Tibetan Buddhism, closed to foreigners until forcibly opened up by the British under Francis Younghusband in 1904.

---

[1]The "Panjdeh incident" of 1885, in which a Russian takeover of an area around Afghanistan's Oxus River nearly provoked a war with Britain, led to the establishment of the Anglo-Russian Boundary Commission and a formal border for northern Afghanistan.

thing connected with the Russians, their Government, and their military prowess. I took the hint and set about collecting facts and figures bearing on the subject. By the end of May last, I had written a book in Urdu—a language I considered to be the best medium for conveying to the masses those facts and impressions respecting the Russians which I found embalmed in the works of various authors consulted. These I have chosen from all parts of the civilized world, including Russia itself. The views of English writers alone, I thought, would not go down with the masses so easily. The whole subject has been treated *pro* and *con*; and, moreover, in the form of a contrast between the Russian system of rule and the British. . . . I was pressed by certain friends of mine to bring out an English version of the book as well . . .

Opinion Regarding the Book

We beg to acknowledge the receipt of a pamphlet, entitled "The Truth about Russia and England," . . . The author has, at the outset, very clearly and impartially portrayed the oppression and violence practiced by the Russian Government on its subjects, as well as the grossly outrageous conduct of the Russian officers and soldiery towards the fair sex of a conquered country [Poland]. Afterwards, he describes the main features of British rule in India, and, in a thoroughly loyal and independent spirit and with much truthfulness, points out both its sins and virtues. In the course of this criticism, he gives a list of the grievances of the people which have conduced to alienate their sympathise (sic) from the British Government. But he does something more. He traces those grievances to their legitimate causes, and where they are ascribable to the folly or misapprehension of the people themselves and where to the errors of the Government, he does not hesitate to say so. . . .

The Hon'ble Syed Ahmed Khan Bahadur, C.S.I.,[2]
in the Aligarh Institute Gazette, of 30th March 1886.

from *Hand-book of General Instructions for the Survey of India Department*

The Survey of India, the British government office responsible for mapping India and surrounding regions, was set up by the British East India Company in 1767. In 1865 Thomas Montgomerie began training Indians and disguising them as monks, replacing traditional 108-bead Buddhist

[2]Companion of the Star of India, a British honor.

rosaries with 100-bead rosaries suitable for pacing off distances. The training Kim would have received for his work on the Survey is reflected in this second edition, prepared by Colonel J.R. Hobday, I.S.C., Deputy Surveyor General, and published in Calcutta by the Office of the Superintendent of Government Printing, India in 1900.

from Chapter 1 Section 1—Admission to the Imperial Service

The Imperial Service is open to officers of the Royal Engineers and the Indian Staff Corps, who are appointed by the Government of India, on the recommendation of the Surveyor General of India according to the following extract from Army Regulations . . . The preliminary examination will embrace the following subjects . . .

I— Arithmetic, including involution and evolution; arithmetical and geometrical progression; proportion, or the rule of three; vulgar and decimal fractions; logarithmic calculations; and mensuration of surfaces.

II— Elementary geometry; first four books of Euclid.

III— Algebra, as far as quadratic equations, inclusive.

IV— Elements of plane trigonometry.

V— Topographical, mechanical, or civil drawing, to be executed in the presence of examiners.

* * *

The final examination to be held at the close of the period of probation will comprise—

I— The satisfactory execution, unassisted, of a small area of country, including the computation and entire mapping involved in the same.

II— Perfect use and knowledge of all the instruments employed in the department, and adjustment of the same.

III— Familiarity with the details of the several calculations for the reduction of the observations which are commonly used in the Survey Department.

IV— The elements of practical astronomy, sufficient for ascertaining time, azimuth, latitude, and longitude.

V— A fair knowledge of all rules in force for the general conduct of the Survey establishments.

Each candidate will also be required to produce a certificate of having passed the higher standard examination in any vernacular language prescribed by the Government of India. . . .

* * *

No application can be entertained from any individual whose age at the time of completion of the examination is under 18 or above 22 years, except in the case of natives whose maximum age is fixed at 24 years; no person who is married or likely to be soon married will be admitted, excepting candidates of pure Asiatic origin. . . .

As surveyors are liable to much exposure and to work in trying climates, the medical certificate should particularly specify that the candidate is of good physique and is likely to stand hard work, such as riding or walking long marches. . . .

All maps of trans-frontier countries are in the first instance to be considered absolutely confidential, and no copies of such maps are to be made or rendered to local civil officers, or to subordinate Governments before submission to the Supreme Government, and without the special sanction of the Surveyor General.

* * *

Appendix 4—Rules for crossing the N.W. Frontier of India.

The following extract from the Proceedings of the Government of India, in the Foreign Department, No. 1682-F., dated 1st November 1889, is circulated for departmental information and guidance . . .

Observations—The Viceroy and Governor General in Council observes that the progress of events during recent years has rendered it desirable that on the North-Western Frontier of India some modification should be made in the orders restricting British officers from visiting countries beyond the border.

In parts of the North-Western Frontier, more especially south of the Vihowa Pass, the attitude of the frontier tribes towards the British Government has undergone a considerable change for the better; and though this may not be the case in other parts, it has nevertheless become a matter of necessity that the Government should obtain a fuller knowledge of the country beyond the border, and endeavour to establish closer relations with its inhabitants. The restrictions hitherto in force cannot yet be wholly withdrawn, as excursions beyond the border will still in many cases be attended with risk; but the Governor General in Council is of opinion that, with proper local precautions and arrangements, much may be done to decrease this risk and to promote friendly intercourse between British officers and the border tribes.

Sir Hugh Clifford

Beginning his career in Malaya at age seventeen in 1883, Clifford rose to become the British Resident at Pahang, then Governor of North Borneo, Colonial Secretary of Trinidad, and Governor of the Gold Coast, Nigeria, and Ceylon, before his final post as British High Commissioner in Malaya (1927-30). Throughout his life, he wrote extensively about his experiences in colonial service, especially in Malaya. "Up-Country" is from In Court and Kampong *(London, Grant Richards, 1897).*

from "Up-Country"

It has been said that a white man, who has lived twelve consecutive months in complete isolation, among the people of an alien Asiatic race, is never wholly sane again for the remainder of his days. This, in a measure, is true; for the life he then learns to live, and the discoveries he makes in that unmapped land, the gates of which are closed, locked, barred, and chained against all but a very few of his countrymen, teach him to love many things which all right-minded people very properly detest. The free, queer, utterly unconventional life has a fascination which is all its own. Each day brings a little added knowledge of the hopes and fears, longings and desires, joys and sorrows, pains and agonies of the people among whom his lot is cast. Each hour brings fresh insight into the mysterious workings of the minds and hearts of that very human section of our race, which ignorant Europeans calmly class as "niggers." All these things come to possess a charm for him, the power of which grows apace, and eats into the very marrow of the bones of the man who has once tasted this particular fruit of the great Tree of Knowledge. Just as the old smugglers, in the Isle of Man, were wont to hear the sea calling to them; go where he may, do what he will, the voice of the jungle, and of the people who dwell in those untrodden places, sounds in the ears of one who has lived the life. Ever and anon it cries to him to come back, come back to the scenes, the people, the life which he knows and understands, and which, in spite of all its hardships, he has learned to love.

The great wheel of progress, like some vast snowball, rolls steadily along, gathering to itself all manner of weird and unlikely places and people, filling up the hollows, laying the high hills low. Rays of searching garish light reflected from its surface are pitilessly flashed into the dark places of the earth, which have been wrapped around by the old-time dim religious light, since first the world began. The people in whose eyes these rays beat so mercilessly, reel and stumble blindly on in their march through life, taking wrong turnings at every step, and going woefully astray. Let us hope that succeeding generations will become used to the new conditions, and will fight their way back to a truer path; for there is no blinking the fact that the first, immediate, and obvious effects of our spirit of progress upon the weaker races, tend towards degeneration. . . .

To all dwellers in the desolate solitude, which every white man experiences, who is cast alone among natives, there are two "up countries"—his Heaven and Hell, and both are of his own making. The latter is the one of which he speaks to his fellow race-mates—if he speaks at all about his solitary life. The former lies at the back of his heart, and is only known to himself, and then but dimly known till the time comes for a return to the Tents of Shem.[1] Englishmen, above all other men, revel in their privilege of being allowed to grumble and "grouse" over the lives which the Fates have allotted to them. They speak briefly, roughly, and gruffly of the hardships they endure, making but little of them perhaps, and talking as though their lives, as a matter of course, were made up of these things only. The instinct of the race is to see life through the national pea-soup fog, which makes all things dingy, unlovely, and ugly. Nothing is more difficult than to induce men of our race to confess that in their lives—hard though they may have been— good things have not held aloof, and that they have often been quite happy under the most unlikely circumstances, and in spite of the many horrors and privations which have long encompassed them about.

Let us take the Hell first. We often have to do so, making a virtue of necessity, and a habit is a habit; moreover, our pains are always more interesting than our pleasures—to our neighbours. Therefore, let us take the dark view of up-country life to start upon. In the beginning, when first a man turns from his own people, and dwells in isolation among an alien race, he suffers many things. The solitude of soul—that terrible solitude which is only to be experienced in a crowd—the dead monotony, without hope of change; the severance from all the pleasant things of life, and the want of any substitutes for them, eat into the heart and brain of him as a corrosive acid eats into iron. He longs for the fellowship of his own people with an exceeding great longing, till it becomes a burden too grievous to bear; he yearns to find comradeship among the people of the land, but he knows not yet the manner by which their confidence may be won, and they, on their side, know him for a stranger within their gates, view him with keen suspicion, and hold him at arm's length. His ideas, his prejudices, his modes of thought, his views on every conceivable subject differ too widely from their own, for immediate

---

[1]"God shall enlarge Japheth, and he shall dwell in the tents of Shem; and Canaan shall be his servant" (Genesis 9.27).

sympathy to be possible between him and them. His habits are the habits of a white man, and many little things, to which he has not yet learned to attach importance, are as revolting to the natives, as the pleasant custom of spitting on the carpet, which some old-world Rajas still affect, is to Europeans. His manners, too, from the native point of view, are as bad as his habits are unclean. He is respected for his wisdom, hated for his airs of superiority, pitied for his ignorance of many things, feared for what he represents, laughed at for his eccentric habits and customs, despised for his infidelity to the Faith, abhorred for his want of beauty, according to native standards of taste, and loved not at all. The men disguise their feelings, skillfully as only Orientals can, but the women and the little children do not scruple to show what their sentiments really are. When he goes abroad, the old women snarl at him as he passes, and spit ostentatiously, after the native manner when some unclean thing is at hand. The mothers snatch up their little ones and carry them hurriedly away, casting a look of hate and fear over their shoulders as they run. The children scream and yell, clutch their mothers' garments, or trip and fall, howling dismally the while, in their frantic efforts to fly his presence. He is Frankenstein's monster, yearning for love and fellowship with his kind, longing to feel the hand of a friend in his, and yet knowing, by the unmistakable signs which a sight of him causes, that he is indescribably repulsive to the people among whom he lives. Add to all this that he is cut off from all the things which, to educated Europeans, make life lovely, and you will realise that his is indeed a sorry case. The privations of the body, if he has sufficient grit to justify his existence, count for little. He can live on any kind of food, sleep on the hardest of hard mats, or on the bare ground, with his head and feet in a puddle, if needs must. He can turn night into day, and sleep through the sunlight, or sleep not at all, as the case may be, if any useful purpose is to be served thereby. These are not things to trouble him, though the fleshpots of Egypt are very good when duty allows him to turn his back for a space upon the desert.[2] Privations all these things are called in ordinary parlance, but they are of little moment, and are good for his liver. The real privations are of quite another sort. He never hears music; never sees a lovely picture; never joins in the talk and listens lovingly to conversation which strikes the answering sparks from his sodden brain. Above all, he never encounters the softening influence of the society of ladies of his own race. His few books are for a while his companions, but he reads them through and through, and cons them o'er and o'er, till the best sayings of the best authors ring flat on his sated ears like the echo of a twice-told

[2]"Would to God we had died by the hand of the Lord in the land of Egypt, when we sat by the flesh pots, and when we did eat bread to the full; for ye have brought us forth into this wilderness, to kill this whole assembly with hunger" (Exodus 16.13).

tale. He has not yet learned that there is a great and marvellous book lying beneath his hand, a book in which all may read if they find but the means of opening the clasp which locks it, a book in which a man may read for years and never know satiety, which, though older than the hills, is ever new, and which, though studied for a lifetime, is never exhausted, and is never completely understood. This knowledge comes later; and it is then that the Chapter of the Great Book of Human Nature, which deals with natives, engrosses his attention and, touching the grayness of his life, like the rising sun, turns it into gold and purple.

Many other things he has to endure. Educated white men have inherited an infinite capacity for feeling bored; and a hot climate, which fries us all over a slow fire, grills boredom into irritability. The study of oriental human nature requires endless patience; and this is the hardest virtue for a young, energetic white man, with the irritable brain of his race, to acquire. Without it life is a misery—for

> It is not good for the Christian's health
> To hurry the Aryan brown,
> For the Christian riles and the Aryan smiles,
> And he weareth the Christian down;
> And the end of that fight is a tombstone white,
> With the name of the late deceased,
> And the epitaph clear, A fool lies here
> Who tried to hustle the East.[3]

Then gradually, very gradually, and by how slow degrees he shudders in after days to recall, a change comes o'er the spirit of his nightmare. Almost unconsciously, he begins to perceive that he is sundered from the people of the land by a gulf which they can never hope to bridge over. If he is ever to gain their confidence the work must be of his own doing. They cannot come up to this level, he must go down to the plains in which they dwell. He must put off many of the things of the white man, must forget his airs of superiority, and must be content to be merely a native Chief among natives. His pride rebels, his prejudices cry out and will not be silenced, he knows that he will be misunderstood by his race-mates, should they see him among the people of his adoption, but the aching solitude beats down one and all of these things; and, like that eminently sensible man, the Prophet Mohammed, he gets him to the Mountain, since it is immovable and will not come to him.

Then begins a new life. He must start by learning the language of his fellows, as perfectly as it is given to a stranger to learn it. That is but the first step in a long and often a weary march. Next, he must study, with

[3]This is a misquote of the epigraph to chap. 5 of Kipling and Balestier's novel *The Naulakha.*

the eagerness of Browning's Grammarian,[4] every native custom, every native conventionality, every one of the ten thousand ceremonial observances to which natives attach so vast an importance. He must grow to understand each one of the hints and *doubles ententes*,[5] of which Malays make such frequent use, every little mannerism, sign and token, and, most difficult of all, every motion of the hearts, and every turn of thought, of those whom he is beginning to call his own people. He must become conscious of native Public Opinion, which is often diametrically opposed to the opinion of his race-mates on one and the same subject. He must be able to unerringly predict how the slightest of his actions will be regarded by the natives, and he must shape his course accordingly, if he is to maintain his influence with them, and to win their sympathy and their confidence. He must be able to place himself in imagination in all manner of unlikely places, and thence to instinctively feel the native Point of View. That is really the whole secret of governing natives. A quick perception of their Point of View, under all conceivable circumstances, a rapid process by which a European places himself in the position of the native, with whom he is dealing, an instinctive and instantaneous apprehension of the precise manner in which he will be affected, and a clear vision of the man, his feelings, his surroundings, his hopes, his desires, and his sorrows,—these, and these alone, mean that complete sympathy, without which the white man among Malays, is but as a sounding brass and as a tinkling cymbal.

It does not all come at once. Months, perhaps years, pass before the exile begins to feel that he is getting any grip upon the natives, and even when he thinks that he knows as much about them as is good for any man, the oriental soul shakes itself in its brown casing, and comes out in some totally unexpected and unlooked-for place, to his no small mortification and discouragement. But, when he has got thus far, discouragement matters little, for he has become bitten with the love of his discoveries, and he can no more quit them than the dipsomaniac can abandon the drams which are killing him.

Then he gets deep into a groove and is happy. His fingers are between the leaves of the Book of Human Nature, and his eager eyes are scanning the lines of the chapter which in time he hopes to make his own. The advent of another white man is a weariness of the flesh. The natives about him have learned to look upon him as one of their own people. His speech is their speech, he can think as they do, can feel as they feel, rejoice in their joys, and sorrow in their pains. He can tell them wonderful things, and a philosophy of which they had not dreamed. He never offends their

[4]See Robert Browning's poem, "A Grammarian's Funeral," 1855.

[5]*Doubles ententes* or *doubles entendres*: (French) Words or phrases with double meanings.

susceptibilities, never wounds their self-respect, never sins against their numerous conventionalities. He has feasted with them at their weddings, doctored their pains, healed their sick, protected them from oppression, stood their friend in time of need, done them a thousand kindnesses, and has helped their dying through the strait and awful pass of death. Above all, he *understands*, and, in a manner, they love him. A new white man, speaking to him in an unknown tongue, seems to lift him for the time out of their lives. The stranger jars on the natives, who are the exile's people, and he, looking through the native eyes which are no longer strange to him, sees where his race-mate offends, and in his turn is jarred, until he begins to hate his own countrymen. Coming out of the groove hurts badly, and going back into it is almost worse, but when a man is once well set in the rut of native life, these do not disturb him, for he is happy, and has no need of other and higher things. This is the exile's Heaven.

As years go on the up-country life of which I write will become less and less common in this Peninsula of ours, and the Malays will be governed wholly by men, who, never having lived their lives, cannot expect to have more than a surface knowledge of the people whose destinies are in their hands. The Native States will, I fancy, be none the better governed, and those who rule them will miss much which has tended to widen the lives of the men who came before them, and who dwelt among the people while they were still as God made them.

And those who led these lives? The years will dim the memories of all they once learned and knew and experienced; and as they indite the caustic minute to the suffering subordinate, and strangle with swaddlings of red-tape the tender babe of prosperity, they will perchance look back with wonder at the men they once were, and thinking of their experiences in the days of long ago will marvel that each one of them as he left the desert experienced the pang of Chillon's prisoner . . .

> Even I
> Regained my freedom with a sigh.[6]

Edwin Lord Weeks
from "Hindoo and Moslem,"
Harper's Monthly Magazine, October 1895

Illustrated as well as written by Edwin Lord Weeks (see p. xxi), the page reproduced here showcases popular Western views of "baboos" and Indian intellectual culture. Kipling, who also wrote for Harper's, *shared a Calcutta*

[6]The last lines (391-92) of *The Prisoner of Chillon* (1816), by George Gordon, Lord Byron. Having been chained in a dungeon underneath the waters of Lake Geneva for six years, the speaker has come to make psychological accommodation with his plight.

publisher with Mohindronauth Mookerjee, whose 1873 memoir of Onoocool Chunder Mookerjee Weeks quotes here. Though Weeks characterizes Mookerjee's language as already outdated, it would remain a stock resource for jokes about "baboo English": see Mark Twain's 1897 Following the Equator.

HINDOO WOMEN, SUBURBS OF BOMBAY.

many years connected with the management of one of the northern railways does not think that they are actually supplanting Europeans, but that, on the contrary, they are often elbowed out by "poor whites," a class which formerly did not exist, the sons of Europeans, or "Eurasians," for the most part laborers and mechanics, when they can find employment. On the other hand, fewer Europeans now fill the posts of station-masters, engine-drivers, or guards, and natives trained for the work are rapidly replacing them. Natives, particularly the Baboo class, now hold a larger number of official appointments than was formerly the case, in accordance with recent official decisions. My informant thinks that they are excellently organized for office and routine work, though not reliable in case of emergencies, and personally he would rather employ a native for any post worth under 100 rupees a month than a European, as he can procure a better stamp of man in a native at that price. But these adaptive and versatile Hindoos are rapidly crowding out Europeans from minor clerkly employments, since they can make a better appearance on less money. Among their ranks may be found journalists, politicians, and scribes of every description, advocates, attorneys, and judges. Many have achieved distinction at the bar, in politics, and in literature. The poetess Toru Dutt, whom Edmund Gosse calls a "fragile, exotic blossom of song," was the daughter of the Baboo Govin Chunder

as in their journals, for they are usually endowed with the gift of volubility and rapid utterance, and freely express their minds in "hifalutin" and more or less Shakespearian English. With the steady progress of modern ideas and education the examples of Baboo English which once delighted Anglo-Indian readers are becoming rarer, and we may never have another book equal to the well-known biography of Onoocool Chunder Mookerjee.* A gentleman who has been for

* The writer cannot do better than quote the opening lines of this remarkable work for the instruction of those not familiar with the author's style. "The Memoir of the late Hon'ble Justice Onoocool Chunder Mookerjee. "Let me hold my *Penna* after a few months, to write the memoir of the individual above-named: but quid agis? if any one put me such a query, I will be utterly thrown into a great jeopardy and hurley-burley, and say—a fool of myself! As a spider spins web for its own destruction, or as when the clown who was busy in

digging a grave for "Ophelia," was asked by Hamlet, "Whos grave's this Sirrah?" said, "Mine Sir," so in writing one's memoir I am as if to dig my own grave in it. To write one's memoir, or to write in such a way as the literary public may fall in love with, is a task difficult in the extreme, especially of such a man as the late Hon'ble Justice Mookerjee. He was no poet that I may put some such writing in print, full of poetical thoughts, which the public did not see, or recite some such stirring events, as induced him to write into measured lines some such subjects, which the public are already in possession of and thereby please them."

An official while in town left a pony in charge of a native subordinate, from whom it escaped. The native explained the matter in a letter to his "sahib": "I have the honour to report that the little horse, since your honour's departure, has assumed a devil-may-care attitude and has become violently obstreperous. This morning at 6 A.M. the said little horse eloped from my custody but, with the favour of Heaven he may return."

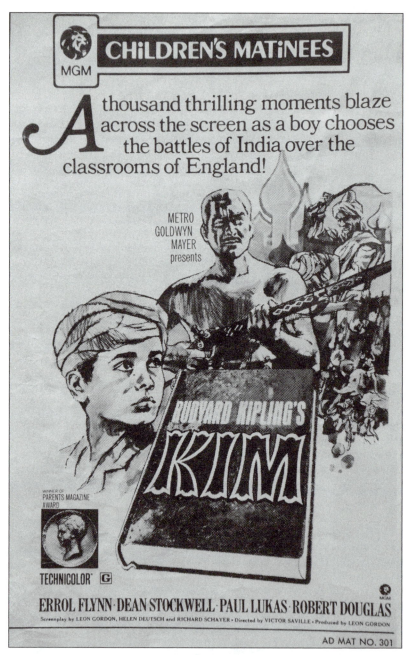

Kim © Turner Entertainment Co.
A Warner Bros. Entertainment Company. All rights reserved.
Advertisement for the 1971 reissue of the 1950 film as a Children's Matinee.

Kipling and Kim

Kim is a novel by a travel writer, poet, short story writer, propagandist—and, not least, a reporter. A meeting point for "all the world" of Kipling's writing, the book owes much to nostalgia for the India of his childhood and to ongoing conversations with his parents, as his memoir makes clear. Yet as "Home" and "The Edge of the East" demonstrate, Kipling's most successful novel also draws deeply on the cultural observations of a professional newspaper writer. *Kim* pulls together themes, genres, and even figures from Kipling's earlier career, yet it often does so in ambiguous ways. For example, Hurree Chunder Mookerjee, Mahbub Ali, Lispeth, and Strickland all appear in stories or poems before *Kim*, but what relationship do these characters bear to their later counterparts? In these earlier texts, we see scenes of overt sexuality, calculated physical cruelty, or blunt racial and religious hostility, of a sort that *Kim* omits or elides. The fate of the first "Lispeth" invokes a woman's unexplored interior life. The tortures of "The Ballad of the King's Jest" and "The Mark of the Beast" move the grotesque and the gothic to center stage; the cruel, politically hostile humor of "What Happened" suggests new readings of Kipling's Bengali babu. Above all, perhaps, the strains of Kipling's famous hymn, "Recessional," considered in conjunction with the brutal scene that Kipling discarded in revising his draft of "Kim o' the Rishti," (here published for the first time), help dramatize Kipling's deliberateness in shaping *Kim* as the novel he thought his empire needed.

Rudyard Kipling

First published in the Civil and Military Gazette *in 1891, Kipling's account of his return to his parents in Lahore begins with his landing in the south of India, which he had never seen before.*

from "Home"

The longing began at least a league off shore from Colombo, when the *Chusan*, Calcutta bound, swung out round the breakwater

255

under the *Valetta's* nose, and we who were Anglo-Indians separated ourselves a little from the crowd. A smell came up over the sea—a smell of damp earth, coconut oil, ginger, onions and mankind.

It spoke with a strong voice, recalling many things; but the most curious revelation to one man was the sudden knowledge that under these skies lay home and the dearest places in all the world. Even the first sniff of London had not caused so big a choke in the throat, or so strict a tightening over the heart. . . .

As a second wind to a runner, or wine to a wearied man, was this second view of the city of Lahore—the oldest and surely the most picturesque city in the world. Thomas—of the K.O.S.B.'s[1]—was on guard at the main gate of the Fort[2] (I wonder which of us best knew the guard-room on the wall) and the sunlight was splashing the mouldering tile work of the main face—the gay tile-wrought angels and elephants of Akbar. The minars of Shadera where Jahangir lies dead, [3] and with him the memories of many moonlight picnics and wild words under the roses, showed above the belt of green by the Ravi.[4] Thomas—a spot of vermillion— was loafing down the sunk way to the gate, his dog at his heels. Thomas with a *chilumchee*[5] and bare headed—will nothing teach Thomas that he must not play even with the cold weather sun?—was scuffling from barrack to barrack, and Thomas (fever-stricken Thomas) in his great coat was hanging over the balcony of the hospital, half a dozen superb Pathan soldiers in undress were swinging across the path by the glaring native guard room where Sikh sepoys rested near their speckless rifles, rising to salute and standing one bar of blood red against the whitewashed wall. It is awful to think that in England they have never seen any of the primary colours, and that they know nothing of the drapery, the folds of well worn unsewn clothing that falls in great laps and curves, and gathered round the neck and under the armpit in robes of richest deep shadowed wrinkles. The square of the Naulakha[6] pavilion ached in the sunshine, and there tramping across the white marble, his belt well over his hips, his coat open and helmet at the back

[1]"Tommy Atkins," the generic Cockney imperial soldier, appears here as enlisted in Kipling's brother-in-law's regiment, the King's Own Scottish Borderers, 25th Regiment of Foot. See Kemp and Lewis, *Writings on Writing*, p. 173.

[2]Surrounded by massive fortifications built for Emperor Jalaluddin Muhammad Akbar, ("Akbar the Great," 1542-1605), the Lahore Fort's lavish complex of palaces, gardens, ceremonial spaces, and courtyards had been occupied by the British since 1846. A masterpiece of Mughal art and architecture, it is now a U.N. World Heritage site.

[3]Minarets on the tomb of Jahangir, Akbar's son.

[4]One of five rivers for which the Punjab ("five waters") is named.

[5]Metal basin.

[6]Famous white marble structure; Kipling used this name for both his house in Vermont and his co-authored novel with Wolcott Balestier.

of his head, was Thomas—affable and a citizen of the world—Thomas with four years service and very pronounced views on men and things. We talked together sitting under the painted, mirror-inlaid ceilings till he said with cheerful irrelevance that it was near canteen opening time. O Thomas, Thomas! to think that I should have been taken in by that stale old trick. But it was Simla beer, and no muddy English porter.

There was a glimpse of the fort barrack room with its monstrous understrutting of masonry—and the spider-legged cots disposed in the hall of dead kings, the pillars of black and white marble defiled with whitewash, and the marvellous painted relief work daubed out of all knowledge. In the vast cool silence of this echoing hall, Thomas in every stage of undress came and went; and Thomas's dog lay on the cot and barked. The verandah arches showed pure raw sunlight and blue, and Thomas stood there in red, the points of light twinkling off his accoutrements as he went to relieve guard. It was home indeed! . . . .

If the Civil station hinted at the memories of years, the city shouted them aloud. House upon piled house, the time worn wood tracery standing askew on the rotten brickwork, well gulley mouth, ruinous dead wall and crumbling heap of sheer stark red-rotten rubbish overrun by the crowd, the cattle and the asses—all spoke with the voice of the years. Here lived the Jews of Shushan, there, arrogant and unashamed was Lalun's naughty little house, Azizan of the Douri Bagh was a little beyond, and the house of Suddhoo[7] was not far off the ringing roaring gulley of the coppersmiths, where the lean traders sat by piles of beaten gold vessels selling the splendour of the East for a few annas. Here were the Pathan horse-dealers chattering with the seal-cutters for a new signet ring. Not till one understands in some small measure the heart of the city, does one realize how much the poorest country in the world has to spend on fripperies—four-anna embroidered caps for the babies, cheap jewellry, bats and stumps (a new industry since my time—cricket is more than ever naturalised with us), kites, cheap lithographs of the gods, tinsel-stuck shoes and slippers, necklaces, beads, mirror-rings, and a hundred other toys. Here and there through the jostling crowd where buffalo calves and led ponies share all the rights of way with men, a face passes that I know, and once or twice an old friend stops me to give greeting. The Dubbi Bazaar is full of old friends, from the fat bunnia among the turmeric heaps to the policeman with the *kullam*[8] and the green-glazed inkpot in his hand. They don't know me, but I know them.

[7]All places and characters from Kipling's work: see, for example, "Jews in Shushan" (*Life's Handicap*, 1891); "On the City Wall" (*Soldiers Three: The Story of the Gadsbys in Black and White*, 1888); and "In the House of Suddhoo" (*Plain Tales from the Hills*, 1888).

[8]*Qualam*; pen. See Kemp and Lewis, p. 174.

How shall one describe the sun-lit river bed of people whose daily passage has oil polished the wooden posts of the shop boards, smoothed the angles of the brickwork and faced the very ground with glair[9] as a glacier polishes a rock. As if its own beauty were not enough, the dyers have spread filmy muslins of palest blue and pink across the street, and you look down upon the old witchery of the old life through the pearl tinted mists of dawn. It is noon and past, and high overhead a boy's yellow paper kite is sawing and jigging into the restful blue like a big sulphur butterfly. Below there is the hurry and the shouting, the broken waves of colour, the deep shadows that heighten colour as velvet displays the diamond, and apart from all, as a prayer from a tortured heart, the mosque of Wazir Khan flings up its four minars to heaven. What need to cry four times a day that God is great?

At the shadow of the Delhi Gate the picture of the city ends for the sight—to be graven deeper into the mind. Again comes the memory of the murmurs of a little city called London—a city where there is neither colour nor light nor air. Who was the particular *pagal*[10] over there who wrote of extravagance of description and the Lord knows what else? If he were here now—between that broken-hatted, unbuttoned English loafer slinking red nosed in the sunshine and the dusty swaying plantain leaves of the Badami Bagh[11]—here when I stand looking at the heaped-up roofs of the city, the proud arch of the gateway and the torrent of turbulent colour that rolls beneath it, what would he write? And if he had seen that Jubilee night in '87,[12] when the city of Lahore flamed out of the dusk as a jewelled queen from the door of the palace of night—dome, minaret, bastion, wall and house-front drawn in dotted fire, what he would have said of extravagance then? But who can show a blind man colour?

from "The Edge of the East"

> "The Edge of the East" *opens a series of syndicated travel letters from Kipling's honeymoon, published nearly simultaneously in Lahore, London, and New York. This excerpt from* The Times *of* London, July 2, 1892, *ends where* Kim *begins: with "The Buddha at Kamakura." A substantially revised version of the poem also appears in Kipling's* Complete Verse.

This that follows happened on the coast twenty miles through the fields from Yokahama, at Kamakura, that is to say, where the great

---

[9]Egg white; used for glazes and to fix gold leaf in bookbinding.

[10]Madman.

[11]Section of Lahore; by the 1880s, home to an important railway station.

[12]Queen Victoria's Golden Jubilee. For the Diamond Jubilee, see p. 280.

bronze Buddha sits facing the sea to hear the centuries go by.[1] He has been described again and again—his majesty, his aloofness, and every one of his dimensions, the smoky little shrine within him, and the plumed hill that makes the background to his throne. For that reason he remains, as he remained from the beginning, beyond all hope of description—as it might be, a visible god sitting in the garden of a world new made. They sell photographs of him with tourists standing on his thumb nail,[2] and apparently, any brute of either gender can scrawl his or her ignoble name over the inside of the massive bronze plates that build him up. Think for a moment of the indignity and the insult. Imagine the ancient orderly gardens with their clipped trees, shorn turf, and silent ponds smoking in the mist that the hot sun soaks up after rain, and the green-bronze image of the Teacher of the Law wavering there as if half seen through incense clouds. The earth is all one censer, and myriads of frogs are making the haze ring. It is too warm to do more than to sit on a stone and watch the eyes that, having seen all things, see no more—the down-dropped eyes, the forward droop of the head, and the colossal simplicity of the folds and the robe over the arm and knee. Thus, and in no other fashion, did Buddha sit in the old days when Ananda asked questions and the dreamer began to dream of the lives that lay behind him ere the lips moved, and as the Chronicles say:—"He told a tale." This would be the way he began, for dreamers in the East tell something the same sort of tales to-day:— "Long ago, when Devadatta was King of Benares, there lived a virtuous elephant, a reprobate ox, and a King without understanding." And the tale would end, after the moral had been drawn for Ananda's benefit:—"Now the reprobate ox was such an one, and the King was such another, but the virtuous elephant was I myself, Ananda." Thus, then, he told the tales in the bamboo grove, and the bamboo grove is here to-day. Little blue and gray and slate robed figures pass under its shadow, buy two or three joss sticks, disappear into the shrine, that is, the body of the god, come out smiling, and drift away through the shrubberies. A fat carp in a pond sucks at a fallen leaf with just the sound of a wicked little worldly kiss. Then the earth steams, and steams in silence, and a gorgeous butterfly, full six inches from wing to wing, cuts through the steam in a zig-zag of colour and flickers up to the forehead of the god. And Buddha said that a man must look upon everything as illusion—even light and colour—the time-worn bronze of metal against the blue-green of pine and pale emerald of the bamboo—

[1] A monumental 13th-c. statue of the meditating Amida Buddha, the *Daibutsu* ("Great Buddha") of Kamakura, Japan has drawn pilgrims for centuries.

[2] Such photographs were widely circulated. See, for example, pioneering American travel lecturer John L. Stoddard's much-reprinted *Lectures* (New York: Belford, 1897).

the lemon sash of the girl in the cinnamon dress, with coral pins in her hair, leaning against a block of weather-bleached stone—and last, the spray of blood-red azalea that stands on the pale gold mats of the teahouse beneath the honey-coloured thatch. To overcome desire and covetousness of mere gold, which is often very vilely designed, that is conceivable; but why must a man give up the delight of the eye, colour that rejoices, light that cheers, and line that satisfies the innermost depths of the heart? Ah, if the Bodhisat had only seen his own image.

At the entrance to the gardens there is a quaint little printed appeal, half pathetic and half dignified, put forward by the priests of the place, for reverence and decent behavior on the part of the visitors.[3] It might, perhaps, be done into rhyme, something after this style:

Oh ye who tread the narrow way
By Tophet-flare to Judgment Day
Be gentle when the heathen pray
    To Buddha at Kamakura,—

To him the Way, the Law, Apart,   5
Whom Maya held beneath her heart,
Ananda's Lord the Bodhisat,
    The Daibutz(u) of Kamakura

For though he neither burns nor sees
Nor hears ye thank your Deities   10
Ye have not sinned with such as these
    His children at Kamakura,

Yet spare us still the Western joke
When joss-sticks turn to scented smoke
The little sins of little folk   15
    That worship at Kamakura,

The gray-robed, gay-sashed butterflies
That flit beneath the Master's eyes—
He is beyond the Mysteries
    But loves them at Kamakura.   20

And who so will, from Pride released
Despising neither man nor beast,
May hear the soul of all the East
    Breathe round him at Kamakura.

[3]"Stranger, whosoever thou art, and whatsoever be thy creed, when thou enterest this sanctuary remember thou treadest upon ground hallowed by the worship of ages. This is the temple of the Buddha and the gate of the Eternal, and should therefore be entered with reverence" (Countess Iso Mutso's translation, 1918; see Cortazzi and Webb, p. 207).

Yea, every tale Ananda heard,   25
Of birth as fish or beast or bird
While yet in life the Master stirred,
    The warm wind brings Kamakura.

With voice of every soul that clung
To life that strove from rung to rung,   30
When Devadatta's rule was young,
    In worship at Kamakura.

Till drowsy eyelids seem to see
Far-flaming near her golden *hlee*[4]
The Shwe-Dagon[5] flare easterly   35
    From Burmah to Kamakura

And down the loaded air there comes
The thunder of Thibetan drums,
And droned:—"*Om mane padme hums*"
    A world's width from Kamakura.   40

Yet Brahmans rule Benares still,
Buddh-Gaya's ruins pit the hill,[6]
And beef-fed zealots[7] threaten ill
    To Buddha and Kamkura.

A tourist's-show, a legend told,   45
A rusting bulk of bronze and gold,
So much, and scarce so much, ye hold
    The meaning of Kamakura;

But when the morning-prayer is prayed
Think, ere ye pass to strife or trade,   50
Is God in man's own image made
    No nearer than Kamakura?

---

[4]*Htee* or *hti*: golden, bud-shaped tops of Burmese pagodas. Annexed in 1886, Burma became an independent British Indian province beginning in 1897.

[5]Or *Shwedagon*, a pagoda in Rangoon. Kipling deeply admired this most sacred of Burmese Buddhist monuments.

[6]However widely Buddhist worship may extend elsewhere, great Buddhist Holy Places (the Deer Park near Benares and Buddh-Gaya) in India are no longer home to believers, and are neglected.

[7]Western Christians (especially beef-loving British), here cast as aggressively extending a history of disrespect for sacred Buddhist art.

from *Something of Myself*

As early as October 1892, Kipling began to correspond with American author and editor Mary Mapes Dodge about his idea for Kim: *a "tale of the Thibetan lama and Kim o' the Rishti." In his memoir* Something of Myself *(1937), Kipling recounts the story of the novel's composition.*

In a gloomy, windy autumn *Kim* came back to me with insistence, and I took it to be smoked over with my Father. Under our united tobaccos it grew like the Djinn released from the brass bottle,[1] and the more we explored its possibilities the more opulence of detail did we discover. I do not know what proportion of an iceberg is below waterline, but *Kim* as it finally appeared was about one-tenth of what the first lavish specification called for.

As to its form there was but one possible to the author, who said that what was good enough for Cervantes was good enough for him.[2] To whom the Mother: 'Don't you stand in your wool-boots hiding behind Cervantes with *me*! *You* know you couldn't make a plot to save your soul.'

So I went home much fortified and *Kim* took care of himself. The only trouble was to keep him within bounds. Between us, we knew every step, sight, and smell on his casual road, as well as all the persons he met. Once only, as I remember, did I have to bother the India Office, where there are four acres of books and documents in the basements, for a certain work on Indian magic which I always sincerely regret that I could not steal. They fuss about receipts there.

At 'The Elms,' Rottingdean, the sou'wester raged day and night, till the silly windows jiggled their wedges loose. . . . But I was quite unconcerned. I had my Eastern sunlight and if I wanted more I could get it at 'The Gables,' Tisbury.[3] At last I reported *Kim* finished. 'Did *it* stop, or you?' the Father asked. And when I told him that it was *It*, he said: 'Then it oughtn't to be too bad.'

He would take no sort of credit for any of his suggestions, memories, or confirmations—not even for that single touch of the low-driving sunlight which makes luminous every detail in the picture of the Grand Trunk Road at eventide. The Himalayas I painted *all* by myself, as the children say. So also the picture of the Lahore Museum of which I had once been Deputy Curator for six weeks—unpaid but immensely

---

[1]In one of the tales of the Arabian Nights, a fisherman opens a bottle, unknowingly releasing a fierce *djinn* (or genie), who threatens to kill him. When the fisherman professes not to believe that such a huge genie could have fit into so small a bottle, the genie proves it by returning to the bottle, upon which the clever fisherman retraps him.

[2]Miguel de Cervantes' celebrated *Don Quixote* (1605) is an episodic narrative.

[3]Kipling's parents' house.

important. And there was a half-chapter of the Lama sitting down in the blue-green shadows at the foot of a glacier, telling Kim stories out of the Jatakas, which was truly beautiful but, as my old Classics master would have said, 'otiose,' and it was removed almost with tears.

But the crown of the fun came when . . . the Father. . . had the notion of making low-relief plaques and photographing them afterwards.[4] Here it was needful to catch the local photographer, who, till then, had specialized in privates of the Line with plastered hair and skin-tight uniforms, and to lead him up the strenuous path of photographing dead things so that they might show a little life. The man was a bit bewildered at first, but he had a teacher of teachers, and so grew to understand. The incidental muck-heaps in the stable-yard were quite noticeable, though a loyal housemaid fought them broom-and-bucket, and Mother allowed messy half-born 'sketches' to be dumped by our careless hands on sofas and chairs. Naturally when he got his final proofs he was sure that 'it all ought to be done again from the beginning,' which was rather how I felt about the letterpress, but, if it be possible, he and I will do that in a better world, and on a scale to amaze Archangels.

There is one picture that I remember of him in the tin tabernacle, hunting big photos of Indian architecture for some utterly trivial detail in a corner of some plaque. He looked up as I came in and, rubbing his beard and carrying on his own thought, quoted: 'If you get simple beauty and naught else, You get about the best thing God invents.'[5] It is the greatest of my many blessings that I was given grace to know them at the time, instead of having them brought to my remorseful notice too late. . . .

And so much for *Kim* which has stood up for thirty-five years. There was a good deal of beauty in it, and not a little wisdom; the best in both sorts being owed to my Father.

from "Kim o' the Rishti"

In 1892, the year Kipling first mentioned Kim, some 160 African-Americans died at the hands of mobs. This excerpt from the manuscript of Kim *in the British Library, which ends with Kim and his narrator, in explicitly, violently racist language, celebrating the degradation and murder of a "Negro, wearing the Arab fez," reminds us that* Kim *was composed during America's notorious lynching era. It also dramatizes how decisively omission, no less than creation, determined the* Kim *we now read. Compare this scene to pp. 162–167.*

All ellipses are in the manuscript. Our glosses and comments are in square brackets. Illegible text is indicated by [???].

---

[4]These would illustrate *Kim* (see p. 235).
[5]From Robert Browning's "Fra Lippo Lippi" (1855).

But at Somna road the fates sent him something to think about. ~~An ekka drove across the plain at a gallop, and~~ There tumbled into the compartment just as the train was moving a mean lean little Mahratta, so far as Kim could judge by the cock of ~~his small turban and~~ the tight turban – ~~a xxx~~ who had been driven across the plain in an ekka. He had no time to take any ticket and was followed by yells + shouts from the ~~native staff~~ platform. ~~Xxxxxxxxxxxstationhe was willing to pay fare that thexxxcollector hadxxxxxxxxxxxxxxThe thing seemed to trouble him beyond measure, though in the of course he could have paid fare with a few annas to the ticket collector at the next station.xxxxxxpprevent the xxxxxxxxxxxxxthe company. He was going to Delhi to wherehis son lived,but and that the ekka had upset and xxxx~~ His face was cut in two places, his muslin upper garment was badly torn, and one leg was bandaged. He told the company that the <u>ekka</u> had upset ~~as he~~ and very nearly slain him. He was going to Delhi where his son lived. Kim watched him closely. If as he said he had been rolled over and over on ~~xxx~~ the earth, there should have been signs of gravel-rash on the skin. But all his injuries seemed clean cuts and a mere upset from a cart could not ~~xxx~~ cast a man into such extremity of terror. As he knotted up the cloth about his neck with shaking fingers Kim caught the glimmer of an amulet. Now amulets are common enough but they are not generally strung on a ~~copper wire xxx~~ plaited copper wire, and still fewer amulets are black enamel on silver. ~~All at~~ For the moment ~~only the Kamboh and the lama were~~ there were none ~~xxx~~ except the Kamboh and the lama in the compartment. Kim made as to ~~reach in his bosom~~ scratch in his bosom and thereby ~~showed his own amulet~~ lifted <u>his</u> own amulet. The Mahratta's face – it was not lovely – ~~took~~ changed altogether, at the sight.

"Yes" he went on to the Kamboh – "the ekka driven by a bastard Muslim, bound its wheel in a water cut and besides the harm done to me, ~~xxx my~~ there was lost a full dish of <u>tarkeeyan</u>.

That was a great loss' said the Kamboh without interest. His experiences in Benares had made him suspicious of hungry people.

"Was it cooked by a woman by any chance?" said Kim.

"Assuredly. ~~Therein lay xxxxx~~ said the Mahratta swiftly raising his eyes to Kim.

But all women cook <u>tarkeyan</u> said the Kamboh. "It is good curry as I know."

Oh yes, it is a good curry," said ~~Kim. "Even poor men can cook tarkeeyan.~~ The Mahratta — ~~xxx~~ "And cheap!" said Kim.

Assuredly. Even poor men can cook – at tarkeeyan," the Mahratta replied. In whose service art thou?"

In the service of this holy one" Kim pointed to the drowzy lama, who woke with a bob.

Ah. He was sent from heaven to lead me. He is called the friend of all the world. He is also called the friend of the stars.

And a son of the charm" said Kim under his breath as the Kamboh made haste to prepare a pipe lest the Mahratta should beg.~~for food~~

~~"And who is he?"~~

"Who is ~~he~~ that?" the Mahratta asked, glancing sideways nervously.

One whose child I – we have cured. Who lies under great debt to us. Sit by the window, thou."

"Humph! I have no desire to mix with chance-met wastrels. My ears are not long. I am not a woman wishing to overhear secrets." The Jat slid himself heavily into a far corner.

The man is cut and bruised all over. I go about to cure him" ~~said~~ Kim retorted ~~xxx~~. None interfered between thy babe and me.

Have mercy. I am rebuked" said the Kamboh meekly. "I am thy debtor for the life of my son."

Show me the cuts! Kim bent over the Mahratta's neck, his heart nearly choking him, ~~for this~~ for this was the Great Game with a vengeance. "Now tell thy tale swiftly."

"I am come from the South," the Mahratta muttered, between blued lips. I having found that which I was sent to seek I came away. ~~My companion in the service they slew by the roadside.~~ My ~~predecessor~~ mate they slew by the road-side. ~~Didst thou know" Kim shook his head.~~ Hast thou heard?" Kim shook his head. Next, as the order was, I took up the search but a woman betrayed me.~~as I believe~~. They of the palace went about to kill me ~~and I escaped from that city~~ but I escaped from that city alive, and came to ~~rejoin~~ Mhow. I lay a week in ~~Chuxx~~ Chitor – the old city because I knew that the stars were against me. I came from Chitor by night – judge ~~by that~~ how closely they followed me. Hence I was hunted northward like a wet jackal."

"Who are the hunters?"

~~All men as I believe. How~~ All the land as I believe. How – how can I tell that this is not another trap?

Kim put the question aside and remembering the white stallion's pedigree asked – "What dost thou carry upon thee which they desire? Is it by chance some letter or word?"

Nay. I got rid of that in Chitor. ~~Xxxxnd by now it should be safe~~ It is my life that they seek. ~~Telt is no mere thing of a To accomplishxxxx~~ To get to my ends it was necessary to – There was a woman of the household." In spite of his fear ~~a cxxxx~~ the little man for a moment put on the deprecating smirk of a professional breaker of hearts. . . . Thus it touches the King's honour. <u>Therefore</u> they follow me to the death."

One of the drawbacks of all ~~services~~ departments is that employees are human and E.23, a man externally of unlucky aspect was even more human than most."

"But why not have thrown them off by doubling?"

Thou art young. Thou hast never had a price on thy head. Who shall stand against the anger of a King and the zeal of his ~~xxxx~~ derran (his prime minister) as I was when I [fled] the city I am now. There has been no breathing space even for a change of raiment. ~~In Chitor I was stricken with fever. They followed me through the xxxxxxx. In Ch~~ In Chitor I was ~~omor~~ in Kings' country, for Kotah to the East is beyond ~~xxx~~ the Sirkar's law; and east again ~~like~~ lie Mewar, Jaipur and Gwalior. I was a hare among tigers, but I broke through at Bandakui and came by Agra. I took the ekka in the fields and there sprang up an armed man from a ditch and cut at me ~~it~~ — as thou seest. It is a game they play – else they could have caught me an hundred times. They jest with my fear. ~~At Delhi they m~~ by day and night. At Delhi they will lay hold upon me and I shall be borne south to my punishment. So the man told me who rode by the side of the ekka slashing my legs. Would I had never seen the girl's face."

Kim pondered deeply. He had no experience of the interesting fate that follows a man who has tampered with royal households but he remembered how much in request was Mahbub Ali. The train slowed for the next station ~~The Mahratta felt in his belt to xxx~~, which was one where they did not collect tickets. The Mahratta looked out and his face turned ashy grey. ~~Behold, he sa~~A large ~~Arab Negro Arab~~ Negro, ~~with~~ wearing the Arab fez stalked slowly down the platform, leering into every compartment.

"Ha!" said he ~~and~~ staring at the Mahratta ~~"The bird has hidden here" and he waddled in. took his seat immediately opposite the collapsed man.~~

with inflated nostrils The bird has flit in here" and took his seat opposite the collapsed Mahratta. The Kamboh drew close. He had a mild creed-objection to a Moslem, and the Asiatic's ~~xxxx~~ bitter contempt for the nigger, who looked round with an equal scorn.

We go as far as Delhi together" he volunteered. "It is a good road to Delhi." No one ~~overmuch was~~ answered. "But overmuch worn [???] by beggars he went on cocking his fez rakishly askew.

"Ay – beggars, goats, and <u>hubshees</u> (niggers)" said Kim quietly. The Kamboh chuckled~~.~~ as he dandled his child. ~~"The~~

The answer was something in bastard Arabic that did not sound like a blessing. "If I had thee at the King's court to the southward I could change thy voice for all thy days" the brute ~~growled squeaked~~ growled.

~~Was it thus that they changed thine then? Kim asked.~~

Ah, ~~but~~ this is no King's country but the Sirkars" said the Kamboh. We do not stomach down-country rufflers, we Jats. Not even when they ~~x~~ are of our own people much less –

"Let the prince alone" said Kim. He does not like the sound of thy voice. It is too deep. Didst thou never hear the story of the jackal that lost his tail? Ho, woolly one, when did they change thy voice?"

The negro's eyes grew red and he lowered his head like a bull~~s~~ but there was little satisfaction in the farmer's great hard shoulder or Kim's steady eyes so he called them both unspeakable names a plenty.

"It wearies me" said Kim. We were here all friends. Comes then a woolly one who is not a man from God knows what trumpery princeling's court in the South and lords it over us upcountry folk." ~~Hearkye Herakeye~~-Harkee, Hubshee, there is one master in this land and that is the Sirkar who is not an eunuch nor a –

Knifes!" said the Kamboh dropping a ~~hand like a~~ hand on the black wrist that ~~went to~~ stole into the negroe's bosom. ~~xx~~ What iron age has come back here? ~~Hold the babe~~ Hold the babe."

[The next paragraph is crossed out and hard to read]: ~~He thrust it into the lama's lapone arm round the Negroe's neck borethrust him down upon the floor. Kimxxxxxxxxx throat and xxxxxxx bore down with all his weight. The Mahratta fled to the end of the carriage compartment and looked with gleaming eyes.~~

He thrust it into the lama's lap and flung an arm round the negroe's neck.

Here! cried the Mahratta leaping to the far end of the carriage. "He will stab! He will slay!" The negro ~~hit out wildly~~ struggled wildly for an instant~~. then~~ and then the muzzle of Kim's revolver prodded the centre of his stomach. Evidently he knew the [???]s of the weapon for he stiffened where ~~the~~ he lay under the Kamboh's shoulder.

There was a knife in his hand" snorted the farmer. "He might have slain my babe. For a little friendly talk he might have killed.

Open the door" said Kim to the Mahratta ~~will~~ who obeyed with zeal. ~~Xxxxx up~~-Push him out." He is an offense to honest men." Kim's loose sleeve ~~hid the [???]~~ and the niggers fat hid the hard-pressed pistol.

"Out" said Kim. "Take thy luck of a broken neck or a broken belly. Next time remember – this came to him as an inspiration – "it is even the death that thou didst intend."

The man's eyes rolled and goggled horribly as the ~~the Kamboh with~~ farmer with strong feet kicked him towards the swaying door.

This is the Sirkar's country" he grunted. A woolly one to lord it over <u>us</u>. Oh swine! Oh son of a male ass!"

A push and a heave ended the ~~strug~~ struggle. The negro ~~slid out over the xxx~~ rolled out over the foot-board – Kim remembered the amazement and question in his great white eyeballs – rolled down the embankment like a shot rabbit and lay still in the borrow pit. The Mahratta ~~xxx~~ had helped valiantly ~~in the last~~ overcome his last objections. The ~~bab~~ child ~~half xxx~~ between crying and laughter, clapped his hands in the lama's lap; the Kamboh adjusted his shoulder-cloth, still snorting like a fighting-buffalo; Kim slid the revolver back into his bosom and they all quibbled indignantly at the presumption of the woolly-haired ~~reeking negro~~ strong scented negro. The Kamboh was most eloquent. Even the lama, when thoroughly xxed[???]to the situation, admitted that, since the offender was a negro, ~~and therefore as devoid of of necessity as soulless as an ape,~~ he had been mercifully dealt with.

~~And for honor's the~~ And I took all his money at the last" the Mahratta whispered to Kim. I felt him most thoroughly. We did that well. ~~He will~~ If his neck is not broken he will find it hard to come by food.

Kim's eyes, alight, danced in his head. ~~Xxxx xxxx~~ for ~~xx xx~~ joy of the game. He even overlooked the Mahratta's "we." "Now what further have we to fear at Delhi?"

~~It was~~ How do I know? Belike he was sent to play with me on the road till ~~xx~~ I am handed over to those who wait at Delhi."

~~"Then why to Delhi at all?~~
~~If I go elsewhere they will come XXXXXXXonly it is pleasant to look at the sun while one may.~~

"Then why to Delhi?"

Where else. This is not a matter of stealing mere news but as I have said, of a woman. I am as dead already."

"And thou hast no fear?"

My very liver is dissolved to water by the thought of it which has followed me twenty days," said the Mahratta, simply, and Kim, looking him over marvelled.

None the less — for I see thou art a somebody in this business – carry my word into the office that that which I was sent to seek is hid in Chitor under the stone of which they know – the Ranee's stone. It is a small thing besides some which I have accomplished: and no man will give me credit therefore as they did to some of our brethren in the great game. But I beg thee say nothing of the woman if my name be blotted out."

"We must fight that also" said Kim.

"As thou wilt. I am spent – I am spent ~~"He took a handful of xxx~~ Twenty days of fear and fever. As thou wilt." He took an opium pill from a tin box in his waist belt and dropped into the slumber of the ~~drugxxDecide E.23 wasxxxxx~~ merciful drug.

~~When they reached Ghaziabad Kim found himself with a full blown situation on his hands – one xxxxxxxxxxxxxxxxxx~~

And now" said the Kamboh "since he has no tikkut he will say ~~that we have stolen it while he was senseless~~ when they ask him that he stole it while we lay senseless [Kipling reversed "he" and "we"] and there will be a lawsuit – all these Mahrattas are alike. He is cut and bruised furthermore and ~~he~~ that will be good evidence we [inkblot obscures text here] him. I am scratched over my hands by that [???] Hubshee, which is yet more evidence. Brothers we must change swiftly into another carriage. We are poor men." The [thought] of a hand to hand tussle with quarterstaves, or a skirmish with his own plough buffaloes would not have shaken his pulse but the thought of arrest on the wayside turned the big man into an abject coward.

"What Happened"

This early poem, first collected in Departmental Ditties *(1886), was later described by Kipling as "forecasting the result of Indians of mixed castes dealing in arms." "When you write 'native,' what do you mean?" he asked Margaret Burne-Jones in the mid-1880s; "Which one of all the thousand conflicting tongues, races, nationalities and peoples between the Khaibar Pass and Ceylon do you mean? There is no such thing as the natives of India. You may rest assured that if we didn't hold the land in six months it would be one big cock pit of conflicting princelets."[1]*

Hurree Chunder Mookerjee, pride of Bow Bazar,
Owner of a native press, "Barrishter-at-Lar,"
Waited on the Government with a claim to wear
Sabres by the bucketful, rifles by the pair.

Then the Indian Government winked a wicked wink,   5
Said to Chunder Mookerjee: "Stick to pen and ink.
They are safer implements, but, if you insist,
We will let you carry arms wheresoe'er you list."

[1]*Letters of Rudyard Kipling*, ed. Thomas Pinney (Palgrave, 2004), 6: 127; 1: 97–98.

Hurree Chunder Mookerjee sought the gunsmith and
Bought the tubes of Lancaster, Ballard, Dean, and Bland,[2]   10
Bought a shiny bowie-knife, bought a town-made sword,
Jingled like a carriage-horse when he went abroad.

But the Indian Government, always keen to please,
Also gave permission to horrid men like these— [3]
Yar Mahommed Yusufzai, down to kill or steal,   15
Chimbu Singh from Bikaneer, Tantia the Bhil;

Killar Khan the Marri chief, Jowar Singh the Sikh,
Nubbee Baksh Punjabi Jat, Abdul Huq Rafiq—
He was a Wahabi; last, little Boh Hla-oo
Took advantage of the Act—took a Snider too.[4]   20

They were unenlightened men, Ballard knew them not.
They procured their swords and guns chiefly on the spot;
And the lore of centuries, plus a hundred fights,
Made them slow to disregard one another's rights.

With a unanimity dear to patriot hearts   25
All those hairy gentlemen out of foreign parts
Said: "The good old days are back—let us go to war!"
Swaggered down the Grand Trunk Road into Bow Bazar.

Nubbee Baksh Punjabi Jat found a hide-bound flail;[5]
Chimbu Singh from Bikaneer oiled his Tonk *jezail*;   30
Yar Mahommed Yusufzai spat and grinned with glee
As he ground the butcher-knife of the Khyberee.

Jowar Singh the Sikh procured sabre, quoit, and mace,
Abdul Huq, Wahabi, jerked his dagger from its place,
While amid the jungle-grass danced and grinned and jabbered   35
Little Boh Hla-oo and cleared his *dah*-blade from the scabbard.

---

[2]Showy range of Western arms: Lancaster rifled cannon; Ballard single-shot rifle; guns from well-known London arms firms Dean and Bland.

[3]In addition to the Sikh and Jat fighters of *Kim*, Kipling invokes the Pathan Yusufzai tribe, who won fame battling Sikhs and the British; the Singhs, British supporters who ruled the internally embattled western state of Bikaner; the Bhils, whose fame as warriors traced back to ancient times; and the Marri tribes, who repeatedly attacked British forces. Abdul Huq Rafiq's Wahabism may suggest histories of conflict within Islam; Boh Hla-oo's name echoes those of Boh-Shwe and Hla-oo, two leaders of *dacoits* (armed robbers).

[4]Snider-Enfield rifle.

[5]The list of deadly weapons that follows includes the *jezail*, a long-barrelled, often handmade Afghani musket much used against the British; the quoit or *chakra*, a sharp, circular, missile-like Sikh projectile; and the *dah*-blade, a heavy Burmese knife.

What became of Mookerjee? Soothly, who can say?
Yar Mahommed only grins in a nasty way,
Jowar Singh is reticent, Chimbu Singh is mute,
But the belts of all of them simply bulge with loot.

What became of Ballard's guns? Afghans black and grubby
Sell them for their silver weight to the men of Pubbi;[6]
And the shiny bowie-knife and the town-made sword are
Hanging in a Marri camp just across the Border.

What became of Mookerjee? Ask Mahommed Yar
Prodding Siva's sacred bull down the Bow Bazar.
Speak to placid Nubbee Baksh—question land and sea—
Ask the Indian Congress[7] men—only don't ask me!

"The Native-Born"

"It is as the poet of the native-born," wrote economist John Davidson in 1900, "that [Kipling] has done most for empire."[1] First collected in The Seven Seas *(1897), this series of ambivalent, increasingly aggressive toasts officially speaks to the "Native-born" of the "four new nations" (Canada, Australia, New Zealand, and South Africa) and "the islands" (presumably including Polynesian islands and the West Indies). Still, Kipling's own status as one of the "native-born" is far from the only reason to suspect that the sentiments voiced here may have wider application.*

We've drunk to the Queen—God bless her!—
  We've drunk to our mothers' land;
We've drunk to our English brother
  (But he does not understand);
We've drunk to the wide creation,   5
  And the Cross[2] swings low to the morn,
Last toast, and of obligation,
  A health to the Native-born!

---

[6]Northwest Frontier village, now in Pakistan.

[7]The Indian National Congress. Members strenuously opposed the Arms Act of 1878, which banned or severely restricted Indians' access to firearms, while waiving licensing requirements for Europeans and Anglo-Indians.

---

[1]See *Commercial Federation and Colonial Trade Policy* (S. Sonnenschein, 1900), p. 114. The "native-born" are people of British descent, born in the colonies.

[2]Constellation: the Southern Cross.

They change their skies above them,
  But not their hearts that roam!   10
We learned from our wistful mothers
  To call old England "home";
We read of the English sky-lark,
  Of the spring in the English lanes,
But we screamed with the painted lories[3]   15
  As we rode on the dusty plains!

They passed with their old-world legends—
  Their tales of wrong and dearth—
Our fathers held by purchase,
  But we by the right of birth;   20
Our heart's where they rocked our cradle,
  Our love where we spent our toil,
And our faith and our hope and our honour
  We pledge to our native soil!

I charge you charge your glasses—   25
  I charge you drink with me
To the men of the Four New Nations,
  And the Islands of the Sea—
To the last least lump of coral
  That none may stand outside,   30
And our own good pride shall teach us
  To praise our comrade's pride.

To the hush of the breathless morning
  On the thin, tin, crackling roofs,
To the haze of the burned back-ranges   35
  And the dust of the shoeless hoofs—
To the risk of a death by drowning,
  To the risk of a death by drouth—
To the men of a million acres,
  To the Sons of the Golden South.   40

To the Sons of the Golden South, (Stand up!)
  And the life we live and know,
Let a fellow sing o' the little things he cares about,
If a fellow fights for the little things he cares about
  With the weight of a single blow!   45

[3]Bright Australasian parrots.

To the smoke of a hundred coasters,
  To the sheep on a thousand hills,
To the sun that never blisters,
  To the rain that never chills—
To the land of the waiting springtime,   50
  To our five-meal, meat-fed men,
To the tall, deep-bosomed women,
  And the children nine and ten!

And the children nine and ten, (Stand up!)
  And the life we live and know,   55
Let a fellow sing o' the little things he cares about,
If a fellow fights for the little things he cares about
  With the weight of a two-fold blow!

To the far-flung, fenceless prairie
  Where the quick cloud-shadows trail,   60
To our neighbour's barn in the offing
  And the line of the new-cut rail;
To the plough in her league-long furrow
  With the grey Lake gulls behind—
To the weight of a half-year's winter   65
  And the warm wet western wind!

To the home of the floods and thunder,
  To her pale dry healing blue—
To the lift of the great Cape combers,
  And the smell of the baked Karroo.[4]   70
To the growl of the sluicing stamp-head—[5]
  To the reef and the water-gold,
To the last and the largest Empire,
  To the map that is half unrolled!

To our dear dark foster-mothers,   75
  To the heathen songs they sung—
To the heathen speech we babbled
  Ere we came to the white man's tongue.
To the cool of our deep verandas —
  To the blaze of our jewelled main,   80
To the night, to the palms in the moonlight,
  And the fire-fly in the cane!

[4]South African semidesert.
[5]Heavy cast-iron mining equipment.

To the hearth of our people's people—
  To her well-ploughed windy sea,
To the hush of our dread high-altars   85
  Where The Abbey makes us We;
To the grist of the slow-ground ages,
  To the gain that is yours and mine—
To the Bank of the Open Credit,
  To the Power-house of the Line![6]   90

We've drunk to the Queen—God bless her!—
  We've drunk to our mothers' land;
We've drunk to our English brother
  (And we hope he'll understand).
We've drunk as much as we're able,   95
  And the Cross swings low to the morn;
Last toast—and your foot on the table!—
  A health to the Native-born!

A health to the Native-born, (Stand-up!)
  We're six white men arow,   100
All bound to sing o' the little things we care about,
All bound to fight for the little things we care about
  With the weight of a six-fold blow!
By the might of our cable-tow,[7] (Take hands!)
  From the Orkneys to the Horn,[8]   105
All round the world (and a little loop to pull it by),
All round the world (and a little strap to buckle it),
  A health to the Native-born!

"The Ballad of the King's Jest"

*Like the more famous "Ballad of East and West," this poem invokes the
wild country near Afghanistan where teenaged journalist Kipling went to
Fort Jumrood (Jamrud) in 1885 to cover the entry of Afghan Amir Abdur
Rahman Khan into British India. The "Iron Amir" and his military commander-in-chief, Gholam Hyder Khan, like the fictional Mahbub Ali,*

[6]Like customers with open credit, colonies draw on British wealth without needing to
pledge anything as security; the powerhouse sends electricity down the entire line.

[7]The telegraph, a symbol of British technological superiority.

[8]The Orkney Islands lie north of the Scottish mainland; Cape Horn is the southern tip
of South America.

(portrayed here through the eyes of a spy for the British), figure repeatedly in Kipling's later writing. The poem was collected in Barrack-Room Ballads and Other Verses *(1889–91).*

When spring-time flushes the desert grass,
Our *kafilas*[1] wind through the Khyber Pass.
Lean are the camels but fat the frails,[2]
Light are the purses but heavy the bales,
As the snowbound trade of the North comes down   5
To the market-square of Peshawur town.

In a turquoise twilight, crisp and chill,
A kafila camped at the foot of the hill.
Then blue smoke-haze of the cooking rose,
And tent-peg answered to hammer-nose;   10
And the picketed ponies, shag and wild,
Strained at their ropes as the feed was piled;
And the bubbling camels beside the load
Sprawled for a furlong adown the road;
And the Persian pussy-cats, brought for sale,   15
Spat at the dogs from the camel-bale;
And the tribesmen bellowed to hasten the food;
And the camp-fires twinkled by Fort Jumrood;
And there fled on the wings of the gathering dusk
A savour of camels and carpets and musk,   20
A murmur of voices, a reek of smoke,
To tell us the trade of the Khyber woke.

The lid of the flesh-pot chattered high,
The knives were whetted and—then came I
To Mahbub Ali the muleteer,   25
Patching his bridles and counting his gear,
Crammed with the gossip of half a year.
But Mahbub Ali the kindly said,
"Better is speech when the belly is fed."
So we plunged the hand to the mid-wrist deep   30
In a cinnamon stew of the fat-tailed sheep,
And he who never hath tasted the food,
By Allah! he knoweth not bad from good.

[1]Caravans. [Kipling's note]
[2]Baskets.

We cleansed our beards of the mutton-grease,
We lay on the mats and were filled with peace,   35
And the talk slid north, and the talk slid south,
With the sliding puffs from the hookah-mouth.

Four things greater than all things are,—
Women and Horses and Power and War.
We spake of them all, but the last the most,   40
For I sought a word of a Russian post,
Of a shifty promise, an unsheathed sword,
And a grey-coat guard on the Helmund ford.[3]
Then Mahbub Ali lowered his eyes
In the fashion of one who is weaving lies.   45
Quoth he: "Of the Russians who can say?
When the night is gathering all is grey.
But we look that the gloom of the night shall die
In the morning flush of a blood-red sky.
Friend of my heart, is it meet or wise   50
To warn a King of his enemies?
We know what Heaven or Hell may bring,
But no man knoweth the mind of the King.
That unsought counsel is cursed of God
Attesteth the story of Wali Dad.   55

His sire was leaky of tongue and pen,
His dam was a clucking Khattack[4] hen;
And the colt bred close to the vice of each,
For he carried the curse of an unstaunched speech.
Therewith madness—so that he sought   60
The favour of Kings at the Kabul Court;
And travelled, in hope of honour, far
To the line where the grey-coat squadrons are.
There have I journeyed too—but I
Saw naught, said naught, and—did not die!   65
He hearked to rumour, and snatched at a breath
Of "this one knoweth" and "that one saith,"—
Legends that ran from mouth to mouth
Of a grey-coat coming, and sack of the South.
These have I also heard—they pass   70
With each new spring and the winter grass.

[3]The longest river in Afghanistan. Russian control of the ford could have grave military consequences.

[4]Or *Khatak*: A Peshawar district tribe known for British Indian Army service.

Hot-foot southward, forgotten of God,
Back to the city ran Wali Dad,
Even to Kabul—in full durbar[5]
The King held talk with his Chief in War.   75
Into the press of the crowd he broke,
And what he had heard of the coming spoke.

Then Gholam Hyder, the Red Chief, smiled,
As a mother might on a babbling child;
But those who would laugh restrained their breath,   80
When the face of the King showed dark as death.
Evil it is in full durbar
To cry to a ruler of gathering war!
Slowly he led to a peach-tree small,
That grew by a cleft of the city wall.   85
And he said to the boy: "They shall praise thy zeal
So long as the red spurt follows the steel.
And the Russ is upon us even now?
Great is thy prudence—await them, thou.
Watch from the tree. Thou art young and strong.   90
Surely thy vigil is not for long.
The Russ is upon us, thy clamour ran?
Surely an hour shall bring their van.
Wait and watch. When the host is near,
Shout aloud that my men may hear."   95

Friend of my heart, is it meet or wise
To warn a King of his enemies?
A guard was set that he might not flee—
A score of bayonets ringed the tree.
The peach-bloom fell in showers of snow,   100
When he shook at his death as he looked below.
By the Power of God, Who alone is great,
Till the seventh day he fought with his fate.
Then madness took him, and men declare
He mowed in the branches as ape and bear,   105
And last as a sloth, ere his body failed,
And he hung as a bat in the forks, and wailed,
And sleep the cord of his hands untied,
And he fell, and was caught on the points and died.

[5]Formal audience at the royal court.

Heart of my heart, is it meet or wise   110
To warn a King of his enemies?
We know what Heaven or Hell may bring,
But no man knoweth the mind of the King.
Of the grey-coat coming who can say?
When the night is gathering all is grey.   115
Two things greater than all things are,
The first is Love, and the second War.
And since we know not how War may prove,
Heart of my heart, let us talk of Love!"

"The Mother-Lodge"

Voiced by "Tommy Atkins," this Masonic "New Barrack-Room Ballad" was first collected in The Seven Seas (1897). *In* Something of Myself, *Kipling wrote that through entry into his own first (or "mother") lodge at Lahore in the mid 1880s, he came to know "Muslims, Hindus, Sikhs, members of the Arya and Brahmo Samaj, and a Jew . . . So yet another little world opened to me which I needed." Indian access to the masculine "little world" of Freemasonry had been hard-fought.*

> There was Rundle, Station Master,
>   An' Beazeley of the Rail,
> An' 'Ackman, Commissariat,
>   An' 'Donkin o' the Jail;
> An' Blake, Conductor-Sargent,   5
>   Our Master twice was 'e,[1]
> With 'im that kept the Europe shop,[2]
>   Old Framjee Eduljee.
>
> Outside—"Sergeant! Sir! Salute! Salaam!"
> Inside—"Brother," an' it doesn't do no 'arm.   10
> We met upon the Level an' we parted on the Square,
> An' I was Junior Deacon in my Mother Lodge out there![3]
>
> We'd Bola Nath, Accountant,
>   An' Saul the Aden Jew,
> An' Din Mohammed, draughtsman   15

[1]Master Mason; an elevated degree.

[2]Outlet for European goods.

[3]Appointed assistant officer.

Of the Survey Office too;
There was Babu Chuckerbutty,
    An' Amir Singh the Sikh,
An' Castro from the fittin'-sheds,
    The Roman Catholick!   20

We 'adn't good regalia,
    An' our Lodge was old an' bare,
But we knew the Ancient Landmarks,[4]
    An' we kep' 'em to a hair;
An' lookin' on it backwards   25
    It often strikes me thus,
There ain't such things as infidels,
    Excep', per'aps, it's us.

For monthly, after Labour,
    We'd all sit down an' smoke   30
(We dursn't give no banquits,
    Lest a Brother's caste were broke),
An' man on man got talkin'
    Religion an' the rest,
An' every man comparin'   35
    Of the God 'e knew the best.

So man on man got talkin',
    An' not a Brother stirred
Till mornin' waked the parrots
    An' that dam' brain-fever-bird;[5]   40
We'd say 'twas 'ighly curious,
    An' we'd all ride 'ome to bed,
With Mo'ammed, God, an' Shiva
    Changin' pickets in our 'ead.

Full oft on Guv'ment service   45
    This rovin' foot 'ath pressed,
An' bore fraternal greetin's
    To the Lodges east an' west,
Accordin' as commanded,
    From Kohat to Singapore,   50
But I wish that I might see them
    In my Mother Lodge once more!

[4]Unchanging core precepts and practices of a Masonic order.
[5]Hawk cuckoo; disliked for its shrill, incessant call.

I wish that I might see them,
  My Brethren black an' brown,
With the trichies smellin' pleasant[6]   55
  An' the *hog-darn*[7] passin' down;
An' the old khansamah[8] snorin'
  On the bottle-khana floor,[9]
Like a Master in good standing
  With my Mother Lodge once more!   60

Outside—"Sergeant! Sir! Salute! Salaam!"
Inside—"Brother," an' it doesn't do no 'arm.
We met upon the Level an' we parted on the Square,
An' I was Junior Deacon in my Mother Lodge out there!

"Recessional"[1]

As Something of Myself *reports, Queen Victoria's extravagant 1897 sixtieth anniversary Diamond Jubilee celebrations struck Kipling as betraying "a certain optimism that scared me." His poetic response, conceived "in the nature of a* nuzzur-wattu, *(an averter of the Evil Eye)," and sent to* The Times *of London free of charge, immediately became a national hymn. Said to have been sung by British troops in June 1900 to celebrate Pretoria's capture from the Boers, "Recessional" quickly entered the Church of England hymnal as well as* The Oxford Book of English Verse.

God of our fathers, known of old,
  Lord of our far-flung battle-line,
Beneath whose awful Hand we hold
  Dominion over palm and pine—
Lord God of Hosts, be with us yet,   5
Lest we forget—lest we forget![2]

The tumult and the shouting[3] dies;
  The Captains and the Kings depart:
Still stands Thine ancient sacrifice,

---

[6]Cheap, square-cut cigars.
[7]Cigar-lighter. [Kipling's note]
[8]Butler. [Kipling's note]
[9]Pantry. [Kipling's note]

---

[1]Withdrawal hymn played after the end of sacred services.
[2]"Then beware lest thou forget the Lord, which brought thee forth out of the land of Egypt, from the house of bondage" (Deuteronomy 6.12).
[3]Literally, the Jubilee celebration, but see Job 39.25.

An humble and a contrite heart.[4]   10
Lord God of Hosts, be with us yet,
Lest we forget—lest we forget!

Far-called, our navies melt away;
   On dune and headland sinks the fire:[5]
Lo, all our pomp of yesterday   15
   Is one with Nineveh and Tyre![6]
Judge of the Nations, spare us yet,
Lest we forget—lest we forget!

If, drunk with sight of power, we loose
   Wild tongues that have not Thee in awe,   20
Such boastings as the Gentiles[7] use,
   Or lesser breeds without the Law—[8]
Lord God of Hosts, be with us yet,
Lest we forget—lest we forget!

For heathen heart that puts her trust   25
   In reeking tube and iron shard,[9]
All valiant dust that builds on dust,
   And guarding, calls not Thee to guard,
For frantic boast and foolish word—
Thy mercy on Thy People, Lord!   30

"Lispeth"

Published in the Civil and Military Gazette *on November 29, 1886 and collected as the first of the* Plain Tales from the Hills *(1888), "Lispeth" treats Anglo-Indian communities on the boundaries of the world of* Kim: *civilian missionaries, travelers, and British women. Clearly, the central figure of this story bears some connection to the character of Lispeth in* Kim; *but we get a very different perspective on her here.*

---

[4] "The sacrifices of God are a broken spirit: a broken and a contrite heart, O God, thou wilt not despise" (Psalms 51.17).

[5] After the Jubilee's close, marked by a naval review of unprecedented force, the fleet disperses. On land, throughout the empire, Jubilee bonfires and fireworks sink to ash.

[6] Powerful Assyrian and Phoenician cities laid waste, in biblical accounts, by God's wrath. See the book of Nahum, and Isaiah 23.

[7] In biblical terms, pagans.

[8] A controversial line: Many read "lesser breeds" as racial; others, including George Orwell, have pointed to the Germans, whose rising military power Kipling feared.

[9] Raw weaponry: If the "reek" of gun barrels comes in part from animal fat, it evokes the 1857 Rebellion (see p. xiii).

Look, you have cast out Love! What Gods are these
    You bid me please?
The Three in One, the One in Three? Not so!
    To my own Gods I go.
It may be they shall give me greater ease
Than your cold Christ and tangled Trinities.

The Convert[1]

SHE was the daughter of Sonoo, a Hill-man of the Himalayas, and Jadéh his wife. One year their maize failed, and two bears spent the night in their only opium poppy-field just above the Sutlej Valley on the Kotgarh side; so, next season, they turned Christian, and brought their baby to the Mission to be baptized. The Kotgarh Chaplain christened her Elizabeth, and "Lispeth" is the Hill or *pahari* pronunciation.

Later, cholera came into the Kotgarh Valley and carried off Sonoo and Jadeh, and Lispeth became half servant, half companion, to the wife of the then Chaplain of Kotgarh. This was after the reign of the Moravian missionaries in that place, but before Kotgarh had quite forgotten her title of "Mistress of the Northern Hills."

Whether Christianity improved Lispeth, or whether the gods of her own people would have done as much for her under any circumstances, I do not know; but she grew very lovely. When a Hill-girl grows lovely, she is worth travelling fifty miles over bad ground to look upon. Lispeth had a Greek face—one of those faces people paint so often, and see so seldom. She was of a pale, ivory colour, and, for her race, extremely tall. Also, she possessed eyes that were wonderful; and, had she not been dressed in the abominable print-cloths affected by Missions, you would, meeting her on the hillside unexpectedly, have thought her the original Diana of the Romans going out to slay.

Lispeth took to Christianity readily, and did not abandon it when she reached womanhood, as do some Hill-girls. Her own people hated her because she had, they said, become a white woman and washed herself daily; and the Chaplain's wife did not know what to do with her. One cannot ask a stately goddess, five foot ten in her shoes, to clean plates and dishes. She played with the Chaplain's children and took classes in the Sunday School, and read all the books in the house, and grew more and more beautiful, like the Princess in fairy tales. The Chaplain's wife said that the girl ought to take service in Simla as a nurse or something "genteel." But Lispeth did not want to take service. She was very happy where she was.

When travellers—there were not many in those years—came into Kotgarh, Lispeth used to lock herself into her own room for fear they might take her away to Simla, or out into the unknown world.

[1]Kipling's lines; "The Convert" appears in his collected poems.

One day, a few months after she was seventeen years old, Lispeth went out for a walk. She did not walk in the manner of English ladies—a mile and a half out, with a carriage-ride back again. She covered between twenty and thirty miles in her little constitutionals, all about and about, between Kotgarh and Narkunda. This time she came back at full dusk, stepping down the breakneck descent into Kotgarh with something heavy in her arms. The Chaplain's wife was dozing in the drawing-room when Lispeth came in breathing heavily and very exhausted with her burden. Lispeth put it down on the sofa, and said simply, "This is my husband. I found him on the Bagi Road. He has hurt himself. We will nurse him, and when he is well, your husband shall marry him to me."

This was the first mention Lispeth had ever made of her matrimonial views, and the Chaplain's wife shrieked with horror. However, the man on the sofa needed attention first. He was a young Englishman, and his head had been cut to the bone by something jagged. Lispeth said she had found him down the hillside, and had brought him in. He was breathing queerly and was unconscious.

He was put to bed and tended by the Chaplain, who knew something of medicine; and Lispeth waited outside the door in case she could be useful. She explained to the Chaplain that this was the man she meant to marry; and the Chaplain and his wife lectured her severely on the impropriety of her conduct. Lispeth listened quietly, and repeated her first proposition. It takes a great deal of Christianity to wipe out uncivilised Eastern instincts, such as falling in love at first sight. Lispeth, having found the man she worshipped, did not see why she should keep silent as to her choice. She had no intention of being sent away, either. She was going to nurse that Englishman until he was well enough to marry her. This was her programme.

After a fortnight of slight fever and inflammation, the Englishman recovered coherence and thanked the Chaplain and his wife, and Lispeth—especially Lispeth—for their kindness. He was a traveller in the East, he said—they never talked about "globe-trotters" in those days, when the P. & O. fleet[2] was young and small—and had come from Dehra Dun to hunt for plants and butterflies among the Simla Hills. No one at Simla, therefore, knew anything about him. He fancied that he must have fallen over the cliff while reaching out for a fern on a rotten tree-trunk, and that his coolies must have stolen his baggage and fled. He thought he would go back to Simla when he was a little stronger. He desired no more mountaineering.

[2]The Peninsular & Oriental Steam Navigation Company, founded in the 1830s, delivered passengers to the Mediterranean port of Alexandria in Egypt. Travelers then went up the Nile to Cairo, from there by shallow-draft vessels to Cosseir, then by mule to Port Suez, then overland to India. The Alexandria-Suez railway, completed in 1858, considerably shortened the journey, opening it up to more "globe-trotters." "Lispeth" would thus seem to be set in an earlier era than *Kim*.

He made small haste to go away, and recovered his strength slowly. Lispeth objected to being advised either by the Chaplain or his wife; therefore the latter spoke to the Englishman, and told him how matters stood in Lispeth's heart. He laughed a good deal, and said it was very pretty and romantic, but, as he was engaged to a girl at Home, he fancied that nothing would happen. Certainly he would behave with discretion. He did that. Still he found it very pleasant to talk to Lispeth, and walk with Lispeth and say nice things to her, and call her pet names, while he was getting strong enough to go away. It meant nothing at all to him, and everything in the world to Lispeth. She was very happy while the fortnight lasted, because she had found a man to love.

Being a savage by birth, she took no trouble to hide her feelings, and the Englishman was amused. When he went away, Lispeth walked with him up the Hill as far as Narkunda, very troubled and very miserable. The Chaplain's wife, being a good Christian and disliking anything in the shape of fuss or scandal,—Lispeth was beyond her management entirely,—had told the Englishman to tell Lispeth that he was coming back to marry her. "She is but a child you know, and, I fear, at heart a heathen," said the Chaplain's wife. So all the twelve miles up the Hill the Englishman, with his arm round Lispeth's waist, was assuring the girl that he would come back and marry her; and Lispeth made him promise over and over again. She wept on the Narkunda Ridge till he had passed out of sight along the Muttiani path.

Then she dried her tears and went in to Kotgarh again, and said to the Chaplain's wife, "He will come back and marry me. He has gone to his own people to tell them so." And the Chaplain's wife soothed Lispeth and said, "He will come back." At the end of two months, Lispeth grew impatient, and was told that the Englishman had gone over the seas to England. She knew where England was, because she had read little geography primers; but, of course, she had no conception of the nature of the sea, being a Hill-girl. There was an old puzzle-map of the World in the house. Lispeth had played with it when she was a child. She unearthed it again, and put it together of evenings, and cried to herself, and tried to imagine where her Englishman was. As she had no ideas of distance or steamboats, her notions were somewhat wild. It would not have made the least difference had she been perfectly correct; for the Englishman had no intention of coming back to marry a Hill-girl. He forgot all about her by the time he was butterfly-hunting in Assam. He wrote a book on the East afterwards. Lispeth's name did not appear there.

At the end of three months, Lispeth made daily pilgrimage to Narkunda to see if her Englishman was coming along the road. It gave her comfort, and the Chaplain's wife finding her happier thought that she was getting over her "barbarous and most indelicate folly." A little later, the walks ceased to help Lispeth and her temper grew very bad. The Chaplain's wife thought this a profitable time to let her know the real state of affairs—that the Englishman had only promised his love to keep her quiet—that he had never meant anything, and that it was wrong and improper of Lispeth to think of marriage with an Englishman, who was of a superior clay, besides being promised in marriage to a girl of his own people. Lispeth said that all this was clearly impossible because he had said he loved her, and the Chaplain's wife had, with her own lips, asserted that the Englishman was coming back.

"How can what he and you said be untrue?" asked Lispeth.

"We said it as an excuse to keep you quiet, child," said the Chaplain's wife.

"Then you have lied to me," said Lispeth, "you and he?"

The Chaplain's wife bowed her head, and said nothing. Lispeth was silent, too, for a little time; then she went out down the valley, and returned in the dress of a Hill-girl—infamously dirty, but without the nose-stud and ear-rings. She had her hair braided into the long pigtail, helped out with black thread, that Hill-women wear.

"I am going back to my own people," said she. "You have killed Lispeth. There is only left old Jadeh's daughter—the daughter of a *pahari* and the servant of *Tarka Devi.*[3] You are all liars, you English."

By the time that the Chaplain's wife had recovered from the shock of the announcement that Lispeth had 'verted to her mother's gods, the girl had gone; and she never came back.

She took to her own unclean people savagely, as if to make up the arrears of the life she had stepped out of; and, in a little time, she married a woodcutter who beat her after the manner of paharis, and her beauty faded soon.

"There is no law whereby you can account for the vagaries of the heathen," said the Chaplain's wife, "and I believe that Lispeth was always at heart an infidel." Seeing she had been taken into the Church of England at the mature age of five weeks, this statement does not do credit to the Chaplain's wife.

Lispeth was a very old woman when she died. She had always a perfect command of English, and when she was sufficiently drunk, could sometimes be induced to tell the story of her first love-affair.

It was hard then to realise that the bleared, wrinkled creature, exactly like a wisp of charred rag, could ever have been "Lispeth of the Kotgarh Mission."

---

[3]Tara (not Tarka) Devi is a powerful maternal Hindu goddess who is fond of blood.

"The Mark of the Beast"

Described by the author himself as "a rather nasty story," and reviled as well as celebrated by generations of critics, "The Mark of the Beast" draws its name from the Bible's book of Revelation.[1] The critical challenges posed by this account of religious disrespect, retaliation, and torture are now more significant than ever. First published in India in 1890, Kipling's story appears here as collected in Life's Handicap *(1891).*

Your Gods and my Gods—do you or I know which are the stronger?

Native Proverb.

EAST of Suez, some hold, the direct control of Providence ceases; Man being there handed over to the power of the Gods and Devils of Asia, and the Church of England Providence only exercising an occasional and modified supervision in the case of Englishmen.

This theory accounts for some of the more unnecessary horrors of life in India:[2] it may be stretched to explain my story.

My friend Strickland of the Police, who knows as much of natives of India as is good for any man, can bear witness to the facts of the case. Dumoise, our doctor, also saw what Strickland and I saw. The inference which he drew from the evidence was entirely incorrect. He is dead now; he died in a rather curious manner, which has been elsewhere described.[3]

When Fleete came to India he owned a little money and some land in the Himalayas, near a place called Dharmsala.[4] Both properties had been left him by an uncle, and he came out to finance them. He was a big, heavy, genial, and inoffensive man. His knowledge of natives was, of course, limited, and he complained of the difficulties of the language.

He rode in from his place in the hills to spend New Year in the station, and he stayed with Strickland. On New Year's Eve there was a big dinner at the club, and the night was excusably wet.[5] When men foregather from the uttermost ends of the Empire, they have a right to be riotous. The Frontier had sent down a contingent o' Catch-'em-Alive-O's[6] who had not seen twenty white faces for a year, and were

---

[1] The beast's followers "receive a mark in their right hand, or in their foreheads" (13.16). At the Apocalypse, as the vials of God's wrath are poured "upon the earth," there falls "a noisome and grievous sore upon the men which had the mark of the beast" (16.2).

[2] An ambiguous, possibly ironic claim: Does this theory "account for" unnecessary horrors by accurately identifying their source? Or might it, in fact, *be* their source?

[3] See "By Word of Mouth," *Plain Tales from the Hills* (1888).

[4] A once-popular colonial hill station in the Himalayan foothills; now the Dalai Lama's home in exile.

[5] Drunken.

[6] Militia recruits.

used to ride fifteen miles to dinner at the next Fort at the risk of a Khyberee bullet where their drinks should lie. They profited by their new security, for they tried to play pool with a curled-up hedgehog found in the garden, and one of them carried the marker round the room in his teeth. Half a dozen planters had come in from the south and were talking "horse" to the Biggest Liar in Asia, who was trying to cap all their stories at once. Everybody was there, and there was a general closing up of ranks and taking stock of our losses in dead or disabled that had fallen during the past year. It was a very wet night, and I remember that we sang "Auld Lang Syne" with our feet in the Polo Championship Cup, and our heads among the stars, and swore that we were all dear friends. Then some of us went away and annexed Burma, and some tried to open up the Soudan and were opened up by Fuzzies in that cruel scrub outside Suakim,[7] and some found stars and medals, and some were married, which was bad, and some did other things which were worse, and the others of us stayed in our chains and strove to make money on insufficient experiences.

Fleete began the night with sherry and bitters, drank champagne steadily up to dessert, then raw, rasping Capri with all the strength of whiskey, took Benedictine with his coffee, four or five whiskies and sodas to improve his pool strokes, beer and bones[8] at half-past two, winding up with old brandy. Consequently, when he came out, at half-past three in the morning, into fourteen degrees of frost, he was very angry with his horse for coughing, and tried to leapfrog into the saddle. The horse broke away and went to his stables; so Strickland and I formed a Guard of Dishonour to take Fleete home.

Our road lay through the bazaar, close to a little temple of Hanuman, the Monkey-god,[9] who is a leading divinity worthy of respect. All gods have good points, just as have all priests. Personally, I attach much importance to Hanuman, and am kind to his people—the great gray apes of the hills. One never knows when one may want a friend.

There was a light in the temple, and as we passed, we could hear voices of men chanting hymns. In a native temple, the priests rise at all hours of the night to do honour to their god. Before we could stop him, Fleete dashed up the steps, patted two priests on the back, and was gravely grinding the ashes of his cigar-butt into the forehead of

[7]In 1885, the Third Anglo-Burmese War ensured the full annexation of Burma as a British Indian province; in 1890, the British left Suakin, their last outpost in the Egyptian-controlled Sudan. "Fuzzies" were Sudanese warriors.

[8]Equivalent of bar food, made with beef bones.

[9]Hindu deity in the form of a mighty ape; Rama's ally in the epic *Ramayana*, revered as a courageous protector against evil.

the red stone image of Hanuman. Strickland tried to drag him out, but he sat down and said solemnly

"Shee that? 'Mark of the B-beasht!' I made it. Ishn't it fine?"

In half a minute the temple was alive and noisy, and Strickland, who knew what came of polluting gods, said that things might occur. He, by virtue of his official position, long residence in the country, and weakness for going among the natives, was known to the priests and he felt unhappy. Fleete sat on the ground and refused to move. He said that "good old Hanuman" made a very soft pillow.

Then, without any warning, a Silver Man came out of a recess behind the image of the god. He was perfectly naked in that bitter, bitter cold, and his body shone like frosted silver, for he was what the Bible calls "a leper as white as snow."[10] Also he had no face, because he was a leper of some years' standing, and his disease was heavy upon him. We two stooped to haul Fleete up, and the temple was filling and filling with folk who seemed to spring from the earth, when the Silver Man ran in under our arms, making a noise exactly like the mewing of an otter, caught Fleete round the body and dropped his head on Fleete's breast before we could wrench him away. Then he retired to a corner and sat mewing while the crowd blocked all the doors.

The priests were very angry until the Silver Man touched Fleete. That nuzzling seemed to sober them.

At the end of a few minutes' silence one of the priests came to Strickland and said, in perfect English, "Take your friend away. He has done with Hanuman, but Hanuman has not done with him." The crowd gave room and we carried Fleete into the road.

Strickland was very angry. He said that we might all three have been knifed, and that Fleete should thank his stars that he had escaped without injury.

Fleete thanked no one. He said that he wanted to go to bed. He was gorgeously drunk.

We moved on, Strickland silent and wrathful, until Fleete was taken with violent shivering fits and sweating. He said that the smells of the bazaar were overpowering, and he wondered why slaughterhouses were permitted so near English residences. "Can't you smell the blood?" said Fleete.

We put him to bed at last, just as the dawn was breaking, and Strickland invited me to have another whiskey and soda. While we were drinking he talked of the trouble in the temple, and admitted that it baffled him completely. Strickland hates being mystified by

---

[10]In 2 Kings, 5.27, the phrase describes a holy healer's servant, cursed with leprosy for disobedience and corruption. In Exodus 4.6–7, God renders Moses' hand leprous, then heals it as proof of divine power.

natives, because his business in life is to overmatch them with their own weapons. He has not yet succeeded in doing this, but in fifteen or twenty years he will have made some small progress.

"They should have mauled us," he said, "instead of mewing at us. I wonder what they meant. I don't like it one little bit."

I said that the Managing Committee of the temple would in all probability bring a criminal action against us for insulting their religion. There was a section of the Indian Penal Code which exactly met Fleete's offence. Strickland said he only hoped and prayed that they would do this. Before I left I looked into Fleete's room, and saw him lying on his right side, scratching his left breast. Then I went to bed, cold, depressed, and unhappy, at seven o'clock in the morning.

At one o'clock I rode over to Strickland's house to inquire after Fleete's head. I imagined that it would be a sore one. Fleete was breakfasting and seemed unwell. His temper was gone, for he was abusing the cook for not supplying him with an underdone chop. A man who can eat raw meat after a wet night is a curiosity. I told Fleete this and he laughed.

"You breed queer mosquitoes in these parts," he said. "I've been bitten to pieces, but only in one place."

"Let's have a look at the bite," said Strickland. "It may have gone down since this morning."

While the chops were being cooked, Fleete opened his shirt and showed us, just over his left breast, a mark, the perfect double of the black rosettes—the five or six irregular blotches arranged in a circle—on a leopard's hide. Strickland looked and said, "It was only pink this morning. It's grown black now."

Fleete ran to a glass.

"By Jove!" he said, "this is nasty. What is it?"

We could not answer. Here the chops came in, all red and juicy, and Fleete bolted three in a most offensive manner. He ate on his right grinders only, and threw his head over his right shoulder as he snapped the meat. When he had finished, it struck him that he had been behaving strangely, for he said apologetically, "I don't think I ever felt so hungry in my life. I've bolted like an ostrich."

After breakfast Strickland said to me, "Don't go. Stay here, and stay for the night."

Seeing that my house was not three miles from Strickland's, this request was absurd. But Strickland insisted, and was going to say something when Fleete interrupted by declaring in a shamefaced way that he felt hungry again. Strickland sent a man to my house to fetch over my bedding and a horse, and we three went down to Strickland's stables to pass the hours until it was time to go out for a ride. The man who has a weakness for horses never wearies of inspecting them;

and when two men are killing time in this way they gather knowledge and lies the one from the other.

There were five horses in the stables, and I shall never forget the scene as we tried to look them over. They seemed to have gone mad. They reared and screamed and nearly tore up their pickets; they sweated and shivered and lathered and were distraught with fear. Strickland's horses used to know him as well as his dogs; which made the matter more curious. We left the stable for fear of the brutes throwing themselves in their panic. Then Strickland turned back and called me. The horses were still frightened, but they let us "gentle" and make much of them, and put their heads in our bosoms.

"They aren't afraid of us," said Strickland. "D'you know, I'd give three months' pay if Outrage here could talk."

But Outrage was dumb, and could only cuddle up to his master and blow out his nostrils, as is the custom of horses when they wish to explain things but can't. Fleete came up when we were in the stalls, and as soon as the horses saw him, their fright broke out afresh. It was all that we could do to escape from the place unkicked. Strickland said, "They don't seem to love you, Fleete."

"Nonsense," said Fleete; "my mare will follow me like a dog." He went to her; she was in a loose-box; but as he slipped the bars she plunged, knocked him down, and broke away into the garden. I laughed, but Strickland was not amused. He took his moustache in both fists and pulled at it till it nearly came out. Fleete, instead of going off to chase his property, yawned, saying that he felt sleepy. He went to the house to lie down, which was a foolish way of spending New Year's Day.

Strickland sat with me in the stables and asked if I had noticed anything peculiar in Fleete's manner. I said that he ate his food like a beast; but that this might have been the result of living alone in the hills out of the reach of society as refined and elevating as ours, for instance. Strickland was not amused. I do not think that he listened to me, for his next sentence referred to the mark on Fleete's breast, and I said that it might have been caused by blister-flies, or that it was possibly a birth-mark newly born and now visible for the first time. We both agreed that it was unpleasant to look at, and Strickland found occasion to say that I was a fool.

"I can't tell you what I think now," said he, "because you would call me a madman; but you must stay with me for the next few days, if you can. I want you to watch Fleete, but don't tell me what you think till I have made up my mind."

"But I am dining out to-night," I said.

"So am I," said Strickland, "and so is Fleete. At least if he doesn't change his mind."

We walked about the garden smoking, but saying nothing—because we were friends, and talking spoils good tobacco—till our pipes were out. Then we went to wake up Fleete. He was wide awake and fidgeting about his room.

"I say, I want some more chops," he said. "Can I get them?"

We laughed and said, "Go and change. The ponies will be round in a minute."

"All right," said Fleete. "I'll go when I get the chops—underdone ones, mind."

He seemed to be quite in earnest. It was four o'clock, and we had had breakfast at one; still, for a long time, he demanded those underdone chops. Then he changed into riding clothes and went out into the verandah. His pony—the mare had not been caught—would not let him come near. All three horses were unmanageable—mad with fear—and finally Fleete said that he would stay at home and get something to eat. Strickland and I rode out wondering. As we passed the temple of Hanuman, the Silver Man came out and mewed at us.

"He is not one of the regular priests of the temple," said Strickland. "I think I should peculiarly like to lay my hands on him."

There was no spring in our gallop on the racecourse that evening. The horses were stale, and moved as though they had been ridden out.

"The fright after breakfast has been too much for them," said Strickland.

That was the only remark he made through the remainder of the ride. Once or twice I think he swore to himself; but that did not count.

We came back in the dark at seven o'clock, and saw that there were no lights in the bungalow. "Careless ruffians my servants are!" said Strickland.

My horse reared at something on the carriage-drive, and Fleete stood up under its nose.

"What are you doing, grovelling about the garden?" said Strickland.

But both horses bolted and nearly threw us. We dismounted by the stables and returned to Fleete, who was on his hands and knees under the orange-bushes.

"What the devil's wrong with you?" said Strickland.

"Nothing, nothing in the world," said Fleete, speaking very quickly and thickly. "I've been gardening—botanising, you know. The smell of the earth is delightful. I think I'm going for a walk—a long walk—all night."

Then I saw that there was something excessively out of order somewhere, and I said to Strickland, "I am not dining out."

"Bless you!" said Strickland. "Here, Fleete, get up. You'll catch fever there. Come in to dinner and let's have the lamps lit. We'll all dine at home."

Fleete stood up unwillingly, and said, "No lamps—no lamps. It's much nicer here. Let's dine outside and have some more chops—lots of 'em and underdone—bloody ones with gristle."

Now a December evening in Northern India is bitterly cold, and Fleete's suggestion was that of a maniac.

"Come in," said Strickland sternly. "Come in at once."

Fleete came, and when the lamps were brought, we saw that he was literally plastered with dirt from head to foot. He must have been rolling in the garden. He shrank from the light and went to his room. His eyes were horrible to look at. There was a green light behind them, not in them, if you understand, and the man's lower lip hung down.

Strickland said, "There is going to be trouble—big trouble—tonight. Don't you change your riding-things."

We waited and waited for Fleete's reappearance, and ordered dinner in the meantime. We could hear him moving about his own room, but there was no light there. Presently from the room came the long-drawn howl of a wolf.

People write and talk lightly of blood running cold and hair standing up and things of that kind. Both sensations are too horrible to be trifled with. My heart stopped as though a knife had been driven through it, and Strickland turned as white as the tablecloth.

The howl was repeated, and was answered by another howl far across the fields.

That set the gilded roof on the horror. Strickland dashed into Fleete's room. I followed, and we saw Fleete getting out of the window. He made beast-noises in the back of his throat. He could not answer us when we shouted at him. He spat.

I don't quite remember what followed, but I think that Strickland must have stunned him with the long boot-jack or else I should never have been able to sit on his chest. Fleete could not speak, he could only snarl, and his snarls were those of a wolf, not of a man. The human spirit must have been giving way all day and have died out with the twilight. We were dealing with a beast that had once been Fleete.

The affair was beyond any human and rational experience. I tried to say "Hydrophobia,"[11] but the word wouldn't come, because I knew that I was lying.

We bound this beast with leather thongs of the punkah-rope, and tied its thumbs and big toes together, and gagged it with a shoe-horn, which makes a very efficient gag if you know how to arrange it. Then we carried it into the dining-room, and sent a man to Dumoise, the doctor, telling him to come over at once. After we had despatched the

---

[11]Rabies.

messenger and were drawing breath, Strickland said, "It's no good. This isn't any doctor's work." I, also, knew that he spoke the truth.

The beast's head was free, and it threw it about from side to side. Any one entering the room would have believed that we were curing a wolf's pelt. That was the most loathsome accessory of all.

Strickland sat with his chin in the heel of his fist, watching the beast as it wriggled on the ground, but saying nothing. The shirt had been torn open in the scuffle and showed the black rosette mark on the left breast. It stood out like a blister.

In the silence of the watching we heard something without mewing like a she-otter. We both rose to our feet, and, I answer for myself, not Strickland, felt sick—actually and physically sick. We told each other, as did the men in *Pinafore*, that it was the cat.[12]

Dumoise arrived, and I never saw a little man so unprofessionally shocked. He said that it was a heart-rending case of hydrophobia, and that nothing could be done. At least any palliative measures would only prolong the agony. The beast was foaming at the mouth. Fleete, as we told Dumoise, had been bitten by dogs once or twice. Any man who keeps half a dozen terriers must expect a nip now and again. Dumoise could offer no help. He could only certify that Fleete was dying of hydrophobia. The beast was then howling, for it had managed to spit out the shoe-horn. Dumoise said that he would be ready to certify to the cause of death, and that the end was certain. He was a good little man, and he offered to remain with us; but Strickland refused the kindness. He did not wish to poison Dumoise's New Year. He would only ask him not to give the real cause of Fleete's death to the public.

So Dumoise left, deeply agitated; and as soon as the noise of the cart-wheels had died away, Strickland told me, in a whisper, his suspicions. They were so wildly improbable that he dared not say them out aloud; and I, who entertained all Strickland's beliefs, was so ashamed of owning to them that I pretended to disbelieve.

"Even if the Silver Man had bewitched Fleete for polluting the image of Hanuman, the punishment could not have fallen so quickly."

As I was whispering this the cry outside the house rose again, and the beast fell into a fresh paroxysm of struggling till we were afraid that the thongs that held it would give way.

"Watch!" said Strickland. "If this happens six times I shall take the law into my own hands. I order you to help me."

He went into his room and came out in a few minutes with the barrels of an old shot-gun, a piece of fishing-line, some thick cord, and his heavy

---

[12]In act 2 of Gilbert and Sullivan's comic opera *H.M.S. Pinafore* (1878), eloping lovers and supporters sing, "'Goodness me - / Why, what was that ?'/ 'Silent be, / It was the cat!'" It was not; they have been caught. A famous spoof on English patriotism follows.

wooden bedstead. I reported that the convulsions had followed the cry by two seconds in each case, and the beast seemed perceptibly weaker.

Strickland muttered, "But he can't take away the life! He can't take away the life!"

I said, though I knew that I was arguing against myself, "It may be a cat. It must be a cat. If the Silver Man is responsible, why does he dare to come here?"

Strickland arranged the wood on the hearth, put the gun-barrels into the glow of the fire, spread the twine on the table, and broke a walking-stick in two. There was one yard of fishing-line, gut, lapped with wire, such as is used for *mahseer*-fishing,[13] and he tied the two ends together in a loop.

Then he said, "How can we catch him? He must be taken alive and unhurt."

I said that we must trust in Providence, and go out softly with polo-sticks into the shrubbery at the front of the house. The man or animal that made the cry was evidently moving round the house as regularly as a night-watchman. We could wait in the bushes till he came by, and knock him over.

Strickland accepted this suggestion, and we slipped out from a bath-room window into the front verandah and then across the carriage-drive into the bushes.

In the moonlight we could see the leper coming round the corner of the house. He was perfectly naked, and from time to time he mewed and stopped to dance with his shadow. It was an unattractive sight, and thinking of poor Fleete, brought to such degradation by so foul a creature, I put away all my doubts and resolved to help Strickland from the heated gun-barrels to the loop of twine—from the loins to the head and back again—with all tortures that might be needful.

The leper halted in the front porch for a moment and we jumped out on him with the sticks. He was wonderfully strong, and we were afraid that he might escape or be fatally injured before we caught him. We had an idea that lepers were frail creatures, but this proved to be incorrect. Strickland knocked his legs from under him and I put my foot on his neck. He mewed hideously, and even through my riding-boots I could feel that his flesh was not the flesh of a clean man.

He struck at us with his hand and feet-stumps. We looped the lash of a dog-whip round him, under the arm-pits, and dragged him backwards into the hall and so into the dining-room where the beast lay. There we tied him with trunk-straps. He made no attempt to escape, but mewed.

When we confronted him with the beast the scene was beyond description. The beast doubled backwards into a bow, as though he had

[13]Game fish; Indian carp.

been poisoned with strychnine, and moaned in the most pitiable fashion. Several other things happened also, but they cannot be put down here.

"I think I was right," said Strickland. "Now we will ask him to cure this case."

But the leper only mewed. Strickland wrapped a towel round his hand and took the gun-barrels out of the fire. I put the half of the broken walking-stick through the loop of fishing-line and buckled the leper comfortably to Strickland's bedstead. I understood then how men and women and little children can endure to see a witch burnt alive; for the beast was moaning on the floor, and though the Silver Man had no face, you could see horrible feelings passing through the slab that took its place, exactly as waves of heat play across red-hot iron—gun-barrels for instance.

Strickland shaded his eyes with his hands for a moment, and we got to work. This part is not to be printed.

* * *

The dawn was beginning to break when the leper spoke. His mewings had not been satisfactory up to that point. The beast had fainted from exhaustion and the house was very still. We unstrapped the leper and told him to take away the evil spirit. He crawled to the beast and laid his hand upon the left breast. That was all. Then he fell face down and whined, drawing in his breath as he did so.

We watched the face of the beast, and saw the soul of Fleete coming back into the eyes. Then a sweat broke out on the forehead, and the eyes—they were human eyes—closed. We waited for an hour, but Fleete still slept. We carried him to his room and bade the leper go, giving him the bedstead, and the sheet on the bedstead to cover his nakedness, the gloves and the towels with which we had touched him, and the whip that had been hooked round his body. He put the sheet about him and went out into the early morning without speaking or mewing.

Strickland wiped his face and sat down. A night-gong, far away in the city, made seven o'clock.

"Exactly four-and-twenty hours!" said Strickland. "And I've done enough to ensure my dismissal from the service, besides permanent quarters in a lunatic asylum. Do you believe that we are awake?"

The red-hot gun-barrel had fallen on the floor and was singeing the carpet. The smell was entirely real.

That morning at eleven we two together went to wake up Fleete. We looked and saw that the black leopard-rosette on his chest had disappeared. He was very drowsy and tired, but as soon as he saw us, he said, "Oh! Confound you fellows. Happy New Year to you. Never mix your liquors. I'm nearly dead."

"Thanks for your kindness, but you're over time," said Strickland. "To-day is the morning of the second. You've slept the clock round with a vengeance."

The door opened, and little Dumoise put his head in. He had come on foot, and fancied that we were laying out Fleete.

"I've brought a nurse," said Dumoise. "I suppose that she can come in for . . . what is necessary."

"By all means," said Fleete cheerily, sitting up in bed. "Bring on your nurses."

Dumoise was dumb. Strickland led him out and explained that there must have been a mistake in the diagnosis. Dumoise remained dumb and left the house hastily. He considered that his professional reputation had been injured, and was inclined to make a personal matter of the recovery. Strickland went out too. When he came back, he said that he had been to call on the temple of Hanuman to offer redress for the pollution of the god, and had been solemnly assured that no white man had ever touched the idol and that he was an incarnation of all the virtues laboring under a delusion. "What do you think?" said Strickland.

I said, "'There are more things . . .'"[14]

But Strickland hates that quotation. He says that I have worn it threadbare.

One other curious thing happened which frightened me as much as anything in all the night's work. When Fleete was dressed he came into the dining-room and sniffed. He had a quaint trick of moving his nose when he sniffed. "Horrid doggy smell, here," said he. "You should really keep those terriers of yours in better order. Try sulphur, Strick."

But Strickland did not answer. He caught hold of the back of a chair, and, without warning, went into an amazing fit of hysterics. It is terrible to see a strong man overtaken with hysteria. Then it struck me that we had fought for Fleete's soul with the Silver Man in that room, and had disgraced ourselves as Englishmen for ever, and I laughed and gasped and gurgled just as shamefully as Strickland, while Fleete thought that we had both gone mad. We never told him what we had done.

Some years later, when Strickland had married and was a church-going member of society for his wife's sake, we reviewed the incident dispassionately, and Strickland suggested that I should put it before the public.

I cannot myself see that this step is likely to clear up the mystery; because, in the first place, no one will believe a rather unpleasant story, and, in the second, it is well known to every right-minded man that the gods of the heathen are stone and brass, and any attempt to deal with them otherwise is justly condemned.

[14]*Hamlet* 1.5: "There are more things in heaven and earth, Horatio, / Than are dreamt of in your philosophy."

Further Reading

By Rudyard Kipling

Kipling's Japan: Collected Writings, eds. Hugh Cortazzi and George Webb. Athlone, 1988.

Something of Myself and Other Autobiographical Writings, ed. Thomas Pinney. Cambridge UP, 1990.

The Definitive Edition of Rudyard Kipling's Verse. Hodder and Stoughton, 1940.

The Letters of Rudyard Kipling, ed. Thomas Pinney. 6 vols. Macmillan, 1990–2004.

The New Readers' Guide to the works of Rudyard Kipling, Kipling Society, http://www.kipling.org.uk/bookmart_fra.htm. Initiated and guided by George Webb; gen. ed. John Radcliffe, verse ed. John Walker, project group: D. Page, J. Slater, A.Wilson, P. Havholm, M. Hamer, and L. Ormond.

The Sussex Edition of the Complete Works in Prose and Verse of Rudyard Kipling. 35 vols. Macmillan, 1935–37.

Writings on Writing, eds. Sandra Kemp and Lisa Lewis. Cambridge UP, 1996.

About Rudyard Kipling

Bristow, Joseph. *Empire Boys: Adventures in a Man's World*. Harper Collins Academic, 1991.

Carrington, Charles. *Rudyard Kipling: His Life and Work*. Macmillan, 1955.

Dillingham, William B. *Rudyard Kipling: Hell and Heroism*. Palgrave Macmillan, 2005.

Feeley, Margaret Peller. "The *Kim* Nobody Reads," *Studies in the Novel*. Vol. 13 (Fall 1981) 278–9.

Gilbert, Elliot L., ed. *Kipling and the Critics*. New York UP, 1965.

Gilmour, David. *The Long Recessional: The Imperial Life of Rudyard Kipling*. Farrar, Straus and Giroux, 2002.

Green, Roger Lancelyn. *Kipling; The Critical Heritage*. Barnes & Noble, 1971.

Havholm, Peter. *Politics and Awe in Rudyard Kipling's Fiction*. Ashgate, 2008.

Hopkirk, Peter. *Quest for Kim: In Search of Kipling's Great Game*. U Michigan P, 1997.

Keating, Peter. *Kipling the Poet*. Secker & Warburg, 1994.

Lewis, Lisa. "The Manuscript of *Kim*." Kipling Society, http://www.kipling.org.uk/rg_lewiskim.htm.

McBratney, John. *Imperial Subjects, Imperial Space: Rudyard Kipling's Fiction of the Native-born.* Ohio State UP, 2002.

Montefiore, Jan. *Rudyard Kipling.* Northcote House, 2007.

Moore-Gilbert, B. J. *Kipling and "Orientalism."* St. Martin's P, 1986.

Nagai, Kaori. *Empire of Analogies: Kipling, India, and Ireland.* Ireland: Cork UP, 2006.

Parry, Ann. *The Poetry of Rudyard Kipling: Rousing the Nation.* Open UP, 1992.

Randall, Don. *Kipling's Imperial Boy: Adolescence and Cultural Hybridity.* Palgrave Macmillan, 2000.

Sullivan, Zohreh T. *Narratives of Empire: The Fictions of Rudyard Kipling.* Cambridge UP, 1993.

Tompkins, J. M. S. *The Art of Rudyard Kipling.* Methuen, 1959.

On Empire

Baucom, Ian. *Out of Place: Englishness, Empire, and the Locations of Identity.* Princeton UP, 1999.

Bhabha, Homi K. *The Location of Culture.* Routledge, 1994.

Brantlinger, Patrick. *Rule of Darkness: British Literature and Imperialism, 1830–1914.* Cornell UP, 1988.

Burton, Antoinette, ed. *Politics and Empire in Victorian Britain: A Reader.* Palgrave, 2001.

David, Deirdre. *Rule Britannia: Women, Empire, and Victorian Writing.* Cornell UP, 1995.

Hobsbawm, E. J. *Age of Empire, 1875–1914.* Pantheon, 1987.

Leoshko, Janice. *Sacred Traces: British Explorations of Buddhism in South Asia.* Ashgate, 2003.

Loomba, Ania. *Colonialism/Postcolonialism.* Routledge, 1998.

Low, Gail Ching-Liang. *White Skins/Black Masks: Representation and Colonialism.* Routledge, 1996.

Parry, Benita, and Michael Sprinker, eds. *Delusions and Discoveries: India in the British Imagination, 1880–1930.* Verso, 1998.

Richards, Thomas. *The Imperial Archive: Knowledge and the Fantasy of Empire.* Verso, 1993.

Roy, Parama. *Indian Traffic: Identities in Question in Colonial and Post-colonial India.* U California P, 1998.

Sharpe, Jenny. *Allegories of Empire: The Figure of Woman in the Colonial Text.* U Minnesota P, 1993.

Said, Edward. *Orientalism.* Pantheon, 1978.

———. *Culture and Imperialism.* Knopf-Random House, 1993.

Suleri, Sara. *The Rhetoric of English India.* U Chicago P, 1992.

Viswanathan, Gauri. *Masks of Conquest: Literary Study and British Rule in India.* Columbia UP, 1989.

Williams, Patrick, and Laura Chrisman. *Colonial Discourse and Post-Colonial Theory: A Reader.* Columbia UP, 1994.